HOUSEHOLD
ENCYCLOPAEDIA

HOUSEHOLD
ENCYCLOPAEDIA

Comprising
MEDICAL and GARDENING information
COOKERY and HOUSEHOLD recipes
A guide to ETIQUETTE
Hints for the TOILET
etc., etc., etc.

Edited by
W. H. STEER

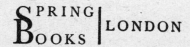

SPRING
BOOKS | LONDON

Published by

SPRING BOOKS

SPRING HOUSE · SPRING PLACE · LONDON N W 5

Printed in Czechoslovakia

PREFACE

This Encyclopaedia is intended as a handy book of reference for the average household, and its present sale of over 250,000 copies shows that it has been found of inestimable value to housewives.

The compilers, while endeavouring to include all that necessary and useful information which the housewife will require, have yet been limited to the scope of a single volume, so that the reader must bear in mind that only such information has been included as is likely to be required in the management of the average household.

Each subject, however, has been dealt with in a manner that will enable the reader to turn to the work for effective assistance in any ordinary domestic activity or where difficulty or emergency arises.

The alphabetical arrangement of the subject-matter will be found particularly simple and attractive, eliminating as it does the necessity for a separate index or the classification of the subjects dealt with under separate sections.

The necessity for yet another reprint of the Household Encyclopaedia afforded an opportunity of making an entirely new edition. It has, accordingly, been reset and revised throughout, and is calculated to be of constant guidance in every aspect of domestic activity.

The whole has been brought into line with the latest usage and information, including a wealth of up-to-date items of popular inquiry, while the many hints and recipes which for long have been accepted, have not been ignored.

AARON'S BEARD. Popular name for St. John's Wort, a hardy, attractive plant with yellow flowers, growing freely in sandy soil, suitable for rock gardens or for bordering on slopes. The reptant variety flowers in July and is of trailing habit: easily cultivated and full flowered. They are perennial and increased by division.

AARON'S ROD. A hardy biennial, blooms second year, with yellow flowers of varying shades. Gardeners know it as the yellow variety of the Verbascum or Mullein. It is tall, 3 to 5 feet, will flower all the summer, grow in any soil. Sow seed in boxes covered with glass till second leaf shows. Do as well in herbaceous border. For newer pink variety *see* VERBASCUM.

ABERNETHY BISCUITS, PLAIN. Named after the famous doctor, and supposed to be from his recipe, these are wholesome for any on a strictly plain diet. Take 1 lb. flour (not self-raising), 1 egg and 2 table-spoonfuls sugar, with a ¼ lb. butter and very little milk (2 dessertspoonfuls). Make a stiff paste by rubbing the egg and butter into the flour, adding the sugar. Roll out and make into thin rounds by pressing the rim of a drinking glass into the dough. Bake for 10 minutes in a moderate oven. According to taste, the sugar can be lessened or increased, and some prefer to add a scattering of caraway seeds.

ABRASIONS. Grazing, scratching or otherwise breaking the surface of the skin. Thoroughly bathe with boracic lotion to cleanse all dirt or grit, then apply iodine and bind up till the skin has reformed. Watch daily in case inflammation sets in, when apply hot fomentations at intervals.

ABRONIA. A half-hardy annual of the verbena family, having a delicate perfume and small star-like flowers. Makes a suitable edging and also looks well massed in the rockery. Start seed in pots covered with glass in May and plant out in light soil. Height about 10 inches.

ABSCESS, homely remedy. Boil a fair-sized parsnip to a pulp. Bathe the affected part with the water in which the parsnip has been boiled and then apply the parsnip pulp itself as hot as can be borne.

ABUTILON, INDIAN MALLOW. This half-hardy greenhouse perennial is useful for training on conservatory walls. The Thompsonii variety may be transferred to open borders for the summer. Sow under glass in February or March in pots; replant when about an inch high, setting well into the earth, or they may be propagated from cuttings in sand in autumn. The plant needs plenty of water and room.

ACACIA. *See* MIMOSA.

ACANTHUS. A fairly hardy perennial, remarkable for the beauty of its foliage. Thrives well in shade, but requires sun to produce good flowers. May be raised from seed, but is more easily increased by division of roots.

ACHILLEA. Also known as the Milfoil. It produces all the summer plentiful sprays of white or yellow flowers, and will thrive in any plot that is not sunless, but prefers a heavy soil. The dwarf sorts are 6 inches high, and a giant yellow variety, *A. filipendulina*, attains a height of 4 feet. Other varieties are 2 feet high. Being perennial they are increased by division. Fresh stock is by seed sown in open in spring.

ACIDITY OF THE STOMACH. Heartburn, flushings of the face, and other disagreeable sensations are symptoms of this disorder. It is best cured by taking 2 teaspoonfuls of magnesia in a tumbler of milk or $\frac{1}{2}$ teaspoonful of bicarbonate of soda in fairly hot water, preferably the former.

ACID ON CLOTHES. To counteract the effects, immediately moisten the spot with spirits of ammonia.

ACNE. *See* BLACKHEADS.

ACONITE. *See* ERANTHIS.

ACROCLINIUM. *See* IMMORTELLE.

ADENOIDS. These are fleshy growths at the back of the nose (in children). Salt and water sniffed up or injected into the nose relieve, but most cases require operation. This should be followed by breathing exercises. The child closes its mouth, and takes a long breath through the nose, holds the breath for a moment, after which the mouth is opened and the air allowed to escape.

ADIANTIFOLIUM THALICTRUM. Known as the hardy perennial Maidenhair. This plant will grow in almost any soil or situation, and increase in size and beauty each year. It has elegant fern-like foliage, and when cut and placed in water is more lasting than fern fronds: excellent foliage for decorative effect with cut flowers. Start by buying roots, then divide up each season.

ADONIS, PHEASANT'S EYE. These useful rock plants thrive in a shady position if sown in March and planted out in a mixture of loam, peat and leaf-mould. It has feathery foliage and crimson flowers, averaging 12 inches in height.

ADULT HEIGHT AND WEIGHT, comparisons. Men and women differ in regard to their average weight in relation to height. The following table affords a dependable average:

MEN		ST.	LB.
Five feet two inches	about	9	0
Five feet three inches	„	9	7
Five feet four inches	„	9	13

8

						St.	Lb.
Five feet five inches	.	.	.	.	about	10	2
Five feet six inches	.	.	.	.	,,	10	5
Five feet seven inches	.	.	.	.	,,	10	8
Five feet eight inches	.	.	.	.	,,	11	1
Five feet nine inches	.	.	.	.	,,	11	7
Five feet ten inches	.	.	.	.	,,	12	1
Five feet eleven inches	.	.	.	.	,,	12	6
Six feet	.	.	.	.	,,	12	10

WOMEN

						St.	Lb.
Five feet	.	.	.	.	,,	7	5
Five feet one inch	.	.	.	.	,,	7	10
Five feet two inches	.	.	.	.	,,	8	0
Five feet three inches	.	.	.	.	,,	8	7
Five feet four inches	.	.	.	.	,,	9	0
Five feet five inches	.	.	.	.	,,	9	7
Five feet six inches	.	.	.	.	,,	9	13
Five feet seven inches	.	.	.	.	,,	10	6
Five feet eight inches	.	.	.	.	,,	10	12
Five feet nine inches	.	.	.	.	,,	11	2

AGAPANTHUS (AFRICAN LILY). A bulbous-rooted plant with graceful foliage and large heads of blue or white blossom. The blue variety is the most successful in this country. The bulbs should be stored in winter and planted out in early spring, to flower in August, they are mostly grown in pots or tubs. Water abundantly in summer with weak liquid manure.

AGERATUM. Neat, compact little annuals, blue or white flowers showing couple of months from sowing if raised under glass in boxes of fine compost. Prick out the seedlings to about 3 inches apart. Do not sow outdoors.

AGNAILS, to prevent. Use an orange-stick to loosen the semi-circular skin of the nails. Avoid touching the quick. Now dip the tips of the fingers in lukewarm water and press the skin back with a towel and rub in some cuticle oil. If this is done every day, the formation of agnails will be prevented and the general appearance of the hands will be improved.

AGROSTEMMA. The perennial variety of this branch of the lychnis family is familiarly known as the Rose Campion and also as the Flower of Love. It has crimson flowers, with grey, hairy foliage and grows to about 2 feet. They thrive in any soil and are raised from seed sown in position in spring. Self-sown seed increases the supply year by year.

ALBUMEN WATER. For diarrhoea or digestive prostration, take an absolutely new-laid egg, break it carefully and separate the white from the yolk. Whisk the white until it is a stiff froth, then add half a pint of cold water, cover with a saucer and leave it for an hour to give the white time to dissolve. Give the patient a teacupful at a time.

A pinch of salt or a dash of lemon juice are an improvement if either is allowed.

ALLOTMENTS. Where the Secretary of an allotment association is unknown, application should be made to the local municipal offices. An allotment garden is usually 10 rods in extent, or say 30 feet by 90 feet, ample space for supplying the vegetable needs of an average family. Particulars of the most economical planting lay-out of the area are issued by the Ministry of Agriculture, Whitehall, London, S.W.1, who also send free leaflets advising on the culture of allotments, seed quantities and directions for growing the most useful vegetables.

Those having an allotment are expected to keep it in good cultivation, and particularly, for the common good, to keep it free from weeds and rotting leaves which foster insect pests.

Throughout this Encyclopaedia are ample directions for every cultural activity and for growing vegetables of every kind, as well as directions for destroying insects and combating plant diseases.

ALLSPICE. (Alternatively called Jamaica Pepper, or Pimento.) This is a spice made from the dried berries of a tree largely cultivated in Jamaica, and must not be confused with Mixed Spice. It is used in the making of pickles, curing of hams, and often as an ingredient for stews. It is also one of the components of curry powder.

ALMOND PASTE.

1 lb. ground almonds
1 lb. castor sugar
2 eggs
few drops of almond essence
1 tablespoonful of flavouring, such as orange-flower water or rose water

Mix almonds and sugar, then add flavouring and essence, and lastly the eggs thoroughly whisked. Knead well, place on cake and roll level with rolling-pin.

Almond paste may be made into small fancy shapes, flavoured and coloured as liked.

ALMOND TARTLETS.

2 oz. ground almonds
2 oz. cake-crumbs
2 eggs
2 tablespoonfuls sherry
castor sugar
short crust
strawberry jam

Line some patty tins with the pastry and put a teaspoonful of strawberry jam in each. Separate the yolks from the whites of eggs, mix the ground almonds, crumbs, sherry, yolks and sugar (to taste) together and put some in each tart. Whip the whites stiffly, add some castor sugar and a few drops of almond essence; pile some of this meringue on top of the almond mixture, and bake in a moderate oven about 30 minutes.

ALMONDS. To blanch and peel, place either in cold water and bring to the boil, or in boiling water and let them remain for about 6 or 7 minutes. Take out, remove skin and throw into cold water. If to be used immediately dry with a cloth. If to be pounded, or stored for a few days, dry them off in a cool oven.

ALMONDS, BURNT. Chop or shred the blanched almonds, put them on a baking sheet and bake them a nice brown in moderate oven. They should be moved constantly so that they are an even colour; and they burn very quickly, so must be carefully watched.

ALMONDS, DEVILLED.   Put enough butter in a small pan to give a depth of 1 inch when melted. Bring to boiling heat and, after blanching the almonds, throw them in all together.   Mix salt and a little cayenne on a piece of paper.   Remove almonds from the pan and roll them in the salt, shaking them well until almost cold.

ALMONDS, SALTED.   Prepare exactly as for Devilled Almonds, but omit the cayenne.

ALOYSIA (SWEET VERBENA).   A perennial, usually classed as a greenhouse plant, but in southern counties it may be left out of doors during the winter if well protected by a covering of straw.   It is worth cultivation for the lemon aroma of its leaves and the delicate tint of its foliage.   Propagate by cuttings.   Grow in sandy loam.

ALPINES.   An Alpine section is a novel attraction in the garden. It can take the form of a Rockery (which see, for construction), or it can be a level stretch of silver sand, gravel and grit over a prepared bed, with a foundation of small stones and filled in with soil suited to the particular species of Alpines favoured.   The Moraine bed gently rises and falls like a tiny valley slope, and some ambitious enthusiasts build the foundation so that water can percolate through underneath the surface at only sufficient depth to irrigate the roots.   If this is tried, some means must be provided for turning off the flow as needed.   Suitable plants, apart from special sorts as seedsmen would recommend according to locality, conditions of climate, etc., are anemone, rock jasmine, aubretia, acaena, dwarf columbine, thrift, sandwort, draba, dryas, cyclamen, gypsophila, dwarf linaria, primulas, sedum, thyme, dwarf veronica and the maidenhair plant.   Put in your selection in spring or autumn, watering the pockets first, and spreading the roots well down with firmness.   Add a little compost to each pocket well packed in above the roots.   The compost should include sand, loam and well-matured and broken-up top spit.

ALSTROMERIAS (PERUVIAN LILY).   Popular perennial for cut flowers and excellent border plants of very easy culture.   Will increase and last for many seasons, and are propagated by division.   Colourings: rose, crimson, salmon, orange, yellow and pink, often spotted, splashed or edged with contrasting colours.   They must be given a well-drained sandy soil in a warm and sheltered position.

ALYSSUM.   The annual variety, sweet alyssum and compactum, are invaluable as edging plants, their white blossom being prolific and on short stems.   Sow in spring in open in ordinary soil.   The perennial sorts, saxatile, grow to 9 inches, and quickly spread.   They throw up sprays of orange, or pale yellow blossom in April and May.   Sunshine and a loose, friable soil are best, and they should not be disturbed.

AMARANTHUS (LOVE-LIES-BLEEDING, PRINCE'S FEATHER).   Annual, easily raised from seed sown in March in gentle heat. Love-lies-bleeding is a fine variety, 2 to 4 feet when cultivated in rich soil. Prince's Feather is mostly grown as a pot plant.   The leaves of each are richly variegated.

11

AMBROSIA. Mix 2 oz. cornflour with a little milk. Pour on a pint of milk that has boiled with 2 oz. butter. Return to saucepan and cook thoroughly, adding 1 wineglass sherry and 2 oz. sugar. Pour into a wet mould.

AMERICAN BLIGHT. The apple and the oak are most subject to this pest. It is more correctly known as the Woolly Aphis, a woolly-looking substance of insect growth, infesting the bark of the tree and piercing the sap vessels, and ultimately destroying the branch it attacks. It lies dormant at the foot of the tree during winter, but in the spring it renews its ravages and will spread throughout the tree if its progress is not stopped. The best remedy is the free use of paraffin, rubbed into the crevices of the bark with a hog-hair paint-brush wherever the insect appears; and in the winter, to prevent a recurrence of the trouble, a spray of soft soap and paraffin, with a little soda, may be applied.

AMERICAN COWSLIP. *See* DODECATHEON.

AMMONIATED TINCTURE OF QUININE. *See* QUININE.

ANAEMIA. *See* BLOODLESSNESS.

ANCHOVIES. These ared used, either whole or filleted, for hors d'œuvres and savoury dishes.

ANCHOVY EGGS.

2 eggs	anchovy paste
butter	cayenne
chopped parsley	rounds of bread either fried
	or toasted and buttered

Hard boil the eggs, place in cold water for a few minutes and then remove shells. Cut eggs in halves across, not lengthwise. Scoop out the yolks and well pound with a little butter, anchovy paste and a pinch of cayenne. Cut bread into neat rounds and either fry or toast and butter. Cut a small piece off the bottom parts of the cups of whites of eggs to make a flat base, and then stand the whites of the eggs on the rounds of bread, filling these egg cases with the mixture with the aid of a forcing bag and fancy tube. Sprinkle over with chopped parsley and serve on a dish garnished with cress.

ANCHOVY SAUCE. *See* SAUCES.

ANCHOVY TOASTS.

8 anchovies 6 or 7 croûtons of bread
2 tablespoonfuls tomato sauce

Skin, fillet and pass the anchovies through a sieve, mix with tomato sauce, spread thickly on rounds of toast or croûtons of fried bread and serve very hot.

ANCHUSA. Growing to a height of 3 feet, with spikes of light-blue flowers. The Cape Anchusa has pale-blue flowers. The plants like a friable rich soil in sunny position. Flowers late May to July. It is hardy, and propagated by division.

ANGELICA, to prepare. Angelica should be soaked a for minute or so in boiling water; this removes all the sugar and makes it pliable, otherwise it cracks when bent.

12

ANISEED. This is a spice used largely in confectionery and for flavouring and colouring liqueurs and cordials.

ANTHEMIS. *See* CAMOMILE.

ANTIRRHINUM. *See* SNAPDRAGON.

ANTISEPTICS. As the name implies, these are used to prevent any wound, etc., becoming septic. The following are the antiseptics in most common use to-day:

PEROXIDE OF HYDROGEN.—This is always in liquid form and is obtainable from any chemist. It is non-poisonous and, as it is sold in various strengths, the proportion to be used in water is stated on each bottle.

BORACIC ACID.—One tablespoonful to a pint of water.

PERMANGANATE OF POTASH.—One teaspoonful to the pint, and kept as a stock mixture. For washing wounds, or as a gargle, use one part of the stock mixture to twelve parts of water. Being poisonous, care must be taken not to increase strength.

CARBOLIC ACID.—One tablespoonful to a pint and a half of water for sick room cleansing. Must not be taken internally.

FRIAR'S BALSAM.—Should be used undiluted. The bottle containing the antiseptic should be labelled and kept out of the way of children.

ANTS, in house. Sometimes ants invade the house and it is difficult to trace their nests to destroy them. In such cases a scattering of powdered borax where the ants collect will be found effective in driving them away.

ANTS, to destroy. If the nests appear in the turf, boiling water should be poured in. When ants attack ripening wall fruit, lay a broad band of tar, mixed with a little sugar, on the bottom of the wall and around the stem of the trees. Bands drawn in white chalk will have the same effect.

APERIENTS.

LIQUID PARAFFIN.—1 or 2 dessertspoonfuls.

CASTOR OIL.—1 teaspooonful to 2 tablespoonfuls.

SENNA TEA.—2 to 4 tablespoonfuls.

CONFECTION OF SULPHUR.—1 to 2 teaspoonfuls.

SYRUP OF CASCARA.—$\frac{1}{2}$ to 2 teaspoonfuls.

MAGNESIA.—$\frac{1}{2}$ to 1 teaspoonful.

LICORICE POWDER.—$\frac{1}{2}$ to 1 teaspoonful.

APHIDES. *See* PLANT-LICE.

APHIS (GREEN FLY), to remove. Nothing is better than a pair of soft brushes joined together with a cane bow, so that by pressure of the hand they are brought in contact and the bud between them is cleared. *See also* INSECTS ON PLANTS, to destroy.

APOPLEXY. Bleeding into the brain. It occurs most frequently in men, and is a disease of middle and advanced life.

The head and shoulders should be raised a few inches from the ground. If the breathing is bad he should be turned on his side; a wet towel may be placed round his head. The patient should be kept quiet until again conscious, and stimulants of any sort avoided.

APPLE CHARLOTTE (for 4 or 5 people).

apples	2 oz. butter
stale bread	sugar
3 or 4 cloves	custard sauce

Stew the apples (peeled and cored) till tender, with sugar and cloves. Line a cake-tin with bread dipped in 2 oz. clarified butter; join the edges together with egg. Pour in the stewed apples and cover with a round of bread dipped in butter. Then cover with buttered paper and bake in a quick oven, turning round to brown all sides alike.

APPLE CHIPS.
Peel and core the apples, cut into thin slices and bake in an oven till quite hard. They will then keep for years. Steep in hot water before using.

APPLE DUMPLINGS (for 6 or 8 people).

6 or 8 apples	pinch of salt
8 oz. flour	6 or 8 cloves
4 oz. lard and butter	sugar
water	

Make the pastry with flour and butter and lard; add pinch of salt, mix stiffly with water, cut into as many pieces as apples, allowing roughly 1 oz. of pastry to each apple. Peel and core the apples, keeping them whole; place each on a piece of pastry and fill the hole with sugar and a clove. Work the pastry round the apple, brush over with water and sprinkle with sugar. Bake about 20 minutes.

APPLE FLAN.

½ lb. short pastry	1 oz. butter
5 medium-sized cooking apples	grated rind of about ½ a lemon
2 tablespoonfuls of sugar	

Peel and core 4 of the apples and cut them into thin slices. Place in pan with the butter, sugar and lemon rind, cooking over very gentle heat until the apple becomes pulp, when allow to cool. Make short pastry and line flan ring with same. Place in the pastry the pulped apple. Prepare the uncooked apple by peeling, coring and cutting into thin slices. Place these thin slices on the top of the cooked apple until it is completely covered. Bake in fairly hot oven until the pastry is nicely browned. Can be served either hot or cold.

APPLE FOOL.
Peel and core the apples, stew till tender, beat to a pulp, gradually adding either 1 pint milk custard or ½ pint cream and ½ pint milk.

APPLE FRITTERS. *See* FRITTERS.

14

APPLES, BAKED. Remove the cores from the apples and fill the cavity with sugar and pour enough grape juice over them to baste them while they are being baked. Serve the apples with whipped cream.

Before putting the apples in the oven run a knife round each one, just cutting the peel. This will prevent the apples from bursting.

APPLES, to dry. Peel the apples and cut into slices. Then spread on cloths or boards and dry outside if the weather is fine. Portable frames are an advantage. They can be used either in drying indoors or outside. After the apples are pared, quartered, and cored, string them in lengths to reach twice across the frame; the ends of the twine should then be tied together and the string hung on the nails across the frame. As the apples dry they can be taken from the string and others substituted. Dried apples have a slight brownish tinge; the taste, however, is not affected.

APPLES, to peel easily. If scalding water is poured over apples the skins will peel off more easily.

APPLES, to preserve the colour of. If apples are soaked for quarter of an hour in cold water to which a little lemon juice has been added they will retain their colour during cooking.

APPLES, to store. Lay the fruit on the floor or shelf so that they do not touch one another. They should be frequently examined and any that show signs of decay should be removed. Rough skinned apples such as russets keep best.

APPLES, DUNFILLAU.

4 oz. flour	2 lb. cooking apples
3 oz. butter	2 oz. castor sugar
1 egg	1 gill milk
	1 teaspoonful baking-powder

Stew apples and place them in a buttered pie-dish. Rub butter into flour sifted with baking-powder and pinch of salt. Beat egg and sugar together. Add milk and stir into flour with a wooden spoon. Pour batter on top of apples and bake in a moderate oven ½ an hour. The batter can be flavoured with any essence, preferably vanilla.

APPLES, PROVENCE.

8 red apples	juice of 1 orange
1 cupful castor sugar	½ lemon

Cook apples in boiling water till soft. Remove skins and place apples in a dish. Add to the water sugar, grated lemon rind and orange juice. Simmer until reduced to a cup. Cool and pour over apples.

APPLE SNOW (for 4 or 5 people).

¾ lb. apples	rind of 1 lemon
½ oz. gelatine	juice of ½ lemon
4 oz. castor sugar	whites of 2 eggs
½ gill water	

Peel, core and slice the apples. Stew them with the sugar, dissolve the gelatine in the water and add with the grated rind and juice of lemon. Whip the whites to a stiff froth and stir lightly. Put into a mould. Turn out when set, and serve with custard sauce.

15

APPLE-TREE PESTS. When the blossom is in the pink-bud stage the ravages of pests and diseases can be combated by spraying with nicotine, derris or lime sulphur.

Apple scab, the commonest fungus disease, is controlled by spraying with lime sulphur.

APPLE WATER. Bake apple till quite soft, then pulp and pour upon it a pint of boiling water. Beat it up with a little sugar and strain when cold. This gives a refreshing drink for sick people.

APRICOT COCKTAIL.

1 tin apricots	1 orange
½ cupful sugar	pistachio nuts or almonds

Cook 1 cupful apricot syrup with minced orange rind and sugar for 5 minutes or until very thick. Cool and add juice and pulp of orange. Cut in pieces 18 apricot halves and put in 6 cocktail glasses. Cover with apricot-orange syrup and garnish with bits of pistachio nuts or almonds.

AQUARIUS (THE WATER-CARRIER). Eleventh sign of the Zodiac, influencing persons born between 22nd January and 21st February. Such possess fascination and friendliness, with enjoyment of life on conventional lines. They lack concentration, are apt to dwell on personal slights and show a tendency toward miserliness.

AQUILEGIA. *See* COLUMBINE.

ARIES (THE RAM). First sign of the Zodiac, influencing persons born between 22nd March and 21st April. Such are loyal, patriotic, courageous, highminded, but apt in some circumstances to be boastful, vain and bad-tempered.

ARROWROOT BLANCMANGE. Take 2 tablespoonfuls of arrowroot to 1 quart of milk, and a pinch of salt. Scald and sweeten the milk and then stir in the arrowroot, which must first be moistened with some milk. Let it boil once. Orange water, rose water or lemon peel can be used to flavour it. Pour into moulds to cool.

ARROWROOT CUSTARD, for invalids. Mix 1 tablespoonful of arrowroot with a little cold milk. Then add 1 pint milk, and boil. Stir in the arrowroot, an egg and a tablespoonful of sugar, well beaten together. Let it scald, and pour into cups to cool. A little cinnamon boiled in the milk flavours it pleasantly.

ARTICHOKES, to choose. Break off one of the stalks. Young and good artichokes will break off clean; old ones will be stringy.

ARTICHOKES, GLOBE. The globe variety gives larger heads and more fleshy edible parts than the oval. They can be grown from seed sown in spring. Plant the young shoots in ground that has been well worked and manured. Place in rows about 5 feet apart and 2 feet between the plants and give plenty of water. Trim the tops and roots before planting. They do not mature till the next season. Plant a row or two each year to secure a succession of crops from June to October.

16

Bring to a large head by cutting off the side suckers when about as large as an egg. Gather when the scales open and before the flowers appear at the centre. Break down the stems close to the ground after gathering. Stock is increased by suckers.

ARTICHOKES, JERUSALEM, to boil. Wash, peel and cut the artichokes in oval or pyramid shapes. Put at once into cold water with a little lemon juice or vinegar. Put them in boiling water with salt and lemon juice, and boil gently from 30 to 40 minutes. When tender drain well, put them in a hot vegetable dish, and serve with white sauce.

ARTICHOKES, JERUSALEM. A row of artichokes set about 18 inches apart makes an excellent screen for an ugly fence. They will grow in almost any soil so, readily that it is difficult to clear the ground of them again. Propagation is by sets or cutting of the roots as for potatoes. Plant them in rich soil 4 or 5 inches deep in rows a yard apart, allowing about 2 feet distance in the rows. They may be had throughout the autumn and winter.

ARTIFICIAL RESPIRATION. Turn the patient on his face, and drain the water out of the mouth and air passages. The finger should be swept round the back of the throat to see there is no obstruction to the entrance of air, such as water, weeds or false teeth. The tongue should be grasped and drawn forward, and then the patient turned on his back, and a firm pillow or rolled-up coat put between the shoulder blades, and the head pulled backwards. Grasp the arms at the elbows, and draw them over his head, and keep in the position for two seconds. Lower arms to the side of the chest, and press them against the ribs to expel the air; after remaining in the position two seconds, draw the arms over the head again. The movements should be done fifteen times a minute. Smelling salts should be put under the nose, and hot and cold water dashed alternately on the face. The body should be rubbed with towels. When respiration has been restored the patient should be covered with blankets, and given hot tea or brandy and water.

ARUM (SNAKE-ROOT). This plant is so called from its stem which resembles a serpent's skin. It bears very large dark-purple flowers, and will grow in any soil that is deep and rather moist. It is hardy, should not be disturbed, and protected from frost by straw over root area. Propagate by division.

ASPARAGUS. Wash and scrape the white part of the asparagus; tie in bundles with tape, cutting the stalks an even length. Place in a saucepan of boiling water (stand the bundles up if possible) with salt and a pinch of carbonate of soda. Boil very gently for about 20 to 30 minutes, taking care not to break the heads. Lift out the bundles, drain, untie, and place on a slice of toast in a hot vegetable dish. Serve with melted butter or Hollandaise sauce.

ASPARAGUS. Sow seed in April; grow in a light easily-worked soil and in a situation open to the sun. Divide off into beds 4 or 5 feet wide and leave a 2-foot path between each bed. Dig in plenty of rotted manure before planting matured roots the following March. Always keep beds free from weeds. Give fertilizers in spring.

The following are bandages which can be applied at home without the aid of a surgeon, or nurse:

4. *Finger Bandages.*—Width about ½ inch to 1 inch. Wind first around wrist, then bring up the back of the hand, wind around finger from tip to base, down back of hand again and around wrist in the opposite direction from the first winding, so that the ends may be tied to secure the bandage.

5. *Wrist Bandages.*—Placing one end at the base of the palm of the hand, take bandage over the hand between the thumb and first finger, then completely round hand between thumb and first finger again, down back of hand, round wrist, gradually winding up the arm as far as necessary, reversing the bandage to keep it flat on the arm.

6. *Head Bandages.*—Wind bandage once or twice round the head and then once under chin to prevent bandage from slipping. Tie the ends over the spot where the most pressure is needed.

7. *Arm Sling.*—As is well known this can be made from a large handkerchief formed into a triangle, the point of the triangle being fastened behind the elbow and the ends of the handkerchief knotted behind the neck. Endeavour always to arrange bandage so that the hand is of slightly higher level than the elbow.

8. *Eye Bandage.*—A narrow folded bandage is best. Place centre of bandage over the eye, then take one end of the bandage below the ear and the other diagonally across the forehead to the back of the head, where the ends should be crossed, brought round again, and tied over the eye. If both eyes have to be bandaged, a broader bandage should be used taken straight across the eyes round to the back of the head, ends crossed, brought to the front and tied.

BANNOCK. Mix together 1 cupful each of oatmeal and flour, ½ teaspoonful of ginger, and the same amount of salt, 1 tablespoonful of treacle, a little soda, and enough buttermilk to make into a stiff paste. Bake on an iron plate over the fire. Pease or barley meal may similarly be used for making bannock.

BARLEY SUGAR ROCK. 1 lb. loaf sugar and 1½ gills water should be boiled together until it whitens and bubbles. Stir for a few minutes, adding the juice of a lemon. Drop a little into cold water, and if it breaks off crisply it is ready to be poured on a greased tin. Whilst cooling it should be cut into long strips and twisted.

BARLEY WATER.

2 tablespoonfuls pearl barley	sugar
½ lemon	1 pint water

Well wash the barley, put it into a hot jug with some lemon rind and juice and a little sugar, pour the boiling water over, cover and let it stand for 6 or 7 hours. Strain before use. Or—
Wash 1 oz. pearl barley on cold water and put into a saucepan with ½ pint cold water. When it has boiled for about 15 minutes strain off the water and add 1 quart fresh boiling water. Boil until reduced to half the liquid, and strain. Sweeten and flavour with a little lemon juice.

BASIL. *See* HERBS.

BASIN HOLDER. A simple way to save time and trouble in the kitchen is to have a box with a hole cut in it that will firmly and comfortably hold a cooking basin. For egg-beating, cream-whipping, and many other home-cookery jobs, the firmly-fixed basin just stood on the table will save a deal of needless exertion.

BATH, EFFERVESCENT.

(a) ½ oz. sodium bicarbonate   (c) 1½ oz. sodium chloride
(b) ¼ oz. sodium acid sulphate   (common salt)
(d) ¼ oz. calcium chloride

First dissolve (a), (c) and (d) in a gallon of water; then add sodium acid sulphate and increase the quantity of water to 25 or 30 gallons.

Though the above formula is for one bath, it can, of course, be prepared in larger quantities in the same proportions.

BATH, EMOLLIENT.

1 lb. barley meal   2 lb. wheat bran   1 oz. borax

These ingredients should first be dissolved as far as possible in 2 quarts of warm water and then strained into the bath-tub, afterwards adding sufficient water to make up the bath.

BATH, MUSTARD. Mix 2 tablespoonfuls mustard with a little cold water to a paste, then gradually add hot water for a bath. *See also* MUSTARD BATH.

BATHS, to clean. Tide marks on baths can quickly be removed by rubbing briskly with a cloth dipped in hot water to which a teaspoonful of paraffin has been added.

BATTER, FOR FRYING.

3 oz. flour   1 tablespoonful oil or melted
pinch of salt   butter
2 tablespoonfuls tepid water   whipped white of 1 egg

Put the flour into a basin, add the salt, make a hole in the centre, pour in the oil or melted butter, add the tepid water gradually and stir till smooth; beat for 10 minutes. Let it stand from half an hour to 1 hour. Then add the whipped white lightly and it is ready to use.

Note.—This batter is suitable for coating fish, meat, fruit, fritters, etc., for frying.

BAY LEAVES. These are used either fresh, or dried, for flavouring sauces, soups, stews and sweets. Dried bay leaves should be kept in an air-tight container.

BEAN CROQUETTES (for 3 or 4 people).

½ pint haricot beans   egg and bread-crumbs
½ gill white sauce   salt and pepper

Soak the beans for 12 hours and cook till tender, mash them and mix with the white sauce and season well, form into croquettes, using a little flour, coat with egg and bread-crumbs and fry in hot fat till a golden brown. Drain and serve on a fancy paper, garnish with fried parsley.

patient's back—a little beyond the middle of the bed, that is. The clean undersheet and drawsheet are then spread smoothly over that half of the bed, with the rolled parts close up to the patient's back. The patient must then be very gently rolled over on to his other side, when he will be lying on the clean sheets. After that the clean undersheet and drawsheet are unrolled, straightened out over the second half of the bed and firmly tucked in at the other side. If a mackintosh is being used, it is put in clean with the drawsheet.

BED-SORES. When an illness is of long duration, the position of the patient should be changed from one side to the other to avoid bed-sores. The slightest crease or particle of food in the bedclothes may give rise to bed-sores. The patient should be sponged each day after his bath with equal parts of methylated spirits and oil. Apply the mixture to the back, elbows and any place where there is pressure. Dust all over with starch powder. If there is any soreness, apply the white of egg or lemon juice and put a pad of lint above and below the part to protect it.

BED SPRINGS. New bed and cot springs should be treated with aluminium paint; they will not then rust.

BED TICKS, to clean. Dissolve a very little permanganate of potash in plenty of cold water and rinse the tick in this mixture after washing. Any stains should be removed by means of a weak solution of chloride of lime and water, or a thin paste of starch and water, which should be placed on the stains and brushed off when dry. Well dry and air the ticking. To prevent the feathers coming through rub the inside with a fine piece of beeswax.

BED-WETTING BY CHILDREN. The child should not have anything to drink for 2 hours before bedtime and should be lifted before parents retire. Worms, another cause, should be got rid of. If still persistent a surgeon should be consulted.

BEE BALM. *See* MONARDA DIDYMA.

BEEF, ACCOMPANIMENTS.

For Roast Beef.—Yorkshire pudding and horse-radish either shredded or made into sauce: clear gravy.
For Boiled Fresh Beef.—Carrots, turnips and a green vegetable.
For Boiled Salt Beef.—Carrots, turnips, onions and suet dumplings.

BEEF, BOILED. If after serving a hot joint of boiled beef you put it back into the water in which it was boiled it will be much more tender than if it was put into the larder dry.

BEEF, BOILED, and DUMPLINGS.

beef (silverside)	dumplings
3 carrots	4 oz. flour
3 turnips	2 oz. suet
1 onion	salt and pepper

Well wash the beef to remove the salt, place in tepid water and bring to boiling-point, simmer gently, allowing 20 minutes to the pound and 20 minutes over, skim occasionally. Prepare the vegetables, cut them up neatly, put them in with the meat; the carrots should go in first. Mix the dumplings and cook them with the meat and vegetables about 15 to 20 minutes. Serve the meat on a hot dish with vegetables and dumplings round, some of the liquor in a tureen.

BEEF, to choose. The flesh should be deep red in colour, smooth grained, the lean and fat intermixed. The fat should be of a pale straw colour and somewhat soft. If very yellow it generally denotes the animal was fed on oil-cake. It is rich and greasy, and wastes in cooking, but is quite wholesome.

BEEF, BRAISED.

1 lb. fillet of beef
2 small carrots
½ stick celery
¼ lb. bacon fat
thyme
1 onion
spring parsley
1 bay leaf
1 pint stock

Cut beef into round fillets and lard them. To lard, take a larding needle with a little strip of bacon in it and lard each fillet neatly in rows till one side is covered with strips of bacon. Place scraped, washed and halved carrots in pan, add peeled onion, scraped celery, thyme, bay leaf and parsley. Pour in stock, arrange fillets on top. Take a piece of kitchen paper, the size of a frying-pan and butter it. Place over beef and put frying-pan in hot oven. Lift paper and baste occasionally and cook for about ½ an hour till stock is reduced to half-glaze. Cook slowly in oven till meat is tender, about 1½ hours. Serve on hot dish surrounded by vegetables.

BEEF CAKE. Chop the meat very fine, add pepper and salt to taste, a little parsley, nutmeg, and some finely-chopped lemon peel. Mix well together with bread-crumbs, and bake in the oven for about 1 hour.

BEEF COLLOPS (for 4 people).

½ lb. beef
1 onion
2 oz. rice
½ pint stock
1 oz. butter
vegetables for garnish
salt and pepper

Mince the beef finely, melt the butter in a stewpan and fry the chopped onion; remove it and fry the beef, add the stock and the rice, which must be washed and previously parboiled. Simmer gently till cooked, season well, pile in the centre of a hot dish, garnish with vegetables (carrot and turnip cut in dice or green peas). Serve very hot.

BEEF, FRICANDEAU OF (for 7 or 8 people).

2 lb. fillet or piece of rump
herbs
larding bacon
mushrooms
tomatoes
potatoes
3 cloves
2 blades of mace
salt and pepper
carrot, turnip, onion
wineglassful sherry

25

BEEF, STEWED BRISKET.

5 to 7 lb. brisket	1 head celery
2 carrots	12 peppercorns
2 onions	6 cloves
1 turnip	bunch of herbs
1 leek	salt

Put the meat into a large stewpan with sufficient water to cover; prepare the vegetables and add them, the cloves stuck in the onions, the peppercorns and herbs tied in muslin. Simmer gently from 4 to 5 hours, skimming occasionally. If served hot, take out the meat, thicken some of the liquor and serve as gravy. If to be served cold, take out the bones, press the meat between two boards with a weight on top, strain some of the liquor and reduce it to a glaze, adding a little meat extract. When the meat is cold wipe it with a hot cloth, brush it with the glaze; a drop or two of cochineal added improves the colour of the glaze.

BEER, HERB. Place 2 handfuls of nettles, 1 dozen roots of dandelion (with leaves) and 1 oz. bruised root ginger in 2 gallons of water and boil for 1 hour. Strain through a sieve into a vessel and whilst still hot add 1½ lb. sugar. Allow to cool. Dissolve 2 oz. yeast in sweetened lukewarm water, and when risen mix with the beer. Skim the barm off the beer the next day; bottle, cork and make secure with twine. In two days' time it will be ready for use. Be sure the bottles are perfectly dry.

BEER, NETTLE. Boil 1 peck of nettles, 4 lb. malt, 1½ lb. sugar, 2 oz. hops, ½ oz. ginger in 2 gallons of water. Strain and add a little yeast when nearly cold. Bottle whilst fermenting.

BEER, SPRUCE. Add 4 gallons of boiling water to 4 gallons of cold; add 8 lb. of treacle or molasses and a few tablespoonfuls of essence of spruce. Stir well together. Add 1 gill yeast and leave in a warm room for 2 days with the bung-hole open. Close up the cask, or bottle the beer when it has fermented and it will be ready for use in a few days. This is useful as a preventative against scurvy.

BEET, GLOBE and TAPER. Sow in drills, and 2 inches deep, towards the end of April and again in June in light deep rich soil, which has been well manured for a previous crop and free from recent manuring, in rows of 18 inches apart, and thin out to about 6 inches apart for globe beet and 9 inches for taper beet. The roots should be lifted, without breaking or bruising the skin, before the frost touches them, and stored in dry sand.

BEET, SPINACH. Sow broadcast in an open sunny spot from February to May. Thin out to intervals of about a foot, hoeing between the plants. Sow at three fortnightly intervals to assure continuous supply of these succulent leaves.

BEETROOT. These can generally be purchased already cooked but, if purchased raw, care must be taken to see that the skin has not been broken; otherwise the juice and colour will come out during cooking. Place in boiling water to which salt has been added, and cook until tender. To test whether cooked either press the skin with a finger (if cooked the skin will commence to peel), or try to pierce with a straw. They may be served either hot, as a vegetable, with melted butter or parsley sauce, or cold, thinly sliced, sprinkled lightly with pepper and salt and with a little vinegar or lemon juice poured over.

A teaspoonful of grated horse-radish will give cooked buttered beetroot a very appetizing flavour, especially if serving roast beef with the beetroot.

The easiest way to remove skin from beetroot after boiling is to run cold water into the pot till cold and it will come off quite easily.

BEGONIA. There are two varieties in general use—the tuberous and the fibrous rooted, the tuberous being the greater favourite, rivalling the geranium in popularity. It is classed as a half-hardy perennial, and from seed sown in March in gentle heat good plants may be obtained early in June. The seed is fine and should be sown very thinly, scattered on the surface of the soil, not buried. Germination is slow and irregular, and as soon as a few seedlings are large enough they should be pricked out into shallow boxes and not disturbed again until planted out; they require moderate heat, moisture and shade, and when planted out they should go into a rich soil. After flowering, the tubers should be carefully lifted (the decayed stems being gently removed) and stored in sand in a cool, frost-proof place. For summer bedding the Begonia produces a fine effect, the colours ranging from white to rose, pink, crimson and darkest scarlet.

BEREAVEMENTS. Though death brings sorrow to a family, there are duties and social conventions which cannot be set aside.

At once the head of the family (or whoever shoulders the responsibility) should inform friends and relations of the event, then, when the arrangements for the funeral are decided upon, a further intimation should be sent to all whose presence is wished for at the funeral.

Letters of condolence should at once be written on receipt of the tidings. These must be penned with sympathetic tact.

Only very intimate friends should express any wish to intrude upon the privacy of the mourners before the funeral, unless under exceptional circumstances.

Unless a wish for "no flowers" is expressed, it is usual for relations and friends to send floral tributes, which need not be all white, and to each should be attached a card bearing the sender's name and a brief message of sympathy or affection.

It should be someone's special duty to keep a record of the names of all who send flowers or expressions of sympathy, so that they may be acknowledged in due course.

There is no set rule now as to whether ladies follow to the grave or not, nor is black-bordered stationery used.

BILIOUS ATTACKS. No food whatever should be taken when an attack is on: a full day's fast, in bed if possible, is wise. The stomach should be thoroughly washed out with large draughts of water or soda water and purgatives taken to remove the undigested matter. People who are subject to bilious attacks should live plainly, take plenty of outdoor exercise, keep the bowels free, and drink plenty of water between meals.

Note.—Instead of an egg a little treacle or golden syrup can be used to mix.

BISCUITS, GINGER SNAP. Two cupfuls each of treacle and lard, 1 tablespoonful each of soda and ginger, and sufficient flour to make stiff enough to roll out. Bring the mixture to the boil before adding the flour. This will make them "snappish".

BISCUITS, OATMEAL.

4 oz. flour	2 oz. butter (melted)
2 oz. fine oatmeal	1 egg and a little milk
1 oz. sugar	pinch of salt

Mix the flour, oatmeal and sugar together, stir in the melted butter and beaten egg and if necessary a little milk, but the mixture must be stiff. Roll out thinly, cut into rounds, place them on a greased baking-sheet and bake about 10 minutes.

BISCUITS, RICE.

6 oz. ground rice	6 oz. sugar
6 oz. self-raising flour	6 oz. butter
	2 eggs

Sift the flour and ground rice, rub in the butter, mix with the well-beaten eggs. Roll out thinly, cut into small rounds, put on a floured tin and bake in a moderate oven for 10 to 15 minutes.

BISCUITS, SAVOURY.

6 or 8 water biscuits	mustard
1 oz. butter	3 oz. Parmesan cheese
	salt and cayenne

Mix the grated cheese with the butter, made mustard, salt, and cayenne, spread on one side of the biscuit, place on a baking-tin in a hot oven for 5 minutes, sprinkle well with grated cheese and serve at once.

BISCUITS, SHORTBREAD.

8 oz. flour
5 oz. butter
2 oz. castor sugar

Rub the butter finely into the flour, add the suggar, work together until a stiff dough, turn on to a flour board, and knead thoroughly until quite smooth; roll out till about ¼ inch thick, cut in rounds with a crinkled pastry cutter. Bake on a greased baking-tin in a moderate oven till a pale brown, sprinkle each biscuit with castor sugar, and place on a cake tray to cool. If allowed to stand some time on the baking-tin before baking they do not lose their shape.

BISCUITS, SPONGE.

3 eggs	6 oz. castor sugar
4 oz. well-dried sifted flour	little almond essence to flavour
	pinch of salt

Beat the yolks of the eggs only with the sugar, until very frothy. Whisk the whites separately until quite stiff, and then stir flour and whisked whites gradually into the beaten yolks and sugar, adding the salt and flavouring essence. Dust out some finger-shaped moulds with some castor sugar and flour mixed, and fill with the mixture, dredging a little castor sugar over each. Bake in a quick oven until a very light golden brown, when they should be thoroughly cooked through. Time for baking should be about 15 to 20 minutes.

BISCUITS, VANILLA.

8 oz. flour	2 eggs
4 oz. butter	vanilla essence
4 oz. sugar	glacé cherries

Rub the butter into the flour, add the sugar, mix with the beaten eggs, and add vanilla essence. Knead till smooth, roll out, cut into rounds with a fancy cutter, brush over with water or white of egg, sprinkle with castor sugar, put half a glacé cherry on each biscuit and bake on a greased baking-sheet in a moderate oven—a pale brown.

Note.—Lemon or almond essence can be used instead of vanilla.

BISCUITS, WATER.

½ lb. flour	½ teaspoonful salt
2 oz. butter	water to mix

Sift the flour into a basin, add the salt, rub in the butter finely, mix with water to a smooth paste; turn on to a floured board and knead until quite smooth, roll out very thinly, cut into rounds, prick with a fork, place on a floured baking sheet. Bake in moderate oven till crisp. Keep in tin till used.

BITES, DOG, to treat. As a rule it is only necessary thoroughly to cleanse the wound and to apply a little iodine or weak carbolic. But should there be even the faintest suspicion of rabies, it is absolutely imperative that the circulation should immediately be arrested by a cord tightly drawn above the bite, and the doctor sent for. Give a mild stimulant.

BITES, INSECT. *See* STINGS AND BITES.

BLACKBERRY CORDIAL, for diarrhœa. Boil together 4 lb. white sugar and 1 gallon of blackberry juice. Remove the scum and add 1 oz. cloves, 1 oz. cinnamon and 4 or 5 grated nutmegs. When sufficiently boiled, allow to settle; strain and add 1 pint of brandy. Give 1 tablespoonful to a child and a wineglassful to an adult.

BLACKBERRY VINEGAR. (No. 1.) Allow the fruit to stand for 24 hours covered with vinegar; then strain. To every quart of liquid, add 1 lb. sugar and boil in a porcelain-lined saucepan until the liquid thickens.

BLACKBERRY VINEGAR. (No. 2.)

1½ lb. blackberries
1 pint vinegar (malt)
1 lb. brown sugar

Pour vinegar over blackberries, let stand for 3 days, stirring often. Strain through muslin and boil the vinegar with sugar 10 to 15 minutes; bottle when cold. Good taken with a little hot water when cough is troublesome.

BLACK CLOTHING, to renovate. If black cloth is rubbed with a rag soaked in spirits of turpentine it will effectively remove all shininess. A black dress may be restored by first dusting and brushing. Then remove stains and sponge with hot water, and iron on the wrong side.

BLACKCURRANT JUICE, value of. It is not generally known that weight for weight blackcurrant juice contains double the quantity of Vitamin C as does orange juice. *See* VITAMINS.

BLACKCURRANT TEA.

> 1 tablespoonful blackcurrant jam
> little lemon juice
> ½ pint boiling water

Put the jam into a jug, add the lemon juice, pour over the boiling water, cover for a few minutes, strain it and serve.

BLACK EYE, to treat. Make a solution with hot water and a little bicarbonate of soda and bathe with same.

BLACKHEADS, or ACNE. Blackheads are due to the blocking of the oil glands of the skin. The parts affected should be swabbed three or four times with very hot water to soften the pores, after which the blackheads may be squeezed out by applying a watch-key over them and pressing; afterwards they should be dressed with sulphur ointment, and an aperient taken each morning for a few days.

BLACKLEADING GRATES. If vinegar is used to damp the black-lead for stoves and grates all the grease will come off and the polish will be much better.

BLADDER, INFLAMMATION OF THE (CYSTITIS). It may be caused by stone or by some form of infection which has introduced the harmful bacteria, or it is often caused by a chill, such as prolonged motor-car riding or chilled feet. The following mixture brings relief:

> 15 grains citrate of potash
> ½ oz. infusion of buchu
> 1 tablespoonful three times per day.

The symptoms are pain in the small of the back, frequency of making water, bad smell to the urine, and a whitish sediment. In severe cases there may be high fever and fits of shivering. Send for a doctor. The patient should stay in bed, have hot fomentations, and simple diet with a large quantity of barley water to drink. Give no alcohol.

BLANCMANGE. Recipes for blancmanges made with arrowroot, cornflour or ground rice are given under these three headings.

BLANCMANGE. When making a blancmange or jelly always rinse the mould first with cold water. This makes it easy to get the mould out and gives it a gloss.

BLANKETS, to wash. An ounce of glue should be dissolved in a pint of water and placed in a jug to stand on the stove. Stir the glue water into a bath full of hot water. Place the blankets in the bath, and leave for half an hour, stirring occasionally. This will remove all the dirt. Put through the wringer and rinse in hot water; wring out again and hang out on the line. When washed and thoroughly dried, blankets should be beaten with an ordinary carpet-beater; this makes the wool light and soft and gives the blankets a new and fresh appearance.

BLEEDING, to stop. A handkerchief should be doubled up into a pad, put over the wound, and kept in position by pressure from the hand, or another handkerchief may be tied tightly over it.

If an artery of a limb is cut, and the blood spouts out, a handkerchief should be tied round the limb *above* the wound, and a stick put through the handkerchief and twisted as tightly as possible. The part should be elevated, and the patient should lie down and keep as quiet as possible.

BLEEDING FROM THE NOSE. *See* NOSE.

BLEEDING HEART (DICENTRA). This plant, so general a favourite under its older name Dielytra, requires no recommendation. Its more fitting place is some sheltered nook in the rock garden, where its slender stalks of blood-red flowers could more safely display their peculiar beauty. Plant in leaf-mould and sand. Increased by division.

BLOATERS, to cook. Cut off heads and tails and clean and then wrap each fish completely in a piece of greaseproof or buttered paper with a small bit of fat, plate the fish in a baking-tin and put same in a moderate oven for about 20 minutes. Take fish out of paper and serve. By this method there will be no smell in cooking.

BLOODLESSNESS, or ANAEMIA. This occurs most frequently in females between fourteen and twenty-five. Pallor and palpitations are usual signs. The patient should have plenty of fresh air and easily digested food; rest, both bodily and mentally. Avoid climbing stairs and weight-carrying, and constipation should be relieved by taking a Seidlitz powder or a dose of saline in water every morning before breakfast till the bowels are regular.

Iron must be taken in some form or other. Pills are the most convenient; 1 to 3 aloes and iron pills three times a day after food, or Blaud's pills taken in the same way. A walk should be taken daily in fresh air and a daily bath, using a coarse towel with which to dry briskly to stimulate circulation.

BLOOD STAINS, to remove. Soak the article in several changes of clean cold water before washing in warm soapy water, or, in the case of delicate fabrics, or any article for which the foregoing method is impracticable, lightly sponge the stained part with lukewarm water to which has been added a few drops of ammonia.

BOARDS, to whiten. Add to 1 part of lime, 2 parts of soft soap and 3 parts of silver sand. Sprinkle a little on the boards and well scrub with a wet scrubbing brush. Rinse with clean water and wipe dry. This method will prevent vermin.

BOILERS, HOT WATER. *See* WATER SUPPLY.

BOILERS, LEAKY, to make a cement for. Mix together 2 parts powdered litharge, 2 parts very fine sand, and 1 part slaked quicklime. When required for use, mix the contents with boiled linseed oil and apply immediately, as it hardens very quickly.

BOILERS, RUST IN. Rust can be prevented if, after emptying, the boiler is rubbed with soap, whilst it is still hot.

BOILS. Bring to a head by applying hot fomentations of camomile flowers. Surrounding the boil with sticking plaster perforated to let the pus escape, may help to check the severity of the inflammation. When the boil is ripe it should be opened, taking care not to let the pus remain on the surrounding skin. The condition of the blood should receive attention and the bowels kept open.

BOOKS, to preserve from mildew. A few drops of strong perfumed oil sprinkled in the bookcase will preserve books from damp and mildew.

BOOT POLISH. If the polish cakes and breaks before the tin is finished up, it can be put into the oven or over moderate heat for only a minute or two, when it will soften into paste again and can be used to the last scrap.

BORACIC ACID, or BORIC ACID. This is an exceedingly useful antiseptic, obtainable from any chemist as powder, lotion or ointment.

BORACIC LINT. This is a very handy form of dressing for any wound, and merely requires to be moistened with water before being applied to the wound.

BORECOLE (KALE). Borecole and kale are the same, and are popularly known as winter greens, as they provide abundant supplies of excellent green food even during the severest winters. It requires a deep, moderately rich, well decomposed soil. For first crop sow at the beginning of March, and prick out the seedlings about the end of April. These will have formed sturdy plants, and be ready for final planting towards the latter part of May, for use in early winter. A sowing should be made in the middle of May, pricked out and planted in beds early in July, to furnish a supply during winter and spring. The plants should be from 2 to 2½ feet apart each way, carefully watered when necessary, and in cutting, the top or heart of the plant should be taken first.

BOSTON CREAM.

1 oz. tartaric acid	1 breakfastcupful sugar
2½ breakfastcupfuls boiling water	2 teaspoonfuls essence of lemon
	1 white of egg

Pour boiling water over sugar, stirring occasionally. When cold add acid, the essence and well-whisked white of egg and then bottle the cream. Take 2 teaspoonfuls to 1 tumbler of water, adding ½ saltspoonful carbonate of soda if desired.

BOSTON TOASTS.

3 eggs	1½ oz. butter
½ glass port	2 tablespoonfuls grated cheese
chillies	pepper and salt

Add the yolks of eggs to the butter, stir until it thickens, then add the cheese. Mix well and add the port wine and seasonings. Make thoroughly hot but do not let it boil. Put a thick layer on squares of hot buttered toast, garnish with strips of chillies and serve.

BOTTLES, MEDICINE, to clean. Put some tea leaves in a bottle with a few spoonfuls of tepid water. Shake well and leave for a few minutes. Repeat the operation if smell has not entirely disappeared.

BOTTLE TOPS, STIFF. To remove the screw cover or the lid of a bottle or jar, instead if using a cloth, try gripping with a piece of sandpaper.

BOTTLING OF FRUIT. *See* FRUIT.

BOWELS, INFLAMMATION OF THE. This is mostly confined to children and is prevalent during warm weather. If the child is at the breast it should be fed regularly, but not allowed to overload its stomach; a quarter of an hour is long enough to remain at the breast. A teaspoonful of lime-water may be given before the child begins suckling. In bottle-fed children the milk should be boiled, and the vessels that it is stored in and the feeding-bottle both kept scrupulously clean. Children should not be weaned during hot weather. If they have been and diarrhœa sets in, they should be returned to the breast. If notwithstanding diarrhœa sets in, a dose of castor oil should be given. If bottle-fed, all milk and milk foods should be stopped, and the child fed on albumen water made by adding the white of 1 egg to ½ a pint of cold water, and given in teaspoonful doses. Barley water may be given to quench the thirst. Hot fomentations should be applied to the abdomen and constantly changed. If these simple remedies fail to give relief a doctor should be consulted.

BRAIN, INFLAMMATION OF (MENINGITIS).

Causes.—Injury, burns, during measles, scarlet fever, or erysipelas; sometimes as a complication to discharge from the ear. It is now considered a very serious condition and medical advice should be taken at first symptoms.

Symptoms.—Headache, restlessness, fever, vomiting, convulsions, paralysis.

Treatment.—The patient should be in a darkened room and kept perfectly quiet; put on a milk diet, and every direction of the doctor rigorously carried out.

BRAIN SAUCE.

> ½ pint melted butter
> brains of calf or sheep already cooked
> pinch of salt and pinch of cayenne

Heat the melted butter and add the salt, cayenne and brains chopped small. This sauce is used for serving with sheep's or calf's head.

BRAINS ON TOAST.

calf's or sheep's brains	few sprays of fresh parsley
1 egg	(unchopped)
about 1 teaspoonful parsley	1 oz. butter
(chopped finely)	pinch each of salt and pepper
1 gill milk	squares or rounds of toast

Wash brains in cold water, removing any clots of blood, or bits of loose skin, and allow to soak for about half an hour. Then place in boiling water to which has been added a tablespoonful of vinegar or lemon juice and simmer gently for 10 minutes. Take out, drain and chop fairly coarsely, removing the skin. Make the toast, butter and keep hot. Put the chopped brains into a pan with the butter, chopped parsley, milk and thoroughly beaten egg. Add the pepper and salt and stir over a very gentle heat until the mixture is heated right through, but be very careful that it does not boil, otherwise the egg will curdle. As soon as ready place the mixture on the pieces of toast and serve at once on a hot dish garnished with the sprigs of parsley.

BRASSICA. The family name for vegetables of the cabbage variety—broccoli, savoys, sprouts, cauliflower, cabbage and such.

BRAWN.

1 pig's head	1 teaspoonful mixed spice
1 onion	pepper and salt
6 cloves	1 teaspoonful chopped sage if
2 bay leaves	liked

Well wash the head in salt and water to remove the blood, rub the head with common salt, a little brown sugar, and saltpetre, and leave it for three days, adding a little fresh salt every day. Put it in a stewpan with enough cold water to cover, an onion stuck with cloves and the bay leaves, simmer till quite tender, then remove the bones. Cut the meat up roughly, sprinkle over the mixed spice, sage and plenty of pepper and salt. Skin the tongue, place some of the head in a brawn tin, lay in the tongue, fill with the rest of the head, pour over some of the liquor in which it was cooked, then put away to get cold. Turn it out of the mould when required for use.

The brawn will be improved if two extra tongues are procured and added.

BREAD CUTTING. New bread may be cut into the thinnest slices by first dipping the knife into boiling water.

BREAD, to detect adulteration. Alum is sometimes used in bread to give a pure white colour. This is very harmful because it injures the linings of the stomach and impairs digestion. Its presence may be detected if a piece of the bread is soaked in ammoniacal tincture of logwood. Pure bread becomes pink; adulterated bread turns blue.

BREAD, to prevent burning. If you dredge flour at the bottom of your loaf tins before putting in the dough the bread will not burn. This is also true of tarts, pies and buns.

BREAD, BREAKFAST BUNS.

3 oz. lard	1 lb. flour
½ oz. yeast	2 eggs
2 oz. sugar	¼ lb. currants
2 oz. candied peel	

Rub lard into flour, add yeast, beaten-up eggs, sugar, currants washed and dried, and peel shredded. Warm a little milk; add enough to make a dough. Stand in warm place to rise, work into buns, brush with milk. Bake in hot oven for 20 minutes.

BREAD, BROWN.

1¾ lb. household flour	1 teaspoonful sugar
1¼ lb. whole meal	1 oz. salt
1 oz. German yeast	tepid water (about 1½ pints)

Make as for white household bread.

BREAD, CORN.

1 pint cornmeal (maize meal)	1 pint milk
1 pint flour	2 eggs
3 tablespoonfuls melted butter	1 teaspoonful salt

Mix the cornmeal and flour together in a basin, add the salt, mix with the eggs and beat thoroughly; add the melted butter and the pint of milk. Pour the mixture into a well-buttered tin and bake in a hot oven.

BREAD, DRY AND STALE, seven ways of using. Put all dry pieces of crusts, crumbs, and leavings of the table in a tin pan. When the bread is drawn put in the oven and let it stand all night. When pounded it is called Rusk Crumbs and is good to eat in milk or in any of the following ways:

1. Take apple sauce, stewed pears or peaches, or any kind of small berries and mix them with equal quantities of Rusk Crumbs. Prepare an egg custard, making it very sweet. Mix it with the crumbs and fruit, and bake for 20 minutes as a pudding.

2. Make an egg custard, thicken it with Rusk Crumbs, and bake for 20 minutes. Serve with pudding sauce, flavoured with nutmeg (and wine if desired).

3. Take any kind of cold meats, chop them fine with cold ham, or cold salt pork. Season with salt and pepper, and mix in 2 eggs and a little butter. Mix this up with bread-crumbs or Rusk Crumbs and bake it like a pudding. Or put it in a pan and warm it like hash. Or put it into balls, flatten and fry like forced meat balls.

4. Soak dry bread-crumbs in milk till quite soft. Then beat up 3 eggs and stir in, and put in sliced and peeled apples, or any kind of berries. Flour a pudding cloth, and tie it up and boil it half or three-quarters of an hour, according to size. This pudding does not swell in boiling. Eat with sauce.

5. Take stale bread and crumble it fine, and mix it with an egg and a little milk, and boil it in a large pudding cloth, or put it around small peeled apples, and boil it for dumplings in several smaller cloths.

6. Take bread-crumbs or Rusk Crumbs, and mix them with eggs and milk, and bake them for griddle cakes. If you have raspberries, blackberries, strawberries, or ripe currants, put them in and thicken with a little flour, so as to make *drop cakes*, and bake them (a large spoonful at a time) on a griddle, as drop cakes. Or put them in muffin rings, and bake them. Serve with butter and sugar, or with pudding sauces.

7. Break it into rather small rough pieces, dip each in sweetened milk quickly, and place on a slightly buttered tin in a cool oven until dry and crisp. Hand with cheese or butter.

BREAD, FRENCH ROLLS.

1 quart lukewarm milk
½ teacupful yeast
1 teaspoonful salt

Flour, enough to make a stiff batter
mix thoroughly

Set it to rise and, when very light, work in 1 egg and 2 spoonfuls of butter, and knead in flour till stiff enough to roll.

Let it rise again, and when very light, roll out, cut in strips, and braid it. Bake 30 minutes on buttered tins.

BREAD, MILK ROLLS.

½ lb. flour
1 oz. butter
1 teaspoonful castor sugar

1 teaspoonful baking-powder
½ teaspoonful salt
milk to mix

Mix flour and salt in a basin, rub in the butter lightly, add the sugar and baking-powder, and mix with enough milk to form a dough. Turn the dough on to a floured board, make into fancy shapes, place them on a greased tin, brush over with milk, and bake in a quick oven for 15 minutes.

BREAD, QUICKLY MADE.

1 lb. flour
2 teaspoonfuls baking-powder

1 teaspoonful salt
water or milk to mix

Sift the flour into a basin, add salt and baking powder, mix to a soft dough with water or milk; knead lightly on a floured board; form quickly into loaves, and bake in a hot oven for about half an hour.

BREAD SAUCE. *See* SAUCE, BREAD.

BREAD, VIENNA.

1 lb. Vienna flour
½ oz. yeast
1 oz. butter

1 egg
1 teaspoonful sugar
1 teaspoonful salt
½ pint milk

Cream the sugar and yeast together, warm the milk, add with the beaten egg to the yeast. Sift the flour into a basin, add the salt and rub in the butter, mix to a light dough with the milk and yeast; leave to prove in a warm place from 1½ to 2 hours. Form the dough into fancy shapes, brush over with egg; leave on a greased tin in a warm place for 10 minutes. Bake in a quick oven for 20 minutes.

BREAD, WHITE HOUSEHOLD.

3½ lb. flour
1 oz. German yeast
1 oz. salt (small)

1 teaspoonful sugar
tepid water (about 1½ pints)

Put the flour into a warm basin, make a well in the middle of the flour; add the sugar to the yeast, cream them together until liquid, pour it into the well in the middle of the flour; add some water, stir in enough flour from the sides to form a thick batter, sprinkle over with flour and put the salt round the sides; cover with a cloth and put in a warm place for half an hour. This is called setting the sponge. Knead the whole into a firm dough, using more tepid water if required. The pan should be quite clean. Sprinkle in a little flour, replace the dough, cut it across and put it in a warm place for 2 to 3 hours to prove. The dough should swell to more than double the size. When ready turn it on to a floured board, knead again and form into loaves, put them on a warm floured tin, stand in a warm place for 10 minutes, then bake in a hot oven until they sound hollow when tapped on the bottom.

Note.—For loaves baked in tins the dough need not be so stiff.

BREAM, BAKED. Cut down centre. Thoroughly wash and wipe, fill with veal stuffing and sew up again. Smear over with butter and bake in baking-tin for an hour. Serve on hot dish and garnish with lemon and parsley. The skin must be removed when carving.

BREATH, OFFENSIVE, or onion tainted. In case of offensive breath from stomach disorders take 6 drops of concentrated solution of common salt in a wineglassful of water during the morning toilet.

If the cause is decayed teeth, rinse the mouth well with a teaspoonful of the salt solution in a tumbler of water.

For breath tainted after eating onions, eat a few leaves of parsley dipped in vinegar.

BREWIS, to make. Here is a good way of using up crust and dry fragments of bread. Soak them for some time in hot milk, mash up and eat with salt.

BRIGHT'S DISEASE.

Causes.—Often results from an acute attack of inflammation of the kidneys, or from over-eating, lead poisoning, gout, or excessive alcohol.

Symptoms.—Comes on slowly. Headache, vomiting, general weakness, swelling of legs and puffiness of eyelids. Sometimes goes on for years.

Treatment.—Avoid exposure to cold and, if possible, reside in a warm climate. Alcohol should be taken in moderation only if customary, otherwise it is better left alone. Milk, eggs, fish and chicken should form the principal articles of diet. Eat mutton in preference to beef. Avoid all sudden muscular exertion and strain.

BROAD BEANS. *See* BEANS, BROAD.

BROCCOLI. Cook in the same way as cauliflower.

BROCCOLI. Sow thinly nearly an inch deep in April, but not in same plot as last season, and prick out the young plants when large enough to handle. Transplant in July into rich loamy soil, in rows 2½ feet apart. Give waterings of liquid manure during hot breaks. A sprinkling of salt on the ground in autumn will be beneficial in hard weather. Lower the heads of the plants northwards before frost sets in, disturbing the soil about the roots as little as possible. A new hybrid, *Cauli-Broccoli* produces good white heads; but it is not hardy enough to flourish in cold areas. Treat as Broccoli for culture. *Purple-sprouting Broccoli*, quite hardy, is grown in the same way.

BROCCOLI, to pickle. *See* PICKLES, CAULIFLOWER.

BROKEN ENGAGEMENTS. *See* ENGAGEMENTS.

BRONCHITIS. The patient should be in bed or sitting up in a warm room. An attack of bronchitis can often be thrown off in a few days if the patient remains indoors and takes no risks such as going from a warm room out into cold passages or the open air. The bowels should be kept open and a quarter to a half teaspoonful of ipecacuanha wine taken three or four times a day. Hot milk will loosen the phlegm. Use mustard poultices on the chest, or rub with hartshorn and oil. Children may be given hot home-made lemonade at bedtime, to which may be added 1 or 2 tablespoonfuls of whisky if the patient is an adult. A jug of steaming water to which has been added a teaspoonful of Friar's balsam or a few drops of eucalyptus oil should be prepared, a towel put over the head and the vapour inhaled, keeping the eyes shut meanwhile.

BROOM. *See* CYTISUS.

BROOMS. Always stand head upwards. Wash in hot soapy water about once a fortnight and hang up until thoroughly dry.

BROOMS, OLD. Get some bits of cloth and make a pad rather larger than the broom head. Lay this on the hair, having a larger piece outside, which wrap tightly round the broom's head and secure at top with tack. This makes a capital floor polisher.

BROTH, CHICKEN.

1 old fowl
1 quart water

1 oz. rice or pearl barley
chopped parsley
salt and pepper

Prepare and draw fowl, unless this has already been done by poulterer. Cut off all the meat and cut up into small pieces. Chop the bones and put all into a stewpan with the water. Simmer gently for 2 hours or more, then strain and return to the pan with the rice or pearl barley previously washed in a little warm water and soaked in same. When rice or barley is tender, season with salt and pepper. When serving sprinkle over very finely chopped parsley.

BROTH, SCOTCH (for 4 people).

2 lb. neck mutton
1 quart water
1 onion
1 carrot
1 turnip

2 oz. pearl barley
bouquet garni
seasoning
1 teaspoonful chopped parsley

Cut meat up finely, removing fat and skin, chop the bones, add to the water with onion, seasoning and bouquet garni, and allow to simmer gently for 1 hour. Strain and remove bones, return to the saucepan with the blanched barley, carrot and turnip cut in tiny dice, simmer till carrot is tender; put back some of the meat cut in neat pieces. Season and add parsley just before serving.

BROTH, VEAL (for 10 people).

small knuckle veal
3 quarts water
2 onions
4 oz. rice

4 cloves
slice of lemon peel
salt and pepper

Wash the veal, put it in a stewpan with the cold water. When it boils remove the scum thoroughly, add a little salt, which causes the scum to rise better. Simmer for 1½ hours, then add the onions stuck with cloves and the rice (which must be well washed) and the lemon peel. Cook again for 1½ hours; remove the vegetables and the knuckle, cut the meat into neat pieces, return to the pan, flavour to taste. Serve the broth with rice and meat in it.

BRUSHES, PAINT. After use remove the paint and clean the brushes in turpentine. If the brushes are not to be used again for some time wash them also in soda water, rinse in plain water and moisten with linseed oil. To soften brushes that have become hard soak them in equal parts of turpentine and linseed oil and then in warm soda water, finishing by gently kneading bristles when dry. Do not allow brushes to rest on the bristles when not in use.

BRUSHES, WHITEWASH, cleaning. With cold water wash off the lime from the bristles of the brush; and scrub well with a hard scrubbing-brush the part where the bristles are fixed into the wood. This should be done at once, as soon as the whitewashing for that day is finished. It is far better than to let them soak all night.

BRUSSELS SPROUTS.

sprouts	salt	carbonate of soda

Take off the outside leaves of the sprouts and cut across the stalk, leave to soak in salted water. Place them in boiling water with salt and a pinch of carbonate of soda and cook gently uncovered till tender, drain well in a colander, arrange neatly in a hot vegetable dish.

BRUSSELS SPROUTS. Sow thinly in March and for succession in April and May, and transplant when strong enough in rows 3 feet apart by 2 feet, into soil which has been deeply trenched and liberally manured. Early sowings can be in a cold frame. Transplant 6 inches apart and in May plant out permanently 2½ feet apart, treading in each plant very firmly. Do not cut off the head of the plant till the sprouts are stripped.

BUGS, to kill. Where it is possible to make use of it, boiling water is quite effective for this purpose. In cases where it is not possible to use boiling water, make an emulsion of either petroleum, or benzine, with soap, and apply with either a syringe or brush. To make emulsion use 2 oz. of soft soap dissolved in ½ pint of hot water, then add 3 pints of petroleum oil, or benzine, stirring all well together until it gives a milky appearance. Dilute with 6 parts of water and force into the cracks with either a syringe or brush, as mentioned above.

If it is not possible to use either the boiling water or the foregoing emulsion, the only other method is to fumigate the room by burning in it, on either an old shovel or some other metal utensil, a mixture of brimstone and saltpetre, taking precautions to see that all possible air has been excluded from the room. Do not remain in room.

BULBOCODIUM (SPRING MEADOW SAFFRON). A bulb of the lily tribe, one of the earliest of spring flowers and delightful for its beautiful colour of purplish hue. It should have a place in every spring garden and may be propagated by division in summer.

BULBS. These should be planted at varying depths according to size. A good rule is: 2 inches for anemone, crocus, scilla and snowdrops; 3 inches for hyacinth, iris, montbretia and tulip; 4 inches for gladioli and narcissus and 6 inches for lilies.

BUNIONS. To get rid of bunions successfully the cause must be ascertained and the bunions treated accordingly. If they are due to flat foot, metal plates in shoes will support the arches. If the joints are enlarged owing to gout or rheumatism, heed must be paid to the constitutional condition of the sufferer. In any case, wear stockings and shoes of which the inner edges of the soles are perfectly straight.

A simple treatment for bunions is by using a lotion made from Comfrey powder or root. The comfrey can be obtained from any herbalist. Two tablespoonfuls put into 1 pint of cold water, brought slowly to the boil, then simmered for a half-hour, and strained into a basin. This will make three bathings by adding that proportion to as much hot water as needed. Bathe and soak the bunion for about 5 minutes every morning and evening. This should be followed by rinsing in plain warm water. If the bunion is still distended, even after several weeks' continuous treatment, then consult a chiropodist.

BUNS, BATH.

8 oz. flour
2 oz. castor sugar
2 oz. margarine
1 gill milk
2 oz. peel
1 egg
grated rind of 1 lemon

Heat the milk and mix with it some yeast and 1 tablespoonful sugar, and leave in a warm place for 5 minutes. Add the flour whilst beating and set aside for 30 minutes. Melt the margarine, adding with the egg the remainder of the sugar, and the fruit. Mix into a soft dough and form into the required size. Place on a greased baking-tin and bake in a cool oven for 30 minutes. Bake in a hotter oven, gradually increasing the heat, for another 30 minutes. When baked, brush over with a tablespoonful of brown sugar, dissolved in warm water, and sprinkle a little sugar on top.

BUNS, CHERRY.

6 oz. self-raising flour
2 oz. ground rice
2 oz. butter
2 oz. castor sugar
2 oz. glacé cherries
1 egg
a little milk

Rub the butter into flour, add rice, sugar and cherries, cut in small pieces, keeping back some to decorate the buns. Beat up the egg with a little milk and mix well. Bake in greased patty tins or in heaps on a greased baking-sheet; place half a cherry on each bun. Bake from 7 to 10 minutes.

BUNS, CITRON.

½ lb. self-raising flour
3 oz. butter
1 oz. rice flour
3 oz. sugar
1 oz. chopped almonds
grated rind of ½ lemon
3 oz. citron
2 eggs and a little milk

Rub the butter into the flour, add all the dry ingredients, mix to a stiff dough with the beaten eggs and a little milk, form into buns, and bake on a greased baking-sheet in a quick oven for 10 minutes.

BUNS, COCOANUT.

½ lb. flour	3 oz. butter
4 oz. cocoanut	1 egg
3 oz. castor sugar	a little milk

Cream the butter and sugar together, add the egg and beat well, then the flour and cocoanut, using a little milk if too stiff. Place in small heaps on a greased baking-sheet, using two forks. Bake in a quick oven for 15 minutes.

BUNS, GINGER.

	1 teaspoonful ground ginger
1 lb. self-raising flour	3 oz. golden syrup
4 oz. butter	1 egg
4 oz. sugar	little milk if required

Cream the butter and sugar well together, sift the flour, ginger, beat the egg and add the syrup; mix into the butter and sugar with the sifted flour, etc.; stir lightly and quickly. Divide the mixture into equal parts, roll each portion into a round ball, place on a greased baking-sheet, and bake in a moderate oven for 15 or 20 minutes.

BUNS, HOT CROSS.

Mix together 1½ oz. yeast, 1 pint milk, ½ lb. sugar, ½ lb. flour, 1 pint hot water, and stand in a warm place until it rises and falls again. Rub ½ lb. butter or lard into 3 lb. of flour, and add 12 drops of essence of spice. Mix the whole together and stand in a warm place until dough rises. Then form into buns and place in flat tins; make the cross with the back of a knife. Make the buns rise by means of steam, and bake in a quick oven for about 5 minutes.

BUNS, LEMON.

	2 eggs
1 lb. self-raising flour	grated rind of 1 lemon
4 oz. butter	lemon essence
4 oz. sugar	little milk if required

Sift the flour, rub in the butter, add the sugar and grated lemon rind; beat the eggs, stir into the dry ingredients, adding a few drops of lemon essence and a little milk if necessary. Divide into about twelve portions, form into round shape, and brush over with egg and sprinkle them with sugar. Place them in a greased baking-sheet and bake in a moderate oven for about 20 minutes.

BUNS, RICE.

	2 oz. sugar
2 oz. flour	½ oz. peel grated lemon rind
2 oz. ground rice	1 egg
2 oz. butter	a little milk

Cream the butter and the sugar together, add egg, flour, rice, and beat well, then add chopped peel or grated lemon rind and a little milk if too stiff. Put mixture into greased patty tins and bake in a moderate oven for about 15 minutes.

BUNS, SEED.

½ lb. self-raising flour
2 oz. dripping
½ oz. caraway seeds

2 oz. sugar
½ oz. candied peel
1 egg and a little milk
pinch of salt

Rub the dripping into the flour, add all the dry ingredients, beat the egg, add a little milk and mix to a very stiff dough. Place in rough heaps on a greased baking-sheet. Bake in a quick oven about 15 minutes.

BURIALS. The executors or nearest relatives are responsible for a deceased person's burial: his wishes, if any, must be strictly fulfilled. If he desired cremation he should have left instructions in writing. Failing a parish churchyard he should be buried in the nearest cemetery. Poor persons can be buried at the expense of the County Council or Borough Council. A person found drowned on the seashore is buried at the expense of the parish. It is necessary to register a person's death before burial; for cremation to have the death certified by two doctors.

BURNING, to prevent. A large marble boiled with milk custard or porridge will automatically do the stirring as the liquid cooks and thus prevent burning. Care must be taken to remove it before the food is served.

A tray of water on the bottom shelf of the oven when cooking cakes and pastries will prevent burning.

BURNS. When the burn has been slight and the part is red and blistered, flour or ground starch should be dusted thickly over it to exclude the air; lanoline or castor oil will answer the same purpose. The burn should be covered with a clean handkerchief and protected from injury.

When the burns are deep, the clothes must be removed very carefully. The burn should be bathed in Condy's fluid, boracic acid, or any antiseptic, and stupes of lint smeared with boracic ointment applied. The patient should be put to bed and covered with blankets, and hot-water bottles put to the feet; then give stimulants or strong tea or coffee.

BURNS AND SCALDS. If white of egg be poured over the wound, inflammation will be prevented and the pain alleviated.

BURNS FROM ACIDS. Wash immediately with limewater, carbonate of soda and water, whiting and water, or chalk and water. Failing these, use old mortar and water. Then apply the mixture of chalk and oil. For burns from sulphuric acid bathe with linseed oil for 10 minutes.

BURNS FROM LIME. After bathing with vinegar and water, apply chalk which has been mixed with linseed oil to a thin paste. Renew the treatment at intervals.

BURNT ALUMINIUM PAN. You can clean this by half-filling the pan with water into which odd bits of rhubarb have been put. Boil for 15 minutes.

BURNT DISHES, china, enamel, etc., to clean. Rub them with a damp cloth sprinkled with salt.

BURNT MILK. The best way to use up burnt milk is to make it into a chocolate blancmange when the nasty taste will disappear. It can be made quickly by mixing a little cocoa with cornflour.

BUTTER, to soften. If butter be too hard for spreading, place it in a saucer, put the saucer above a pan containing hot water, and gently stir the butter from time to time.

BUTTER BEANS. Soak ½ lb. butter beans in water, well covering to allow for swelling and leave all night. Cook butter beans in salted water, with a small carrot and an onion. Meantime boil a small head of celery until tender, chop into dice and add to a white sauce (which see). When the butter beans are tender, drain and put into a pan with the celery and sauce, simmer gently for 10 minutes and serve piping hot.

BUTTER, MELTED.

1½ oz. butter	½ pint water
1 oz. flour	salt and pepper

Make as white sauce, season with salt and pepper. Served as a plain savoury sauce for fish, boiled meats and vegetables.

BUTTER, RANCID, to sweeten. Wash first in good new milk and afterwards in cold spring water.

BUTTER, SALT, to freshen. By churning each pound of salt butter with 1 quart of new milk it may be made fresh.

BUTTERSCOTCH.

	vanilla
¼ lb. brown sugar	1 teaspoonful vinegar
1 gill water	½ oz. butter

Place all the ingredients except the vanilla into a pan and boil for 20 minutes. Remove from the fire and add the vanilla. Pour into buttered tins.

BUTTONS. When sewing on buttons, especially on heavy cloth, do not drag the button down tightly. Put a thick pin under it and sew button and pin together. Then release the pin and before securely finishing off, pass the thread several times round that remaining loose under the button. This will prevent any tearing of the cloth by the strain on the button.

CABBAGE. Whether spring or winter cabbages, the culture is the same, the time of sowing being: spring, July to August; winter, April to June. Sow thinly 1 inch deep, keep watered and protected from birds. As soon as the plants have made from four to five leaves they should be planted out from 24 inches apart on a well-manured and deeply-trenched piece of ground; a liberal supply of liquid manure is useful during the growing season. When planting, firmly tread in the young seedlings, both at roots and on surface. The destructive caterpillar must be picked off every evening from first noticing and put into salt and water to make sure of destruction. The pest can be checked in advance by early dustings of Derris powder on the young plants to keep off the white butterfly, which deposits the eggs or larvæ.

Red Cabbage.—Seed should be sown in March, following the procedure above.

CABBAGE AND BACON.

bacon, cheese	½ head cabbage
potatoes	1 cupful milk

The cabbage should be sliced and boiled in milk for 20 minutes. Season with pepper, place in baking-dish and cover with slices of streaky bacon. Place in oven till bacon is browned. Sliced cooked potatoes can be used instead of bacon; cover with grated cheese after potato is browned and serve when cheese is melted.

CABBAGE, RED, to pickle.

1 red cabbage	mace
vinegar	peppercorns
	salt

Choose a fine, tight cabbage and cut it very thin; then take some cold vinegar, three blades of mace, a few white peppercorns and make it fairly thick with salt. Put the cabbage into the vinegar as you cut it, put it into a glass-preserving jar, screw it down tight and it will be fit for use in a day or two.

CABBAGE, RED, to stew.

1 red cabbage	1 gill vinegar
1 slice ham	1 tablespoonful sugar
½ oz. butter	salt
½ pint stock	pepper

Cut the cabbage into thin shreds and put into a pan with a slice of ham and the butter at the bottom. Add the stock and vinegar. Let it stew for 3 hours. Add a little more stock, salt, pepper and sugar. Mix well and boil till the liquor is exhausted, then put it into a dish and serve with fried sausages.

CABBAGE, SAVOURY (for 4 people).

cabbage	4 oz. grated cheese
1½ oz. butter	salt and pepper

Choose a cabbage with a good firm heart, boil in the usual way till tender, drain thoroughly, chop it finely, season well, place in a gratin dish, put the butter on in small pieces, sprinkle over a good layer of grated cheese, bake in a quick oven for ten minutes and serve hot.

CABBAGE, STUFFED (for 3 or 4 people).

1 large cabbage	½ gill brown sauce
3 oz. cold meat	salt and pepper

Mince the meat, mix with the brown sauce, season well, wash the cabbage thoroughly, split open, remove the centre, stuff with the mince, tie up with tape, boil in gravy for 1 hour and serve.

CAKE BAKING. The heat in most ovens is stronger on one side than the other; then the cake should be put farther away from the hotter side as it will draw the cake up more quickly on that side and consequently out of shape.

Every time the oven door is opened, which should be as seldom as possible, turn the cake round gently; this ensures it being cooked and browned evenly, and keeps the shape good. Always open and shut an oven door very gently; the sudden rush of air caused if the door is banged will send a cake down and make it heavy. Never take a cake out of the oven until it is well set, and not then if it can be avoided. Cakes should not be baked at the same time as meat; they may take up the flavour. If a range has two ovens one should be used for meat and one for cakes and pastry.

Heat of Oven.—With one exception only, have a *moderate* oven for cakes. Test the heat with the hand. If more than moderate, reduce it and put the cake in the middle of the oven. If put up too near the top, a hard crust is formed at once, which prevents the cake from rising. If too low down, it burns at the bottom, which is objectionable.

The exception referred to is in the case of a Christmas or Wedding cake. For both it is necessary to start in a hot oven, but only to set the mixture and so prevent the fruit sinking to the bottom. As soon as set, reduce to moderate heat for the rest of the time.

To Test when Done.—An experienced cakemaker can tell by the touch and the smell when a cake is done. For amateurs the safest test is to gently insert a bright skewer. If it comes out clean and dry the cake is sufficiently cooked. If a cake has to be kept a day or two it is well to leave the paper on; it helps to keep it moist.

A cake should be handled very carefully when removing it from the tin. Light mixtures should be allowed to stand a minute or two to shrink from the sides of the tin.

All cakes should be put on a cake-rack or sieve to cool. Failing these stand on a clean, dry cloth, so that the steam may pass off. Otherwise the cake will be sodden.

Some Useful Hints.—Put a pan of water in the oven while baking a fruit cake. The water will keep the cake moist during the baking.

Before turning a cake to cool, especially a chocolate cake, sprinkle some paper with sugar, turn out the cake and slip the cooling rack under it. Remove the paper from the bottom of the cake and again sprinkle lightly with sugar and turn over. Sugar will keep the cake from sticking to paper or cloth.

When greasing the cake-tin, use lard or saltless butter. Salt in the butter causes the cake to burn and stick to the tin.

To remove a cake from the tin without breaking, set the cake-tin on a damp cloth and the moisture created inside the tin loosens the cake until it can be slipped out easily.

To Prevent Burning.—Get the top of a biscuit tin and put half an inch of common salt in it. Place the cake-tin in the centre and heap the salt round the sides and put it in the oven in the ordinary way. The salt can be used again and again.

CAKE ICING AND PIPING. It is easier to do this when a cake has a covering of almond paste (which see) and a smoother surface is achieved. If there is no revolving icing stand put the cake on the back of a plate and stand it on a cake tin turned upside down. When the almond paste is dry and firm put sufficient royal icing on the top of the cake to cover it. Spread this over the cake with a palette knife, getting the sides smooth first. Hold the knife vertically to do this, drawing it round until the surface is smooth; then get the top smooth and even. Put the cake in a warm place to set. It should be thoroughly dry before it is piped.

To pipe a cake use good strong icing-paper to make the bags. To make these satisfactorily requires practice. The icing must be well beaten, and after the pipe is inserted in the bag drop in some icing; close the top of the bag carefully, and press the icing out on the cake in patterns. Much practice is required for elaborate patterns. There are a great many kinds of pipes that can be obtained; the rose, cord, leaf, ribbon are used most.

CAKE MAKING. It is of vital importance to take care in following directions and to give attention to detail if the work is to have success. There are four principal methods of making cakes:

1. The flour is sifted into a basin; the shortening, whether butter, lard or dripping, is rubbed into the flour; all the other dry ingredients are added (sugar, fruit, spices, etc.); the whole mixed with eggs and milk if required. This method is used for *plain* cakes.

2. The butter and sugar are creamed together; the eggs and flour beaten in alternately; the fruit, etc., stirred in last. This is done when making rich fruit, Madeira, wedding, Christmas cakes, etc.

3. The eggs and sugar are whisked together until thick and creamy, the flour sifted in lightly, and the butter—if any—melted and stirred in with the flour. This is the method of making sponge cakes, Genoese pastry, and all light cakes of that nature.

4. All the dry ingredients, such as flour, sugar, spice, etc., are put in a basin; the butter or lard heated in a saucepan with treacle or golden syrup, beaten eggs added and mixed quickly into the dry ingredients, carbonate of soda dissolved in milk and added. This is the method of making all kinds of plain and fancy gingerbreads.

Creaming.—When creaming butter and sugar together, warm the butter slightly if very hard, and beat until white and soft. It is not necessary to beat the eggs first when added in this method as they are beaten well after they are added to the mixture. For plain cakes they must be well beaten first before adding. Never use an egg that smells musty as the musty smell and taste remain even after the cake is baked.

CAKE, hint for making. One egg and 1 tablespoonful of vinegar will serve the place of 2 eggs.

CAKE, to keep moist. Keep the cake in a tin, adding a piece of fresh bread daily.

A sweet apple placed in the cake-tin will also keep cakes moist over a long period.

CAKE, APPLE.

1 lb. flour
½ lb. apples
2 oz. butter
2 oz. sugar
½ oz. yeast
1½ gills tepid water
¼ teaspoonful mixed spice
pinch of salt

Sift the flour into a basin with the salt, cream the yeast with 1 teaspoonful of sugar and pour on the tepid water; mix into the flour and put it into a warm place to rise for 1 to 1½ hours. Peel, core and chop the apples finely, and melt the butter; knead the dough on a floured board for 15 minutes; work in the apples and butter and the mixed spice. Put into a well-buttered cake-tin, allow it to prove for 10 minutes, then bake in a hot oven for a half to three-quarters of an hour.

CAKE, BACHELOR'S.

1 lb. flour
4 oz. butter
5 oz. sugar
¾ lb. currants
2 oz. peel
¼ teaspoonful mixed spice
1 teaspoonful carbonate of soda
about ¼ pint warm milk

Rub the butter into the flour; add the sugar, currants, peel and spice; dissolve the soda in the milk, strain into the dry ingredients, and mix quickly, making a stiff batter. Pour into a tin lined with greased-paper, and bake in a moderate oven for about 1 hour.

CAKE, CHERRY.

½ lb. self-raising flour
4 oz. butter
4 oz. castor sugar
3 oz. glacé cherries
3 eggs
grated rind of 1 lemon
little milk

Cream the butter and sugar well together, sift in the flour and add the eggs alternately, beating well between each addition, add the cherries cut in quarters, grated lemon rind and milk. Put the mixture in a tin lined with buttered paper and bake in a moderate oven for about 1¼ hours.

CAKE, CHERRY GINGER.

10 oz flour
3 oz. glacé cherries
3 oz. crystallized ginger
½ flat teaspoonful carbonate of soda
½ flat teaspoonful ground ginger
1 teaspoonful cream of tartar
6 oz. margarine
6 oz. sugar
2 eggs
milk

Mix flour, tartar, soda and ginger together in a basin. Cream the fat and sugar together. Add eggs and stir quickly and beat well. Then stir in flour and prepared fruit with milk as required—not too moist. Bake for 1¼ hours in moderate oven.

CAKE, CHOCOLATE.

6 oz. self-raising flour
6 oz. chocolate powder
6 oz. sugar
4 oz. butter
4 eggs
vanilla essence

Cream the butter and sugar together, sift in the flour and chocolate powder alternately with the eggs, beating well, add the vanilla essence. Bake in flat sandwich tin in a hot oven for about half an hour. When cold cut open, spread with jam or chocolate filling, and ice with chocolate icing and sprinkle with chopped pistachio nuts.

Note.—This cake can be baked in a cake-tin and iced if preferred.

CAKE, CHRISTMAS.

1 lb. self-raising flour	milk
12 oz. lard	¼ lb. glacé cherries
12 oz. sugar	¼ lb. candied peel
¼ lb. ground or chopped almonds	grated rind of 1 lemon
½ lb. sultanas	½ nutmeg grated
½ lb. raisins (stoned)	pinch of salt
¾ lb. currants	4 eggs
	1 wineglassful brandy

Mix flour, salt. Rub in the lard. Add all the dry ingredients after cleaning and picking the stalks from the currants and sultanas, cutting the cherries in halves and shredding the candied peel. Mix well, thoroughly whisk the eggs and gradually add the brandy to them; then stir into the eggs and brandy about 1 gill of milk. Moisten the cake mixture with this. Put mixture into a well-greased and lined cake-tin. Place in a hot oven for the first 20 minutes. Then lessen the heat slightly and allow the cake to cook for about 3 to 3½ hours longer, lessening the heat still further about 1 hour before the cake is cooked. If the top of the cake is found to be sufficiently brown before the cake is cooked, cover the top with a piece of greaseproof paper.

Note.—This cake improves by keeping, and should be made at the beginning of December. A day or so before it is required cover the cake with a layer of almond paste about 1 inch thick and then coat with Royal Icing. For these recipes see ALMOND PASTE and ICING, ROYAL. Decorate the top of the cake according to taste.

CAKE, DUNDEE.

¾ lb. self-raising flour	6 oz. currants
½ lb. butter	2 oz. peel
½ lb. sugar	½ teaspoonful mixed spice
6 oz. sultanas	grated lemon rind
4 oz. almonds	5 or 6 eggs

Prepare the fruit carefully, cream the butter and sugar together until quite soft, and add the eggs alternately with sifted flour. Beat well, add the fruit, spice and grated lemon rind, mix thoroughly, turn the mixture into a cake-tin lined with thick, buttered paper. Sprinkle over the blanched almonds. Bake in a moderate oven for 2 to 2½ hours.

CAKE, GENOA.

¾ lb. flour	2 oz. almonds
½ lb. butter	3 oz. mixed peel
½ lb. sugar	grated rind of 1 lemon
½ lb. sultanas	5 eggs

Cream the butter and sugar together, beat in the eggs and flour alternately, then the sultanas, peel and grated lemon rind. Pour the mixture into a tin lined with buttered paper. Blanch and split the almonds and sprinkle them on the top. Bake in a moderate oven for 2½ hours.

CAKE, GINGER.

12 oz. self-raising flour
6 oz. sugar
4 oz. preserved ginger
pinch of salt
½ gill ginger syrup
½ gill milk
2 eggs
6 oz. butter, lard or margarine

Mix the flour, sugar and salt. Rub in the fat. Add nearly all the preserved ginger chopped finely. Thoroughly whisk the eggs and then add to them the milk and ginger syrup, stirring well. Pour the eggs, milk and ginger syrup gradually into the cake mixture, beating well. Pour the mixture into a tin lined with buttered paper and decorate the top with the remainder of the preserved ginger cut into small pieces or thin slices. Sprinkle a little castor sugar over and bake in a moderate oven for 1 hour.

CAKE, MADEIRA.

8 oz. flour
5 oz. fresh butter
5 oz. castor sugar
citron or lemon peel
4 eggs

Cream the butter and sugar well together, sift the flour and add it alternately with the eggs, beaten well. Pour the mixture into a tin lined with buttered paper, sprinkle a little castor sugar on the top and place on two pieces of citron. Bake in a moderate oven.

CAKE, MOCHA.

4 eggs
4 oz. castor sugar
4 oz. flour
coffee icing (see Icing)
some chopped almonds

Whisk the eggs and sugar together as for sponge cake, beating for 20 minutes; add the sifted flour lightly. Pour the mixture into a buttered cake-tin and bake in a moderate oven for about 35 minutes. When cold and firm cut into three, and put in layers of coffee icing and press well together, spread thinly with the remainder of the icing, and cover all over with browned, finely-chopped almonds.

CAKE, ORANGE.

½ lb. self-raising flour
3 oz. butter
3 oz. castor sugar
grated rind of 1 orange (2 if
    small)
3 eggs

Cream the butter and sugar, add the eggs and sifted flour alternately, beat well and add the orange rind. Pour the mixture into a tin lined with buttered paper and bake in a moderate oven for about 1 hour.

Note.—This cake can be iced with an icing made of ½ lb. icing sugar mixed with orange juice and sprinkled with blanched and chopped pistachio nuts.

CAKE, PERTH SODA.

½ lb. flour
¼ lb. rice flour
2 oz. lard or dripping
1 oz. butter
6 oz. sugar
6 oz. sultanas
1 oz. peel
pinch of salt
1 egg
½ teaspoonful carbonate
    of soda
½ pint sour milk

Rub the butter and lard or dripping into the sifted flour, mix in well the carbonate of soda, sugar, sultanas and peel. Beat the egg, pour in into the centre of the flour, and use enough milk to mix to a soft dough. Bake in a tin lined with greased paper in a moderate oven for 1½ hours.

CAKE, POTATO.

½ lb. butter
½ lb. sugar
½ lb. potato flour
5 eggs
2 tablespoonfuls rum

Cream the butter and sugar together, sift flour and potato flour together, add alternately with the eggs, beating well all the time; when half the eggs and flour are used add the rum, then continue as before. The cake should be beaten altogether for 20 minutes. Put into a tin lined with buttered paper and bake for 1 to 1½ hours.

CAKE, SEED.

¾ lb. self-raising flour
4 oz. dripping
4 oz. sugar
1 oz. peel
pinch of salt
1 oz. caraway seeds
1 egg
¼ teaspoonful spice
1 gill milk

Rub the dripping into the flour, add the sugar, caraways, peel and spice, mix with the beaten egg and milk, using a little more milk if required. Bake in a moderate oven from 1½ to 2 hours.

CAKE, SIMNEL.

8 oz. self-raising flour
6 oz. lard
6 oz. castor sugar
½ teaspoonful grated
  nutmeg
pinch of salt
grated rind of 1 lemon
¼ lb. sultanas
¼ lb. currants
¼ lb. raisins (seeded)
2 oz. candied peel
4 eggs

Almond paste in accordance with recipe given for this. Sufficient almond paste should be available to permit of a layer about half an inch thick through the middle of the cake and another one about an inch thick on the top.

Cream the butter and sugar, add the lemon rind and then the eggs one by one, well beating after each is added. When three of them have been beaten in, add a little of the flour. Add the remaining egg, then gradually mix in the rest of the flour to which should have been previously added the salt and nutmeg, and lastly the fruit, well-cleaned and the peel shredded. Well grease and line the cake-tin and put in about half of the mixture, levelling the top and putting on it a layer of almond paste about half an inch thick: put the rest of the mixture in on top of the almond paste and bake in a moderate oven for about 3 hours. When nearly cooked remove cake from oven and cover the top with a layer of almond paste about 1 inch thick, mark out the almond paste with a knife into squares, brush over with white of egg or milk. Return cake to oven to finish cooking.

Another method of decorating the top of this cake is to leave the cake in the oven until completely cooked. Then place around the top edge a ring of the almond paste, drawing a fork around it. Make

54

some almond paste into little balls and place these on the ring of paste around the cake, decorating each with half a crystallized cherry. Put into the oven, or under a grill, to brown the edges of the paste.

CAKE, SPICE.

¾ lb. self-raising flour
6 oz. butter
6 oz. sugar
6 oz. currants
4 oz. sultanas
2 oz. peel
½ teaspoonful mixed spice
3 eggs
little milk

Prepare the fruit, sift the flour into a basin, rub in the butter lightly, add all the dry ingredients. Mix with the beaten eggs and a little milk if necessary. Turn the mixture into a tin lined with greased paper. Sprinkle a little castor sugar on the top, and bake in a moderate oven for 1½ hours.

CAKE, SPONGE.

4 eggs
5 oz. castor sugar
5 oz. flour
grated rind of 1 lemon

Whisk the eggs and sugar together in a warm place for 10 minutes, remove to a cooler place and beat for another 10 minutes. Sift the flour in very lightly, add the lemon rind; well butter a cake-tin, sift out twice first with a coating of sugar, then a coating of flour; pour in the mixture, tie a border of paper round the outside of the tin, and bake in a slow oven for 1¼ hours.

CAKE, VANILLA.

4 eggs
4 oz. castor sugar
5 oz. self-raising flour
vanilla essence
royal butter icing (see Icing)
chopped almonds

Whisk the eggs and sugar well together until a stiff froth, stir in the sifted flour, very lightly flavour with little vanilla. Pour the mixture into a buttered square cake-tin and bake in a moderate oven for about half an hour. When cold and firm coat thinly with butter icing flavoured with vanilla, press some browned chopped almonds round the sides; with some of the butter icing pipe half the top with roses close together, colour the rest pale pink, and pipe the other half with pink roses.

CAKE, WAFER OAT.

½ lb. oatmeal
1 gill boiling water
salt

Add about half a teaspoonful of salt to the oatmeal. Pour over it the boiling water, mix quickly into a dough; turn in on to a board sprinkled with oatmeal. Handle as little as possible. Roll out very thinly, cut into rounds or three-cornered shapes. Bake on a girdle or in a hot oven. Oatcakes should after the first day be toasted a little before the fire or crisped in a hot oven so that they may eat quite crisp.

CAKE, WALNUT.

8 oz. self-raising flour	3 oz. fresh butter
6 oz. butter	6 oz. icing sugar
6 oz. sugar	vanilla essence
3 eggs	fondant icing
3 oz. walnuts	

Cream the butter and sugar together until white, add eggs and sifted flour alternately, beating well. Put the mixture in two shallow tins lined with buttered paper; bake in a moderate oven from half to three-quarters of an hour. When the cakes are cold put them together with a layer of walnut filling between. To make the filling beat the fresh butter and icing sugar (sieved) to a cream, add the chopped walnuts and vanilla essence. Ice with fondant icing and decorate with walnuts.

Note.—A few walnuts finely chopped can be added to the cake mixture if liked.

CAKE, WEDDING.

1½ lb. flour	½ lb. French plums
1½ lb. butter	1 lb. citron peel
1½ lb. sugar	pinch of salt
2 lb. currants	10 eggs
1 lb. sultanas	1 gill noyau
½ lb. cherries	1½ gills brandy
¾ lb. almonds	little caramel

Cream the butter and sugar together until it is quite white, beat in the eggs and flour (sifted) alternately, add the fruit very carefully prepared and the brandy and noyau; colour the mixture a pale brown with the caramel; pour the mixture into a tin lined with several thicknesses of buttered paper. Bake in a hot oven at first and cooler afterwards for about 7 or 8 hours.

Note.—It is a good plan to put a thick layer of sand in the bottom of the oven to prevent the cake burning underneath, also to tie a thick layer of brown paper round the outside of the tin.

Three times the above quantity will make a large wedding cake of three tiers, and about 15 lb. of almond icing will be required.

CAKE, YORKSHIRE SANDWICH.

2 eggs	ground rice
their weight in butter	pinch of salt
sugar	jam
self-raising flour	

Cream the butter and sugar, beat in the eggs and flour alternately, bake in two sandwich tins lined with buttered paper in a moderate oven for about a quarter of an hour. When cold spread with jam or lemon curd mixture and place them together. Sprinkle with castor sugar.

CAKES, ALMOND FINGERS

¼ lb. flour	¼ lb. castor sugar
¼ lb. ground almonds	1 egg
	1 oz. sweet almonds

Mix flour, sugar and ground almonds together; add beaten yolk of egg; mix in the white of egg beaten stiff. Roll out and cut into fingers, brush with egg and sprinkle with sweet almonds chopped fine. Bake in moderate oven for 20 minutes.

CAKES, LITTLE CHOCOLATE.

6 oz. flour	3 oz. chocolate
3 oz. butter	3 eggs
3 oz. sugar	vanilla essence

Cream the butter and the sugar well together, sift the flour and grated chocolate, add alternately with the eggs, and beat well; flavour with vanilla essence, and put the mixture into small, well-buttered cake-tins. Bake in a moderate oven for 15 minutes. These cakes can be coated with chocolate icing if liked.

CAKES, QUEEN.

6 oz. flour	1 oz. citron
4 oz. butter	grated rind of lemon
4 oz. sugar	3 eggs
2 oz. currants	pinch of salt

Cream the butter and sugar together, add the eggs and sift in flour alternately and beat well; add the chopped citron, lemon rind and currants and salt and mix well. Put in well-buttered queen-cake tins and bake from 15 to 20 minutes.

CAKES, ROCK.

½ lb. self-raising flour	3 oz. currants
3 oz. dripping	1 oz. peel
3 oz. sugar	1 egg and a little milk
	pinch of salt

Rub the dripping into the flour; add all the dry ingredients. Beat up the egg with a little milk and mix to a very stiff dough. Place in rough heaps on a greased baking-sheet and bake in a quick oven about 15 to 20 minutes.

CAKES, ROSE.

4 oz. self-raising flour	4 oz. butter
4 oz. ground rice	4 eggs
6 oz. sugar	2 teaspoonfuls rose water
	carmine colouring

Cream the butter and sugar well together, sift in the flour and ground rice alternately, adding eggs, and beat lightly; add the rose water and colour a pretty pink with carmine. Put mixture in buttered patty tins and bake in a quick oven from 10 to 15 minutes. Ice with water icing and decorate with cherries.

CAKES, SURPRISE.

1 lb. ground almonds	little brandy or sherry
1 lb. icing sugar	colourings
1 or 2 eggs	angelica
	almonds

Mix the ground almonds and icing sugar together, add the beaten eggs and a little brandy or sherry till the mixture is the right consistency to form into shapes; divide and colour one part green, one part pink, and leave part uncoloured; form into apples, pears, cherries, potatoes, etc. A great variety can be made by taking the real vegetable or fruit as a model. For example, to make a potato, use the uncoloured paste and make a good shape and toss in chocolate powder.

CAKES, YEAST TEA.

1 lb. flour	1 egg
2 oz. lard or butter	1 teaspoonful castor sugar
½ oz. yeast	½ teaspoonful salt
	about 1½ gills tepid milk

Rub the lard into the flour, add the salt, cream the yeast with the sugar and add the beaten egg and tepid milk, knead when well mixed into a dough, set to prove for an hour in a warm place; divide the dough and form into round cakes. Place on a floured tin and allow to prove for 10 minutes, then bake in a quick oven for 15 minutes. Glaze with milk or beaten egg.

CAKE-TINS.
All tins need the most careful drying and storing. If there is a chance they may rust, rub them over with a little lard before putting away. Tin kettles rust very quickly. If you are not going to use them again at once boil up water and turn upside down—heat will dry them thoroughly; the same with saucepan lids.

CALCEOLARIA.
The golden blooms of the shrubby variety are effective for summer bedding; the herbaceous kind are better suited for the greenhouse. Both kinds need plenty of leaf-mould in the soil and abundant watering. Propagation of shrubby calceolarias is by cuttings made during October and kept in sand in a cold frame for the winter. For herbaceous species propagation may be by seed sown in a cool house in June, in pots or pans filled with a rich porous soil.

CALF'S BRAINS, FRIED (for 3 or 4 people).

2 sets of brains	1 tablespoonful vinegar
1 shallot	pepper and salt
chopped parsley	frying batter (*see* Batter)
1 tablespoonful salad oil	tomato sauce (*see* Sauce)

Cleanse the brains thoroughly and remove the skin, place in a stewpan with cold water and salt, boil up and simmer for 10 minutes, remove the brains, rinse them in cold water and allow them to get cold, and then cut into neat pieces, soak the brains for 1 hour in a deep dish with the oil, vinegar, chopped parsley and shallot, take the brains out, dry them, dip in flour lightly and then in frying batter, and fry a golden brown in deep fat, drain carefully and dish on a fancy paper or folded serviette, garnish with fried parsley and serve with tomato sauce.

CALF'S FOOT JELLY. *See* JELLY, CALF'S FOOT.

CALF'S HEAD, BOILED (for 7 or 8 people).

Half a calf's head or a whole one	vegetables and herbs to flavour
bacon	peppercorns
lemon	parsley sauce
salt	

Thoroughly wash the head and let it soak in cold water. Put it in a saucepan with enough cold water to cover. When it boils, add a little salt and remove the scum as it rises; add the vegetables, herbs and peppercorns; simmer gently from 2 to 3 hours till perfectly tender. The brains must be removed and soaked, then tied in muslin and boiled. Take out the head, remove all the bones and the tongue, place the head on a hot dish, coat well with parsley sauce, garnish with the skinned and sliced tongue, chopped brains, bacon fried and cut into dice, quarters of lemon and parsley.

CALF'S LIVER, STEWED (for 3 or 4 people).

½ lb. calf's liver	2 onions
1 oz. butter or dripping	1 apple
1 oz. flour	1 potato
½ pint stock or water	salt and pepper

Melt the butter or dripping in a stewpan; dip the liver, cut in small pieces, in seasoned flour and fry a nice brown; take out the liver and brown the remainder of the flour. Add the stock gradually and stir till it boils; return the liver to the sauce and the vegetables cut neatly; simmer gently for 1 hour, season and serve very hot.

CALIFORNIAN BLUEBELL. *See* NEMOPHILA.

CALIFORNIAN POPPY. *See* ESCHSCHOLTZIA.

CALLIOPSIS (COREOPSIS). A very general favourite hardy annual giving rich yellow or brown flowers. Seed should be sown early in April, in the place where intended to bloom, and by later sowings flowers may be had continuously from July to October.

CAMOMILE. This hardy perennial may be bought as sturdy plants in pots for bedding-out. The bright green foliage is feathery and graceful, and the marguerite-like flowers, white, or some shade of yellow. *A. Kelwayi* has unusually large, deep-hued yellow flowers from June until November. The perennial varieties are about 2 feet high, fairly compact in growth and require staking. They prefer the sun but thrive in any good soil or situation.

CAMOMILE TEA, to make. Put ½ oz. camomile flowers into 1 pint of boiling water and let it simmer for 15 minutes; then strain. When warm it may be used as an emetic, and when cold as a tonic. Take from 1 wineglassful to 1 breakfastcupful.

CAMPANULA (HAREBELL, CANTERBURY BELL). The campanulas are a big family, some biennials, as the Canterbury Bell, the rest perennials. The Bell Flowers, varying from 3 to 6 inches in the Alpine varieties. The taller border plants run to 4 feet and are among those perennials that can be planted with safety right up to the end of April, with care as to watering. Canterbury Bells are hardy biennials and will flower in May and June. They flower—dark and light blues and white—earliest in sunny positions. A rather light, limy soil suits the Campanulas. The root does not expand very quickly and so 1 foot will be enough to allow each way for development for a couple of seasons. These tall species bear the flowers on upright stems that do not need to be staked.

CANAPÉS OF FRESH COD ROE. Wash the roe, simmer in a saucepan with enough water to cover for about 6 minutes. Pound to a smooth paste and add whipped cream, lemon juice and seasonings. Spread on croûtons of fried bread and cover with chopped truffles and parsley.

CANCER (THE CRAB). Fourth sign of the Zodiac, influencing persons born between 22nd June and 21st July. Such have a love' of the sea, are placid, gentle, of quick sympathies, home-lovers, yet drawn to travel. They are not truculent, but if sure of a principle stick to it, yet rather prone to wishful thinking.

CANDYTUFT. *See* IBERIS.

CANTERBURY BELL. *See* CAMPANULA.

CAPE JESSAMINE. *See* GARDENIA.

CAPRICORN (THE GOAT). Tenth sign of the Zodiac, influencing persons born between 22nd December and 21st January. Such are plodding and painstaking, steadfast and faithful, apt to take gloomy views, but keep steadily on in all things. They must guard against brooding over fancied slight.

CAPSICUM. Sow seed in a hotbed in March or April and plant out in a sunny spot in May or early in June at a distance of 1 foot. The pods will be ready for use from July to September.

CARAMEL CREAM.

4 eggs	vanilla essence
1 pint milk	4 oz. castor sugar
1 yolk egg	butter

Melt sugar in a pan till a toffee-brown then run it into the bottom of a warm mould. Butter the sides of the mould. Beat the eggs and the yolk, stir well with the milk and vanilla and fill the mould with the mixture. Cover with buttered paper and steam with boiling water coming half up the sides till set. Large mould requires 1 hour, small moulds 15 to 20 minutes. If any caramel is left in tin, add boiling water, pour round mould.

CARBOLIC. This is a strong disinfectant and poison—especially in its fluid form. Great care should be taken to label any bottle containing this fluid, so that it may not be mistaken for medicine. Carbolic powder is the safer form for household use.

CARBUNCLE.

Causes.—Debility, anæmia, diabetes, gout, or infection of an area of the skin with microbes.

Symptoms.—A carbuncle starts as a hard, painful swelling. The skin becomes red and hot; blisters form on the surface, then burst and allow the contents of the carbuncle to discharge. The constitutional symptoms may be severe and blood-poisoning may supervene.

Treatment.—Good food and a fair amount of stimulants. A teaspoonful of Parrish's food in water three times a day after food. The affected part should be fomented constantly. In bad cases, where blood-poisoning is likely to supervene, it may be necessary to operate.

CARDS, LUCK OF THE. There are those who believe that playing cards have particular meanings, and indeed indicate what may happen. Whether or not this is so, the omens attributed are:

All Aces are unfortunate.
Kings are fortunate for women inquirers.
Queens show good luck for men.
Red Knaves are fortunate to both men and women.
Black Knaves are unlucky.
Odd numbers are fortunate for men and unlucky for women.
Even numbers are fortunate for women.
Tens refer to business, whatever the suits.
Nines to home.
Eights to friends.
Sevens to friends also or perhaps lovers.
Sixes indicate a change of fortune or a removal.
Fives accidents.
Fours news of one sort or another.
Threes a letter.
Twos a gift.

It will be seen that no notice is taken of the suits; only the values of the cards count.

CARNATIONS. Sow seeds 1 inch apart during April or May, in pots of two parts loam and one part cow manure. A little bonemeal and old mortar rubble may also be added. Plant out 10 to 15 inches apart when there are five or six leaves, protecting them from frost during winter. They will be in flower the following summer in a variety of colours.

Propagation is also by layers and cuttings in August in the open or struck in a frame in January. They are of perennial habit and have been much improved in recent years.

Plant in a compost of two parts turfy loam and one part rotted leaf-mould and coarse sand.

Pinks require similar cultivation.

CARPENTRY. To avoid nails bending up before they can be hammered in, dip them first of all in melted lard; this will enable them to be driven in straight without any difficulty.

If a screw refuses to leave the wood in which it is embedded place a screwdriver in the top of it and give it a sharp tap with the hammer. This loosens the wood adhering to it and the screw can be withdrawn easily.

CARPETS, to join. Match the patterns and reverse the carpet. Then buttonhole firmly each edge with flax thread.

CARPETS, to remove grease from. Into 1 pint of hot water put a tablespoonful of ammonia and scrub the grease spots with a clean brush. Rub dry with a clean cloth. Make a paste of Fuller's earth and cold water; lay over the stains and leave until dry; then brush off. This process may have to be repeated if the carpet is very old.

CARPETS, to remove stains. Ink stains can be cleaned with sour milk. Apply the milk direct to the stain and mop up with a clean cloth. Rub with warm water to which a little ammonia has been added. Allow to dry thoroughly and run over with vacuum cleaner.

Oil or grease stains can be removed by covering the affected spot with blotting-paper and pressing with a hot iron. Renew the blotting-paper till the grease is absorbed. Any remaining marks should be rubbed with a flannel dipped in either spirits of turpentine or warm water to which a little ammonia has been added. When quite dry, run over with vacuum cleaner to refresh the pile.

CARPETS, to rid of moth. Put into a bowl of hot water 1 table-spoonful of liquid ammonia; into this immerse a cloth, wring out, fold into four and place on carpet over the patch affected by moth. Then with the electric (or heated flat) iron go over and over again till the cloth is dry. This will also kill any eggs the moths have deposited.

CARROT. The carrot is rich in health promoting vitamins and has deservedly increased in popularity. It requires a good fresh loam, which has been trenched to double spit depth, and manured with thoroughly decayed manure the previous autumn. If natural manure is scarce, use fertilizer when sowing the seed, when too a top dressing of sand and lime will help to prevent maggot. Sow thinly in early April, $\frac{1}{2}$ inch deep in drills 9 inches apart; when the plants are about 3 inches high, thin out to 2 inches apart; after a few weeks to 4 inches apart. Thin once more after a few weeks to 6 inches apart. Early crops can be secured by growing under glass in January. For the open ground sowings finer specimens result if when sowing the dibber is used to make holes, each of which fill lightly with fine sand and loam and bury two seeds just below the surface, thinning out the weaker of the two when they show—a long job but worth it. Keep down weeds, keep soil loose, keep watered. Dust young plants with soot to keep off maggot.

CARROTS.

young carrots	chopped parsley
butter	salt and pepper

Prepare the carrots, boil them in water with salt or in stock till tender, with the lid on the pan; drain well. Melt the butter in the saucepan, and toss the carrots in it. When thoroughly hot sprinkle with chopped parsley and serve them standing upright in a vegetable dish.

CARVING. For successful carving, the following points should be borne in mind:

1. The carving knife must always be sharp.
2. The dish on which the joint is served should always be sufficiently large to take the joint comfortably and to enable it to be manipulated with ease.
3. Always serve gravy separately.
4. Never use a steel knife when carving fish—fish carvers should be of silver.

CARVING—*continued.*

5. When poultry or game has to be carved, a pair of carving scissors should be provided.

6. See that all joints are properly chopped.

The following are directions for carving the more usual joints, fish, etc.:

BEEF.

Rib.—Loosen meat from bone with a sharp knife, then starting at thick end carve parallel to bone. If boned and rolled, Rib of Beef should be carved in accordance with directions for Rounds of Beef.

Round of, and Aitchbone.—Cut into thin slices across from right to left.

Sirloin, Uppercut.—Carve into thin, long slices, parallel to bone, loosening the meat from the bone with a sharp knife.

Sirloin, Undercut.—Carve across the bone—not parallel to it.

MUTTON AND LAMB.

Leg.—Place on table with knuckle to the left of carver. Carve in fairly thick, slantwise pieces, commencing about 3 or 4 inches from the knuckle, cutting the meat right down to the bone. When the other end of the joint has been reached, it should be turned over and carved in a similar way underneath.

Shoulder.—Place in front of carver with knuckle end to the left. Holding meat with the fork as near knuckle as possible, cut as many thin, wedge-shaped pieces as you can from the top of the joint, carving the meat from the blade bone next. When all meat has been carved from this side of the joint, turn it over and carve the underside in a similar manner.

Neck, or Loin.—Carve into chops.

Saddle of.—Either carve slices from neck to tail end, or make a cut down the centre from neck to tail and then carve from the centre outwards.

Breast.—If boned, stuffed, rolled and roasted, carve by cutting into thin slices across from right to left.

VEAL.

Fillet.—Carve in thin slices and serve a piece of fat and a little stuffing to each person.

Neck.—Carve as directed for Neck of Mutton or Lamb.

Loin.—If small, carve as directed for Loin of Mutton or Lamb. If too large for this method, turn the joint with the thin edge towards you and carve as for Sirloin of Beef.

Knuckle.—Serve with underside uppermost. Carve as directed for Shoulder of Mutton or Lamb.

PORK.

Leg.—Carve as directed for Leg of Mutton.

Loin.—Carve as directed for Loin of Mutton.

HAM.—The knuckle end should be nearest the carves. Carve in very thin, slanting slices, down to the bone, commencing about 3 or 4 inches from the knuckle.

CARVING—*continued.*

GAME AND POULTRY.—Always serve with the legs towards the carver.

Capon.—If large, carve in accordance with directions for Turkey.

Fowl.—Holding the leg with carving fork, press away from the side of the fowl with the carving knife, when the joint should break apart and the leg will then only require cutting off. Carve the meat from the breast in long thin slices. To remove the wing, cut down through the breast to the wing joint and then remove in the same way as the leg.

Turkey, Roast or Boiled.—Carve in the same way as a fowl, except that the leg is merely loosened and is not cut off until the breast has been carved. Carving scissors make the removal of the leg easier.

Goose.—Neck end should be on the left-hand side of the carver. Carve the breast first and then loosen and cut off the legs and wings.

Duck.—Carve in the same way as a Goose.

Pigeon.—Carve by cutting the bird into two from end to end. If each half forms too large a portion, cut it again into halves.

Game.—Large game are carved in accordance with the directions given for Fowl, whilst small game about the size of a partridge are carved like pigeons. Larks, quails, etc., are generally served whole and so need no carving.

FISH.

Turbot, Brill and Large Plaice.—Using a fish slice, cut the fish through to the backbone and then cut into pieces from the backbone to the fins, first on one side and then on the other of the backbone. These slices should be carved right down to the bone.

Sole and Small Plaice.—Cut fish down the backbone and again down the fins. Carve from the backbone to the fins and lift off in fillets. When the whole of the top side has been carved, remove bone and carve underside into fillets.

Salmon or Cod.—Place on table with the thick edge away from the carver. Before commencing to carve, the carver should remove the skin from one side of the fish and then cut the fish from end to end about two-thirds of the way from the thick edge. Cutting right through to the bone, carve in fairly thick pieces from the thick edge to the incision. When all the fish has been carved from the top side, remove backbone and underneath side can then be carved in the same way as the top portion.

CASCARA. *See* APERIENTS.

CATARACT. Opacity of the crystalline lens in the eye whereby the sight becomes dim. It occurs most frequently in advanced life. Children may be born with it, but otherwise it is rare amongst the young. A surgical operation is necessary.

CATARRH. Catarrh is an inflammation of the mucous membrane, particularly of the air-passages of the head and throat. The inflammation is accompanied by an exudation on the free surface.

The best time to treat catarrh is during warm or hot weather because it is then that the affected parts heal most quickly. In chronic cases a little boracic acid powder should be snuffed up the nostrils. This attacks the germs and prepares the way for the following soothing and healing liquid remedy, which should be used in an atomizer after about 15 or 20 minutes.

Mix together 12 drops oil santol (English), 15 drops oil gaulth or wintergreen, 8 drops oil cassia or cinnamon, 15 grains menthol and 4 oz. medoline medicated or alboline. Use night and morning if required.

Another simple and effective method of treatment is a solution of 1 teaspoonful common salt in a breakfast cup of warm water, snuffed up the nose at bedtime and first thing each morning. Use soft water preferably.

CATS. As in the case of dogs, cats should not be overfed, neither should they be fed too frequently. They should have plenty of exercise and be kept supplied with plenty of clean water and milk. Their coats should be well combed and brushed—especially if they are long-haired. They are subject to the same diseases and illnesses as dogs, but do not seem to become ill so easily or frequently.

CAULIFLOWER. Sow in mid-August in an open situation on plots well manured previously. The drills should be about 9 inches apart; plant out in November in beds, or in frames with about 3 inches between each plant, or in a very warm border. They will be ready for use in May. Another sowing may be made in heat in February and a third in March for use from June to September. The rows should be 2 feet and the plants $1\frac{1}{2}$ feet apart in permanent quarters. Keep well watered and plant in very firmly. Mulches are beneficial in hot season. When the white heads start forming, tie leaves across to foster bleaching and keep compact.

CAULIFLOWER AU GRATIN.

1 cauliflower	$\frac{1}{2}$ pint white sauce
salt and soda	2 oz. grated cheese
$\frac{1}{2}$ oz. butter	few bread-crumbs

Boil the cauliflower, put into a hot dish, mix 1 oz. of the grated cheese with the white sauce and pour it over the cauliflower. Sprinkle over a few bread-crumbs, next the rest of the cheese and then a few little pieces of butter. Brown nicely in a quick oven and serve at once. This dish can be browned under a gas griller or with a salamander.

CAULIFLOWER IN BATTER.

	2 tablespoonfuls tepid water
1 cauliflower	1 tablespoonful oil or butter
salt and soda	1 white of egg
3 oz. flour	salt and pepper

Boil the cauliflower and divide the flower into neat pieces, dry them and dip in a batter made with the above ingredients, and fry in deep fat, drain on kitchen paper, pile on a hot dish and serve.

CEILINGS. To remedy little bits of whitening falling off the ceiling wash the ceiling over with a quart of water to which 1 oz. of alum has been added. This also helps to whiten the ceiling.

CEILINGS, SMOKED. Smoky patches above the gas globes on a white ceiling should be treated to a good paste of starch and water put on with a clean flannel cloth. Leave it to dry on, then wipe off with a brush or soft duster and no trace of smoke remains.

CELERY. A well-trenched, heavily-manured soil is required for celery. For early use sow on a mild hot-bed in the beginning of February, and for the general crop first week in March. Prick out when sufficiently large, and harden off. Choose suitable weather in May, June or July for planting out, and water freely, should the weather prove dry. Dressings of liquid manure will improve the quality and produce of the crop. When earthing up, choose a dry day and carefully close the stalks to keep out the soil. The trenches should be 8 inches deep and 1 foot wide; or if two plants abreast 18 inches wide, earth up for blanching gradually till October.

CELERY, STEWED.

3 or 4 heads celery	½ pint white sauce
salt	toast

Well wash and trim the celery, split each head lengthways into four, tie firmly into bundles, cut in equal lengths, place in a stewpan with enough boiling water to cover and a little salt. Boil till tender (about 1 hour), drain it carefully, dish in a hot vegetable dish on a slice of toast and pour the white sauce over. Celery can also be boiled in a nice brown stock and a sauce to coat it made of 1 oz. butter, 1 oz. flour (browned), and half a pint of the stock the celery was boiled in. Seasoned and served in the same way.

CELERY, with Fried Fish.

4 cupfuls celery	1 teaspoonful lemon juice
1 tablespoonful orange juice	½ teaspoonful pepper
	1½ tablespoonfuls butter

Remove tough threads from outside stalks of celery. Boil 1 hour in salted water, drain and keep liquid, which should be reduced to 2 cups for soup. Add butter, orange juice, lemon juice and pepper. Return to fire, stirring all the time, and serve with fried fish.

CENTRANTHUS. Hardy perennials popularly known as Valerian, of shrubby growth, 2 feet high. The foliage is grey, and the red, pale pink or white flowers will be borne throughout summer, provided the seed heads are removed promptly. This also is wise to prevent self-sowing, which is profuse. It likes a light, limy soil and sunshine, and if the need arises does not suffer from transplanting at any time.

CERATE, WHITE, to make. Melt together 1 gill of olive oil and ¼ lb. white wax and stir till cold. This makes an excellent soft dressing for cuts, blisters, etc.

CHAMOIS GLOVES. A few drops of olive oil added to the rinsing water when washing these will not only double their life but they will dry beautifully soft.

CHAMOIS LEATHERS. Instead of buying a large piece, buy a small piece and stitch on to the centre of a very soft duster; gather up the sides of the duster in the hand and use the piece of chamois leather for polishing.

CHAMPAGNE CUP. Mix together 1 pint bottle of champagne, 1 bottle soda or seltzer water, powdered sugar to taste, $\frac{1}{2}$ wineglassful of curaçao, ample clear ice, and a sprig of green borage or a little cucumber rind, or a few slices of fruit, such as pineapple, melon or peaches, etc.

CHAPPED HANDS. The hands and wrists should be thoroughly dried after washing, and friction applied. Lanoline should be rubbed in at bedtime and a pair of gloves put on to protect the bed-clothes.

CHAPPED LIPS. Apply vaseline, if not a lipstick user, when winds are cold and also at night.

CHARACTER, told from Playing Cards. The delineation of character as deduced from the six principal cards of a pack is a belief strongly held. It is done by making up twenty-seven cards; twenty-one taken at random after those specially noted below are put aside, and then the whole twenty-seven shuffled together by the person conducting the proceedings.

It is usual to have six others who each draw a card, so that it is possible, though not likely, that each could draw a significant card. If an ordinary card is taken out it means nothing and the drawer is "out" and popularly is counselled not to try for another card. If one of the six cards is drawn, the interpretation of its message can be learned from the following:

The King of Diamonds shows that the one who has drawn the card loves pleasure.

The Queen signifies that the person has many friends and will hold some important post.

The Knave shows a hopeful and cheerful disposition. If drawn by one connected with any of Her Majesty's Forces it is a promise of good luck as well.

The Ace of Hearts has been drawn by someone of exceptional ability but with whom idleness is a besetting sin.

The Two of Hearts if drawn by a man shows he is of an open-hearted and generous disposition. If it is drawn by a woman it shows the reverse. She should be careful not to give way to meanness.

The Three of Hearts is a warning. Trouble threatens the drawer through folly, or perhaps drunkenness. It may not be his or her own, of course, quite likely they will suffer for the faults of others.

CHEESE, to preserve. Mildew on cheese can easily be prevented by placing two pieces of lump sugar underneath the cover of the cheese dish. Cheese will then never get dry and always keep fresh.

CHEESE BALLS (for 4 or 6 people).

3 oz. cheese	$\frac{1}{4}$ pint tepid water
2 oz. flour	1 teaspoonful mustard
$\frac{1}{2}$ oz. butter	salt and cayenne
1 egg	

Mix the flour and mustard, salt and cayenne, separate the yolk from the white of the egg, mix it to the flour with the butter (melted), add the grated cheese a little at a time and the whipped white of egg.

Mix all to a smooth batter; drop a teaspoonful of the mixture into hot fat and fry. Half of this quantity makes a good dish.

CHEESE CAKES. Make a curd by adding a few drops of rennet to 1 pint of hot milk. Press the whey from the curd. Mix with the curd 3 eggs, 3 ratafia biscuits, 4 tablespoonfuls cream, 2 oz. sugar and a few drops of lemon, pound in a bowl with a wooden spoon, and press the curd in a napkin to absorb moisture. Line six patty pans with puff paste; fill up with the custard and place two strips of candied peel on top of each.

CHEESE, CREAM. Put some cream into a damp cloth and hang for a week in a cool place. Then place it in a mould lined with a cloth and press lightly. Turn the cheese twice a day and it will soon be ready for use.

CHEESE DELIGHTS.

2 cupfuls grated cheese	1 tablespoonful butter
1 beaten egg	$\frac{1}{4}$ teaspoonful salt
6 slices bread	$\frac{1}{2}$ teaspoonful mustard
bacon, paprika	1 teaspoonful Worcester sauce

Add butter, eggs, seasonings to grated cheese, mix to a paste, spread thick on bread, put a piece of bacon on top of each and bake in a moderately hot oven from 5 to 9 minutes and serve accompanied by olives.

CHEESE ÉCLAIRS.

choux pastry (see Pastry)	whipped cream
grated cheese	salt and pepper

Make the choux pastry, put into a forcing-bag and force into small éclairs $1\frac{1}{2}$ inches long, bake in a hot oven; when cold, fill the centre with a well-seasoned mixture of grated cheese and whipped cream.

CHEESE FRITTERS. Take 2 oz. margarine, 1 oz. bread-crumbs, 2 oz. cheese, 1 egg, pepper and salt to taste. Grate the cheese and put into a basin. Beat the egg and mix with the other ingredients. Melt some butter in a frying-pan, and when boiling drop the mixture from a tablespoon into it. Fry until fritters are golden brown, drain them and serve hot.

CHEESE AND POTATO PIE. Slice some potatoes. Make 1 pint of thick white sauce and stir in 4 oz. grated cheese. Season with salt and pepper. Arrange in a dish a border of toasted bread, then a layer of potatoes, over which pour some sauce. Repeat until full. Cover the whole with sauce, and sprinkle with grated cheese. Place in the oven for 20 minutes.

CHEESE PUDDING.

4 oz. bread-crumbs	1 pint milk
3 oz. grated cheese	2 eggs
1 oz. butter	salt and pepper

Pour the boiling milk on the bread-crumbs, add the grated cheese, butter, salt and pepper, mix well together; beat the 2 eggs well and add them. Pour the mixture into a buttered pie-dish and bake in a moderate oven about half an hour.

CHEESE SOUFFLÉ (for 4 or 5 people).

3 oz. flour	yolks of 3 eggs
3 oz. butter	whites of 4 eggs
6 oz. cheese (Parmesan)	brown bread-crumbs
¼ pint milk	salt and cayenne

Cook the flour in the butter, add the milk, stir till it boils and thickens. When it cools add the yolks and beat well, then the grated cheese, salt and cayenne and, lastly, the stiffly-beaten whites of eggs; pour into a well-buttered pie-dish, and sprinkle over some bread-crumbs. Bake in quick oven and serve immediately.

CHEESE STRAWS (for 3 or 4 people).

2 oz. flour	½ teaspoonful mustard
2 oz. grated cheese	yolk of 1 egg
2 oz. butter	salt and cayenne

Sift the flour into a basin, add the mustard, salt, cayenne and grated cheese, rub in the butter, mix to a paste with yolk of egg and a little water if necessary, knead slightly, roll out on a pastry board till about an eighth of an inch thick, cut into narrow strips about 3 inches long, place on a greased baking-tin and bake in a quick oven.

CHEIRANTHUS. The Siberian wallflower, as amateurs know it, is a biennial, growing 1 foot high and producing richly coloured orange flowers in May, continuing till early autumn if planted not later than mid-April. Flowers quickest in sunny positions, on rather sandy, light soils; but will flourish almost anywhere. Treat as for Wallflower.

CHERRIES, to bottle. To every pound of fruit add 6 oz. powdered sugar. Put the fruit into jars and shake the sugar over. Tie each jar down with two bladders unless they have screw tops. Place the jars in a boiler of cold water and bring to boiling point. Let them remain in the hot water for 3 hours. Remove to a dry place when cool. This will preserve them for over a year.

CHERRY BRANDY.

Morella cherries	sugar	brandy

Remove the stalks from the cherries, which should be ripe and sound, prick them with a large needle or fork, and drop them into a bottle. To every pound of fruit allow 6 oz. of sugar, or pounded sugar candy. Put this in and fill up the bottles with brandy. The bottles should be three parts full of cherries. Cork down and keep 3 or 4 months, shaking the bottle every now and again. A clove or two added improves the flavour.

CHERRY PIE. *See* HELIOTROPIUM.

CHESTNUTS, BOILED.

1 lb. chestnuts	sufficient boiling water to cover
little butter, pepper and salt	the nuts when in the saucepan

Peel the outside shells from the nuts, then drop them into boiling water and remove the inner skins. Place in boiling water to which salt has been added and boil until tender. Strain and serve in a hot vegetable dish with parsley sauce, or mash with butter, pepper and salt like turnips. This forms an excellent accompaniment for roast beef.

CHESTNUTS, to peel.   Make a cut in the skin of each nut and place them in the oven for about 10 minutes, or place in cold water, bring to the boil and keep boiling for about 3 minutes.   Take out a few at a time and you will find that both the outside and inside skins can easily be peeled off.

CHICAGO SALAD.

1 tin baked beans	1 cupful cold cooked ham in
½ cupful chopped pimentos	squares
½ teaspoonful salt	½ lettuce
½ cupful dressing	chopped parsley

Arrange lettuce on a dish or salad plates, mix ham, salt, beans and peppers.   Arrange in centre of lettuce.   Pour in 1 tablespoonful salad dressing.   Sprinkle dressing with chopped parsley, chill thoroughly and serve.

CHICKEN, BOILED.   Tie the wings and the legs to the body with thread; immerse in milk and water for 2 hours.   Place in cold water and boil slowly for half an hour.   Skim constantly.   Garnish with broccoli and serve with white sauce.   Very plump birds are the most satisfactory for this dish.

CHICKEN BROTH.

	1 oz. rice or pearl barley
1 old fowl	chopped parsley
1 quart water	salt and pepper

Prepare and draw the fowl, cut off all the meat and cut it up finely, chop the bones and put into a stewpan with the water and simmer very gently for 2 hours or more; strain, return to the pan with the rice or barley, previously washed and soaked in a little warm water. When tender season well with salt and pepper and a grate of nutmeg if liked.   Sprinkle over chopped parsley and serve.

CHICKEN, CURRIED.

1 chicken	2 oz. butter
2 tablespoonfuls coconut	2 tablespoonfuls Indian curry
1 tablespoonful lemon juice	powder
1 onion	½ pint gravy or stock
¼ teaspoonful sugar	1 teaspoonful salt

Joint chicken neatly and fry a light brown in the butter, then remove from pan.   Slice the onion and fry, adding all the other ingredients except lemon juice.   Put the chicken back and simmer for half an hour. Add lemon juice and serve with a dish of rice.

CHICKEN ENTRÉE.

1 chicken	1 onion
1 oz. butter	½ teaspoonful sugar
salt and pepper	½ lb. tomatoes
1 oz. flour	slices of bacon

Boil chicken slowly till tender.   Slice tomatoes and onion and fry gently in butter for 3 minutes.   Pour over stock and simmer gently for half an hour.   Rub through wire sieve, thicken with flour; add seasoning.   Boil and pour over chicken.   Cut rind from bacon and roll up.   Place on skewer and cook 10 minutes.

CHICKEN, FRICASSÉE OF (for 6 or 7 people).

1 chicken	2 oz. butter
1 onion stuffed with cloves	2 oz. flour
1 blade of mace	½ pint white stock
bunch of herbs	½ pint milk
1 lemon	salt and pepper

Cut the chicken into neat joints, place in a stewpan with onion, mace, herbs and strip of lemon peel, add the white stock and simmer very gently till tender. Cook the flour in the butter, add the stock the chicken was cooked in and the milk, stir till it boils, season well with salt and pepper and lemon juice. Put back the joints of chicken, serve with a rose border of mashed potato, and garnish with cut lemon and parsley. Cold boiled fowl can be served in this way, using the liquor it was boiled in.

CHICKEN, ROASTED. Singe, and truss by cutting the legs off at first joint. Make an incision in the wings and put the gizzard under the left wing and the liver under the right. Prepare stuffing of 3 oz. bread-crumbs, 2 oz. suet, a few leaves parsley (chopped), 1 egg, pepper and salt. Some prefer chestnut stuffing (which see) or veal or sausage forcemeat. Draw up the legs under the wings and stuff chicken in breast. Dredge flour over, or place a buttered paper over chicken and baste frequently. A couple of slices of bacon placed on the breast keeps it from cracking and makes a tasty addition. Roast for 1 hour or more according to size. When cooked remove trussing string and skewers and serve on a hot dish with good brown gravy and bread sauce.

CHICKEN, VOL-AU-VENT (for 3 or 4 people).

½ lb. puff pastry (*see* Pastry)	ham
cold chicken	salt and pepper
white sauce	

Make an oval vol-au-vent case with the puff pastry, bake it and scrape out the soft paste in the centre, make a savoury mixture with the minced chicken and sauce, chopped ham and seasoning, fill the centre and serve at once.

CHICKEN, to keep fresh. An unskinned onion cut in two and put inside a chicken will keep it fresh for a considerable time.

CHICKEN-POX. On the approach of chicken-pox the child feels ill, and the eruption shows itself in about 24 hours, with small pimples on the scalp, neck, back, chest and shoulders, but rarely on the face. These mature on the third day and begin then to fade—others making their appearance at the same time. Chicken-pox very rarely leaves pit-marks as in the case of smallpox, but boracic acid ointment may be applied to the spots with advantage. The complaint lasts but a few days, and for the first 3 or 4 days the patient should be kept indoors and fed on milk and farinaceous food. On the sixth day, but not before, give a mild aperient.

Chicken-pox cannot be considered dangerous, but it is infectious. The quarantine period being 3 weeks, it is apt to leave the child weak and he should be given a tonic, fresh air and good food.

CHICORY. Cook according to recipe for sea-kale, which it very much resembles.

CHILBLAINS. Here are two useful prescriptions for dealing with chilblains:

1. 1 dr. aconite liniment, 2 dr. belladonna liniment, 5 minims carbolic acid and 1 oz. flexible collodion. Mix and apply each night with a camel hair brush.

2. 2 dr. flexible collodion, 2 dr. castor oil, 2 dr. spirits of turpentine. This should be applied three times daily with a camel-hair brush.

CHILDREN'S LAUNDRY. Children's bibs and pinafores which are stained with egg should be soaked in cold water before they are washed; the marks will then come out without hard rubbing.

CHIMNEY, BURNING. To put out a fire in the chimney which has been caused by a fire in the fireplace, first close all doors, so as to prevent a draught up the chimney; next throw some fine common salt upon the fire in the grate, which will immediately extinguish that in the chimney.

CHIMNEYS. These can be kept reasonably clear of soot if potato peelings mixed with a little salt are burnt in the grate at least once a week. It will form a glaze inside the chimney and thus prevent its becoming clogged.

CHINA. When washing china, use a little Fuller's earth and pearl ash or soda with the water.

To avoid breaking fine china when you wash it put a thick turkish towel at the bottom of the wash-pan.

CHINA, to remove tea-stains on. Place the china in a saucepan of water with a little soda and allow to boil for about 10 minutes.

CHIVES. Divide the roots in the spring or autumn, leaving a few small roots together in each slip, and plant at intervals at about 6 inches.

They multiply quickly, thrive in any soil and come up year after. The taper leaves are used in salad, being of a mild onion flavour.

CHOCOLATE ÉCLAIRS. *See* ÉCLAIRS.

CHOCOLATE MOULD.

3 oz. cornflour	1½ pints milk
2 oz. chocolate powder	vanilla essence
1 oz. sugar	custard sauce

Mix the cornflour and chocolate powder with cold milk, put on remainder of milk to boil, pour on to cornflour and powder and return to the saucepan. Cook thoroughly, add sugar and vanilla essence to taste; pour into a wet mould; turn out when set and serve with custard sauce.

CHOKING. The finger should be put down the throat and an attempt made to hook out the obstruction. If this fails the child should be turned upside down and shaken. A dessertspoonful of mustard in a cup of water may be given to make the patient vomit or a dry crust eaten may remove the trouble. Things that are swallowed generally pass through the bowels, and are got rid of without difficulty.

CHRISTENINGS. Notices in the Press concerning the arrival of a child take the following form:

"*On the 4th inst. at 200 So-and-so Avenue, to the wife of A. B. Dash, a son*" (or a daughter).

The Church of England asks no set fee for baptism, but parents, according to their means and position, give a donation to the church or place a contribution in one of the collection boxes at the entrance door. A little gratuity for the verger is also usual.

Two godfathers and one godmother stand as sponsors for a boy, and one godfather and two godmothers for a girl.

Godparents always give presents to the child, and these, with any other gifts, are displayed when the party returns from the church for whatever hospitality is provided in celebration of the event.

CHRISTMAS ROSE. *See* HELLEBORUS.

CHRYSANTHEMUM. These perennials, which flower so freely in the autumn, require a rich light soil and abundant moisture. Propagation is by root division in early spring, cuttings in March, or in sand under glass in February, and layers in July and August. Those grown by layers may, if transplanted, flower the same year if the autumn is mild. They grow freely in the open and also in the cool greenhouse, the latter producing bigger and purer flowers if kept supplied with liquid manure and grown in extra large pots. Of recent years the strain has been improved both in range of colours and variety of petals. The singles remain popular, though the doubles have greater range of colour and are perhaps more widely grown, particularly the Japanese, the newer Cactus petalled varieties and the Incurves. To get larger blooms the number of buds must be reduced. Budding is expert work, but soon learned. In the spring, when about 1 foot high, take off the top of the plant; then three shoots will grow from top; pinch out any other shoots, and when the crown buds form nip off the leaves around them. These three buds will give fine blooms within 3 months, if all the other buds are removed. Where a large display of flowers is wanted, remove fewer buds; the blooms will, of course, be smaller. The stalks of all chrysanthemums, even when thick, are brittle, and so all plants must be securely staked.

CHUTNEY.

4 lb. apples	2 lb. brown sugar
2 lb. sultanas	4 oz. green ginger or 2 oz.
4 oz. garlic	ground ginger
¼ oz. cayenne	1 quart vinegar

Pare and core the apples; then add the brown sugar and boil to the consistency of jam. Chop finely the sultanas and garlic; add all

73

the other ingredients except vinegar. Mix the whole with the apples and boil for another 10 minutes. Pour into a jar and, while hot, mix well with vinegar, adding salt to taste. Bottle when cold.

CHUTNEY, APPLE.

1½ lb. brown sugar	½ oz. chillies
¼ lb. salt	2 oz. mustard seed
2 oz. garlic	1 lb. raisins
½ lb. onions	3 lb. cooking apples
½ teaspoonful ground ginger	3 pints vinegar (malt)

Peel and core apples and boil until soft in 1 pint of vinegar. Soak chillies overnight, then chop fine with the raisins. Add to other ingredients and boil the whole for 10 minutes.

CHUTNEY, OLD-FASHIONED.

15 large apples	½ lb. raisins, stoned and
1½ lb. brown sugar	chopped
¼ lb. Spanish onions	½ lb. tomatoes
¼ lb. garlic	2 oz. ground ginger
¼ lb. mustard seed	⅔ oz. cayenne pepper
¼ lb. salt	3 pints best brown vinegar

Peel and core the apples and boil them in the vinegar until quite soft. Chop the onions and garlic finely and add, with the other ingredients, to the apples. Boil all together and bottle. Half an hour is usually enough.

CHUTNEY TOAST (for 3 or 4 people).

1 oz. Bengal chutney	1 oz. grated cheese
2 oz. ham	salt and cayenne
2 tablespoonfuls cream	croûtons of fried bread or toast

Mince the ham finely, mix it with the cream, season well, spread in on the rounds of toast or fried bread, put a layer of chutney over and spread thickly with grated cheese. Brown in a quick oven and serve hot.

CHUTNEY, TOMATO.

2½ lb. tomatoes	1 oz. cloves
1 pint vinegar	4 oz. sliced or chopped onions
4 oz. brown sugar	2 oz. preserved ginger
	little pepper and salt

Place layers of sliced tomatoes in a dish, with a sprinkling of salt between each layer and let them stand for a whole day (24 hours). Then drain off all the resulting water. Next put all the ingredients together into a pan and simmer until quite tender. Strain and store in small air-tight containers. This can be used immediately.

CINERARIAS. These should be cultivated as pot-plants, for they flower, blue, red, purple, from December to May. Grow in ordinary light garden soil and keep just moist. The cactus petalled variety is popular and no difficulty to grow. Propagate by root division, cuttings or seed sown in June.

CINNAMON WATER. Allow 1 lb. of cinnamon bark to steep for 4 or 5 days in a gallon of brandy and an equal quantity of water. Distil off 1 gallon.

CISTERN. *See* WATER SUPPLY.

CLARET CUP.

1 bottle claret	2 sprigs borage
1 bottle soda water	1 small lemon sliced
1 bottle lemonade	cucumber peel
2 wineglassfuls sherry	2 oz. castor sugar

Mix all together, adding the sugar last. Ice it either by putting it in a refrigerator or adding lumps of ice.

CLARKIA. This well-known hardy annual is robust, easy of culture and flowers for a long time in delightful pastel colours on 30-inch spikes. A good sandy loam is best and a warm position desirable. It makes an excellent winter plant for the greenhouse and for table decoration by sowing in autumn in a cool house.

CLEMATIS. A profusely flowering climber, much improved of late from the deep blue and always favourite *Jackmanii*, by expert grafting and hybridization. The *Montana* is early flowering and white, and can be increased by cuttings after blooming: the *Coccinea* varieties, pinks and reds and crimsons, flower in July: the *Florida* classes, greys and whites, are best for the greenhouse, and the *Patens* group, ideal for pillars and pergolas, are in various colours. *Jackmanii* can now be had in white, red and claret, as well as the old rich blue, and thrive best if planted early and cut back to within a foot of the ground. The whole species does not thrive on heavy soil, but otherwise gives no difficulty if planted in sunny positions. They repay manuring. The branches are brittle and when being tied as they climb require care in handling. In earliest spring they often seem quite dead, but the first sun soon brings life into the buds.

CLOCHES. The true cloches are bell glasses, but a cheaper kind is simply two sheets of glass resting at an angle to each other and supported by wire. They can be moved about the garden to give protection and warmth to seeds or seedlings as and where required. More of these glasses can be added to give a continuous run.

CLOGGED DRAINPIPE. Pour a little soda over the drain and follow it up with vinegar. The effervescing that ensues will soon clear the clogged pipe.

CLOTHES, to brush. Brush gently with a soft brush all fine fabrics, but a hard one should be used if the clothes are muddy. Always brush in the direction of the nap, with the garment spread over a table. All dirt should previously be beaten off.

CLOTHES, to hang out. Skirts should be hung by the bands, nightdress by the shoulders and stockings by the toes.

To dry a jumper carelessly makes it get out of shape. Squeeze out as much water as possible, but do not wring, and then pass a stick or a coat hanger through the sleeves and hang thus on the line. When nearly dry take down and pull into shape.

If collars, cuffs, pieces of lace, etc., are threaded on a piece of tape or string, and tied on to the clothes line, the ends of the cuffs and collars will not be pulled out of shape. There will be no dirty peg marks, and pieces will not get lost in the wash.

CLOTHES, to remove creases. Hang the creased or crumpled garments in the bathroom on a clothes line, then turn on the hot-water tap until the room is full of steam. Allow them to remain for an hour or so; then remove hem to the open air and complete the drying. Press on the wrong side with a cool flat-iron.

CLOTHES, to remove shininess. Well wash some ivy leaves in cold water and put them in a saucepan with enough cold water to cover well; boil slowly until the leaves are tender. Strain off the liquid and use it for sponging the shiny places, having first thoroughly brushed the garment.

CLOTHES, to whiten. A teaspoonful of cream of tartar to a quart of water makes an excellent recipe for whitening white clothes that have become yellow. The articles should be allowed to soak overnight in the mixture, and when ironed the clothes will be perfectly white.

CLOTHES HANGERS. Loops for hanging garments are always wearing out and breaking, particularly with children's cloaks and coats. To make a durable loop, cut a strip of kid from an old glove, roll into it a piece of coarse string, and sew the edges of kid neatly together. This loop, fastened securely to a garment, will stand any amount of pulling without wearing or breaking.

CLOTHES PEGS. A washing-day hint. To save constantly dipping into the peg bag or stooping to pick up pegs, clip them all round an old raincoat belt and fasten round the waist, from which they can be taken with ease as hanging out proceeds.

CLOVE ESSENCE. Mix together $3\frac{1}{2}$ oz. cloves, $\frac{3}{4}$ pint proof spirits and $\frac{1}{4}$ pint water. Stand for a week, then strain.

COAL. To make coal last longer it should be sprinkled with a solution of soda and water and allowed to dry before using. Use about 1 tablespoonful of soda to 2 quarts of water.

COAT COLLAR, to clean. Rub with cloth or sponge soaked in paraffin or naphtha.

COAT HANGER, another use for. Screw some cup hooks on a wooden coat hanger. Hang on these small brooms, dustpans, whisks and dusters. On the centre hook hang a set of pockets in which place tins of polish; these can be made of crash. The hanger can be carried from room to room when cleaning and hung on a peg behind the door.

COBAEA (CUPS AND SAUCERS). A half-hardy perennial, valuable as a climber. With a little protection it will survive an ordinary winter. It is a useful plant, for in good soil and with liberal watering it will grow rapidly and flower freely during the summer. There are two varieties, the *C. scandens*, with purple bell-shaped flowers, and *C. scandens alba*, with white flowers. Seed should be sown in early spring, in gentle heat, the seedlings potted off as soon as they will bear it, and planted out in June.

COCK-CROWING, to prevent. Loosely suspend a small lath about 1½ feet above the bird's perch, so that when he stretches his neck to crow, his comb will come gently in contact with it; this will stop the noise.

COCKROACHES, to destroy. Mix 2 oz. powdered plaster of Paris with 4 oz. oatmeal and scatter on the floor.

COCKSCOMB, to cultivate. *See* CELOSIA.

COCKTAIL. Here is a recipe for a delicious cocktail that is not too "heady." Mix together equal parts of gin, French vermouth and cointreau, and ice well.

COCONUT ICE. Boil till clear 2 lb. sugar and 1 cupful water. Pour into a basin wetted with cold water, adding 2 cupfuls desiccated coconut. Stir until milky; then spread on a wet or buttered tin. Add cochineal to colour.

COCONUT KISSES. Mix together the whites of 3 eggs, 2 cupfuls each of coconut and powdered sugar, and 2 teaspoonfuls baking-powder. Place upon buttered paper and bake in a brisk oven until slightly brown.

COD, BAKED. Cut the fish into slices ½ inch thick, dip into flour and then into 1 egg beaten in 1 tablespoonful milk, and lastly into bread-crumbs with a seasoning of mixed herbs. Baste with butter melted in the baking-tin and cook for 20 minutes in a hot oven. Serve with caper sauce.

COD, BOILED (for 8 people).

4 lb. cod	vinegar or little lemon juice
salt	lemon and parsley

Well wash the fish in salt and water, place it in hot water with a little vinegar or lemon juice and salt, simmer very slowly until cooked, skimming occasionally, and allowing 10 minutes to the pound and 10 minutes over. Drain well, serve on a hot dish and folded serviette, garnish with cut lemon and parsley and serve with oyster, anchovy or any suitable sauce.

COD, CURRIED. Cut the fish into large slices, and fry to a good colour with sliced onions. Stew them in white gravy to which has been added 1 large tablespoonful curry powder, 2 or 3 spoonfuls of cream, a little flour and butter, a saltspoonful of cayenne pepper, and a pinch of salt.

77

COD, FRIED. Skin and bone the fish and cut into slices about 1½ inches in thickness. Wash thoroughly and dry with clean cloth, dip in well-beaten egg and then in bread-crumbs. Place in boiling fat, but cook slowly afterwards until the fish is cooked through and the outside is nicely browned. After draining off the fat on soft paper, or blotting paper, serve the fish on a paper d'oyley on a hot dish and garnish with slices of lemon and sprigs of parsley. Tomato sauce makes a good accompaniment for this dish.

COD-LIVER OIL. This is best taken in new milk, adding a dram of orange juice to every 8 oz. of oil to disguise the disagreeable flavour.

COD ROE.

1 lb. cod roe	salt and pepper
flour	egg and bread-crumbs

Wash the roe in salt and water, cook gently for 30 minutes, drain, cut into slices, dip in seasoned flour, coat with egg and bread-crumbs, fry a golden brown in hot fat, and drain on kitchen paper. Dish on a hot dish on a fancy paper; garnish with fried parsley. If for a luncheon dish serve a piquant sauce with it.

COFFEE, to prepare in a saucepan. Add 1 dessertspoonful freshly ground coffee to every ½ pint water. Use an earthenware or fireproof china saucepan and bring the coffee almost to the boil. Then remove from the fire, stir well, and again allow nearly to boil. Repeat this twice and a thick scum will have risen to the top. Stand by the side of the fire, cover the pan and allow to settle. Serve with boiling milk.

COFFEE, BLACK. Black coffee (*café noir*) should be made very strong and served in very small cups, well sweetened but never mixed with milk or cream. *Café noir* may be made of coffee essence, by pouring a dessertspoonful into each cup, and filling it up with boiling water. This is a very simple and expeditious manner of preparing coffee for a large party, but the essence for it must be made very good and kept well corked until required for use.

COFFEE GROUNDS. Dry coffee grounds filled into a suitable covering make excellent pin-cushions; the pins and needles stuck therein will never rust.

COFFEE, ICED.

8 oz. coffee	2 eggs
1 quart water	cream
1 pint milk	sugar

Make the coffee and allow it to get cold, beat the eggs very lightly, add them with the milk to the coffee, add cream (about 1 gill) and sugar to taste. Stand in a refrigerator for 5 or 6 hours. A pail containing ice and salt will answer the purpose. The coffee can be stood in it in a jug or milk-can, but it must be allowed to freeze.

COFFEE MOULD (for 3 or 4 people).

¾ pint milk	2 tablespoonfuls coffee essence
½ oz. gelatine	2 tablespoonfuls sugar

Soak the gelatine in a little cold milk; when dissolved add it to the remainder of the milk and coffee essence and boil; add the sugar, pour into a wet mould, turn out when set. Strong coffee can be used instead of essence, but it must be very carefully strained.

COFFEE SOUFFLÉ.

1½ tablespoonfuls granulated gelatine	½ tablespoonful vanilla
2 egg whites	1 pint milk
4 tablespoonfuls sugar	1 cupful whipped cream
	2 tablespoonfuls ground coffee

Soften gelatine in 3 tablespoonfuls of milk. Tie coffee in muslin and scald in a double saucepan with the remaining milk and sugar. Remove coffee, add the gelatine to the scalding mixture and stir until it is dissolved. Cool, fold in the whites of eggs beaten stiff and whipped cream and the vanilla. Turn into a prepared mould and set aside to chill. Unmould and serve plain or with soft custard made from the yolks of the eggs left over from the soufflé.

COLCHICUM (MEADOW SAFFRON). A family of hardy bulbs, valuable because they bloom late in autumn. They are hardy, but do best in a moist situation. Give them a suitable position where the bloom will not be splashed with earth by the autumn rains. A sunny, well-drained spot in the rock garden is excellent.

COLD FRAME. Useful both for raising from seed and for bringing along seedlings. Lettuce sown in a frame in the autumn will survive the winter and provide a tender salad earlier in the spring than otherwise possible. There is not a great deal in the making, and is more than worth the trouble, especially where there is no greenhouse. Adjust the size to a couple of old window frames, which can be picked up for very little. If constructing from the start make a wooden frame 6 feet by 8 feet of a height of 1 foot in front and 18 inches at the back. The depth from back to front will be 6 feet, the width being to accommodate two lights, each 4 feet wide, which makes lifting for airing much easier than if in one piece. The sides, of course, will be made to slope to meet the height of back. When put together get everything as firm as possible. The "Lights" are laid on, not fastened, as they are taken off or raised to give air when there is no frost. The trouble of making the glazed tops of the cold frame can be avoided by getting a pair second-hand, but old window frames are much cheaper.

To use, put a layer of rough earth at base, after digging out to about 1 foot, then 6 inches of friable potting mould, pressed down. Seed sown in the frame will germinate more surely than in the open and the seedlings not get broken by winds; but take care to give air for a time each day so as to avoid the danger of damping off, a greater cause of losing seedlings than frost.

COLEUS. This plant, valued for the beauty of its variegated foliage, is best treated as an annual. Sowings should be made in March—in pots rather than in pans, so as to have depth of earth—in sandy loam with moist heat; water seedlings judiciously, as they are liable to damp off. The final pots should be of moderate size only.

COLIC. The common cause is eating indigestible food, especially unripe fruit. Relief may be obtained by applying hot flannels or hot bran to the stomach and drinking hot lemonade or a wineglassful of peppermint with a pinch of cayenne pepper. Give castor oil or Gregory powder to relieve the bowels.

COLLARS AND CUFFS, to dry and gloss. Do not hang them so that they come in contact with the clothes line. Put a piece of tape through the buttonhole and tie on to the line.

To gloss, iron first of all lightly on the wrong side. Then turn the collar over and rub quickly and evenly with a piece of flannel or cloth made into a small pad and dipped in French chalk, afterwards rubbing over quickly and evenly with a piece of white soap (not ordinary washing soap). If possible complete the ironing on the right side without returning to the under side, and if you have a special glossing iron finish off with this.

COLUMBINE (AQUILEGIA). They are deservedly popular. Each flower can be divided into parts each of which resembles a *columba* or dove and the newest sorts have long spurs. If protected with litter during the winter will thrive in ordinary soil. They are biennial in habit but perennial in fact. Seed sown in July will be strong enough to stand the winter and can be planted out as soon as the frosts disappear. They flower freely and the latest sorts have a grand variety of delicate mixed colours, on wiry stems averaging 3 feet high, with maidenhair-fern-like foliage, doing well either in sunny or shady positions. They are not exacting as to soil, but when once established, they are impatient of removal unless in late autumn and spring. When bedding-out be most careful to leave root ball undisturbed. Water in well, and keep moist until growth has begun again.

COMPLEXION, to improve. Rub into the skin 2 tablespoonfuls of milk mixed with 1 level dessertspoonful of salt. Allow to dry on and remain till the following morning.

COMPOSTING. In a corner of the plot, well away from the house and so situated, if possible, that the most prevalent winds do not carry aromas toward the dwelling, dig a substantial hole, and in it put all garden refuse, mowings from lawn, cabbage and other leaves, the gathered autumn leaves, particularly beech, from nearby copses, and all such vegetable material which by decaying slowly makes what is known as compost. The refuse of this autumn will not be ready as compost for at least twelve months, as rotting takes time, but it can be hastened by throwing salt, soda and lime at intervals as more refuse is thrown in, and a few buckets of water poured over the heap to hasten decomposition. Fork over now and again to let air and damp get in to speed up the rotting process. This mixture, when black and well rotted, can be forked out, mixed with animal manure (humus) and spread over the plot at any time or used as a mulch (which see). In this way the organic chemicals taken out of the earth by one year's growth are ultimately returned. Compost can be used more freely on light soils than on heavy. For heavy clay soils, add sand and lime.

CONCRETE, GRAVEL. Mix to a creamy consistency 4 barrows slaked lime well soaked with water and 7½ barrows sand. Throw in stones of any shape (up to about 9 inches in diameter) and allow to harden.

CONCUSSION. Concussion of the brain caused by a blow or a fall is indicated when the eyes are shut, the face very pale, and the breathing slow. Vomiting frequently follows immediately and this gives relief. The patient should be put to bed, kept warm and given a warm drink. The doctor should be immediately sent for.

CONSOMMÉ.

good stock	2 whites of eggs
1 carrot	2 shells
1 turnip	½ lb. lean beef
1 onion or shallot	sherry
stick of celery	

Shred the beef finely, removing all the fat, put in basin with some of the stock, add the whites of the eggs and crushed shells and whisk all well together; put the remainder of stock in a white-lined pan, add well-prepared vegetables and the clearing ingredients, whisk well together, remove the whisk and allow to boil gently for 20 minutes. When clear pour gently through a cloth which has had boiling water poured through first: the sherry must be passed through the cloth; the garnish, from which the soup takes its name, must be carefully prepared; cooked vegetables must be rinsed with hot water and put in the soup tureen, and the consommé poured in gently.

Consommé as above with strips of vegetables, *Consommé à la Julienne*; with fancy shapes of custard, *Consommé à la Royal*; with small cubes of vegetables, *Consommé à la Brunoise*; with French plums and leeks, *Consommé à la Portugaise*; with vegetables cut in small fancy shapes, *Consommé à la Jardinière*.

CONSTIPATION. Everything should be tried before drugs are used to relieve the condition. It is well to go to stool at the same time each morning and evening whether felt necessary or not, so as to induce a regular motion. Fruit, vegetables, brown or whole-meal bread, oatmeal, salad and oil, should be amongst the articles of diet. Plenty of fluid should be taken with the meals. A glass of cold water at bedtime and another on rising is often enough to correct the condition. A walk should be taken daily, and, if the patient can stand it, a cold bath in the morning. If all these simple remedies fail 1 teaspoonful of Carlsbad salt or a fruit salt should be taken in a tumbler of water every day a half-hour before breakfast, or a half to 1 teaspoonful of the liquid extract of cascara or medicated paraffin at bedtime.

Constipation in infants is often troublesome; olive oil helps or glycerine should be injected into the bowels, or a pointed bit of soap inserted in the anus. A few drops of castor oil is the safest thing to give a newly-born infant if the bowels require moving.

CONVALLARIA MAJALIS. *See* LILY-OF-THE-VALLEY.

CONVERSATION, use of a person's initial only after the prefix Mr., Mrs. or Miss. No lady or gentleman should address or speak of another as "Mr. A.", "Mrs. B." or "Miss C." Such occasions as when the fault is committed intentionally, in fun, are of course not within the scope of rules of etiquette.

It is right to address people by name when you wish to attract their attention, or occasionally during the course of conversation, but constant repetition is ill-bred and irritating.

CONVULSIONS.

Causes.—Usually the result of some physical weakness and generally occurs in children from a few months old up to three years.

Symptoms.—The child grows restless and its limbs twitch—generally beginning with the hands. The eyes become fixed, the body stiff. Breathing is suspended for a moment and the face becomes flushed. Next the child's eyes commence to move, or roll, wildly, the limbs contract in spasms and the child may show froth at the mouth. The attack gradually passes off, when the child either becomes unconscious, or falls asleep through exhaustion. The number of fits to which the child is subjected depends upon the cause. If the fits follow each other in rapid succession, the child may die from exhaustion.

Treatment.—Loosen the clothing and remove anything which may restrict breathing in any way. If necessary place fingers between the gums and force open the child's mouth. If the fit is a really severe one, the child should be placed in a warm bath to which a little mustard has been added and allowed to remain in it for about a quarter of an hour, during which time its head should be sponged with cold water. If this does not relieve, the child should be put to bed and a doctor sent for at once.

COOKING SMELLS. The smell of cooking can be removed by taking a basin of boiling water with a few drops of oil of lavender in it into the room for a few minutes.

To prevent the smell of cooking throughout the house fill a tin cup with vinegar and place it at the back of the stove.

COPPER, CARE OF THE. When this has been emptied it should be rubbed with soap while it is still warm. This will prevent it from rusting and help to form the suds when the copper is again filled.

COPPER UTENSILS, to clean. First wash in hot water, then rub on salt, fine sand and vinegar mixed, with a piece of flannel. Remove all traces of vinegar by washing in warm water. Then dry and polish the exterior with whiting or metal polish. To retain brightness of metal rub a little sweet oil on every few days.

COREOPSIS. *See* CALLIOPSIS.

CORK CARPET. This will not polish; all it wants is a weekly oiling with boiled linseed oil and other days to be swept.

CORK MATS, to clean. Rub them hard with coarse sandpaper and they will look like new. Do not wash them.

CORKS. Push a piece of stout string into the bottle, turn the bottle until the cork is caught in the loop and then pull out the cork forcibly.

To make corks air and water tight soak in oil for 5 minutes.

When corks swell and are too large for a bottle, throw them for a few minutes into a basin of boiling water; they will then soften.

CORNFLOUR MOULD (for 3 or 4 people).

2 oz. cornflour	1 oz. sugar
1 pint milk	flavouring

Mix the cornflour with a little cold milk, add to the milk when boiling, stir until it thickens, then boil for 5 minutes, stirring well all the time; add sugar and flavouring, pour into a wet mould, and turn out when set.

Note.—Ground rice mould can be made as above, using 2½ oz. ground rice to 1 pint milk.

CORNS. A simple remedy is to soak the feet for half an hour, for two or three successive nights, in a strong solution of soda. This will dissolve the hard cuticle which forms the corn.

Mere washing of the feet with soap and water and rubbing the corns well with the fingers will often produce an alleviating effect. In fact, slight corns can be cured in two or three days merely by this simple treatment, and even chronic corns will yield to it provided the process is persevered with and some salt added to the water.

CORNS AND WARTS. A rapid cure is prepared by standing a small piece of potash in the open air until it powders, then mix to a paste with powdered gum arabic and apply on the affected part.

CORNS, SOFT. Always keep the feet scrupulously clean and dry. Be careful to dry between the toes after a bath. Protect the tender place from pressure or friction by placing a pad of wash-leather in position. This can be secured by strips of adhesive plaster.

COTTAGE PUDDING.

	¾ gill milk
¾ lb. self-raising flour	¼ lb. sugar
¼ lb. butter	1 egg

Put flour in basin, rub in butter and add sugar. Beat the egg, add milk and mix with other ingredients. Put mixture into greased cups and bake in moderate oven for half an hour. Turn out and serve with sweet sauce flavoured with lemon rind and juice.

COUGH-CURE. Take the white of an egg, add a pinch of castor sugar and beat to a froth. Take 1 teaspoonful three or four times at hourly intervals.

COUGH MIXTURE.

4 oz. honey	1 gill vinegar
4 oz. golden syrup	2d. paregoric

Mix all together, using a *bone* spoon. Take 1 teaspoonful three times a day, or when the cough is troublesome.

COW HEEL. Wash a cow heel and place it in a saucepan. Cover with salted water and bring slowly to the boil, skimming frequently. Simmer gently for 2 hours; then remove the meat from the bones and serve with parsley sauce.

CRAB. If fresh, it is heavy and stiff; it should never be bought otherwise.

CRAB, DRESSED (for 3 or 4 people).

1 crab	lemon juice
1½ oz. bread-crumbs	salt and pepper
2 oz. butter	coraline pepper
chopped parsley	

Separate the crab, take meat out carefully from the small claws, mix it with the inside of the crab, add the bread-crumbs, butter, lemon juice and seasoning, make it into a paste, wash and dry the shell, put in the mixture, flake the white meat from the large claws finely, pile it on each side, and decorate it with chopped parsley and coraline pepper.

CRAB APPLE JELLY. When making this add a few oak geranium leaves and boil until the required flavour is obtained.

CRAB SAVOURY.

1 pint crab meat	2 tablespoonfuls butter
½ cupful bread-crumbs	½ teaspoonful dry mustard
2 eggs	½ minced pimento
1 cupful cream or milk	salt and cayenne

Melt butter in saucepan. Add bread-crumbs, cream and mustard. Stir till mixture boils, then add crab meat, pimento and beaten yolks of eggs, salt and cayenne. Serve with wafers of hot buttered toast.

CRACKED GLASSES, to avoid. When pouring boiling liquid into a tumbler or other flat-bottomed glass vessel, first place it on a plate, or on any china, earthenware or marble surface, and the glass will not crack. No spoon is required.

CRAMP IN THE LEGS. To relieve, press the feet firmly against the end of the bed or some cold, hard object.

CREAM. Scald without any sugar and it will keep for 24 hours. If sugar is added it will keep for 36 hours, provided that it is kept in a cool, airy place.

CREAM, to whip. Place cream in a cold basin, and keep in a cool place whilst whipping it. Whip gently with a wire whisk until it begins to thicken, then increase the speed. Be careful not to overwhip as it soon turns to butter in warm weather. If, however, this does happen, continue to whip until it becomes butter and use for cooking. If the whipped cream is not required immediately, allow it to drain on a hair sieve in a cool place.

CREAM, ALMOND. Beat together 2 oz. sweet almonds and a few bitter ones. Place in a pint boiling cream, sweeten with sugar, add the juice of a lemon and 6 eggs. Beat to a froth and place in a dish with the froth on top.

CREAM CARTONS. Empty cream cartons, cut to the required size, are useful for baking little cakes. They are grease-proof and do not need to be greased.

They are also useful for potato salad in luncheon baskets.

CREAM, COFFEE (for 5 or 6 people).

½ pint milk	½ oz. gelatine
2 eggs (yolks)	1 gill strong coffee or coffee
2 oz. sugar	essence to taste
½ pint cream	little wine jelly

Dissolve the gelatine in a little water or milk, make a custard with the yolks of eggs and milk, cook till it thickens, add sugar, strain in the gelatine, and add the coffee or coffee essence. When cool add the whipped cream; mask the mould with a little wine jelly. Allow it to set before pouring in the cream. To unmould dip in warm water and turn on to a cold dish.

CREAM, PINEAPPLE (for 5 or 6 people).

¼ pint milk	½ pint cream
3 yolks of eggs	¾ oz. gelatine
2 oz. sugar	3 or 4 oz. pineapple
¾ pint pineapple syrup	1 wineglassful noyau
lemon jelly	

Make a custard with the milk and yolks of eggs, stir till it thickens, add the sugar, dissolve the gelatine in the syrup, and strain into the custard. When cool add the whipped cream and pulped pineapple; flavour with noyau. Mask the mould with lemon jelly. Then pour in the cream.

CREAM, RASPBERRY (for 5 or 6 people).

raspberry jam	sugar
½ pint cream	noyau
½ oz. gelatine	carmine colouring
lemon juice	lemon jelly

Heat the jam, rub it through a hair sieve—enough to make half a pint of purée—dissolve the gelatine in a little water, strain into the purée, add lemon juice and noyau, and colour with carmine. Whip the cream, stir to the purée, mask the mould with lemon jelly, and pour in the cream. Turn out when set and garnish with chopped jelly.

Note.—Fresh raspberries can be used. One pound should make a half-pint of purée.

CREAM, RHENISH (for 5 or 6 people).

6 yolks of eggs	1 oz. gelatine
½ pint sherry	rind and juice of 2 lemons
1 pint boiling water	sugar to taste

Dissolve the gelatine in the boiling water, allow it to cool, add to the beaten yolks, cook in a double saucepan until it thickens, add the grated lemon rind, juice, sherry and sugar to taste. Pour into a wet mould.

CREAM, STRAWBERRY (for 5 or 6 people).

1 lb. strawberries	pistachio nuts
½ pint cream	carmine colouring
½ oz. leaf gelatine	lemon juice
2 or 3 oz. sugar	lemon or wine jelly

Rinse a fancy mould with water, cover the bottom with jelly and set on ice; arrange some whole small strawberries with some chopped pistachio nuts and set with some more jelly. Pick the strawberries and rub them through a fine sieve, to the purée (about half a pint); add the lemon juice and gelatine dissolved in water and strained. Whip the cream and add to the other ingredients, sweeten and colour it; pour into the mould.

Note.—A little brandy may be added if liked; and strawberry jam can be used instead of the fresh fruit.

CREAM, VANILLA (for 5 or 6 people).

¾ pint cream	vanilla essence
½ oz. gelatine	preserved fruits to decorate
½ gill water	wine jelly
½ oz. sugar	

Rinse the mould with cold water, pour in a little melted wine jelly, and set on ice. When firm make a pretty decoration of preserved fruits, cover with jelly and allow to set. Dissolve the gelatine in a little water, whip the cream, strain in the gelatine, add the sugar and vanilla to taste, stir all together carefully and pour into the mould.

CRESS. *See* MUSTARD AND CRESS.

CRICKETS. *See* BEETLES.

CROQUETTES, EGG (8).

3 hard-boiled eggs	1 gill milk
1 oz. butter	salt and pepper
1 oz. flour	egg and bread-crumbs

Chop the hard-boiled eggs, make a panada with the butter, flour and milk, add the eggs, season with salt and pepper, mix well, place on a wet plate, divide into equal portions, set aside to cool; form into cork shapes, coat with eggs and bread-crumbs, and fry a golden brown in hot fat. Serve on a hot dish on a fancy paper; garnish with fried parsley.

CROQUETTES, FISH (8).

¾ lb. cold fish	anchovy essence
1 oz. flour	salt and pepper
1 oz. butter	egg and bread-crumbs
1 gill milk	parsley

Remove all skin and bones from the fish, flake finely, make a panada with the butter, flour and milk, add anchovy essence and season nicely; add the fish, turn the mixture on to a wet plate, divide into equal portions and allow it to cool; form into croquettes, cork shape, coat with egg and bread-crumbs, and fry a golden brown in deep fat. Serve on a hot dish with fancy paper; garnish with fried parsley.

CROQUETTES, MEAT (for 4 or 5 people).

½ lb. minced meat	1 teaspoonful chopped parsley
1 oz. butter	1 teaspoonful Worcester sauce
1 oz. flour	1 teaspoonful anchovy sauce
1 egg	little nutmeg
¼ lb. mashed potatoes	salt and pepper
1 gill stock	egg and bread-crumbs

Make a panada with the butter, flour and stock, mix with the meat and potatoes, add the flavourings and the raw egg and season well. Place the mixture on a wet plate, divide in equal portions and allow it to cool. Form into cork-shaped pieces, coat with egg and bread-crumbs, fry in hot fat, serve on hot dish with fancy paper and garnish with fried parsley.

CROUP. A teaspoonful of ipecacuanha wine to be taken every 10 or 15 minutes till vomiting begins. Two doses will usually suffice to quieten a child for the night. Repeat when child cough during the next few days. Rub the chest, windpipe and between shoulders with warm olive oil. Soak a piece of new flannel in olive oil and lay on both back and chest.

CROÛTES. These are large pieces of fried, or toasted and buttered, bread on which entrées are frequently served.

CROÛTES À LA LYRIC. Cut out some rounds of hot buttered toast and lay on each a grilled mushroom. Curl round the mushroom a lightly fried soft herring roe.

CROÛTONS. These are small fancy-shaped pieces of bread, either fried or toasted and buttered, which are sometimes used for serving hors-d'œuvres, but more frequently for decorating mince, hash or entrées.

CRUMBS, BUTTERED. Melt a half-ounce butter in a frying pan, not too quickly, stir in a cupful of bread-crumbs and stir constantly for about 5 minutes until they are a rich brown and well coated with butter. These are delicious dusted on a dish of scallops.

CRUMBS, USES FOR. *See* BREAD, DRY AND STALE.

CUCUMBER. Sow one pip in a "thumb" in March and plunge the pots into a hot-bed. When the plants are in early leaf, admit air and finally plant in rich turfy loam. Frame-grown plants should be on mounds from which the shoots will radiate. The ridge varieties should be sown in gentle heat about the beginning of May, and gradually hardened off, afterwards planting out on ridges of manure surfaced over with about 1 foot of good turfy loam. The secret of success depends on allowing nothing to check rapid growth. The temperature should not fall below 60 degrees at any time. Never allow roots to get dry and always use water the same temperature as the house.

CUCUMBERS, slicing for salads, etc. Always commence at the thick end—not at the stem end. If the whole of the cucumber is not being used at once, cut a very small piece off the stem end and stand in water. This will prevent the cucumber from becoming flabby.

CUPBOARD HANDLES. When the catch of a cupboard door handle wears away the wood so that the door cannot be shut securely, fasten a small piece of stiff cardboard over the ragged wooden edge with a couple of drawing pins. The catch will then hold and the cardboard being inside the repair will be invisible.

CUPS AND SAUCERS. *See* COBAEA.

CURDS AND WHEY. To 1 pint new milk (boiling) add a cupful of sour milk and boil briskly. Allow to simmer for a few minutes when it will become curds and whey. A simpler method is to add 1 dram citric acid to 1 quart milk.

CURRANT BUSHES, BLACK. With the blackcurrant the pruning for fruit production is quite different from that of red and white currants. On the blackcurrant the fruit comes from the young growth, the growth of the previous year. It follows, therefore, that an annual thinning out of the old wood must be made, so as to get new fruit-bearing wood for each successive season. While with red and white currants the object in view is to produce good spurs of wood, with the blackcurrant no spurs must be permitted, for as the fruit is produced from the wood of the second year the growth of new wood must be encouraged and the bush kept well open in the centre to light and air. Finally, it should be borne in mind that the blackcurrant bush is a strong grower and therefore requires a good soil and heavy dressing of manure to enable it to produce fine fruit.

CURRANT BUSHES, RED AND WHITE. In the case of red and white currants the fruit is borne by the old wood, and as soon as the requisite form of the bush has been attained the pruning should consist in cutting away annually the young shoots, leaving only those which may be needed as new branches for extending the size of the bush or for retaining its proper form. The lateral shoots should be cut back to within half an inch of the bed, the effect of which will be to cause large clusters of spurs to be formed in due time, and from these spurs the bunches of fruit are produced. As the bush grows old the spurs may perhaps become overcrowded, and it will then be necessary to thin them out, while any old moss-grown wood should be removed as soon as it appears.

The pruning may be done at any time from November to February, but not later, and in the autumn the ground should be manured and gently forked over. In the spring, as soon as the buds begin to swell, a good dressing of soot should be given both to the bushes and ground, as this is a preventative against the attacks of caterpillars and is also beneficial as a manure.

CURRANT JUICE. Select the largest currants and put them into a jar which should be stood in a saucepan of boiling water. Simmer till all the juice is extracted and then strain.

CURRANTS AND SULTANAS, to clean. Put the fruit on to a wire sieve, sprinkle them with flour, rub gently; this will remove most of the stems as well as clean the fruit. Pick it over carefully and remove all remaining stalks. Sultanas must never be washed.

CURRANTS, to dry. Beat up the whites of eggs or a little gum arabic in water, and after dipping in the bunches and letting them get a little dry, roll in finely-powdered loaf sugar. Now place them on a sieve in an oven to dry, and keep turning and adding sugar until they are thoroughly dried. Red, white and black currants and even grapes in bunches may be thus dried and preserved. They should be carefully kept dry in paper-lined boxes.

CURRY OF COLD MEAT (for 5 or 6 people).

1 lb. cold meat	¾ pint stock
1 apple	lemon juice
1 onion	salt
1 oz. flour	¼ lb. Patna rice
1 oz. curry powder	parsley
2 oz. butter	

Trim the meat, cut it into neat slices; melt the butter in a stewpan; cook the finely-chopped apple and onion, remove it and cook the flour and curry powder from 15 to 20 minutes. Add the stock gradually, stir till boils, then allow it to simmer gently with the apple and onion. Season well with lemon juice and salt, put in the meat, reheat but do not boil. Serve in the centre of a border of well-cooked rice; garnish with cut lemon and parsley.

CUSTARD, BAKED. Prepare as for steamed custard, but pour into a small buttered pie-dish, grate a little nutmeg on the top, and bake in a moderate oven until just set. On no account allow it to boil—otherwise the egg will curdle.

CUSTARD, CARAMEL (for 3 or 4 people).

4 yolks of eggs	10 lumps of sugar
¾ pint milk	½ gill water
1 oz. sugar	1 teaspoonful lemon juice
vanilla essence	

To make the caramel put the water, sugar and lemon juice in a saucepan and boil together until a rich brown. Pour into a warm mould and turn the tin round until it is coated all over. For the custard beat up the yolks of eggs, add the sugar and vanilla essence, add the milk, strain it into the mould, cover with greased paper and bake very slowly in a moderate oven, standing the mould in a flat tin with water in it. Turn out carefully and serve hot or cold.

CUSTARD, CHOCOLATE. This is a tempting and wholesome sweet for very young children. Make a boiled custard with 1 pint milk, 3 whole eggs well beaten, 3 tablespoonfuls of sugar, 1 oz. grated chocolate or cocoa moistened with milk, and when cooked, flavour with vanilla essence.

CUSTARD, STEAMED.

1 egg	1 gill milk
butter	1 teaspoonful sugar

Beat the egg, add the milk and sugar, pour into a buttered cup or mould, cover with buttered paper and steam for about 20 minutes.

CUSTARD SAUCE. Mix the beaten egg with the sugar in the bowl, then pour the scalded milk over the egg mixture slowly, stirring constantly. Now put the custard mixture in the top of the double boiler and cook until the mixture coats the spoon.

CUTLERY. *See* KNIVES.

CUTLETS, DURHAM (for 4 or 5 people).

¼ lb. minced meat	½ pint stock
1 oz. butter	1 dessertspoonful Worcester
1 oz. flour	sauce
3 or 4 tablespoonfuls bread-crumbs	salt and pepper
	egg and bread-crumbs

Make a thick sauce with the butter, flour and stock, mix with the meat and bread-crumbs, add flavouring and season well. Put the mixture on a wet plate, divide into equal portions and allow to cool. Form each portion into a neat cutlet shape, put an inch of raw macaroni into the end of each to represent the bone, coat in egg and bread-crumbs and fry in hot fat. Arrange in a circle round a high croûton of fried bread on a hot dish with fancy paper, and garnish with fried parsley.

CUTS. The smallest cut should never be neglected. The wound should be sucked and then put under the tap, and afterwards bathed in Condy's fluid or other antiseptic. Friar's balsam will stop the bleeding, and is antiseptic also.

CYCLAMEN. The small variety, grown in the open from corms, are hardy and like shade. Grow in good loam, with a little lime. Plant corms in little groups, 3 inches below surface, and let them develop on their own account. The hothouse variety in pots is larger and brought on from seed.

After flowering, store corms of both in dry sand. Seed sown in October or early in November, in pans filled with good loam and leaf-mould with a liberal addition of sand.

CYSTITIS. *See* BLADDER.

CYTISUS, BROOM. This beautiful flowering shrub is well worth cultivation and is most useful for clothing rough banks of dry or poor ground where many other plants would soon perish. Its rich blossoms nowadays in mixed colours as well as yellow give a fine effect of colour, and by selection a succession of bloom may be obtained from early spring to late autumn. Many kinds will grow freely from seed, but seedlings require protection and staking in their early growth. Prune in January.

DAFFODILS. *See* NARCISSUS.

DAHLIA. Seed sown in February and started in heat will quickly develop into seedlings which will flower as early as plants grown from tubers. Sow thinly in pans of ordinary compost and cover with a light sprinkling of earth. Pot off when about 1 inch high and gradually harden for transfer to the open. The soil should be a good, rich hazel loam. Lift the tuber roots at first frost, store in sand, protected from frost. In May, when shoots appear, plant out 18 inches apart. Cover over with leaf litter, or cinders, as a precaution against frost. Flowering should begin from the middle of July and continue until frosts cut down the plants if the seed heads are removed as soon as formed. The taller sorts need staking. Earwigs and insects which spoil buds can be trapped if small pots half filled with moss are placed inverted on the tops of stakes. These should be emptied daily into boiling water.

DAMP. If damp is suspected in a room, place a block of camphor in each corner. In a week the camphor will have disappeared and so will the dampness. This has proved successful where fires have failed.

DAMP IN CUPBOARDS. Place a box of quicklime in the cupboard and it will rapidly absorb the moisture.

DAMP WALL. *See* WALL.

DANCING ETIQUETTE. Nowadays dancers often take along their own partners. At certain public balls and dances, however, where admission is gained by tickets which anyone can buy, it is an accepted custom for stewards or M.C.s to be present for the purpose of finding partners for those without them, the necessary introductions being then made merely for the sake of allowing partnerless visitors the pleasure of joining in the diversion of the moment without in any way constituting a definite acquaintance.

Dances arranged by various clubs and societies, and by many business organizations for employees and their friends, may have individual rules and points of etiquette which should be carefully observed, but the actual etiquette of dancing remains much the same everywhere.

DANDELION, DECOCTION OF. Take 2 oz. freshly sliced dandelion root and boil in 1 quart water until reduced to 1 pint. Take in doses of from 2 to 4 oz. for sluggish liver.

DANDRUFF. The head should be washed in warm water and soap, and sulphur ointment sparely applied. If there is caking, almond oil should be put on the head at night to soften and the head well washed the next morning. Repeat this until the head is free from scurf. *See also* SCURF IN THE HEAD.

DARNING. To darn neatly stretch the material over the glass bulb of an electric torch and then hold the sides with an elastic band. If necessary switch on the light for a few moments and it will be quite clear which way the strands of the material go. Delicate materials can be repaired easily in this way.

DEAFNESS. Wax in the ear is a frequent cause. Two or three drops of olive oil should be put in the ear two or three times a day for two days, and then the ear syringed with lukewarm water. Temporary deafness resulting from a cold or accumulation of wax in ears can be allayed by the use of liquid paraffin. Make a small ball of cotton-wool, tie it firmly on to the end of a penholder, or some such slender handle, dip the cotton-wool into the paraffin and well anoint—do no prodding—the inside of the ears, letting it soak; then clear with warm water. To attempt to remove the wax from the ear with knitting needles or hairpins is a dangerous practice.

DEATH. *See* BEREAVEMENTS.

DEATHS, REGISTRATION OF. Information should be given to the Registrar within 5 days by nearest relative present at the death or during the last illness. The Registrar will require to see the doctor's certificate of death before registering, and the Registrar's certificate must be shown to the officiating clergyman at the interment. Special rules apply to cremation, including certification by two doctors.

DELPHINIUM. Seed should be sown in May and transferred to the border in readiness for early bloom in the following summer. They will succeed anywhere, but a deep friable soil, well manured, is best. Every two or three seasons they should be raised, divided and replanted in early spring. A long continuance of bloom may be obtained by cutting off the spikes as soon as they have done flowering. Although of the same origin, Larkspur (which see) is now sold as a distinct annual variety.

DEODORANTS. To keep the air in a sick-room sweet-smelling spray eau-de-Cologne or lavender water into the room, or burn in the room pastilles sold for this purpose by almost any chemist or drug stores.
For sinks, etc., pour down a solution of household ammonia or permanganate of potash in water.

DERBYSHIRE NECK, or GOITRE. This is a swelling in the neck just below the Adam's apple. It occurs most frequently in young females.
If the local water comes through limestone, the patient should remove from the district. The swelling must be painted with iodine, and iodine taken internally as directed by a doctor. If the goitre presses on the windpipe or gullet, it may be necessary to remove it.

DIABETES, SUGAR.
Causes.—Mental anxiety, exposure to cold, abuse of alcohol. Fair persons are more liable to it than dark.
Symptoms.—The person first of all complains that he drinks more fluid and passes more water than he used to and that he is getting thinner. He is constantly thirsty and drinks fluids at all hours of the day and night. The appetite may be enormous, and although the amount of food taken may be great the person continues to lose weight. The lips and tongue are dry, and there is a sweet taste in the mouth.
Treatment.—Under hospital direction insulin is the right treatment. Starch and sugar must not be taken in any form. The following articles of food must *not* be taken; baker's bread (a special diabetic bread is obtainable), potatoes, rice, arrowroot, sago, tapioca, macaroni, carrots, parsnips, peas, broad beans, cabbage, artichokes, beetroot, fruit, oysters, crabs, lobsters, liver, milk, beer, sweet or sparkling wines, liqueurs, lemonade, or other sweetened drinks.

DIANTHUS. A compact border plant of about 8 inches in height and flowering rather like a carnation, but not on spikes. The colours favour the dark reds and often are variegated. They bloom all the summer if the dead flowers are picked. They are perennials and do well in light soil with some lime content and in a sunny spot. Plant not too closely, about 8 inches apart, and this will allow for runners to be brought along for increasing stock. They are easily grown from seed sown in April or preferably May. The Indian Pink is a good variety. It should be noted that carnations and pinks come under this general classification.

DICENTRA. *See* BLEEDING HEART.

DIGGING. Whether in garden or allotment, digging must be thorough, especially if soil is being turned up for the first time.

The right time for digging is the late autumn, so that the winter snows and frosts can purify (sweeten is the gardener's term) and break up the clods, making it easier in the spring to get the necessary tilth or fineness for sowing and for root growth.

Digging is of various kinds; single spit; double spit (a spit is a spade's depth); trenching; bastard trenching; skimming; ridging, as may best suit character of soil and what is to be grown.

Single Spit.—Where the soil is found to be of good quality and shallow-rooted plants desired to be grown on that particular plot, single spit digging can be adopted, though always double spitting is best. Or it may be the soil itself is shallow and there are stones below the depth of one spit. Dig out a spadeful and put it beside the line of working; the second spadeful is thrown into where the first has come from and so on down the length to be dug. Having dug the length, put the soil of the first spadeful into the end of the trench. Start again at far end and continue till the required width is turned over. In single spitting, manure is simply dug in.

Double Spit.—Here the digging is to the double depth of the spade. Dig out one spit, put it aside, as in single spitting, then dig, but do not bring out the second spit. Instead, turn it over, break roughly and dig in some rotted leaves or grass cuttings. Proceed in this way to full length, filling in as proceeding, and then bring the first spadeful to the end, continuing till width is dug. By manuring the lower spit at this stage a lot of digging is saved in the spring, and only surface manuring will be necessary, whether by compost or artificials.

Trenching.—Here the digging goes to a depth of three spits. Instead of working a single width at a time, a double width is dug. Both widths are turned out for the first spit; when digging second spit, dig first the left spit and turn out on surface, dig the spit below it (*i. e.* three spit lot) but do not remove, then dig right-hand second spit and put it on the left-hand over the disturbed third spit, dig the exposed right-hand third spit, and so proceed with the whole plot in this way, filling in second and first spits as digging is done, and bringing from starting point the first spadefuls to complete at the finishing point. Manure between third and second spits.

Bastard Trenching.—This proceeds on much the same lines as trenching, except that it is mostly done on clayey or heavy ground, and in consequence, to secure better drainage, small stones, broken

93

brick and plaster are dug into the lower of the three spits before the earth from the second spit is thrown over it. Manure as in trenching.

Skimming.—This operation refers to the slicing off of turf where virgin soil is being dug. If the soil is shallow, the turves are placed face down and the dug soil thrown on top, the whole left to mature during the winter. Where there is a good depth of soil and particularly if compost is scarce, the skimmed turves are placed aside and stacked in some corner exposed to the weather so that they can rot and provide compost for future use—not less than a year—when they have rotted. The uncovered soil can be treated in any of the methods described for digging. To skim turf, cut with the spade about 3 inches through the surface for the width of the spade and for about 18 inches length on either side, insert the blade of the spade into the width-cut, easing up the turf till the spade can almost flatly be thrust along to free turf for the 18 inches, to the depth of the grass roots only. Go on in this way till area desired is "skimmed."

Ridging.—This mainly applies to cultivated ground. After lifting crops, dig over but do not leave level. Work up into a series of ridges, much as earthing potatoes, and so expose a greater area of soil to the beneficial effects of frost and weather.

In whatever class of digging, it is better to get rid of the weeds as proceeding. If ignored they will multiply so quickly as to make the labour tenfold the next year. Small weeds can be dug in, they then die, but those with large or deep roots must be extracted, roots and all, and burned.

Inexperienced gardeners dig too long and too furiously. Do half an hour steadily at it, then rest the muscles by getting out the stones and deep-rooted weeds; do another half-hour, and then take another rest for 10 minutes.

Always clean and polish the spade after use; it makes all the difference in working.

DIGITALIS (FOXGLOVE). These perennials are invaluable for shady spots, flowering best in moderate sunlight. They like a rich, leaf soil compost. The flower stem grows to 3 feet or more, and the hybrids produce many lovely tints. They flower in June and July, and young plants rapidly spring up from self-sown seeds. They are poisonous to animals.

DINNER, to arrange a special. *See* MENU.

DIPHTHERIA. A feeling of heaviness; headache, chiefly over the eyes. There may be fever and delirium at night. There may or may not be hoarseness, and difficulty in swallowing. The tonsils and uvula are swollen and redder than usual. Then an exudation will be noticed in the throat and palate which gradually grows until there is a membrane. The glands under the jaw are often enlarged. It should be borne in mind that frequently there is *no fever*.

On the slightest suspicion of diphtheria isolate the patient, put him to bed (flat on the back and without a pillow) and send for the doctor. Everything depends upon the immediate administration of antitoxin, and only a doctor can give it.

DISEASES, recognition of. *See* RASHES.

DISHES AND BASINS, to prevent from cracking through heat. In the case of pie-dishes and pudding-basins place in cold water and bring to the boil; leave in the water and allow to get cold. If this is done when new before they are used, they will not crack when subjected to heat in cooking.

In the case of glass dishes, etc., for holding stewed fruit, either hold the dish in the hand while pouring in the hot fruit, or place it on a wet cloth.

DISHMARKS ON POLISHED TABLES, to remove. Procure ½ pint of linseed oil and heat for about 10 to 15 minutes—do not boil, just simmer. Let cool slightly, then mix in ½ gill of turpentine. Apply this mixture to the mark fairly frequently and rub off each time with a soft cloth.

DIURETIC DROPS. Mix ½ oz. aromatic tincture with 1 oz. sweet spirits of nitre, and take 50 drops three times daily in a glass of water to promote a natural flow of urine.

DIVISION, to propagate plants by. It is best to divide plants either in October and November after flowering or in March and April as new growth starts. Lift the clumps, keeping the roots as intact as possible and, after lifting carefully, divide the plant into crowns with a sharp knife. By washing out the earth (putting clump in a pail) division is easier. Do not use a spade for this purpose. Keep and replant the new outer crowns.

DOCUMENTS, to preserve. A thin coating of gutta-percha solution brushed over the back and front of documents will render them damp-proof.

DODECATHEON (AMERICAN COWSLIP). A beautiful hardy perennial that is easily raised from seed or bulbs in sandy peat in a cool situation.

DOGS. Do not overfeed them: for dogs used in sport, or kept on a leash, and consequently not getting a great deal of exercise, boiled meat with thickened gravy once a day forms an excellent diet. For household pets, toy dogs, etc., meat is almost unnecessary, and their diet should consist chiefly of potatoes, gravy, green vegetables, bread, milk, etc., and a very little meat. Dog biscuits form an excellent food for all dogs. Give a dog bones to gnaw at least two or three times a week, as they assist in cleaning the dog's teeth. All dogs should be given plenty of clean water to drink and plenty of exercise.

Distemper.—Dogs are liable to this from the age of about four months to four years. Some of the symptoms are shivering, loss of appetite, cough, loss of brightness of the eyes, and very frequently fits. In any event it is best to consult a veterinary surgeon.

Hydrophobia or Rabies.—The first symptoms of this disease in dogs are generally thirst, fever, restlessness, languor and convulsive starts during sleep. Later the dog becomes sulky and savage, and often tears into shreds anything of which it can get hold. A dog in this condition will frequently snap at imaginary objects or persons. In another form of the disease the dog loses its voice altogether and drops its lower jaw. It is far better to have the dog painlessly destroyed.

Mange.—A contagious disease very difficult to get rid of. The symptoms are intense itching, and small red spots on the skin. These spots later become mattery and the dog's hair falls out. A beneficial method of treatment is to apply sulpho-vaseline.

Licences.—A licence valid for the year must be obtained, through any post office, for any dog kept, with the following exceptions:

1. Any dog under six months old.
2. Sheep or cattle dogs.
3. A dog used for guiding a blind person.
4. Hound puppies which are under twelve months old and are not part of a pack of hounds.

Omission to obtain a licence renders the person liable to a fine.

DOMES OF SILENCE. Put these on the ends of the wooden ribs that cross your trunks. They will slither along platforms and into railway vans and last twice as long.

DOORS, DRAUGHTY. When doors do not close properly, but leave cracks through which draughts enter, place a strip of putty along the jambs, cover the edge with chalk, and shut it. The putty will then fill up all spaces. Chalk rubbed on the edges prevents adhesion. The putty is left in places where it soon dries and leaves a perfectly fitting jamb.

DOORS, to stop from creaking. Apply a little graphite grease to the hinge, or a little softened soap on the end of a pencil, rubbing in the lead of the pencil as well.

DOORSTEPS, to keep free from ice. When washing doorsteps add a cupful of methylated spirits to every pailful of water used.

DOOR-STOP. Take an empty cotton reel and cover it neatly with cloth to match the carpet. Pass a long brass-headed nail through the hole and fasten it to the floor about 3 or 5 inches from the wall behind the door. It will make an excellent door-stop and prevent the handle of the door from injuring the wall.

DORONICUM. *See* LEOPARD'S BANE.

DOUGHNUTS.

1 lb. flour	½ oz. German yeast
2 oz. lard	½ pint milk
½ teaspoonful salt	2 eggs
	jam

Put the lard and milk in a saucepan, test the yeast with a teaspoonful of sugar, make a well in the centre of the flour, pour in the milk and lard and well-beaten eggs, add the yeast and mix to a dough; put in to rise in a warm place for 1 hour. Roll out on a floured board, cut into rounds a quarter of an inch thick; put a little jam on one piece, moisten the edges, cover with another round, press together, and fry in hot fat. When cooked, drain and roll in castor sugar.

DRAINPIPE. *See* CLOGGED.

DRAINS, to test. If oil of peppermint be mixed with hot water and the mixture poured down the upper end of joints, any defects will be discovered, because the smell of peppermint about the house will indicate that there is a possibility of sewer gas entering. In that case, send for a plumber immediately.

DRAWERS, to prevent from sticking. Rub some hard soap over the lower edges of the drawers and on the grooves. Then highly polish these parts to make the drawers slide easily.

DRESSMAKING. A little eucalyptus oil will remove grease and machine oil from any fabric without injury.

DRIED FRUITS. When stewing prunes or any dried fruits do not sweeten them until just before they are removed from the stove and use golden syrup instead of sugar.

DRIED FRUITS. To cut up dried fruits, such as dates, candied fruits, etc., first put the knife in cold water and you will find this does away with a great deal of the stickiness.

DRIPPING. To clarify dripping pour some boiling water on to melted dripping, and, when cold, the impurities will be found at the bottom, whilst the good dripping will be at the top.

DROPSY. Has many causes, hence treatment varies. It may be confined to a certain part, and then it is generally due to some obstruction in the flow of the blood. General dropsy occurs in disease of the kidneys and heart. Large quantities of fluid may accumulate in the abdomen when the liver is affected. A doctor should always be consulted.

DROWNING. *See* ARTIFICIAL RESPIRATION.

DRUNKENNESS, to cure.

5 grains sulphate of iron	11 drams peppermint water
10 grains magnesia	1 dram spirits of nutmeg

This acts as a tonic and stimulant and, by partly taking the place of the accustomed liquor, prevents the physical and mental prostration that follows a sudden breaking off from drink. Start with 12 drops on a lump of sugar and increase until 2 teaspoonfuls are taken at one time twice a day.

DUCK, BRAISED, WITH TURNIPS (for 4 or 5 people).

1 duck	stock
3 turnips	1 glass white wine
1 carrot	2 oz. butter
1 onion	salt and pepper
½ pint brown sauce	croûtons of bread

Truss the duck as for roasting, place in a baking-tin with the butter and partially roast it, allow it to cool and cut into neat joints, put the brown sauce in a stew pan, add the carrot and onion sliced, the wine and seasoning and simmer gently for 30 minutes, dish on a hot dish, strain the sauce over, garnish with fried croûtons of bread and the turnips cut in quarters, boiled, drained and fried.

DUCK, MINCED, AND TOMATOES (for 3 or 4 people).

½ lb. cold duck
4 or 5 tomatoes
some good brown sauce

salt and pepper
rice

Peel the tomatoes, cook for 10 minutes in the brown sauce, then add the duck minced finely, season and reheat, serve with a border of boiled rice.

DUCK, ROAST (for 4 or 5 people).

1 duck
sage and onion stuffing
watercress

gravy
apple sauce

Draw the duck, cut off the legs at the first joint, wipe and put in the sage and onion stuffing, take off the wings at the first joint, truss it firmly, roast in the oven from 1½ to 1¾ hours according to age and size, basting well; dredge with flour and froth and brown it well before dishing. Put the giblets in a saucepan with a sage leaf, onion and some stock, simmer them, using the stock for the gravy, which can be made as for roast meat or thickened if preferred. Put the duck on a hot dish, remove the string, garnish with watercress, and serve with the gravy in a tureen and apple sauce. If a couple of ducks are cooked it is advisable to stuff one only.

DUMPLINGS, DOUGH. Prepare the dough as for bread, and cut it into small pieces. Drop into boiling water and boil for 20 minutes. Serve with treacle or butter and sugar.

DUMPLINGS, DROP. Add 1 gill milk to 2 or 3 beaten eggs. Mix to a stiff batter with ½ lb. flour and a little salt. Gradually drop the batter into the liquor in which meat is being cooked. Boil for 10 minutes and serve with the meat.

DUST BINS. Wrap all meat or vegetable refuse in a piece of paper before placing in the bin and shake a small quantity of chloride of lime over the contents of the bin each day. This will prevent the contents of the bin from giving forth an unhealthy smell and breeding flies.

DUSTERS. When washing these put a good dash of paraffin in the rinsing water; they will dust and polish better. Also add paraffin to the water when washing linoleum; it quickly removes the dirt.

DUSTY VELVET. Rub it with a piece of coarse black crêpe. This takes out the dust much more quickly than a brush.

DYSENTERY. This is a serious disease and is not by any means uncommon among children. If diarrhœa is not promptly attended to, it may develop into dysentery, which will be recognized by the motions being slimy and containing blood and, in bad cases, consisting entirely of slime and blood. Medical attention is absolutely necessary and, though the patient ought not to be treated except under the doctor's advice, large hot fomentations or poultices may be applied to the abdomen should there be pain in that region.

DYSPEPSIA. *See* INDIGESTION.

EARACHE. The ear should be gently syringed with warm water, and a hot flannel applied to the side of the head; a mustard leaf may be put just behind the ear. Do not tamper with the inside of the ear.

EARWIGS. Dahlias are the favourite haunt of these insects, but any flowers of sufficient size are utilized by them for shelter. The best and simplest trap is that of a small flower-pot, stuffed with a little dry moss and inverted on the top of a stake. It should be examined every morning and evening and its catch of earwigs destroyed by plunging it into hot water. Another simple device is a roll of corrugated straw-board, one end thrust into a matchbox cover. *See also* INSECTS OF PLANTS, to destroy.

EAU-DE-COLOGNE. *See* PERFUME, COLOGNE WATER.

EBONY BRUSHES. Thoroughly rub the wood of these with vaseline before washing, to prevent being spoiled.

ECHINOPS (GLOBE THISTLE). A fine hardy plant, growing from 3 to 5 feet high and useful for making ornamental groups in the wild garden. There are several varieties, *E. ritro* and *E. banalicus* being very good, but perhaps the best is *E. ruthenicus*, with its round-headed flowers of beautiful blue. It is easily increased by division or raised from seed, and it thrives in any soil.

ÉCLAIRS.

choux paste
cream

sugar
vanilla essence
chocolate icing

Make the pastry as for Spanish Puffs. Put the mixture into a forcing-bag with a plain tube, force it through on to a greased baking-tin in three-inch lengths, and bake in a hot oven for half an hour: cover with another tin to keep them air-tight. When done place on a pastry rack to cool; whip and flavour the cream, raise the pastry on one side of the éclair and fill it with cream, make the chocolate icing, dip the éclair in it and allow it to dry.

ÉCLAIRS, CHEESE. *See* CHEESE.

ECZEMA, relieving. Well wash a large handful of watercress. Put into a clean saucepan and cover with cold water. Bring to the boil and let it simmer until the goodness is extracted and it is quite tender. Strain through muslin and allow to cool before using. Bathe the affected parts two or three times every day, using a clean cloth every time. This may be used for rough skin caused by the wind.

The diet should be regulated, and the bowels opened. The part should not be washed in soap, but gently sponged with lukewarm water and oatmeal. Scratching should be avoided. In children the hands may be put in gloves or tied to the side. If there are crusts and scales they should be removed by applying strips of linen soaked in olive oil. The trouble, if persisting, should be treated medically.

EELS. Always choose the smallest for boiling. Remove gut, heads and skin; wash well and simmer in a little salt and water with chopped parsley. Decorate with sprigs of parsley and serve with parsley sauce.

EELS, FRIED (for 7 or 8 people).

2 eels	salt and pepper
little flour	egg and bread-crumbs

Skin and thoroughly cleanse the eels and allow to soak in salt and water some time. Cut in three-inch lengths, dip them in seasoned flour, coat in egg and bread-crumbs and fry in deep fat. Serve on a hot dish on a fancy paper, garnish with fried parsley, and serve with tartare or piquante sauce.

EELS, STEWED (for 3 or 4 people).

1 eel	little lemon juice
1 gill stock	½ oz. flour
2 tablespoonfuls port wine	1 dessertspoonful mushroom
blade of mace	ketchup
2 cloves	pepper and salt
1 shallot	½ oz. butter

Thoroughly cleanse the eel and cut in pieces 3 inches long, cook them in a stewpan in the stock and port wine, adding the mace, cloves, chopped shallot and lemon juice. Simmer for about 1 hour, strain and thicken the gravy with the butter and flour; boil up and add ketchup and salt and pepper; dish the eel in a circle and pour the sauce over.

EGG CUSTARD.

To prevent from turning out "watery looking" place the vessel containing the custard inside a larger vessel containing water and bring up to boiling point in a quick oven.

EGG KROMESKIES.

2 hard-boiled eggs	thin slices of bacon
½ gill white sauce	salt and pepper
	frying batter

Chop the hard-boiled eggs finely, moisten with the white sauce and season well, roll some of the mixture in thin slices of bacon, dip into frying batter and fry a golden brown in hot fat, drain well, dish on a fancy paper, garnish with fried parsley.

EGGS, to beat.

When beating eggs add a little hot water; the beating will occupy less time and the cakes and puddings will be much lighter.

EGGS, CRACKED, to prevent boiling out.

Wrap a piece of clean white tissue paper round a cracked egg to prevent boiling out. As soon as wet the paper adheres to the egg shell, and so keeps it together.

Alternative methods are to rub the crack over with salt or butter before putting in the water, or put a teaspoonful of vinegar in the water in which the egg is to be boiled.

EGGS, CURRIED (for 3 or 4 people).

3 or 4 hard-boiled eggs	½ pint milk
1 small onion	lemon juice
1 small apple	salt
½ oz. curry powder	croûtons of fried bread
½ oz. flour	

Fry the finely-chopped apple and onion in the butter, add the curry powder and flour, cook for 10 minutes; add the milk and simmer for another 10 minutes; season with lemon juice and salt and a pinch of castor sugar. Cut the eggs in halves, put each half on a croûton, round side up, coat carefully with the curry sauce, and garnish with white of egg cut in fancy shapes.

EGGS, POACHED.

> 2 or 3 eggs
> salt
> buttered toast

Break the eggs one at a time in a cup, pour gently into a shallow saucepan or frying pan of boiling water with a little salt, and cook very gently. When just set take out the eggs, place them on a round of buttered toast, trimming them so that they are the same size as the toast. Serve immediately. An egg-poacher is useful. It keeps the egg a better shape. Just stand it in a pan of water and pour the egg into it. If the eggs are placed in boiling water for a few seconds before breaking the shells, it will prevent the yolks breaking.

EGGS, to preserve.

1. Be quite sure the eggs are fresh and, if possible, rub them over with butter as soon as they are laid. Put them into a stone jar with the narrow ends downwards and pour over the following brine: ½ pint slaked lime, ½ pint salt, 1 oz. cream of tartar and 2 gallons water. The ingredients should be boiled together for 10 minutes and skimmed. Pour the liquid carefully over the eggs when cold. This quantity of brine is enough for 75 eggs. Eggs may also be kept in salt if they are tightly packed, but not allowed to touch.

2. Use vaseline in place of water-glass. Cracked eggs may be included as the vaseline well rubbed over the egg closes all cracks and pores. Eggs preserved in this way keep quite fresh for a considerable time. The eggs may be packed in cardboard boxes, etc. A pot of vaseline costing 6d. will preserve 200 eggs.

3. As an alternative to water-glass, take good fresh eggs and rub them over with melted lard, thus closing the pores in the shell. Then put a layer of oats or bran in a box, then a layer of eggs, setting them on the small end, and not allowing them to touch each other, separating them by oats or bran. Alternate these layers until the box is full.

EGGS, SCALLOPED (for 3 or 4 people).

> 3 or 4 hard-boiled eggs   bread-crumbs
> ½ pint white sauce   grated cheese
> ½ oz. butter   salt and pepper

Cut the hard-boiled eggs in dice, add to the white sauce, season well with salt and pepper. Well butter some scallop shells, place some of the mixture in each, sprinkle over some fresh bread-crumbs, then a little grated cheese and lastly some small pieces of butter. Brown in the oven and serve hot.

EGGS, SCRAMBLED (for 2 people).

> 3 eggs   little milk or cream
> 1 oz. butter   salt and pepper
> little chopped parsley   buttered toast

Put the butter into a saucepan, well beat the eggs, season with salt and pepper, add the chopped parsley and cream or milk. When the butter has melted pour in the eggs, and stir over the fire until the mixture begins to thicken. Put it on to the hot buttered toast and serve at once.

EGGS, SCRAMBLED, an economy recipe. Break 2 eggs into a basin and add 1 cupful of milk and 1 teaspoonful of semolina. Mix thoroughly and scramble in the usual-way. This makes 2 eggs go as far as 4.

EGGS, to whip whites of. Separate the yolks from the whites carefully so that the yolks are not broken. Put the whites into a basin, beat with a whisk, slowly at first, then more quickly, until the whites are stiff enough to allow the basin to be turned upside down without the eggs falling out.

EGGS, SCOTCH (for 4 people).

2 eggs	salt and pepper
½ lb. sausage meat	egg and bread-crumbs
1 or 2 tomatoes	croûtons of bread

Hard boil the eggs, put them in cold water for a few minutes, remove the shells, dry them well with flour, coat with sausage meat, then with egg and bread-crumbs, rolling them into a nice shape. Fry well in hot fat, allowing time for the sausage meat to be well cooked. Cut off a little of each end of the egg, then cut in half and stand each half on a croûton of fried bread on which is placed a round of tomato. Serve on a fancy paper; garnish with parsley.

EGGS, SHELLING HARD-BOILED. *See* HARD-BOILED.

EGGS, SWISS (for 2 or 3 people).

4 eggs	½ oz. butter
1 gill cream	1 teaspoonful parsley
2 oz. grated cheese	salt and pepper
few bread-crumbs	

Break the eggs one by one, slide gently into a well-buttered fireproof dish, whip the cream slightly, well season it with salt and pepper, pour over the eggs, sprinkle over the chopped parsley and grated cheese a few bread-crumbs and lastly small pieces of butter. Cook in a slow oven till the eggs are set but not hard, and serve hot.

EGG WHITE SUBSTITUTE. A teaspoonful of gelatine (powdered) in 2 tablespoonfuls of hot—not boiling—water. Use when cold.

EGG YOLK, to keep. If you are using only the white of an egg and will not be using the yolk during the same day, beat the yolk up with just a little cold water and cover the basin with a piece of muslin. The yolk will then keep for 2 or 3 days.

EIDERDOWN, to wash. A little liquid ammonia should be added to a lather of hot water and soap jelly. The quilt should be steeped in this mixture for 10 minutes, then squeeze well and "souse" until quite clean. It may be necessary to use several lots of suds. Rinse in 2 warm waters to which should be added a little ammonia. After passing carefully through the wringer, hang out to dry; whilst drying take down and shake well several times.

ELDERBERRY WINE. *See* WINE, ELDERBERRY.

ELECTRIC CURRENT, Value of Fuses. If the light or current suddenly ceases, turn off at meter without delay. Close to meters, safety devices known as fuses are fitted into an easily opened box. These fuses are of weaker wire than carries the house current, and if some strain on current takes place, the fuses "blow out", thus preventing trouble to the rest of the installation. It is seldom all the fuses blow out at the same time (there will be a fuse for upstairs, one for down and one for power; or some such arrangement). Open the fuse box, see which fuse has blown and repair it, then the meter can be turned on again. A fuse is repaired by putting in a new piece of fuse wire (the meter, of course, being turned off). The fuses are porcelain plugs, with the fuse wire running between screw connections at either end. When a fuse is pulled out of its socket, if it is blown, the very thin wire will be seen burned through. Release each fragment from the screw connections, fix in a new fuse, put back and turn on meter. The "fuse" itself is the piece of wire fitted between the two connections. Make sure the fuse wire is of the right gauge; a coil can be obtained from any electrician. It is a good thing as soon as taking a house, to note the type of fuses; to ascertain which lights or power each controls, how the wire is fixed, and that a coil of the right size of spare fuse wire is kept beside the meter.

ELECTRIC METER, to read. To read an electric meter note the figures on the various dials. There is a very small dial, of which take no notice. The left-hand dial tells the single units; the other three the tens, hundreds and thousands. The count is taken from the last figure passed; thus if the left dial shows between 4 and 5, the used amount is 4; the next dial will show, say, exactly 6, and the hundreds dial between 7 and 8, while the thousands will stand at 2. Thus the reading will be 2764 units. This is not the amount burned, but the progressive total. The Electric Company officer "takes" the meter and records it on a card, which it is wise to check. Thus, if at the previous check the dials showed 2624, the difference between this and 2764, gives the units used—140. When taking a house always note immediately the reading before using any current, and if it differs from the record notify the Electric Company.

ELECTROPLATE, to clean. Add a little ammonia to hot water and use as a wash. Take some finely-powdered whiting and rub over the plate. Polish with a soft rag.

EMETICS. Simply explained, these are used to cause vomiting. In cases of poisoning they should be administered immediately, and may consist of strong salt and water, strong mustard and water, or an adult dose of ipecacuanha wine. It is important to note (*see* Poisons) that in burning poisons *no* emetic should be administered.

A very safe emetic for getting rid of indigestible food is readily obtained by mixing a half tablespoonful of mustard in a large cupful of hot water, or 2 tablespoonfuls of common salt dissolved in tepid water.

For Children.—Ipecacuanha wine in teaspoonful doses may be given. (Two tablespoonfuls for adults.) Emetics should be administered with caution to the aged and debilitated. It may be necessary to give a little brandy afterwards.

ENAMELLED WARE. Thoroughly scrub all enamelled articles—both inside and out—in hot soda water, and rinse in clean water. To remove stains sprinkle salt on the pulp of a lemon from which the yellow rind and juice have been removed. A little salt sprinkled on a rag soaked in vinegar is also effective in removing stains.

When enamel saucepans get burnt, soak in water for some time then rub them with a smooth piece of pumice-stone. Burnt patches will come off quite easily. Scorched fireproof dishes may have the stains removed by soaking in strong borax and water.

ENDIVE. Esteemed for salads. Generally speaking, treat as if growing lettuce. Sow in shallow drills in April for early use, or for late use in June or July. When 2 or 3 inches high, transplant into friable ground or thin out 1 foot apart. When nearly full-grown, they must be blanched, to be fit for the table, by gathering and tying the leaves together to exclude the light and air from the inner leaves, which must be done when quite dry, or they will rot. In 3 or 4 weeks they will be blanched. For winter use the green curled variety is most suitable.

ENEMAS. The enema is used to effect a movement of the bowels, particularly with patients who are in bed, and this is a simple operation for which no special prescription is required. The patient should lie in bed on his left side with the knees well drawn up, and the nurse must see that the basin containing the enemata is ready on a chair or table by the bedside. The air should be squeezed out of the syringe so that the fluid to be injected has been drawn into the syringe instead, then the mouthpiece of the syringe, having been oiled with vaseline, must be gently inserted, and the bulb squeezed, so that the fluid is forced slowly into the body. The most usual preparations thus injected are the following:

Soap Enema.—Dissolve 1 oz. of good quality soap flakes or pure yellow soap in 1 pint of warm water.

Castor Oil Enema.—Mix 1 oz. of castor oil with 1 pint of thin starch.

The above are the ordinary enemas to induce an action of the bowels, but where nourishment has to be given in this way, a doctor should do so. The following is the usual preparation:

Nutritive Enema.—Dissolve 1 oz. of white sugar in 1 pint of beef-tea, add 2 tablespoonfuls of cream and 1 of brandy. Inject warm.

Enema for Thread Worms in Children.—Mix strong salt and water and give from a wineglassful to a teacupful.

ENGAGEMENTS. The breaking off of a definitely-announced engagement when the wedding-day is drawing near causes a good deal of worry and trouble.

Invitations and announcements have to be cancelled, the usual course being to send out cards notifying that "The marriage arranged between Mr. A and Miss B will not take place."

Wedding presents must be sent back, with a brief note mentioning the reason, and the couple return each other's presents, including the engagement ring—unless they come to some other mutual arrangement, which is nobody's business but their own.

If the engagement has been announced in the Press, notices that it is at an end should be inserted.

When no definite announcement has been made, the matter chiefly rests between the two people most concerned.

ERANTHIS (WINTER ACONITE). Even before the first spring flowers appear winter aconite gladdens us with its bright-yellow blossoms, and its beautiful shining foliage is in itself an ornament. It flourishes best on a warm chalky soil, in a half-wild state on banks, or under trees and, to gain its full effect, it should be planted in large bold patches. Though the surface of the soil should be renewed every other year, the aconite should not be disturbed too often. Lift a large patch when transplanting in order to make sure you have enough "eyes" for propagation. This is a plant which should not be grown where there are children, for both yellow and blue aconites are poisonous.

ERICA. *See* HEATH.

ERIGERON (FLEABANE). A quick-flowering perennial of varying heights. The border types grow from 6 inches, although about 9 inches to a foot is more usual. They should be planted not later than March, in a sunny position, and will flower from June, not being particular as to soil, and root growth is fairly rapid. The flowers are borne, however, on single stems from the centre spike, and are always single, with yellow disc, though the colour may be pale lilac, pale blue, white, yellow or pink. The taller erigerons run up to 3 feet; are of sturdy, upright growth, and give grand massed effects in beds and borders.

ESCHSCHOLTZIA (CALIFORNIAN POPPY). The Californian poppy has been much improved of late. Average height 1 foot, with feathery, grey foliage has practically all shades from palest yellow to fiery orange, and from palest pink to carmine, as well as white, in single and double blossom, flowering 3 months from seeds sown outdoors in sunny sites. This hardy annual will thrive on dry, stony soils, or light, sandy soils. The seed should be sown late in April.

EVERLASTING FLOWERS. *See* IMMORTELLE AND HELI-CHRYSUM.

EVERLASTING PEAS. *See* PEAS, EVERLASTING.

EXECUTOR, to Will. Anyone can be appointed as an executor except a bankrupt. It is better to appoint an executor (or two if estate is large) and a suitable sum is usual to be named in recognition of the service rendered. Where no executor is named Letters of Administration have to be taken out by someone appointed by the Courts. An executor will be able to obtain necessary forms of affidavit for swearing the will from the Registrar of his district (or from Somerset House, Strand, London), who will also advise as to procedure necessary to prove the will and obtain probate. An executor has also to see to payment and collection of all debts. He has, too, to make the funeral arrangements.

EYE. Where the eye has become inflamed from cold or draught, a boracic lotion, made of a half teaspoonful dissolved in a cupful of boiling water is beneficial. Let the solution cool and then bathe gently.

EYELASHES, to improve. Clip them about once in every four weeks if you wish to lengthen and strengthen them.

EYELIDS, INFLAMED. Bathe in lukewarm water and Condy's fluid, and a small piece of "golden ointment," as big as a pea, applied night and morning to the inflamed lids. It may be necessary to wear a shade or green spectacles.

EYES, to remove foreign bodies from. Dust or insects may often be removed from the eye merely by drawing the upper lid as far down as possible over the lower one. If this is not successful a second person should separate the eyelids with the thumb and first finger. Remove the irritant with the corner of a handkerchief.

In some cases it may be necessary to turn the eyelid inside out. The operator places a matchstick lengthways in the middle of the upper eyelid. The other hand grasps the eyelashes and pulls upwards; at the same time the match is pressed in a downward direction. A drop of olive or castor oil should be put in the eye afterwards.

EYES, BLOODSHOT, lotion. With 3 oz. rose water mix a pinch of boracic crystals. The lotion should be well worked into the eyes by rapidly opening and closing the lids whilst bathing.

EYES, NEW-BORN BABY'S. If the eyes of a newly-born baby become inflamed a doctor should immediately be consulted, as the results may be serious if the matter is not dealt with promptly.

EYE WASH. After removing anything that has got into the eye, or when the eyes are inflamed, or after a severe strain, wash the eye with warm salt water to cleanse and soothe it; ½ teaspoonful of salt to 1 pint of water. If the smarting is objected to, use same proportion of boracic acid and water.

FABRICS, to test. The most common test for wool is to unravel a few threads and apply a lighted match to it. If it smoulders slowly and gives off the smell of burnt feathers, the material is wool. If, on the other hand, it burns fairly freely, emits a smell resembling burning paper, and leaves a whitish ash, then it is cotton.

Silk also burns slowly and with a faint smell resembling burnt feathers.

Linen burns freely, but as a rule the extinguished end is rounded and blunt, whereas cotton is tufted.

It is also possible to test materials by biting. When bitten, wool is harsh and gritty; silk cuts cleanly.

Artificial silk can often be detected if moistened, for this considerably weakens the fibres, as is not the case with real silk.

FAINTING FITS. An attack may be averted in time by drinking a glass of cold water. If the fit develops, the head should be kept low and smelling salts applied to the nose, and cold water sponged over the face. If the unconsciousness is prolonged the patient should be kept warm and hot bottled put to the extremities. Give as much air as possible and loosen the clothing. On recovery, brandy and water or a cup of strong coffee or tea should be given.

FAT, CLARIFYING.

3 or 4 lb. beef and mutton fat
½ pint water

Cut up the fat in small pieces, put into a saucepan with barely the half-pint water, cook until all the fat is melted out and only the skin remains; stir occasionally; strain into a clean basin or pan. This fat is useful for inexpensive pastry and cakes, also for frying.

FEATHER CUSHIONS. To prevent feathers from working through choose closely-woven material for the inside lining and rub the wrong side with dry soap.

FEEDING-BOTTLES. *See* INFANTS.

FEEDING-BOTTLES, to keep the teats in condition. Immediately after use the teats should be rinsed in cold water and rubbed with common salt—inside and out. Place them for a few seconds in boiling water, remove, put in a clean saucer that has been in boiling water and cover with a cup or tumbler.

FEET, BLISTERED. Relief may be secured by changing socks, left foot to right, and *vice versa*, after rubbing soles of socks with dry soap; where blisters break treat with boracic ointment. A frequent cause is ill-fitting shoes and socks too large, which chafe.

FEET, FOOT-BATH. To soothe hot or aching feet, boil a quart of bran in 1½ gallons of water for 5 minutes and leave to cool enough to immerse feet, then soak till water is lukewarm. It should not be strained.

FEET, OFFENSIVE. Bathe the feet every night in one of the following solutions:

1. Plenty of borax and water (tablespoonful to 1 quart).
2. Permanganate of potash (a pinch) in 8 oz. water.
3. Common soda and water (tablespoonful to 1 quart).

After drying, powder with talcum.

FEET, TENDER. Sponge the feet both morning and night with a solution of either carbonate of soda and water, or salt and water, mixed in the proportion of 2 tablespoonfuls to 1 pint.

FELT. Cornflour is effective in cleaning felt hats. Spread the hat on a piece of paper and sprinkle with cornflour. Then brush the hat well and you will find it free of dirt.

FERMENTATION. Add a small piece of sulphate of potash to stop any fermentation of liquors, preserves, syrups, etc.

FERTILIZING. Manuring is the use of decayed garden refuse, animal humus, bonfire ash, etc. Fertilizers are the modern equivalent, used where natural compost is difficult to obtain. They give quicker results, are easier to obtain, and can be applied with less labour.

Fertilizers are mainly of three classes, each possessing distinctive cultural functions; potash promotes growth, nitrogen increases yield, phosphate strengthens roots and ensures more full ripening.

The average proportion for all classes of fertilizers is 1 oz. to the square yard.

The method of using is to mix in small proportions with the tilth and to scatter over the ground among growing plants.

For use in the vegetable plots, phosphates are scattered over the dug areas a week or two before seed sowing. Give an annual dressing for 10 rods (an average allotment) of 30 lb. superphosphate, 20 lb. sulphate of potash applied at the beginning of the season. A dressing of 1½ lb. of sulphate of ammonia per rod will be needed, but this should be applied to the growing crops. Green crops and potatoes require an additional dressing of sulphate of ammonia. Basic slag is a satisfactory alternative to superphosphate if applied during the winter at the rate of 50 lb. per 10 rods.

Another method of applying fertilizers is as the trenches are dug for putting in the young vegetables. A scattering is made—bone meal, dried blood, and so on—along the bottom of the trench and covered with earth, so that the young roots do not get to the fertilizing material till they are established and need extra nourishment to make sturdy growth.

Different plants, flowers as well as vegetables, have their preferences, and while a general fertilizer is always beneficial, mixtures can be obtained from seedsmen to suit this or that particular need.

Although these fertilizers are generally known to gardeners as artificials, they are in reality the concentrated elements of natural soil.

It is because of the different chemical needs of varying classes of vegetable produce that the system of Rotation (which see) is so usefully employed.

FEVER, to relieve. The bed covering should be light, and the temperature may be lowered by sponging the body with tepid or cold water. If the temperature persists, send for a doctor.

FEVERS, cooling drink for. Take ¼ oz. cream of tartar, a few pieces of lemon and orange, and ¼ oz. sugar candy, pour on 1 quart of boiling water and decant the clear liquid when cool.

FILTER. Take an ordinary large flower-pot. Stop the hole with a piece of sponge; then put a layer of powdered charcoal about 1 inch thick and a similar quantity of silver sand; then a layer of small stones and gravel about 2 inches thick. This serves admirably as a filter for impure water.

FINGER-NAILS. To cure an ingrowing nail, every time it is trimmed a notch should be cut in the middle. This will tend to draw the nail up from the sides.

Discoloured nails may be cleansed by rubbing with a slice of lemon at intervals till normal.

Brittle nails should be rubbed with sweet oil or vaseline.

FIRE. (Hints from a Home Office Pamphlet.)

A dog sleeping in a house is a safeguard.

To remove an unconscious person from an upstairs room to downstairs: "Turn him on his back on the floor, tie his wrists together, kneel astride his body and place one's head through the loop formed by his arms. In this kneeling position it is then possible to remove from the scene of danger a person whom it would not be possible to lift."

A person whose clothes are on fire should not remain standing. If such a person starts to run he should be tripped up, rolled on the floor in a rug, coat or blanket until the flames are subdued.

If it is necessary to escape from a window, do not jump. Sit on the window-sill with the legs outside; turn over, facing downwards, and slide out gradually until the fingers grip the sill and then let go. The falling distance is thus reduced.

By keeping close to a wall it is often possible to move safely about a room or corridor or staircase which have been weakened by fire.

If escape by the stairs is cut off, it is safer to stay in a room with the door shut.

Keep all doors and windows closed, especially doors communicating with the open air.

Near the floor the air will be comparatively free from smoke, and also cooler. Therefore, always progress as close to the floor as possible.

A policeman's whistle kept in an upper floor is of great assistance in rousing others or summoning outside assistance.

FIRE, to make last. Either bank up with a good supply of well-damped small coal, or put on a small quantity of lumps of coal and sprinkle about a handful of common salt over them.

FIREPROOFING. Any materials used for nursery curtains, coverings, etc., can be made reasonably fireproof if soaked in a solution of alum. The process needs to be repeated after the materials have been washed.

FISH, to choose and keep. It is most essential that fish should be fresh and in full season; it decomposes more quickly than any food. It is in best condition, most plentiful and cheapest when in season. When fish is kept on ice it is difficult to detect if it is stale; but after it has been removed it quickly loses its apparent freshness and can be judged by its smell and appearance. No one can mistake the smell of stale fish. If in good condition the flesh should be firm and plumb, of a good even colour, eyes bright, gill and spots red. There are a few kinds that can be kept for a short time, such as turbot, cod and halibut; but they must be kept in a cool place in a current of air, and not in water. Fish may need soaking before cooking, but must not lie long in water, as this impoverishes the flavour and the fish becomes flabby. If fish is slimy, especially fresh-water fish, rub it with dry salt, as well as thoroughly wash it. Mackerel is unfit for food unless quite fresh. Salmon is best cooked as soon as possible after it is caught.

FISH, to fry in batter (for 5 or 6 people).

fillets of whiting or plaice	2 tablespoonfuls tepid water
2 oz. flour	white of 1 egg
1 tablespoonful oil or melted butter	salt and pepper

Wash and dry the fillets in flour, place the flour in a basin, add salt, add the oil, then mix smoothly with the tepid water, beat it well, and if possible stand aside for some time; just before using add the beaten white of egg. Dip in each fillet, fry them in deep fat without using a basket. Drain well; garnish with fried parsley.

FISH, to scallop.

any cold fish

For Sauce.:

1 oz. butter

½ pint milk

little butter

few bread-crumbs

1 oz. flour

salt and pepper

Remove skin and bones from fish and flake it. Make a white sauce and flavour it nicely, add it to the fish, butter some scallop shells, put in some of the mixture, and sprinkle over some bread-crumbs. Put small pieces of butter on the top, and bake till a nice brown in a quick oven. A little grated cheese can be sprinkled over before baking if liked.

FISH, to steam.

1 sole, whiting or any
white fish

salt

lemon juice

white sauce

parsley

Thoroughly cleanse the fish, remove any skin, place between two buttered plates, squeeze over a few drops of lemon juice, and sprinkle with a pinch of salt. Place the plates over a saucepan of fast-boiling water and cook until the flesh will leave the bone. Place carefully on a hot dish, strain some sauce over, garnish nicely with parsley and lemon and serve hot.

FISHBONE IN THROAT. If a bone should stick in the throat whilst eating fish, take half a lemon and suck the juice, allowing it slowly to trickle down the throat. This gives speedy relief. If it can be seen, use tweezers carefully to extract.

FISH CAKES (10 or 12).

½ lb. each of cold fish and
potatoes

½ teaspoonful chopped
parsley

½ teaspoonful anchovy

little butter

salt and pepper

egg and bread-crumbs

Remove all bones and skin, flake the fish finely, mash the potatoes, mix them together, add the butter and flavourings, form in small cakes, using a little flour; coat with egg and bread-crumbs, fry in hot fat, garnish with fried parsley.

FISH CHOWDER.

1½ lb. white fish

4 potatoes

2 cupfuls milk

2 cupfuls chopped carrots

¼ lb. salt pork

1 chopped onion

Cut pork in small pieces and fry with onion for 5 minutes. Put pork, onion, carrots and potatoes in a saucepan and add boiling water to cover. Cook till vegetables are tender then add milk and the fish boned and cut in small pieces. Cook for about 10 minutes.

FISH CURRY (for 4 or 5 people).

1 lb. cooked fish

1 apple

1 small onion

2 oz. butter

1 oz. flour

½ oz. curry powder

1 oz. desiccated coconut

lemon juice

salt

1 dessertspoonful curry paste

4 oz. Patna rice

Boil the rice and dry it thoroughly, melt the butter in a stewpan, well cook the apple and onion finely chopped, add the flour and curry powder and cook for 15 to 20 minutes, then add the milk and stir till it boils: infuse the coconut in a little of the milk for some minutes, then strain it into the curry; add the curry paste, lemon juice and salt and a pinch of sugar, flake the fish and stir in gently not to break the flakes. Serve on a hot dish with a border of the rice, and garnish with cut lemon and parsley.

To Boil the Rice.—Well wash the rice, put in fast-boiling water to which has been added salt and a little lemon juice; when tender drain on to a sieve, pour cold water over to separate the grains and dry thoroughly.

FISH CUTLETS, BAKED.

2 lb. thick fish cutlets (halibut, salmon or cod)	1 tablespoonful butter
¼ cupful flour	2 teaspoonfuls mustard
1 cupful milk	2 cupfuls grated cheese
½ teaspoonful pepper	1 teaspoonful salt

Melt butter, add flour and milk. Mix well with pepper, salt, mustard and cheese and cook till thick, when pour over skinned and boned fish. Bake half an hour in moderate oven. Serve with new potatoes and a green salad.

FISH FILLETS, à la Bohemienne (for 3 or 4 people).

fillets of sole or plaice	1 tablespoonful cream
2 oz. butter	lemon juice
1 oz. flour	salt and pepper
1 gill milk	parsley
¼ lb. tomatoes	

Lay the fillets, cut in half or rolled, on a greased tin, sprinkle a little lemon juice and pepper on each, cover with greased paper and bake in the oven from 15 to 20 minutes. Cook the sliced tomatoes in 1 oz. butter; when tender pass them through a sieve. Make a sauce with the remainder of the butter, flour, milk and tomato purée, boil, then add seasoning and cream. Put the fillets on a hot dish, coat with the sauce and garnish with cut lemon and parsley.

FISH FILLETS, à la Maitre d'Hôtel (for 3 or 4 people).

fillets of plaice or sole	chopped parsley
1 oz. flour	lemon juice
1 oz. butter	salt and pepper
½ pint milk	

Skin and fillet the fish, bake in the oven on a greased tin sprinkled with lemon juice and pepper. Make a sauce with the flour, butter and milk, add the chopped parsley and lemon juice, season well. Place the fillets on a hot dish, coat them with the sauce, and garnish with cut lemon and parsley.

FISH, FINNAN OMELETTE.

2 eggs	1 tablespoonful cream
salt	2 tablespoonfuls cooked finnan haddock
pepper	1 dessertspoonful butter

111

Beat the eggs, mix with haddock, cream, pepper, and salt. Melt butter in omelette pan. Pour in mixture and stir till almost set. Gather to one side of pan, cook quickly till set. Turn over and lightly brown the other side.

FISH, FRICASSÉE OF (for 4 or 5 people).

1 lb. cold cooked fish	1 gill cream
1 oz. butter	lemon juice
1 oz. flour	salt and pepper
1 gill milk	mashed potatoes

Remove skin and bones from fish and roughly flake it, make a white sauce with butter, milk and cream, season well and add lemon juice. Make a border of mashed potato, using a rose tube and forcing-bag; place the mixture in the centre; garnish with lemon and parsley. Another suitable garnish is the flaked yolk of hard-boiled egg.

FISH PASTY.

equal quantities cold fish and potatoes	some anchovy sauce or white sauce
pepper and salt	

Remove skin and bones from fish, flake and add to the sauce, season well and place mixture in a greased pie-dish, mash the potatoes smoothly, place it on the top of the fish, decorate it nicely and brush over with egg or milk, cook till a nice brown in a hot oven.

FISH PATTIES.

6 oz. cold cooked fish	½ gill thick white sauce
flaky pastry	anchovy essence

Mix fish with sauce. Add a little anchovy and cool. Line some patty pans with pastry. Place some of the fish mixture in each and cover with pastry. Make a hole in the top of each and brush them over with beaten egg. Bake for 20 minutes in hot oven.

FISH SALAD.

2 eggs	½ teaspoonful sugar
2 cupfuls minced boiled fish	¼ cupful vinegar
	1 tablespoonful powdered gelatine
1 teaspoonful salt	½ cupful cold water

Beat the eggs well. Add salt, vinegar, sugar and water, boil in a double saucepan till thick. Soften gelatine in cold water, add to the hot dressing. Add fish. Place in some small wet moulds or one large one and put in a cold place till firm. Place on lettuce leaves, garnish with tomatoes and serve with mayonnaise.

FISH, white sauce for.

2 tablespoonfuls flour	½ teaspoonful salt
2 tablespoonfuls butter	½ teaspoonful pepper
1 cupful milk	

Melt the butter in a saucepan, add flour and seasoning, gradually stir in milk. Keep on stirring till thoroughly cooked. You can add a finely-chopped hard-boiled egg or egg and tablespoonful chopped parsley, or chopped cucumber or tablespoonful horse-radish grated and moistened with lemon juice.

FLANNEL DUSTERS. Take an old piece of flannel and let it soak for several hours in paraffin. Wring it out tightly and then wash it in tepid water and let it dry. It will gather all the dust and give a good polish to furniture and floors.

FLANNELS, to remove grass stains. Apply to the stains equal parts of yolk of egg and glycerine; allow to remain for an hour or so; then wash the flannels in the usual way.

For slighter stains on white flannels and serge costumes, put powdered magnesia on dry, brush off after laying aside for a day, and shake well.

FLAP JACKS.

1 egg	1 teaspoonful melted butter
1 cupful milk	¼ teaspoonful salt
2 teaspoonfuls baking-powder	1 cupful flour

Mix dry ingredients together, beat egg, add milk, stir in butter, make a hole in dry ingredients and gradually stir in liquid. Beat batter till smooth. If not thin enough use more milk. Then heat an iron girdle, grease it with a piece of suet, pour cakes on from the end of a large spoon, keeping them as round as possible. When full of bubbles turn with a flexible knife and brown on the other side. Wipe girdle with dry cloth and grease again between each batch of cakes. Serve hot.

FLAT FOOT. The sole of the foot should be rubbed with embrocation and exercises done daily. The patient should turn his toes inwards and raise the body on tiptoe. The exercise should be gone through several times every morning; as the muscles get stronger the number of exercises should be increased. A sharp walk should be taken every day. A pad or metal spring as supplied by chemists or bootmakers may be worn in the boot or shoe.

FLATULENCE. A teaspoonful of bicarbonate of soda in a tumbler of hot water should be taken. Peppermint water will also give relief.

FLAVOURING FOR TRIFLES. A good imitation maraschino flavouring for trifles, etc., can be made from the strained juice of a large orange, 6 drops of lemon juice, a teaspoonful of vanilla essence, 1 tablespoonful of sugar and 1 teacupful of hot water.

FLAX. *See* LINUM.

FLEAS. A liberal sprinkling of Keating's powder will keep fleas away from bedding.

FLIES, to drive away. The following are various approved methods:

1. Get 1 oz. of oil of lavender. Put a little on a cloth, and with it rub the window-sill and sides of the window-frame. Also treat the door jambs the same way. The odour does not please flies.

2. A fresh bunch of stinging nettles hung up in the window will prevent the entrance of flies.

3. Cloves placed in a coarse open muslin bag and hung in the places frequented by flies are most useful in ridding the house of them. A spray of bruised elder hung up in a larder will prevent flies settling.

4. By washing your windows in March with a strong solution of carbolic you can keep off flies during the summer months. Carbolic destroys their eggs and by reason of its strong smell keeps flies away. When the warm weather comes use it also to wash your woodwork.

FLOOR POLISH. Put half contents of a tin of floor polish into another tin and fill each with paraffin. Melt slowly, taking care not to place the tin near a naked flame and then put aside to cool. The polish gives the same results as before and a great economy is effected.

FLOORS, STAINING. Colours for staining white wood can be obtained prepared at any oil-shop, but the quantity required is often more than anticipated. By far the cheapest way to stain flooring is to buy 1 oz. of permanganate of potash and dissolve sufficient for use in warm water; then paint the wood with it, and it will leave a stain not unlike dark oak or walnut. It must not be allowed to touch the hands, as it will dye them deep brown. The result on the wood will be a dull surface, but if a polished appearance is preferred it can be painted over with a coating of white varnish, and then will be found to look very well.

FLOORS, DAMP. When linoleums are laid on tiled floors damp frequently rises. To prevent this, get a quantity of the cork in which grapes are packed. Scatter this about quarter of an inch thick between the floor and the linoleum and the moisture will not again appear.

FLOORS, TILED. When cleaning new tiles add a little paraffin to the water. Cement marks on newly tiled floors and porches can be removed by applying spirits of salt with a rag tied on to a stick so as not to get the hands into contact with the salts, which are caustic.

FLOUR, to test. Pass the flour through a fine sieve after warming for $1\frac{1}{2}$ hours; if it is not lumpy and has a pleasant smell the flour is good.

FLOWERS, to keep fresh. An aspirin or a little starch dropped into the water in which flowers are placed will keep the stems upright.

Flowers will last longer by cutting a small piece off the stem every day and splitting hard woody stalks about 1 inch from the bottom. Do these operations with a sharp knife, not scissors. Add a little soda and salt to the water to freshen the flowers. Several sheets of damp newspaper should be wrapped round flowers sent by post.

FLY-PAPERS, to make. Take pieces of strong, thick paper, smear with treacle, and place in prominent positions. Always burn fly-papers after use.

FOMENTATIONS, HOT. Take a towel and lay it in a basin. Put a piece of flannel inside, pour boiling water over it and then wring out the towel with the flannel inside it. Apply flannel as hot as can be borne, cover with a piece of oilsilk and keep warm with a piece of cotton-wool large enough to cover it. Where hot fomentations are necessary replacements must be prepared before the previous ones have had time to get cold. When the hot fomentations are discontinued, a piece of flannel or pad of cotton-wool should be wrapped round the part to prevent a chill.

FOOT VALUES. *See* VITAMINS.

FOOT SCRAPER. Nail a scrubbing brush upside down on to a board outside the door and everyone can wipe his shoes thoroughly before coming indoors.

FORCEMEAT BALLS.

2 tablespoonfuls bread-crumbs
1 tablespoonful chopped suet
1 teaspoonful chopped parsley
½ teaspoonful chopped herbs
little grated lemon rind
little nutmeg
1 egg

Mix all the ingredients together, bind with egg, and form into small balls.

FORCEMEAT, CHESTNUT.

½ lb. chestnuts
¼ lb. bread-crumbs
½ lb. butter
stock
nutmeg
salt and pepper

Peel and boil the chestnuts until the skin can be removed, stew them in some stock; when cold pound them with the bread-crumbs, add butter, nutmeg, salt and pepper, and bind with egg.

FORCEMEAT, VEAL.

4 oz. bread-crumbs
2 oz. suet
1 teaspoonful chopped parsley
½ teaspoonful mixed herbs
little grated-lemon rind
1 egg
salt and pepper

Chop the suet, add bread-crumbs, parsley, herbs and lemon rind, mix with beaten egg, and season.

FORGET-ME-NOT (MYOSOTIS). A hardy perennial which, once started, sows itself freely and gives a profusion of blue flowers.

FOXGLOVE. *See* DIGITALIS.

FRACTURES.

SIMPLE.—When the bone is broken, but the skin remains intact.

COMPOUND.—When both the bone and the skin are broken. The ends of the bone may protrude through the opening.

COMMINUTED.—When the bone is broken in several places.

COMPLICATED.—When other structures, such as nerves and arteries, are injured.

The collar bone is the bone which is most liable to fracture.

Symptoms.—The signs of the injury, pain, bruising, swelling, inability to use the part, and sometimes deformity and displacement. The ends of the bones, upon manipulations, can be heard grating together. Shock will be present and varies with the extent of the injury.

Treatment.—Where a fracture is obvious or even suspected, it should never be handled by an unskilled person—otherwise this may lead to further injury to the part and a simple fracture may be made compound. If it is necessary to move the person before the arrival of a surgeon, a splint should be put on. This may consist of anything handy, such as an umbrella or walking-stick to support each side of the fracture. In the case of a compound fracutre a clean handkerchief should be placed over the wound in the skin.

FRAMES, GILT, to restore. Add to 1½ pints of water sufficient flour or sulphur to give a golden tinge, and in this boil 4 or 5 bruised onions. Strain off the liquid, and allow to cool. Apply with a soft brush and leave to dry.

FREESIA. This is a half-hardy bulbous plant flowering in winter and spring with beautiful white, or yellow, flowers of delicious fragrance. Raised from seed sown in a rich compost, but as the roots are very brittle, use care in transplanting. From seeds sown in February or March flowers may be obtained the same year, while a further sowing in August will supply plants for the following spring.

FRENCH BEANS. *See* BEANS.

FRITTERS, FRUIT.

apples or bananas	2 tablespoonfuls tepid water
3 oz. flour	white of 1 egg
1 tablespoonful oil	pinch of salt

Put the flour and salt into a basin, make a well in the centre, pour in the oil, add the water gradually and mix smoothly; beat well. Let it stand for an hour if possible, then add the whipped white of egg lightly. Peel the apple, cut into slices, take out the core, leaving a ring, dip in the batter, fry in hot fat: drain well. Dish on a lace paper, sprinkle with castor sugar. Serve at once.

Note.—Bananas, oranges, apricots, pineapple may be used instead of apples.

FRITTERS, GROUND RICE.

6 oz. ground rice	1 heaped teaspoonful finely-chopped onion
1 heaped teaspoonful chopped parsley	6 eggs

First cook rice thoroughly in 3 gills of water, strain, mix with other ingredients, form into fritters and fry in boiling oil.

FRITTERS, POTATO.

1 lb. potatoes
4 eggs
1 heaped tablespoonful bread-crumbs

Cook potatoes and mash, mix with the other ingredients, form into fritters and fry in boiling oil.

FRITTERS, SAVOURY.

¼ lb. onions	pepper, salt
little dried and powdered sage	4 eggs
	¼ lb. bread-crumbs

Pour a little boiling water over bread-crumbs and allow to soak for 1 hour. Thoroughly cook onions and then chop finely. Strain off any surplus water from the bread-crumbs, well beat the eggs and then mix all ingredients together. Make into fairly large fritters (about 2½ inches long and ½ inch thick) and fry in boiling oil.

FROZEN PIPES. Screw up and light a newspaper and pass it slowly along the pipe. This gives a quicker result than the application of hot water, but where not convenient, wrap some old clothes round the frozen pipe and pour hot water on them. The clothes will hold the heat and the pipes will thaw out in a few minutes.

FRUIT, to bottle. Fill the bottles with fruit that has been wiped with a dry cloth, and then cover with cold syrup and cork tightly. Loosen the corks and place the bottles in a steamer of cold water and boil slowly for about 1½ hours. After removing them from the steamer, tightly seal the bottles and store them in a dry, cool place.

FRUIT, to peel. Before peeling oranges put them in the oven for a moment; this will loosen the white inner skin and make peeling easy.
To peel apples and tomatoes first immerse them in boiling water for a minute.

FRUIT, to preserve. Blackberries, whortleberries, currants, raspberries, peaches, plums, apples, pears, and quinces can all be preserved by drying them in the sun, and then storing in bags in a cool, dry place.
Green currants and green gooseberries can be preserved thus. Gather when perfectly dry, put into very dry bottles when free from stems and eyes, put the bottles uncorked into a pan of cold water, then bring to the boil. Cork the bottles (the fruit should come up to the cork), and seal them with beeswax and resin. Store in a dry place, where they will not freeze. Everything depends on success in excluding *air and water*. The surest mode of storing bottles is to put them in boxes, and to fill the spaces with dry sand.

FRUIT, COMPOTE OF.
fruits (all kinds in season)
½ lb. loaf sugar
½ pint water
lemon juice
noyau or any liqueur

Make a syrup with the sugar and water, boil for 10 minutes; prepare the fruit carefully, cut into neat dice or fancy shapes and stew *very slightly*. Turn into a basin and allow to stand till cold, add noyau or any other liqueur to taste; put in a salad bowl or glass dish, piling up fruit in centre. Colour the syrup with a few drops of carmine; decorate with blanched and shredded almonds and pistachio nuts.

FRUIT CUP. Mix together 1 bottle raisin wine, juice of 1 lemon, and 1 tablespoonful each of rum and noyau. Sweeten as desired, adding 1 wineglassful of crushed ice and a bottle of soda water. Stir well. Decorate with slices of bananas, grapes and preserved fruits, and serve in cups.

FRUIT PIES. If the edge of a fruit pie is damped with milk instead of water the juice will not run out.
To prevent the bottom crust of fruit pies from becoming sodden with the juice, when you have lined your dish with paste brush it over with a beaten egg and allow it to stand a few minutes before putting in the fruit. You will find the bottom crust as "short" as the top.

FRUIT PUDDINGS. *See* PUDDINGS, BOILED FRUIT.

FRUIT SALAD. *See* SALAD.

FRUIT STAINS. To remove these from light dresses cover the stain with glycerine, leave it on a few minutes and then wipe off the glycerine with a cloth dipped in warm water.

Fruit stains on table linen can generally be removed by stretching the piece across a basin and pouring boiling water from a kettle on the spot. Wring it out, turn it over and pour on the reverse side.

FRUIT, STEWED. *See* STEWED FRUIT.

FRUIT TARTS. *See* TARTS, FRUIT.

FRUIT TREES, PRUNING. Nearly all fruit trees would bear heavier crops of better fruits if more branches were cut away, particularly from the middle of the trees to let in more air and sunshine.

The chief pruning of fruit trees is done between leaf fall and the bursting of the buds in spring. That is the time to inspect them to see which branches ought to be cut out.

If the main branches are 12 inches apart all will be well. If they are not, any that seem ill-placed should be cut right out. Then prune on the following lines.

The leading shoots which extend the main branches are cut back by one-third or even one-half if they are not vigorous, and the long side shoots are pruned to within about three buds of the base. Shoots which are short and possess fruit buds need no pruning.

It is easy to distinguish between blossom buds and leaf buds. The former are large, somewhat rounded and conspicuous, the latter small, pointed and pressed closely against the shoots. To improve set of next year's branches prune just above a bud that points outwards, for that helps to keep the middle of the tree free from useless and hindering branches.

Apple, pear, plum and sweet cherry are pruned in much the same way, but plum and cherry are most satisfactory when pruning is light.

FRUIT TREES, TRANSPLANTING. Fruit trees may be transplanted at any time of the year, but it has been proved that best results are obtained by moving them at night. The earth about the roots should be disturbed as little as possible.

FRYING. If a little salt is sprinkled in the frying-pan before the fat is put in, this will prevent splashing. Fat must be boiling, *i. e.*, a thin blue smoke must rise from it, for successful frying—otherwise the food will appear greasy.

FRYING-PAN. To clean a greasy frying-pan, put a little boiling water and a teaspoonful of soda in it and let it boil for a few minutes.

FUCHSIA. It is quite easy to raise fuchsias from seed, which, if sown in January or February, will produce plants ready to bloom in July or August. Early sowings must be made in heat, and for the soil in which the seedlings are potted off a mixture of cow-dung is advised. Cuttings taken, after flowering, at joints will root in sand under glass.

FUDGE.

2 cupfuls sugar	2 squares chocolate
⅛ teaspoonful cream of tartar	1 cupful milk or water
	1 teaspoonful vanilla

Mix the sugar, cream of tartar, chocolate and milk, and place over a warm fire. Stir steadily until the mixture begins to boil, and afterwards stir occasionally. Test by dropping a little into cold water; if it can be rolled into a soft ball between the fingers, the fudge is ready. When lukewarm, add the vanilla and stir until the mixture is thick. Pour into a buttered tin and cut into squares.

FUNERALS. *See* BEREAVEMENTS.

FUR HINTS. A fur that is constantly worn often gets very shabby-looking round the back. This can largely be prevented by shaking it in front of a fire for a few seconds every time after wearing. All expensive furs, such as sable and skunk, etc., can be cleaned to look like new by being well rubbed with hot silver sand. After a good rubbing thoroughly shake and beat the fur.

Never cut with scissors or the fur will be spoiled. Turn on the wrong side and cut with either a safety razor blade or a sharp knife. When sewing fur have a small piece of cardboard between two edges that are being sewn together. Keep the fur down with this as you sew the edges together and move it along as you sew.

To renovate fur, take some cornflour and brush it through the fur with the grain.

Another way is to brush it with a stiff whisk broom. Then saturate a clean cloth with petrol and rub well. Afterwards use the whisk broom and then hang the fur in the sun to dry. The latter is not always a good method particularly with coloured or dyed furs. It should be done out of doors and you must be very careful when using this inflammable medium.

FUR IN KETTLES. *See* KETTLES.

FURNITURE. When dusting dark furniture a little oil on the duster keeps the articles treated more free from dust.

FURNITURE, to remove finger marks. These will disappear if rubbed lightly with a cloth dipped in paraffin.

FURNITURE, to remove hot plate marks. Though it is very difficult indeed entirely to remove these marks, they may be made less evident if rubbed with linseed oil and the table afterwards polished with spirits of wine. Repeat the process several times if necessary.

FURNITURE, to remove scratches. Make a mixture of equal parts of linseed oil and turpentine and apply to the scratches, rubbing gently with a piece of soft rag.

FURNITURE, to remove worms. *See* WORMS.

FURNITURE, BAMBOO. Clean with a soft brush dipped in salt water and, after drying with a soft rag, rub over with a drop of linseed oil.

GAILLARDIA. The annual Gaillardias grow to about 16 inches if in sunshine, and in a sandy loam for root run. Their dark crimson or yellowish flowers borne on stiff stems above the pointed, light-green foliage are distinctive. Sow in April to flower in July or August until November. Gaillardias are quite easy to raise from seed by sowing thinly in sandy soil. They dislike crowding, whether as seedlings or fully grown. The perennial Gaillardias should be planted in March to produce a supply of large, daisy-like yellow and crimson flowers throughout the summer. Height about 3 feet. A sandy loam suits them, and a sunny position. The clumps should be lifted and divided every spring. Suitable for large borders.

GALANTINE.

1 lb. raw pork
½ lb. raw steak
1½ teaspoonfuls chopped onion
stock to moisten
¾ cupful bread-crumbs
salt, pepper, celery, salt and paprika
1 egg
2 oz. chopped bacon fat
3 hard-boiled eggs
1 teaspoonful tomato catsup

Put meats through a mincer, stir in crumbs, catsup, seasoning, beaten egg, moisten with stock (¾ cupful). Arrange shelled eggs down the centre, place in a pudding cloth wrung out of hot water and dredged with flour, spread out flat, roll up, fasten securely and simmer in hot stock or water, adding an oxo cube, an onion and some soup vegetables for 2 hours. Then place in fresh cloth, weight and cool. Glaze, decorate with butter.

GALL-STONES. Gall-stones may exist for years and give rise to no symptoms at all, but if they are forced from the gall-bladder into the bowels their passage causes excruciating pain. They occur in middle and advanced life, and women are more liable to them than men.

Symptoms.—The person is suddenly seized with agonizing pain in the lower part of the right chest, right shoulder and back. The person vomits, becomes collapsed and perspires profusely. The attack passes off, the stone having either passed into the bowel, or slipped back into the gall-bladder.

Gall-stones may be removed by operation and all further trouble thus avoided.

To prevent the formation of gall-stones, the amount of fat and starchy foods, such as potatoes, arrowroot, bread, rice, sago, should be limited, and 1 or 2 teaspoonfuls of sulphate of soda should be taken in water every morning before breakfast.

GALVANIZED BUCKETS, etc. A little paraffin will clean these effectively.

GAME, to buy and keep fresh. Most of the tests for the age of poultry can be applied to game; but game should always be bought in its feathers, never after it is plucked. Game is greatly improved in tenderness and flavour by hanging; it is not considered worth eating while fresh. The length of time for hanging depends on the weather and the larder. In cold, dry, windy weather it will keep for some weeks, according to the taste of the consumer; but if the atmosphere is moist and warm it decomposes quickly and becomes unwholesome and unfit to eat. Birds should be hung by the neck and sprinkled with pepper to keep away the flies and hung in a safe in the open air if possible.

Waterfowl, such as wild duck, snipe, teal, etc., should not hang more than a day or two.

A good method is to place near the game some muslin bags filled with powdered charcoal, and to renew them daily.

GAME PURÉE.

1 cupful cooked game	pepper and salt
½ cupful stock	½ cupful cooked ham
½ cupful cooked rice	¼ cupful evaporated milk
	¼ cupful grated cheese

Put game and ham twice through mincer before measuring. Add half the stock, then press mixture through a sieve. Stir in seasoning and milk. Heat in saucepan, add rest of stock. Pour into fireproof baking-dish, cover with rice, sprinkle with grated cheese and brown.

GARDENING. Throughout this encyclopædia the manifold activities of gardening, flowers or vegetables will be found under their most appropriate headings. Thus, the first operation of breaking the ground is detailed under Digging, fertilizers under F, the raising of annuals under A and so on. Directions for the growing and propagation of individual plants also appear in rightful alphabetic order: thus Anemone under A, Zinnia under Z; or in vegetables, Broccoli under B and Vegetable Marrow under V.

In this way the gardener will be able to discover all he wants to know about flower and vegetable gardening, with the added satisfaction that the instruction is dependable and up to date.

GARGLES. Gargles are generally used to combat sore throats, and when the trouble is slight it is immaterial whether the solution is employed hot or cold. If the sore throat is severe it is better the gargle should be warm. When it is desired to assist suppuration the gargle should be as hot as possible.

Borax Gargle.—Add a pinch of borax and one of kitchen salt to half a tumblerful of cold water. Stir till dissolved, then use as a gargle. It is a good plan to use this gargle every morning. By its use the muscles and cords of the throat will be strengthened.

Chlorate of Potash Gargle.—Put 2 oz. chlorate of potash into a tumbler of cold water. Only a little will dissolve, but after gargling with the solution, fill up afresh each time with water until all the potash has been dissolved. Cover tumbler when not in use.

Gargle for Thrush.—One part of glycerine to eight of warm water. Use frequently. If any difficulty in gargling, apply with a camel-hair brush.

Gargle to Promote Suppuration. (To assist an abscess in the throat to burst.)—Wash 1 tablespoonful of pearl barley and 1 of whole linseed. Put into a covered pan with 1 pint of water and simmer till reduced to half. Use the gargle hot and as freely as possible. If too thick, a little more water may be added.

When the abscess has burst, use the following:

Healing Gargle.—Add 2 drams tincture of myrrh to a breakfast-cupful of barley water. Use warm.

Nitre Gargle. (For simple sore throat.)—Two drams of purified nitre to 1 breakfastcupful of barley water. Use frequently.

Alum Gargle. (An astringent for use when the mouth is ulcerated or there is relaxation of the mucous membrane of the throat, tonsils or uvula.)—Powdered alum 80 grains, tincture of myrrh half an ounce, water 8½ oz.

Glyco-Thymol brings relief to sore throats.

GARLIC. Plant out the cloves of the root in February, about 9 inches apart, in rich soil. Take up and store in July.

GARNISHES, suitable for various dishes.

BEEF, ROAST.—Horse-radish.

BEEF, BOILED.—Sliced carrot, or beetroot.

CALF'S HEAD.—Sliced lemon.

LAMB, ROAST.—Mint.

MUTTON, ROAST.—Red currant jelly.

VEAL, ROAST.—Sliced lemon.

COLD MEAT OF ANY KIND.—Parsley.

GAME.—Barberries.

WILD DUCK, Etc.—Sliced lemon, or sliced Seville orange.

TURKEY, FOWL OR CAPON.—Fried sausages or forcemeat balls.

FRIED FISH.—Sliced lemon.

TURBOT.—Fried smelts.

SALMON AND MACKEREL.—Fennel.

BOILED FISH.—Parsley.

GOOSE OR TURKEY.—Chestnuts.

MINCED MEAT.—Croûtons of bread.

GAS, a table for converting cubic feet into therms:

Cubic Feet	Therms
100	.5
200	1.0
300	1.5
400	2.0

and so on.

GAS LEAKAGE, precautions against. Gas has a strong smell and the smallest leak is quickly detected. If there is an escape of gas in the house the supply should be turned off at the meter immediately. The taps of all gas appliances should be turned off and the windows opened wide to clear the gas from the room. The Gas Company should be notified at once of an escape. Never bring a naked light of any kind into a room in which an escape of gas is suspected. If any person has inhaled enough gas to become unconscious, or nearly so, loosen the patient's collar and dress, and send for a doctor. Until his arrival try artificial respiration.

GAS MANTLE, to strengthen. Run a thread through the loop at the top, then dip the mantle in a tumblerful of vinegar. When it has been thoroughly soaked hang it up to dry in a safe place. After it has been placed on the burner light the gas before putting on the globe. This will improve the light and make the mantle last much longer.

GAS METER, to read. The gas meter has an index with three or four dials in a row and one small dial above. In reading the meter pay no attention to the top dial. Taking the lower dials in their order from left to right, write down the figures shown by the hands. If the hand is between two figures, always write down the lower; but if the hand is between 9 and 0 always write down 9. Add 00 to the end and you will have the correct reading of the meter. If the previous reading of the meter is subtracted from the present reading the result will give the amount of gas consumed in the period between the readings.

GAS PIPES, LEAKAGE. To stop a leak in a gas pipe moisten some common soap and press tightly over the leak; or you can use a paste of yellow soap and whiting mixed with water.

GAS RING, for roasting. Roast meat or chicken can be as well done in a roasting-tin, with a cover, over a gas ring as in an oven. After a quarter of an hour turn the gas low and allow a quarter of an hour extra time for cooking.

GEESE, STUFFING FOR.

1 qt. stale bread-crumbs
1 tablespoonful minced onion
¼ cupful minced celeriac
pepper and ground ginger
gizzard heart and liver
½ cupful strained stewed tomatoes
2 tablespoonfuls fat
grated nutmeg
salt
1 egg

Soak bread in cold water. Squeeze dry. Heat fat in frying-pan, add crumbs, fry a little, stir in minced giblets, onion, celeriac, tomatoes, teaspoonful of salt, pepper, ginger and nutmeg. Add 1 dessertspoonful of minced parsley. Mix well, stir in a beaten egg and use as stuffing.

GEMINI (THE TWINS). Third sign of the Zodiac, influencing persons born between 22nd May and 21st June. Such have similar dispositions as those born under the sign Pisces (Feb.-Mar.) being discerning, somewhat psychic and adaptable. In addition, Gemini folk are strong mentally, and able to remember in detail, though restless and changeable.

GENTIAN. For the Alpine and rock garden the beautiful little gentians seem almost indispensable, and though the dwarf kinds which are those most suitable for the rock garden and edging are less easily grown than the larger sort, they need but a little care to establish them in healthy tufts. They must not be overshadowed by taller plants; fresh air and sunlight are essential to their welfare. The Vernal Gentian likes a soil of sandy loam but cannot endure much drought, and will benefit, therefore, by a few pieces of broken limestone being so placed as to retard evaporation. The Bavarian Gentian, with its flowers of iridescent blue, is another lovely example. It demands a moist, peaty soil—as bog-like as possible. Gentians may be raised from seed by sowing in pans in spring and planting out.

GERANIUM. This requires a sunny, open spot and ordinary garden soil that is well drained and light. Sow under glass in March or August, or in the open in April. Increase by division or cutting of matured side shoots may be struck in August in a frame. They seldom withstand frost. Water freely.

GERMAN MEASLES. *See* MEASLES, GERMAN.

GEUM. A perennial which produces richly-coloured scarlet or orange flowers, single and double, in summer on flowering spikes which rise to 12 or more inches, looking well in groups. Plant in good loam early spring. They increase yearly, but seed sown in summer will give flowering plants the following year. A good plant for cutting for the vase.

GEYSERS. The modern geyser is fitted with a device which makes it impossible to have an accident resulting in an explosion. The latest are made to fix on to the water supply in the kitchen, and give a full volume of hot water in a few moments.

GIBRALTAR PUDDING.

$\frac{1}{4}$ lb. dried figs	$\frac{1}{4}$ cupful stale bread-crumbs
$\frac{3}{4}$ teaspoonful salt	$\frac{1}{4}$ lb. stoned dates
$\frac{1}{2}$ lb. suet	2 eggs
$\frac{3}{4}$ cupful flour	$\frac{1}{2}$ cupful sugar
$\frac{1}{2}$ cupful milk	1 teaspoonful ground ginger
	1 teaspoonful ground cinnamon

Pass dates and figs through a mincer. Mix in suet, flour, crumbs, sugar, salt and spices; then stir in beaten eggs and milk and steam in a well-buttered mould 2 hours. Serve with white sauce flavoured with lemon juice.

GILT, to clean. Badly-discoloured brass or gilt ornaments may be made to look like new by mixing a piece of soft soap the size of an egg in a pint of hot water with a tablespoonful of ammonia. Carefully wash article in the mixture prepared, rinse well with cold water, and dry with a soft cloth.

Another way to clean gilt is to rub it gently with a sponge dipped in oil of turpentine. Let the oil dry on the gilt and afterwards rub with a clean duster.

GINGER BEER. Boil together for 1 hour, 1 gallon water, 1 oz. bruised ginger and 1 lb. sugar. Skim the liquor and pour into a jug containing $\frac{1}{2}$ sliced lemon and $\frac{1}{4}$ oz. cream of tartar. Allow to cool and then add $\frac{1}{2}$ teacupful yeast and let it work for 2 days. Strain and bottle, tying the corks firmly down. It will be ready for use in a few days.

GINGER BEER POWDER.

30 grains carbonate of soda	1 dram refined sugar
5 grains powdered ginger	2 drops essence of lemon

Dissolve in half a tumbler of cold water and add 30 grains tartaric acid.

GINGERBREAD.

2 breakfastcupfuls flour	2 teaspoonfuls ground ginger
1 oz. sugar	1 oz. carbonate of soda dissolved
1 tablespoonful treacle	in a little hot milk
1 oz. lard	1 cupful milk
	1 egg

Follow generally as for American gingerbread. Bake 1 hour.

GINGERBREAD. Use cold coffee instead of milk when mixing gingerbread, spiced fruit-cakes or steamed ginger pudding. It makes the colour richer and gives a most delicious flavour.

GINGERBREAD, AMERICAN.

½ lb. flour
4 oz. butter
¼ pint golden syrup
2 oz. castor sugar
1 tablespoonful ground ginger
1 tablespoonful mixed spice
1 teaspoonful carbonate of soda
¼ gill milk
3 eggs
4 oz. almonds
pinch of salt

Rub the butter into the flour, and mix in all the dry ingredients except the soda, which must be dissolved in the milk. Beat the eggs, add to the syrup, and mix into the other ingredients, and lastly the dissolved soda. Pour the mixture into a Yorkshire-pudding tin lined with buttered paper, and bake in a moderate oven. Glaze with a little syrup and warm water.

GINGER CREAMS.

4 oz. preserved ginger
1½ gills cream
2 eggs
¾ pint milk
½ gill ginger syrup
3 oz. castor sugar
½ oz. gelatine
½-pint packet lemon jelly

Dissolve jelly in hot water, making it barely half a pint. Leave it to set. Whisk eggs, heat milk. When just off the boil, add milk to eggs and turn them into a jug, standing in pan of hot water.

Cook custard till it thickens, keeping it well stirred; turn it into a basin and let it cool; when cold add ginger cut in small pieces. Soak gelatine in ½ gill of water, add ginger syrup and dissolve them over a low burner. Whisk the cream till thick and add sugar. Stir in the custard mixture gradually and then strain in the gelatine. When the mixture begins to thicken turn into wet moulds. After they are set arrange the moulds on a dish with the jelly roughly chopped round them.

GINGER TEA. Pour ½ a pint of boiling water on to 1 teaspoonful of ginger; add sugar and milk to taste.

GLADIOLUS. A light, friable loam, enriched with well-rotted manure, is best, and the situation should be fully open to the sun but sheltered from wind. Plant in March and April, as the bulbs then planted produce flowers in August and September. Stake well. But if early flowering kinds are desired the bulbs should be set in November, and protected from frost by a suitable litter. Take up bulbs in October or November and store.

GLANDS, ENLARGED. Paint the swelling with a tincture of iodine to lessen it and give cod-liver oil to nourish. If the parts become red, painful, or inflamed, medical advice is necessary.

GLASS, to cut or break. File a notch on the edge of the glass at the place it is desired to start the break. Then to the notch apply a red-hot iron and slowly draw it in the required direction. A crack will follow the iron.

GLASS, to cut. Put the glass in water and cut it with a pair of scissors while it is underneath the water. It can then be cut with ease.

GLASS, to powder. Heat glass until it is red hot and throw it in cold water. It will at once go into powder. Then sift and dry.

GLASS, to wash. It is best either to wash glass in cold water or to wash it first in warm water and then rinse in cold. This gives a brighter and clear appearance than when it is washed with warm water. If washing glass in a bath, place a towel beneath it, to avoid risk of breakage.

GLASS BOTTLES, to clean. Break egg-shells into small pieces and put a small quantity into a bottle or decanter that is discoloured. Add a little water and shake well and the marks will disappear.

GLASS STOPPER, to loosen. Rub a little oil round the stopper and place bottle near a fire. Tap stopper lightly and it may easily be removed.

GLASSES, to avoid cracking. *See* CRACKED GLASSES.

GLAUCIUM (HORNED POPPY). Will flourish in a poor soil. It is of the poppy family, a biennial, sown about May to provide vigorous plants for the following year. Handsome foliage of silvery white. *G. luteum* has large orange-red flowers, while another variety *Asia Minor* bears flowers of bright scarlet.

GLAZING FOR HAMS. Boil a knuckle of veal with salt, pepper and a few cloves for 12 hours in 2 gallons of water. Boil also a shin of beef for the same time and in the same quantity of water. Add the gravy from the veal to the shin of beef and boil down to 1 quart. Heat a quantity as required and spread over the ham with a feather.

GLOBE THISTLE. *See* ECHINOPS.

GLOVES. To make these last longer place a small piece of cotton-wool in the tips of the fingers and thumbs. This will prevent the nails rubbing them into holes so soon.

GLOVES, to clean. Fuller's earth is excellent for cleaning suède or doeskin gloves. Put the gloves on the hands and rub the earth in well with a small soft brush. An old nail or tooth brush will do. Bread-crumbs can also be used or a mixture of Fuller's earth and powdered alum.

GLOVES, HOGSKIN, to clean. Wash on the hands, using a good glove soap and dry on glove stretchers. When quite dry apply some white furniture cream and polish with a soft clean duster. The gloves will come up like new and last clean a long time.

GLOVES, LIGHT KID, to wash. Lay the gloves on a clean folded cloth. Dip a piece of flannel in some skimmed milk, rub on a little yellow soap, then rub the gloves, working downwards from the wrist. When dry lay on a clean towel pulling them to shape.

GLOVES, WASH-LEATHER, to wash. To remove dirt quickly add a few drops of salad oil to the soapy water. Rinse in another lather, squeeze in a towel, and hang in the air. This will prevent the gloves from becoming hard.

GLOXINIA. These lovely plants are perennials and though chiefly greenhouse plants may be used in bedding for summer and autumn flowering, but only in a warm situation. They can be brought into bloom at practically any season in heat. Give a rich fibrous loam, peat, and silver sand compost, and be most careful to leave the root ball undisturbed. Once the plants are in flower do not give liquid manure but in the early budding state it is helpful. Gloxinias are about a foot high, of compact growth, the handsome, large flowers, of many brilliant colours, growing singly on thin stems.

GLUE. After opening a bottle of glue or cement rub mutton fat on a sound cork before inserting it in the bottle. This will prevent the cork from sticking fast to the neck of the bottle when an attempt is made to open it again.

GNAT BITES. *See* BITES.

GODETIA. Showy hardy annuals in two distinctive types, the bushy, and the tall, both of which flower freely throughout the summer. Sown mid-March. The bushy types are about 1 foot high, the tall from 18 inches to 2 feet. The latter should be staked. May be sown where they are to bloom, or transplanted, with 6 to 8 inches each way. The cone-shaped flowers have generally dark blotches of colour at the hearts, and are some shade of pink, red, mauve or lavender. They do not thrive in the shade, but otherwise have no preferences of position or soil.

GOITRE. *See* DERBYSHIRE NECK.

GOLDEN ROD (SOLIDAGO VIRGAUREA). A useful plant for hiding sheds, being about 5 feet high and having profuse feathery yellow blossom, etc. It is propagated by root division; it flowers in the autumn and will grow in any kind of soil.

GOLDEN WEDDINGS. A golden wedding, marking fifty years of married life, is naturally less frequently encountered than a silver wedding. It may be quite a gay and brilliant affair or just a quiet family reunion, this depending entirely upon the wish of those most closely concerned.

A dinner may be given, but there is really no definite form or ceremonial prescribed and, especially in the case of an aged couple, conventional usages would be set aside in favour of consideration for the comfort and wishes of the two who have weathered the storms of life through so many years.

GOOSE. A goose for roasting should be young, when the bill and feet will be yellow and, if freshly killed, the feet will be pliable. The bill and feet become red when the goose gets older. Never buy a goose which is over twelve months old as it is not then fit for eating.

GOOSE, ROAST.

1 goose (drawn and trussed)	dripping for basting
sage and onion stuffing	waterscress or chestnuts

Stuff the goose and fasten up securely at both ends. Place in hot oven and cook quickly for about 20 minutes. Then lessen the heat and continue cooking, basting often with the dripping. About a quarter of an hour before the bird is cooked dredge the breast with a little flour and baste again. When cooked, after removing all strings and skewers, place goose on hot dish and garnish with either watercress or chestnuts. Apple sauce also makes a good accompaniment. Serve a good thick gravy separately in a tureen. If liked, gooseberry sauce may be served in place of apple sauce.

GOOSEBERRIES, to bottle. Wipe the fruit and put it into bottles which must be clean and dry. Add 1 oz. sugar to each pint bottle. Fill a large saucepan with cold water, tie a little straw or hay round each bottle and then put them in the boiler. Put the saucepan on the fire and as the water gets hot the juice will come out and cover the fruit. In about 20 minutes remove the bottles, seal corks and keep in cool, dry place.

GOOSEBERRIES, to preserve. *See as* STRAWBERRIES.

GOOSEBERRY BUSHES. The best plan to adopt pruning the gooseberry bush is to leave last season's growth at full length, though it may be shortened if it extends beyond the space at command. A thinning should be made annually by cutting out old limbs which have any sign of decay and by removing any young wood which may obstruct admission of light and air, cutting back this young wood to within a few buds from the stem. Any suckers which may appear should be carefully eradicated from the very base and not merely cut back to the surface of the ground. The digging of the ground between gooseberry bushes should never be done with the spade, a gentle loosening of the earth with a fork, to the depth of 6 or 8 inches, and an occasional use of the dutch hoe to keep down the weeds, is quite sufficient.

GOOSEBERRY FOOL (for 6 or 7 people).

2 lb. gooseberries	1 gill water
½ lb. sugar	½ pint custard or cream

Make a syrup by boiling water and sugar together, put in the gooseberries and cook till tender. Rub through a sieve, mix with the cream or custard, pour into a glass dish and serve cold.

GOUT, to relieve pain. Citrate of lithium in 5 to 10 grain doses in a tumbler of water before breakfast will prevent the accumulation of the poison of gout. Hot fomentations will bring relief. During an acute attack the foot should rest on a stool, painted with glycerine and belladonna, and wrapped in thick cotton-wool. An aperient pill at night, followed by a seidlitz powder the following morning, should be given. Ten drops of tincture of colchicum every four hours will relieve the pain.

GRAFTING WAX, COBBETT'S. Take 4 parts of pitch and resin, 1 part beeswax and 1 part tallow; melt and mix the ingredients together and use when just warm.

GRAFTING WAX (as given by C. H. Middleton). For covering the cuts after grafting, or to stop bleeding in heavy pruning, a mixture can be made of 1 lb. resin, 3 oz. beef fat, heated together till dissolved, and when cool added to 1 pint of methylated spirit. Apply as soon as possible after cutting.

GRAMOPHONE RECORDS, to clean. Wipe with a soft rag moistened with a very little paraffin. Allow records to dry before putting them away.

GRAPE FRUIT, to prepare and serve. Cut fruit in halves across (not from top to bottom). Cut round core and remove, taking care not to cut through the skin at the bottom of each half. Loosen the fruit from the rind but allow to remain in. Cut fruit from centre to inside of skin into fairly small sections to render it easier of manipulation when being eaten. If liked, fill the hole in the centre (from which the core has been removed) with a tablespoonful of fine sugar, placing on the top a maraschino cherry. Pour over a little port wine, or maraschino. Serve either on separate plates or in glass grape-fruit holders.

GRAPE PUNCH. This very agreeable beverage is made by mixing three parts of ginger ale with one of grape juice.

GRASS, to keep green. A little nitrate of soda dissolved in water and sprinkled over the surface occasionally will be found of great assistance in keeping grass green. *See also* LAWNS.

GRAVEL. Small, sand-like concretions in the kidneys or bladder. Generally caused by a tendency to gout or to a sluggish liver, or an over-indulgence in rich food or drink.

Avoid sweets, creams, wine, malt liquors and red meat. The diet should consist of white fish, mutton, chicken, green vegetables and onions. As much barley water as possible should be drunk. Soda and milk may be taken for a change, but barley water is of special value.

GRAVY, FOR ROAST JOINT. When the joint is roasted place it on a hot dish in the oven; pour off all the fat, leaving the sediment which is the gravy from the meat. Sprinkle a little salt in the pan, add some water or if preferred well-flavoured stock, a little bovril or colouring if necessary; boil up stirring well all round the pan, dissolving all the brown particles, and strain round the meat.

GRAVY, FOR ROAST VEAL. Pour off the fat, leaving the gravy; pour into the dripping-pan a pint of white sauce with the gravy; boil up and pour over the joint.

GREASE SPOTS, to remove from fabrics. Eucalyptus oil will remove grease or oil from any fabric, however delicate, without the slightest injury to the material.

Grease spots can be removed by sprinkling the spot with talcum powder, placing a clean dry cloth over it and pressing it with an iron. Let the iron rest on it for a few minutes and the spot will vanish.

To remove these from clothing heat a poker till it is red hot then hold above the grease spot (taking care not to hold it near enough to singe the cloth).

When the spot has melted, rub it with another part of the garment and it will disappear permanently.

GREASY PANS. When cleaning very greasy pans and dishes wipe them round first with newspaper which can afterwards be thrown away. This is very much cleaner than putting everything into the washing-up water.

GREASY SOUP. To remove grease from soup, dip in small pieces of clean tissue paper. This will remove all fat.

GREEN FLY. *See* APHIS.

GREENGAGES. These are cooked, bottled, preserved, made into tarts and jams in accordance with the recipes given for plums.

GREENS, to boil. Remember that greenstuff, particularly spinach, shrinks in the most extraordinary way. You need a lot to make a little.

When boiling greens throw in a few bits of bacon rind and remove before serving. It adds a very nice flavour to the greens.

When boiling cauliflowers or Brussels sprouts tie them in clean pieces of old lace or muslin curtains; when cooked they can easily be lifted out with a fork and placed in a colander. The cauliflowers keep whole and the sprouts soon drain dry.

GRIPES. *See* COLIC.

GROUSE, ROAST.

grouse	pepper
butter	gravy
fat bacon	bread sauce
lemon juice	browned bread-crumbs

Pluck, singe and draw the grouse, wiping thoroughly with a damp cloth (game should never be washed); put a small piece of butter with a little pepper and lemon juice inside the birds; truss for roasting. A slice of fat bacon and a vine leaf or two should be wrapped over the breast of each bird. Roast in the oven or before the fire, baste frequently, and remove the bacon and froth just before dishing. Place on a hot dish on a croûton of toast, which should be made and put under the grouse in the dripping-pan; garnish with watercress and serve with bread sauce and browned bread-crumbs.

GRUEL.

1 heaped dessertspoonful fine oatmeal	pinch of salt sugar as liked
½ pint water or water and milk together	

Mix the oatmeal into a smooth paste with a little of the water. Bring the rest of the water to the boil and pour on to the oatmeal. Return all to the saucepan and again bring to the boil, stirring all the time to prevent burning, or sticking to the bottom of the saucepan. Simmer for about 30 minutes, during which time the gruel should be stirred frequently. Then strain, add the salt and sugar and, if liked, a little lemon to flavour.

GUESTS, etiquette towards hostess. *See* HOSTESS AND GUESTS.

GUESTS, UNINVITED. *See* UNINVITED GUESTS.

GUMBOILS. The offending tooth should be extracted as quickly as possible, and the mouth washed out repeatedly with warm Condy's fluid and water. Hot bottles to the side of the face afford relief to the pain. If the abscess is pointing at the side of the gum, a sterilized darning needle may be used to open the abscess when a "head" is formed. Take care not to swallow any of the discharge.

GUMS. To harden gums that have receded, and teeth loosened in consequence, mix a good teaspoonful of bicarbonate of soda and a pinch of alum in a quarter glass of lukewarm water. Wash teeth by holding the fluid as long as possible in the mouth. Use three times a day, weakening the solution according to the condition of the gums.

GYPSOPHILA. The annual types bearing numerous tiny white, pink or rosy flowers, single or double. The delicate foliage of this hardy annual runs to 2 feet in height. It is a general favourite for use in table decorations, or as foliage to mix with other cut flowers.

HADDOCK À LA ST. CLAIR (for 4 or 5 people).

1 smoked haddock	1 gill milk
1 or 2 tomatoes	2 tablespoonfuls cream
1 oz. butter	1 yolk of egg (hard boiled)
1 oz. flour	seasoning

Cook the tomato in slices and arrange round a dish, make a sauce with the flour, butter, milk and cream, cook the haddock and flake it, removing skin and bones; add it to the sauce, put it in the centre of the tomato and garnish with yolk of egg rubbed through a sieve.

HADDOCK, BAKED (for 3 or 4 people).

1 fresh haddock	brown crumbs
veal stuffing	dripping or butter
1 egg or little milk	

Thoroughly cleanse the fish, and fill the inside with veal stuffing. Sew up the opening and truss the fish in the shape of the letter S, place it in a baking-tin, brush it with beaten egg and a little milk, sprinkle with brown crumbs and bake it slowly, basting it frequently with dripping or butter. Serve it on a hot dish; garnish with parsley and cut lemon and anchovy or any other suitable sauce poured round.

HADDOCK CHÂTEAU LAURIER.

large fresh haddock	chopped parsley
sliced onions	butter
vinegar	salt

Bone the haddock and cut into fillets. Boil gently in water with a little vinegar and salt. Serve with sliced onions, fried in hot fat. Shake vinegar over the fish and onions, and pour over some melted browned butter with the parsley added.

HADDOCK, FINNAN. Scald the fish in a dish of hot water. Allow to stand for a few minutes, then drain off water. Sprinkle with pepper and a few pieces of butter; pour over 1 gill milk; cover with a flat dish, and bake from 15 to 20 minutes.

HAIR, to remove grease. Wash well with a good carbolic or coal-tar soap, rinse well in cold, soft water and then rinse in water containing a small handful of borax. Rub the scalp with a flannel soaked in a solution of borax once or twice every week, and dry with a clean towel.

HAIR LOTION. Mix 1 oz. eau-de-Cologne with 8 oz. alcohol. Beat to a froth the white of an egg and shake together with 9 oz. water and 4 oz. ammonia. Finally shake up the whole into a lotion.

HAIR TONIC. This recipe by a famous specialist can be made up by any chemist: 2 oz. eau-de-Cologne, 2 oz. glycerine, 2 oz. rose water, 2 drams tincture of cantharides, 10 drops of oil of rosemary.

A simpler method is by regularly rubbing in a small quantity of vaseline.

HALIBUT. Should be put into cold water and boiled as slowly as possible. Drain, garnish with lemon and serve hot with sauce. Salmon must be put into hot water and boiled.

HAM, to carve. Begin a little distance from the knuckle, and proceed towards the thick end, or blade. A baked ham may be cut much thinner than a boiled one.

HAM AND BACON. The fat of ham and bacon should have a clear pinky appearance; the lean firm; the rind, like the skin of good pork, should be thin. If it looks yellow and the salt is crusted on it, it should be rejected, as it will be rancid and unpalatable.

To test a ham insert a bright steel skewer near the bone. If it comes out clean and free from any unpleasant smell it proves the ham is in good condition. On the other hand if the skewer is not clean and smells unpleasant, the ham should be rejected.

HAM AND BACON, to boil. Soak a ham for several hours, if dry, all night; if bacon is very salt soak for 2 hours before cooking. Place in a saucepan with plenty of tepid water, let it come slowly to the boil, remove the scum and simmer gently till cooked, time allowed according to size—20 minutes to the pound and 20 minutes over. Take it out, remove the skin and sprinkle over freshly-made raspings. When cold lift on to a clean dish.

HAM AND POTATO SCALLOP.

> large slice raw ham
> 2 cupfuls raw sliced potatoes
> 1½ cupfuls milk

Ham should be cut about half an inch thick. If salt, soak in warm water half an hour, then drain, brown on both sides in a frying-pan, then place in baking-dish, add potatoes and pour milk over. Cover and bake 1 hour in a slow oven. Then uncover and bake another half-hour before serving.

HAM, BAKED.

> 1 short lean ham
> egg yolk beaten

bread-crumbs
hot cider
flour and water

Scrub ham with flour and water and soak overnight in clean water. Make a thick paste of flour and water and spread over ham, covering completely. Place on rack in baking-tin and cook in hot oven enough to cook paste. Then lower temperature and cook slowly 5 hours. One hour before it is done make a hole in the paste and pour in a cupful of hot cider; repeat twice during the hour. When ham is done remove crust, brush with beaten yolk, sprinkle with bread-crumbs and return to oven to brown.

HAM OMELETTE.

3 eggs	1 oz. butter
1½ oz. cooked ham	salt and pepper

Beat the eggs well, add the finely-chopped ham and the seasoning, melt the butter in an omelette pan. When hot pour in the eggs, stir till the mixture begins to set, fold over and serve on a hot dish immediately.

HAM SCRAMBLE.

6 eggs	3 tablespoonfuls minced
¼ cupful milk	cooked ham
pepper, salt	3 tablespoonfuls butter

Beat eggs, stir in pepper, salt and ham. Put milk and butter in saucepan, heat, stir in egg mixture, cook until set. Serve on buttered toast.

HAM TOAST.

2 cupfuls ham	1 cupful quartered cooked
1 pimento	mushrooms
1 green pepper	2 hard-boiled eggs
2 cupfuls white sauce	buttered toast

Cook and dice ham; slice eggs, cut pimento in narrow strips. Chop green pepper. Heat white sauce; add green pepper, pimento, mushrooms, ham and eggs. Serve on toast.

HAM TOAST, DEVILLED. *See* DEVILLED.

HAMS, GLAZING FOR. *See* GLAZING.

HAMMER TOE.

Causes.—Wearing short, pointed, high-heeled boots or shoes; paralysis of the muscles of the toes.

Treatment.—Properly fitting boots should be worn, with broad flat heels. If this does not correct the deformity, an operation will straighten the toe, or toes.

HAMMOCK FOR BABY. Get half a corn sack and 2 balls of string. Hem the sack at each end and cut each ball of string into 8 equal parts. Take 8 pieces, double them, tie and bind the centre into a loop; then thread the 16 ends into 1 end of the sack and tie firmly. Do the other end the same way. This makes a hammock which can be hung anywhere on 2 hooks and is much warmer and more comfortable than a cradle.

HANDS, to remove stains. For stains of vegetables, dyes, ink stains, etc., use cold water and a little wood ash. For paint and such stains rub with turpentine and wash with carbolic soap in very hot water. Lemon juice is often effective where other means fail.

HANDS, CHARACTER IN. Observant persons can sum up character at sight by glancing at the hands. There are four distinctive classifications, which, with their indications, are:

The Square Hand.—In this hand the palm itself is square as well as the finger-tips. The person to whom such a hand belongs will be conventional and methodical, set great store on appearances, is law-abiding, persevering, intensely sincere, but apt to be hard in judgments.

The Spatulate Hand is wide at the wrist but tapering upwards so that the palm is comparatively narrow at the base of the fingers. Such a hand is a sign of an intensely practical nature. In some cases the shape is reversed, the hand being wide at the base of the fingers but narrow at the wrist, proof that the person has a dash of adventure mingled with a practical nature.

Always the fingers of a spatulate hand are wider at the tips than at the first joint.

The chief characteristic of people with these hands is tremendous energy and inventiveness. When the hand is hard and firm, it gives a handshake that inspires confidence and denotes the hand of a leader. When the hand is soft it shows irritability, dissatisfaction and lack of concentration.

Frequently a square palm will be accompanied by spatulate fingers, which is an excellent combination: energy and enthusiasm, perseverance and sound common sense.

The Conic Hand.—This hand has a medium-sized palm which narrows slightly toward the fingers. The finger-tips are rounded, but the fingers taper very slightly. Quite often they are almost the same size throughout.

This is the hand of the dreamer. Such will be brilliant in conversation, grasping any subject quickly. They have vivid imaginations and a deep sympathy which is a very lovable trait.

They are intensely responsive to music or poetry, colour; are sympathetic and charitable.

The Psychic Hand is long and narrow, with slender fingers that taper almost to a point. Energy and physical strength are lacking, subject to melancholy, no self-confidence yet very sympathetic toward others. Where the psychic hand has some squareness in its contour it gives strength and practicality to an otherwise dreamy nature.

Variations.—Beyond the four types there is the hand that is of mixed conformation, which will partake in milder degree of the characteristics of what types are observed.

When the palm belongs plainly to one type, especially if to the Square or Spatulate, and only the fingers vary, it is a sign of versatility in many ways, but not of the lack of perseverance. In this case the owner of the hand may win great distinction in one or even in two directions and more than ordinary ability will be shown.

HARD-BOILED EGGS. A very quick way of shelling these is to take them from the boiling water and plunge them straight into cold water. Tap the eggs all over and the shells will come off very easily.

HARE, JUGGED (for 9 or 10 people).

1 hare	3 oz. butter
1½ lb. beefsteak	3 oz. flour
2 onions	2 glasses port wine
2 or 3 cloves	red-currant jelly
bunch of herbs	salt and pepper
strip of lemon rind	forcemeat balls (which see)
stock or water	

Skin the hare, do not wash it; let the blood from the upper part of the body run into a basin and put it aside, then wipe the hare care-

134

fully. Cut into neat joints, dip them in well-seasoned flour and fry a nice brown in butter; put the joints into a large stewing jar with the steak cut in pieces, herbs, onions, cloves, lemon rind. Cover with stock or water, cover the jar closely, and cook gently in the oven for 3 or 4 hours. When ready to serve take out the joints, onion and herbs, mix the flour with some water. Add it to the gravy and boil, then add the wine and the forcemeat balls, lastly the seasoning and blood. Do not boil after the blood is added. Put back the joints to reheat. Dish with joints piled in centre, gravy poured round, garnish with forcemeat balls and serve with red-currant jelly.

HARE, ROAST (for 8 or 9 people).

1 hare	flour
veal forcemeat	½ pint brown sauce
butter	red-currant jelly
½ pint milk	glass of port wine

Choose a young hare for roasting and hang it for a few days without paunching it. When required skin it, leaving on the ears. Wipe it well inside and out if necessary, soak it to remove the blood; make a veal stuffing, add the parboiled and chopped liver, put it in the hare, sew it up and truss. Place it in a meat tin with a little milk, roast in the oven, basting constantly. Flour the hare well and baste with butter to froth the outside. The time allowed will depend on the size of the hare. Place on a hot dish, remove the string, pour the fat off from the tin, sprinkle in a little flour and brown it over the fire; pour in the brown sauce, add the wine, boil for a few minutes and strain it. Garnish the hare with some little balls of forcemeat fried, and serve with red-currant jelly and the gravy in a tureen.

HAREBELL. See CAMPANULA.

HARE-LIP AND CLEFT-PALATE. The two halves of the lip and palate should join together before the child is born, but for some reason they have not united and a space is left between them.

Treatment.—Operation is the only possible treatment, when the child is from six weeks to three months old.

HARICOT MUTTON. See MUTTON, HARICOT.

HARVEST BUGS, to treat bites. The parts should be bathed in warm water, to which a pinch of bicarbonate of soda has been added, and sulphur ointment applied.

HASH (for 6 or 7 people).

1½ lb. cold meat	1½ pints stock
2 oz. butter or dripping	1 dessertspoonful ketchup
2 oz. flour	salt and pepper
1 onion	toast and parsley

Remove all the fat and gristle from the meat and cut it into neat pieces; make the fat hot and fry the onion a nice brown; remove it and fry the flour, brown it well, being careful not to burn it. Add the stock gradually, stir till it boils, return the meat and onion, add the ketchup and seasoning, thoroughly reheat it, but do not allow it to boil. Serve with snippets of toast or fried bread dipped in chopped parsley.

HAT, use for old. *See* SLIPPERS.

HATS, BOWLER, to clean brims of. First rub well with a little fresh butter and clean it off with a solution of 2 oz. rock ammonia dissolved in ½ pint hot water. Then hold the hat under running water for a minute or two; wipe with a soft, clean cloth, brush well *with* the nap, and hang out to dry.

HATS, FELT AND VELOUR, to restore. Thoroughly beat and brush the hat to remove all dust and to raise the surface; hold it over boiling water and steam thoroughly from the inside. Turn the hat slowly so that it shall be steamed all over. Shake well. Give a good final brushing when the hat is dry.

HAY FEVER. A teaspoonful of Friar's balsam to 1 pint of boiling water, and the vapour inhaled affords relief. If the symptoms are chiefly asthmatical, the inhalation of burning nitre paper or the smoking of stramonium cigarettes may be tried.

Boil ½ pint of milk, add 1 glass of sherry. Strain through a piece of muslin and sweeten the whey with white sugar. Take the whey at bedtime.

HEADACHE (1). The patient should lie down in a darkened room with a cold bandage round his head. A few drops of sweet spirit of nitre may be used on a piece of rag and applied to the head. Cover with oiled silk to prevent evaporation and renew the application frequently. Antipyrin in from 5 to 15 grain doses, or 10 grains of phenacetin, may be given. Some cases are benefited by taking a cup of strong tea or coffee.

HEADACHE (2). When you have a bad headache and must go out, lie down beforehand with a hot bottle to your feet and a cold, wet compress on your head. Take an aspirin and when you really must get up drink a cup of strong coffee. Probably you will be cured.

HEADACHE, SICK. A little soda water will relieve a headache due to indigestion, or if it is obstinate take 3 soda-mints half-way between each meal for a day.

HEART, PALPITATION OF THE. Indigestion and flatulence is usually the cause of the trouble. Half a teaspoonful of bicarbonate of soda should be taken in a tumbler of hot water. Tea, coffee, alcohol and tobacco should not be taken. If the patient is anæmic a course of Blaud's pills should benefit. All worry, excitement and over-exertion should be avoided.

HEARTBURN. Half a teaspoonful of bicarbonate of soda in a little peppermint water should be taken, and afterwards a glass of hot water.

HEARTHRUG. A home-made hearthrug or mat made of cloth clippings will be found to wear much longer if it is brushed over with liquid glue on the wrong side after the clippings are put in, then lay the lining on and leave overnight. Next day stitch the lining round the edges, as the glue will have fastened it in the middle. This prevents the clippings working out, and makes the rug last much longer.

HEARTSEASE. *See* PANSY.

HEAD-STROKE. The patient should be treated as for shock, the clothes loosened and plenty of air allowed him, and stimulants administered. If the extremities become cold, hot bottles should be applied, and the patient well covered with blankets. Should no relief ensue, send for a doctor.

HEDGEHOGS. Keep in a cage during the day and release at night if it is desired to use them as beetle-catchers. Feed on bread and milk and an occasional earth-worm.

HELENIUM. Hybrid varieties of this perennial have added attraction and to length of flowering season, the supply of yellow, or yellow and brown flowers, borne on stems about 2 feet high, now being from July onwards, instead of during the autumn only. Heleniums prefer sunny positions but thrive in any good soil. The root clumps do not increase very rapidly, and should be planted by mid-March to bloom the same year.

HELIANTHUS (SUNFLOWER). The sunflower may be divided into two classes—the perennial (sometimes called *Harpalium*) and the annual, both quite hardy. The perennials are of such vigorous growth and increase so rapidly that they should not be introduced into a small garden without consideration, but in the wild garden and in shrubberies they are especially valuable because they flower in late autumn. *H. decapetalus*, a bushy plant some 4 or 5 feet high, with abundance of rich yellow flowers, *H. giganteus*, often attaining a height of 10 feet and bearing large flowers of deep yellow 2 or 3 inches in diameter, and *H. rigidus*, one of the best-known and flowering very freely, are all good examples. Of the annual sunflower there are many varieties, averaging height 4 feet and liking moist soil. Sow seed in open about Easter.

HELICHRYSUM. These everlastings grow to 18 inches and flower in a variety of colours, mainly doubles. Sow April in good light soil. They are annuals and give flowers in three months. For cutting treatment, to preserve, *see* IMMORTELLE.

HELIOTROPIUM (HELIOTROPE or CHERRY PIE). A half-hardy perennial, but more wisely treated as an annual, as by sowing in heat early in March the seedlings will be ready for planting out at the end of May. They need a good dry soil, and by their delightful fragrance and delicate tints of colour they are rightly highly esteemed. Many new varieties have been introduced from time to time, such as Roi des Noirs, a very dark shade; Anna Turrel, a beautiful light kind; and the White Lady, pure white; while the old-fashioned *peruvianum* still holds its own in the affections of most of us.

HELLEBORUS (CHRISTMAS AND LENTEN ROSES). A hardy perennial of much value in the garden, as it flowers in the open when little else is in bloom. *H. niger* is that which has for its bloom the well-known flower which bears the name of Christmas rose, beautiful in its waxy-white and delicate blush tint; but we now have other varieties with blossoms of dark purple and ruby red, such as *H. colchicus*

137

and *H. abchasicus*, and with foliage of marked beauty. All kinds are content with ordinary soil, but will do better in well-manured fibrous loam mixed with coarse sand, for stagnant moisture is not good for them. Propagation may be made by division, July being the best time, when the plants are in full vigour; and they may also be raised from seed sown under glass, the seedlings being pricked out into a shady border of rich soil as soon as they are large enough to bear moving. In the following year they may be transplanted to their permanent quarters, and by the third year they should bloom.

HEMSTITCH. Before drawing threads in linen for hemstitching make a dry lather and apply over the space with a shaving brush; when the linen is dry you will be able to draw out the thread more readily.

HERB BEER. *See* BEER.

HERBS, to dry. Herbs should be gathered on a dry day and just before they flower. Cut off the roots, and wash if necessary. Dry either in a slow oven or in the sun till crisp but not brown. Pick off the leaves and rub through a coarse sieve. Bottle for use.

HERBS. Taste is added to viands by herbs, and most of them have distinct health-promoting qualities. They vary in strength as also in flavour, the user soon learning which to use with a sparing hand. A little chopped mint adds relish to a salad, while a few leaves put into the pot when boiling green peas or into green pea soup as it is put into the tureen imparts an acceptable tastiness to either. Chopped mint is also used in rural districts in apple tart; some, indeed, put a sprinkling into cakes. Basil, chervil, tarragon, thyme, marjoram and sage are each recognized as having a distinctive flavour of their own. The last-named must be used with discretion as it has a very strong flavour, and a couple of leaves is generally quite enough, as any who use it in forcemeat will know. Giblet soup, stewed rabbit, Irish stew, shepherd's pie and rice dishes all have greater relish if herbs are introduced.

HERBS, CULINARY. There is a good variety in the herb family to provide seasoning to suit all tastes. The following are the principal sorts, and a corner in the garden should be reserved for their culture. All can be treated as perennials, and a root to start with, planted in April, will soon give good clumps from which to draw supplies. Sweet marjoram, chervil, parsley and fennel are best treated as annuals and grown from seed. Tansy, rue, sage and rosemary do best from slips; thyme, balm and basil by root division. Sow basil, fennel and dill in May; other herbs in March. The leaved herbs can have their leaves picked and dried and stored for winter use and, of course, can always be used freshly plucked from spring till late autumn. The list includes: mint, basil, chervil, parsley, thyme, fennel, marjoram, sage, chives, rosemary, rue, savory, tarragon, horse-radish, sorrel, balm.

HERBS, MEDICINAL. Unlike our grandparents, we tend to ignore the medicinal value of the many wild herbs of the countryside, as too of numerous familiar cultivated herbs. The list is extensive, but some of them, with their uses, may be given. A little observation and inquiry of countryfolk will soon familiarize with these healing herbs of the woods and hedgerows, sufficient to gather them with intelligent recognition. In the main the leaves, flowers and roots are dried in the sun after thorough cleansing, and powdered or ground for use. The usual way to prepare is by simmering, a handful to a quart of cold water for about 1 hour and taking the resulting liquid. Coltsfoot (l. for colds), dandelion (r. l. for blood conditions and liver and kidneys), gentian (r. general tonic), marigold (f. induces perspiration), burdock (r. skin troubles and kidney complaints), bryony (r. coughs and colds), blackberry (l. diarrhœa), catmint (l. induces perspiration), marshmallow (r. coughs), camomile (f. neuralgia), watercress (l. blood purifier), raspberry (l. tonic and ease for dysentery), celery (seed, rheumatics), plantain (rub leaves on stings), thyme (l. flatulence), yarrow (l. reduces temperature), elder (f. sore throat and inflammation), and many more. The letters in brackets indicate whether root, leaves or flowers are the effective parts.

HERNIA. *See* RUPTURE.

HERRING ROES ON TOAST.

6 herring roes (soft)	½ lemon
1 heaped dessertspoonful flour	1 egg
	salt and pepper
few bread-crumbs	1 oz. dripping
fingers of toast	1 teaspoonful chopped parsley

Mix the flour, pepper and salt on one plate, the parsley and bread-crumbs on another. Wipe the roes with a damp cloth, dip each into the flour mixture, then brush over with the egg, previously well beaten, roll in the bread-crumbs and parsley and then cook in the dripping until a pale brown on each side. Place each roe on a finger of hot buttered toast and serve on a hot dish, garnished with slices of lemon and springs of parsley.

HERRINGS, BOILED. Scrape and wash the fish. Place in a pan with sufficient cold water to cover, adding a dessertspoonful vinegar and some salt; boil for 10 or 15 minutes. Serve with parsley sauce.

HERRINGS, GRILLED (for 6 people).

6 herrings	salad oil

For Sauce:

1 oz. butter	1 teaspoonful made mustard
1 oz. flour	seasoning
½ pint milk	

Remove the heads, wash and clean thoroughly without breaking, score the fish with a knife and brush with salad oil; put on the grill before a clear fire and cook on both sides. Put on a hot dish with a small piece of butter on each and serve with mustard sauce.

HERRING SAUTÉ (for 2 people).

2 herrings	salt and pepper
1½ oz. butter	toast

Skin the herrings and cut in half, remove the bone. Melt the butter in a stew pan, lay in the fish. Cook very gently for 10 minutes. Lay on pieces of toast. Season and serve very hot.

HERRINGS, SOUSED.

5 fresh herrings	1 dozen peppercorns
good pinch of salt	1 blade of mace
1 gill vinegar	½ gill water

Slit open the fish and take out the backbone. Then either lay them in a dish head and tail alternately, or tie each into a roll and place in dish. Add the peppercorns, salt and mace, and pour over the water and vinegar. Bake in a moderate oven half an hour. Allow to get quite cold before serving.

HERRINGS, STUFFED (for 3 people).

3 or 4 herrings	milk
veal stuffing	parsley
brown crumbs	cut lemon

Cut off the head and tail, wash well in salted water, make an incision down the back and carefully remove the backbone, lay some stuffing on the tail end and roll up, bake on a greased tin, brush over with milk and sprinkle with brown crumbs. Serve on a hot dish with fancy paper, garnish with parsley and cut lemon.

HERRINGS. When washing up after cooking herrings, add 1 teaspoonful of dry mustard to the water and the nasty smell which the fish leaves on your utensils will quickly disappear.

HESPERIS. *See* ROCKET.

HICCOUGH. The simplest remedies are holding the breath, drinking a glass of cold water, or pulling the tongue. Or put 3 drops oil of cinnamon on a piece of sugar, hold it in the mouth until it dissolves, then gently swallow it.

HOARSENESS, remedy for. Steaming the throat over hot water is useful, as is a gargle of 1 teaspoonful of salt in 1 teacupful of cold water used three or four times a day. Chlorate of potash lozenges is a popular remedy. The throat may be painted with equal parts of tannic acid and glycerine.

HOLLY. Propagation is by cuttings of half-matured wood struck in August in a cold frame or by layers in summer. Plant in May or September and prune in April. Growth is very slow.

HOME-MADE REFRIGERATOR. To make this, procure a large earthenware jar, and a larger bowl, containing cold water in which to stand it. Cover the jar with a piece of wet flannel, large enough to allow the ends to trail in the water, thus keeping the necessary cool dampness. Place the apparatus in a draught and you have a satisfactory refrigerator.

HONESTY. *See* LUNARIA.

HONEYSUCKLE. The honeysuckle is useful as a climber having, in addition to its fragrant blossoms, the advantage of leafing early. It thrives best in a deep, light loamy soil. The bush varieties may be increased from rooted suckers, cuttings, or layers, as well as by seed.

HORNED POPPY. *See* GLAUCIUM.

HOROSCOPE. Casting a horoscope is a complicated process of astrological calculations based upon the hour and day of birth in association with the signs of the Zodiac. A brief table, however, showing what department of life is governed by each respective sign, reveals:

Aries.—Personality and surroundings.
Taurus.—Money matters.
Gemini.—Relations, correspondence and travel.
Cancer.—Home, parents (especially the mother) and the end of life.
Leo.—Love affairs, children, pleasures, speculation, the father.
Virgo.—Sickness and servants.
Libra.—Marriage, business partnership, legal matters.
Scorpio.—Financial position, legacies, death.
Sagittarius.—Long journeys and foreign affairs.
Capricorn.—Profession or business, position in life.
Aquarius.—Friends and associates.
Pisces.—Secret troubles and restraints.
Personal characteristics will be found under the alphabetic entries of the above signs, where also are given their days of influence.

HORSE-RADISH. To put the well-scrubbed sticks of horse-radish through a mincing-machine saves much time and trouble.

HOT-POT (for 7 or 8 people).

1½ lb. mutton (middle neck)	water or stock
3 lb. potatoes	salt and pepper
½ lb. onions	

Cut up the meat into neat joints—it should be rather lean—slice the potatoes and chop the onions, place them in a jar in layers, season highly, add sufficient water or stock to cover, and cook in the oven for 3 hours. If possible, it should be served in the vessel it is cooked in.

HOT-WATER SYSTEM, remedying troubles. *See* WATER-SUPPLY.

HOUSEMAID'S KNEE. If of the painless variety, soft pads should be worn during working hours, and iodine painted on the swelling every night till it is slightly blistered. If the tumour reaches an inconvenient size, and interferes with the patient's employment, it may be operated on and completely removed.

HUMUS. The name for stable or farmyard manure, not so freely obtainable nowadays. It has to be well rotted, sometimes for over a year, by stacking and weathering, and then spread in the earliest months of the year so that its goodness can soak in and yet not be washed down beyond the root levels as would be the case if put on in the autumn.

HYACINTHS. The hyacinth is quite hardy and will thrive in ordinarily good soil, but a well-drained, rich, sandy loam is preferable. For outdoor blooming, plant bulbs in a sunny position from September to November about 4 inches deep and from 5 to 10 inches apart. Lift the bulbs when the leaves have withered, dry in the sun, and store on dry sand or coconut fibre till the following year. For culture in pots, plant in succession from August to November (to bloom from December to April). Place three bulbs in a 5½-inch pot containing two parts turfy loam and one of well-rotted manure, leaf-mould and sand. They are less suitable for bowls, which are mostly too shallow.

HYDRANGEA. Plant in a light soil with plenty of sand. Renew mould every year if plants are potted. Protect roots during winter with a covering of loose straw. Cuttings will strike easily if copiously watered.

HYDROPHOBIA. *See* BITE, DOG, to treat; *also* DOGS, care of, etc.

IBERIS (CANDYTUFT). Either as a perennial or an annual, in the rock garden or the mixed border, this plant is well worth cultivation. Most of the varieties are quite hardy, thrive in any soil, include a variety of colour, and may easily be raised from seed.

ICE, substitute for. Cloths soaked in equal parts of methylated spirits and milk act as an excellent substitute for ice.

ICE CREAM.

1½ quarts milk
1½ lb. sugar
6 eggs, well-beaten

Mix all together in a tin pail, add a little vanilla, then put the pail into a pan of boiling water and stir the custard all the time until it is quite thick. After it is cooled, add 1 quart of rich cream and then freeze it.

ICE CREAM (Another recipe).

1 quart milk
1½ tablespoonfuls arrowroot

grated peel of 2 lemons
1 quart thick cream

Wet the arrowroot with a little cold milk and add it to the quart of milk when boiling hot. Sweeten well with white sugar, add the grated lemon peel, boil the whole and strain it into the cream. When partly frozen add the juice of 2 lemons. Whites of eggs may be added if desired. This quantity is enough for about 17 people.

ICED CHERRY SOUP.

1 lb. cherries
1 pint cherry jelly

½ bottle chablis
1 grape fruit

Stew cherries gently to draw out the juice which pour over the cherry jelly, *hot*, not boiling. Add the chablis and the juice of the grape fruit. Mix well. Stand on ice. Serve in glasses.

ICING, ALMOND.

½ lb. icing sugar
½ lb. ground almonds
1 egg (or yolk only)
lemon juice

For flavouring:
maraschino, brandy,
essence of amonds,
vanilla or sherry

Pass the icing sugar through a sieve, mix with the ground almonds, add the egg and lemon juice and the other flavourings to taste. Knead all well together and it is ready for use.

Note.—All castor sugar can be used instead of icing sugar if preferred, but it must be very fine, or half icing and half castor sugar.

ICING, CHOCOLATE.

2 bars chocolate	1 gill water
4 oz. loaf sugar	vanilla essence

Dissolve the chocolate in a basin over boiling water, boil the sugar and water together for 5 minutes, mix into the chocolate until a good consistency for coating, add vanilla essence and use at once.

ICING, COFFEE BUTTER.

3 oz. fresh butter	coffee essence or strong coffee
6 oz. icing sugar	to taste

Prepare as chocolate butter icing, substituting coffee essence for the chocolate.

ICING, FONDANT.

$1\frac{1}{2}$ lb. loaf sugar	pinch of cream of tartar
$1\frac{1}{2}$ gills water	or few drops of lemon juice

Put the sugar and acid into a saucepan, dissolve the sugar, then boil up quickly; skim, put on the lid and boil for 1 or 2 minutes. Put in a thermometer and boil to 230° F. Pour it into a basin and stir with a spatula or wooden spoon until it turns white and creamy, then pour it over the cake required to be iced. It can be flavoured with any essence, and coloured any shade desired.

ICING, GLACÉ.

$\frac{1}{4}$ lb. icing sugar
$\frac{1}{2}$ gill water
little lemon juice

Rub the icing sugar through a sieve; put it into a saucepan with the water and lemon juice and allow it to get warm. When it is thick enough to coat the back of a wooden spoon it will be the right consistency for coating a cake. For pink glacé use maraschino or any other flavouring and colour with carmine.

ICING, PINK VIENNESE.

3 oz. fresh butter	little maraschino
6 oz. icing sugar	carmine

Rub the icing sugar through a sieve, cream the butter and sugar together, add the flavouring and colour a pale pink with a few drops of carmine.

ICING, ROYAL.

$\frac{1}{2}$ lb. icing sugar
2 whites of eggs
juice of 1 lemon

Sift the sugar through a hair sieve, slightly whisk the whites of eggs and mix into the sugar, using a spatula or wooden spoon and adding lemon juice as it is required. Mix smoothly and beat the icing till quite white. If too stiff add more lemon juice. Keep it covered with a wet cloth.

143

IMMORTELLE (ACROCLINIUM). This hardy annual grows best on a light soil, and under good conditions flowers in about 6 weeks. Start under glass and transplant to the open in May. They can also be grown to flower in winter by sowing under glass in September. They give white and rose-coloured flowers, and when cut should be hung head downwards till dry, then they will last as vase flowers for months. Cut before fully open. The rose-coloured kind is known as Helipterum, and are less hardy than the white. The white immortelles make attractive pot plants, say four in an ordinary size pot. Helichrysum (which see) is another variety of everlasting flower.

INDIAN CORN, or MAIZE. Remove the outer covering of leaves and all the silky fibre underneath. Choose the best of the husks and tie them around the corn cob. Place in a saucepan with sufficient boiling water to cover the cob, to which has been added 1 teaspoonful of castor sugar and a little salt. Boil very gently until the corn is thoroughly cooked. Serve on a very hot dish. Butter sauce, or oiled butter with a little pepper and salt added, to be handed round separately.

INDIGESTION, remedy for. Have fixed hours for meals and keep them strictly; eat slowly, masticate well—do not drink while eating, but after the meal is finished (no tea). Take sufficient exercise and have as much fresh air as possible—never touch any food which is known to disagree.

INFANTS, a weight and height table.

AGE	BOYS		GIRLS	
	Weight (without clothes)	Height	Weight (without clothes)	Height
	lb.	Inches	lb.	Inches
At birth . .	7½	19½	7	19¼
1 month . .	8¾	20½	8¼	20¼
2 months . .	10¾	21½	10¼	21¼
3 months . .	12¼	22½	11¾	22¼
4 months . .	13¾	23½	13	23¼
5 months . .	15	24	14	23¾
6 months . .	16¼	24½	15¼	24¼
7 months . .	17½	25¼	16½	25
8 months . .	18¾	25¾	17½	25½
9 months . .	19¾	26½	18½	26
10 months . .	20½	27	19	26½
11 months . .	21½	27½	20	27
12 months . .	22½	28	21	27½

INFANTS, ARTIFICIAL FEEDING. The natural food for infants from birth till they are eight or nine months old is the milk from the breast of their own mother. If the mother cannot, or will not, suckle her child, a wet nurse may be employed. Cow's milk may be approximated to human milk by diluting with water and adding sugar.

Age	Strength of Food	Quantity	Time	Feeds in the 24 hours	Total in the day
1 to 4 weeks .	1 of milk 2 of water	2 oz.	$2^{1}/_{2}$ hours	8	12 to 15 oz.
2nd month .	1 ,, 1 ,,	4 oz.	$2^{1}/_{2}$,,	8	20 to 30 oz.
3rd and 4th month .	2 ,, 1 ,,	5 oz.	3 ,,	7	30 to 35 oz.
5th and 6th month	Pure milk	7 oz.	3 ,,	6	35 to 40 oz.

Children from six to twelve months should have 2 pints of pure milk a day, which may be thickened with one of the many patent foods on the market. After twelve months the bottle may be gradually left off, and solid food given; but milk must still be the principal food of the child.

INFANTS, CONSTIPATION. *See* CONSTIPATION.

INFANTS, FEEDING-BOTTLES. If the bottle is not perfectly clean the milk turns sour inside it and gives the child indigestion and diarrhœa. Use a bottle with a detachable teat and thoroughly wash both bottle and nipple after each feeding.

INFANTS, FEEDING. Babies do best if breast-fed. Should the baby show a disinclination to take the breast, he will soon come round if you persevere. Bathe the nipples with a boracic lotion before each feed and keep them clean to avoid thrush. After each feed dry them thoroughly and rub with glycerine.

INFANTS, fruit juice for. Every baby over one month who is not breast-fed should be given a little fresh uncooked fruit-juice each day. Orange juice is the best, but the juice of apples, grapes or lemons may also be given. The juice should be strained through fine muslin and diluted with twice or more the quantity of cold boiled water with a little sugar. Give 7 teaspoonsful daily after the first month and gradually increase to the juice of half an orange after three months. Do not give the juice near milk-feeding time, and if the child is costive, half an hour before the first feed is the best time.

INFANTS, VACCINATION. According to the law of this country every child born must be vaccinated. This can be done either by a private medical practitioner or by the public vaccinator, within six months of its birth, unless a certificate to the effect that the child is not fit to undergo the vaccination is produced. If a parent conscientiously believes that vaccination will be prejudicial rather than beneficial to his child's health, he must make a statutory declaration before a commissioner of oaths, justice of the peace, or other qualified person, to this effect if he wishes his child to be exempted from operation. A fee is charged for this declaration.

INFECTIOUS DISEASES, laws governing notification. Notice of the occurrence of any of the following infectious diseases—cholera, croup (when membranous), diphtheria, dysentery, acute sleeping sickness, erysipelas, the various kinds of fevers, malaria, plague, scarlatina, smallpox—must, according to law, be given to the Medical Officer of Health for the District by the head of the family, any relative, or other person residing in the building in which the patient is living, or anyone in attendance on such patient. The doctor attending such patient must also send to the Medical Officer of Health for the District a certificate giving all necessary particulars. Omission either to notify the occurrence of the disease, or send the necessary medical certificate, renders the person responsible for such omission to a penalty.

The following diseases are governed by special regulations: anthrax cerebrospinal meningitis, cholera, glanders, hydrophobia, plague and yellow fever.

The foregoing list of notifiable diseases may be added to by any local authority subject to the additions being approved by the Ministry of Health.

No one who is suffering from any of the above-mentioned infectious diseases may wilfully enter any public conveyance, place, inn, hotel, shop, or even the street, without taking proper precautions to prevent the spread of the disease. If he contravenes this regulation he renders himself liable to a penalty. Furthermore, any person in charge of such patient who permits such contravention renders himself also liable to the same penalty. Moreover, any person who disposes of, lends, or transmits in any way bedding or clothing, etc., which have been in contact with the patient, without previous disinfections, likewise renders himself liable to the same penalty.

The law provides for a fine of not exceeding £20, or imprisonment for one month, with or without hard labour, in the case of any person who lets a house, rooms or lodgings in which a case of infectious disease has occurred without having previously had same disinfected and received a certificate of disinfection from a doctor or medical practitioner.

Before a child who has been suffering from any infectious disease may return to school a certificate must be obtained to the effect that such child is free from infection.

It is within the powers of any Local Education Authority to close any school in which an epidemic of any infectious disease has occurred, or they may elect to exclude from the school any children who are liable to carry the infection.

146

All clothing, etc., which has been in contact with any person suffering from an infectious disease must be properly disinfected before being sent to any public laundry.

No person suffering from an infectious disease may borrow books from any public or circulating library, neither may they return any previously borrowed until they have had them properly disinfected.

The Local Sanitary Authority is responsible for providing for the disinfection of infected bedding, clothing, etc.

Any person vacating a house in which a case of infectious disease has occurred within six weeks of his vacating same must immediately upon his ceasing to occupy such house advise the owner or landlord, so that it may be properly disinfected.

INFLUENZA.   This is an infectious fever and occurs in epidemics.

Symptoms.—From one to three days after infection there is head-ache, pains in the eyes, body and limbs, and a sensation of cold and aching.   The temperature rises, the tongue is coated with fur, the appetite lost, and the water highly-coloured and scanty.   The tempera-ture remains up for about two days and then falls to normal, leaving the person weak and prostrated out of all proportion to the severity of the illness.   The foregoing are the symptoms in a simple, uncom-plicated case.   Inflammation of the lungs is the most serious com-plication that may arise—especially in middle-aged and elderly people.   A rash resembling measles, or scarlet fever, often appears.   The after-effects of influenza may be serious.   The person is always left weak.   Mental depression, inflammation of the brain, paralysis and insanity sometimes follow.

Treatment.—The person should take to his bed at once.   Inflamma-tion of the lungs and other complications are often brought on by the person trying to keep about and do his work.   A physician should be consulted, as mortality from the disease is great, the complications which may set in are serious and the after-effects grave.   Convalescence is sometimes long and tedious, the person remaining weak and unfit for mental or physical exertions sometimes for weeks and months.   A teaspoonful of Parrish's food in water is a useful tonic in this stage, as also is halibut oil.   Either should be taken three times a day after food.

INSECT BITES.   The itching from insect bites can be relieved by the application of a paste of salt and bi-carbonate of soda, made by adding a little water to ¼ of a glass of salt and ¼ glass of bicarbonate of soda.   Or a salt water bath to which has been added ½ lb. of bicarbonate of soda.   Either of these remedies will provide almost immediate relief from itching and will tend to heal the sores from the bites.

INSECTS ON PLANTS.   *See* PESTS.   *See also* ANTS, to destroy; APHIS, to remove from rosebuds; CATERPILLARS, to destroy; EARWIGS, to destroy; PLANT-LICE (APHIDES), to destroy; ROSE TREES, to clear from blight; TOBACCO WASH (for plants), to prepare; TURNIPS AND SWEDES, to prevent destruction by "fly" in dry weather; WIREWORM, to destroy.

INSOMNIA.   *See* SLEEPLESSNESS.

INTRODUCTIONS. Regardless of rank, a gentleman is always introduced to a lady. Thus you would say to her, "Miss A., may I introduce Mr. B. ?" mentioning both their names distinctly.

When introducing two ladies, one of lesser rank or social importance must be introduced to the other, but when their positions are fairly equal a girl or younger woman is introduced to her elder, and an unmarried lady is introduced to a married one, unless the former is of higher rank or possessed of some more special claim to distinction.

Where both ladies are either married or single and there is no appreciable difference in rank or age, it is immaterial which name is mentioned first, unless one is a relation or more intimate friend of the person making the introduction, when she would introduce her to the other lady.

Upon the majority of introductions it is unnecessary to shake hands, a bow being sufficient.

A lady who is seated does not rise or shake hands when responding to an ordinary introduction, but she will shake hands with her host if he is introduced to her, and in her own home it is correct for her to shake hands when greeting her guests or upon being introduced to strangers, either ladies or gentlemen. A gentleman who is seated rises immediately for an introduction.

As a rule ladies do not shake hands in the street or other public places upon being introduced at a casual meeting. Certainly one of lesser rank or position should not make the first move in the matter, though she would accept the other's hand if offered.

If you do not wish an acquaintance to develop further, a polite little bow upon further meetings will generally meet the case.

When walking with friends there is no need to introduce them to any others you may meet, though it is quite correct to do so if you think this course will be mutually agreeable.

INVALID COOKERY. *See* recipes for the following:

SOUPS.—Lentil, mock turtle, ox-tail, pearl barley, potato, vegetable.

BROTHS.—Chicken, mutton, veal.

MEAT, POULTRY, Etc.—Mutton (boiled), mutton cutlets, lamb cutlets, veal (stewed), veal cutlets, tripe (thoroughly cooked), sweetbreads, brains on toast, chicken (roast or boiled), oysters (raw or scalloped).

Note.—An invalid may also be given steak, provided it is placed between two plates and cooked for about half an hour over a pan of boiling water.

VEGETABLES.—Asparagus, cauliflower, celery, potatoes.

FISH.—Plaice, sole, whiting.

PUDDINGS AND SWEETS.—Apple fool, arrowroot blancmange, arrowroot custard, boiled batter pudding, bread and butter pudding, caramel pudding, custard pudding (steamed or baked), jelly moulds, junket, rice pudding, semolina pudding, sponge pudding, stewed fruit, tapioca pudding.

GRUEL, TEAS, Etc.—Apple water, barley water, beef tea, black-currant tea, calf's foot jelly, camomile tea, egg lemonade, gruel, imperial drink, lemonade, linseed tea, milk (baked), milk lemonade, oatmeal gruel, toast water.

IODINE STAINS. Iodine is frequently used for various ailments, and too often gets spilt on bed-linen, underclothing, etc., leaving an ugly brown mark. When such an accident happens carbolic will entirely remove the stain without injury to the most delicate fabric. Get your chemist to give you about a pennyworth of 1 in 40 strength carbolic, put the stained part in a saucer, and simply pour the carbolic lotion over; the mark will at once disappear.

IODINE, TINCTURE OF. This is very useful for reducing swelling in such cases as swollen glands (when the glands should be painted with it), inflammation resulting from insect stings or bites, water on the knee, etc.

IRIS. This plant may be divided into two groups, the bulbous and the non-bulbous (*rhizomatous*). The varieties have increased of late years both in beauty of colour, height and habit. All are hardy and perennial. The Flag Iris will flourish in almost any soil, and flower year after year. Black Prince, with large, fragrant flowers of light and dark tinged with soft blue; and *Pallida dalmatica*, a fine variety, with tall stems of delicate blue flowers and splendid foliage. The Spanish Iris includes white, blue, yellow and striped. It likes a light, well-drained soil and a warm, sheltered situation, but plenty of sunlight and should not be disturbed.

IRISH STEW (for 5 or 6 people).

1 lb. neck of mutton	little stock or water
2 lb. potatoes	salt and pepper
1 lb. onions	

Wipe the meat, chine it and cut into chops, cut the potatoes into slices and chop the onions, put them into a stewpan in layers, adding plenty of salt and pepper. Add a little stock or water (about ½ pint); simmer gently till cooked.

IRONING. When ironing thin frocks, which have patent fasteners, take care these are not ironed into the material as they are liable to cause holes. A well-padded ironing-board is a great help.

Do not use a very hot iron for a coloured blouse; it makes it look faded. It is a good plan to lay a piece of butter muslin over a silk blouse to be ironed.

IRON RUST, to remove from delicate fabrics. Cover the spot thickly with cream of tartar, then twist cloth to keep cream of tartar over spot. Put in a saucepan of cold water, and bring slowly to boiling point.

IRON RUST, to remove from muslins or white goods. Thoroughly saturate the spots with lemon juice and salt, and then expose to the sun. More than one application is necessary as a rule. If the article is enclosed in a muslin bag when being boiled the rust mark will not reappear.

IRONS. To keep irons smooth, tie some beeswax in a piece of muslin, rub it over the warm iron and then move the iron over a paper sprinkled with salt.

ISOLATION, duration. The following will show how long isolation should be enforced, from the commencement of the first symptoms till the patient is considered non-infectious:

German measles, ten days; measles, two weeks; mumps, three weeks; diphtheria, four weeks; whooping-cough, five weeks; scarlet fever, six weeks. In chicken-pox and smallpox all sores should be healed and the skin free from scales.

ITCH, treatment. Wash thoroughly with carbolic soap in very hot water. Sulphur ointment should be rubbed in at night and washed off the following morning in a hot bath. This is repeated the following nights. Wash towels every time of use in antiseptic and do not let others use. New clothes should be worn and the old ones disinfected by baking in an oven, and not put on again for some time.

IVORY, to bleach. Dip in soapy water, place in the sunlight and take it in before it has dried. Repeat the process as often as may be necessary.

IVORY, to restore colour. Rub with juice and Spanish whiting, and leave for half an hour. Wash off and polish with furniture cream. If greatly discoloured, wet well with soapy water and bleach in the sun; then rinse and polish. White piano keys should be gently rubbed with a little methylated spirits. Avoid using water.

IXIA. This is a bulb which is well worth cultivating for its dainty blue flowers, either in the greenhouse or the open garden in a warm wallbacked border of southern aspect. For early flowering the bulbs should be planted in September or the beginning of October in a light, well-drained soil, and some protection from the frost, such as a covering of bracken litter, should be given as soon as the new growth appears.

JAM-MAKING. If jam or jelly is covered immediately after it is poured into the jars there is no need to use wax tissue paper or other preservatives; the jam will not become mouldy or sugar-coated if kept for years. The jars must not be put into the larder till quite cold.

Jam will not burn in the making if the bottom of the pan is rubbed with olive oil. *See also* PRESERVING.

JAM. Setting qualities of fruit. The firmest results come from black and red currants, apples, gooseberries and damsons.

Of less, but satisfactory setting qualities are apricots, blackberries, logans, plums, greengages and raspberries.

The following possess only poor setting qualities and require "bolstering" as indicated: cherries, pear, strawberries and marrow. A firmer setting can be secured by adding juice of lemon, red currants or gooseberries, with a proportion also of tartaric acid.

Sugar is required in differing proportions according to setting quality: for high-setting power, $1\frac{1}{4}$ lb. sugar to 1 lb. fruit; medium, 1 lb. sugar to 1 lb. fruit; poor, $\frac{3}{4}$ lb. sugar to 1 lb. fruit.

JAM, APPLE. To every pound of fruit (weighed after being prepared) allow $\frac{3}{4}$ lb. preserving sugar, the grated rind of 1 lemon and the juice of $\frac{1}{2}$ a lemon.

Take apples all of one kind, preferably greening apples, and peel, core and slice them very thinly. Place in a jar, stand in a saucepan of boiling water and stew till tender. Put fruit in preserving pan, add the sugar with grated rind and lemon juice, and simmer for half an hour over the fire. Remove all scum as it rises. Pour into jars, tie down and keep air-tight.

JAM, APPLE AND GINGER. Take a quantity of apples, peel thinly, remove core and cut into thin slices. When you have 4 lb. put into a pan with 4 gills of water. Cook till soft and then rub all through a sieve. Measure this and return to the pan with ¾ lb. of sugar to every pint of pulp. Cook slowly until the sugar has dissolved, then bring to the boil and skim. Then add the juice and grated rind of 1 lemon and 4 oz. of preserved ginger cut small. Boil all together until it jellies.

JAM, APRICOT. Cut the apricots in halves and remove the stones, crack them and take out kernels, weigh the apricots, and to every pound of fruit add ¾ lb. of preserving sugar. Put both into a pan and let it stand 12 hours. Then put the fruit and sugar into a preserving pan, bring slowly to the boil, then boil quickly, skimming constantly. When nearly done, add the kernels of half the quantity of apricots used, pour into warm jars, and cover down the next day.

JAM, BLACKBERRY. Allow ¾ lb. sugar to 1 lb. of fruit. Boil the fruit half an hour, then add the sugar and boil all together 10 minutes.

JAM, BLACKBERRY AND APPLE. Proceed in the same way as for apple jam, but instead of apples only use half apples and half blackberries.

JAM, BLACKCURRANT. For each quart of fruit allow 1 pint of water and 3 lb. sugar. Boil for 25 minutes.

JAM, CHERRY. Stone 4 lb. cherries and then weigh, add an equal quantity of sugar and 3 teacupfuls of water. Boil the sugar and water in a jelly-pan for 10 minutes, add cherries and boil for half an hour.

JAM, DAMSON or PLUM.
> 3 lb. damsons or plums
> ½ pint of water
> 2¼ lb. sugar, i. e. ¾ lb. to each lb. of fruit

Make a syrup with the water and sugar. Add the damsons or plums well washed, dried and stoned. Bring to the boil and boil quickly for about half an hour, or until the jam sets when tested. Remove scum, bottle and store in the usual way.

JAM, GOOSEBERRY.
> 4 lb. gooseberries
> 3 lb. sugar
> 1 pint water

The gooseberries should not be fully ripe for this purpose. After having well washed, topped and tailed the gooseberries make the jam in accordance with the recipe for damson or plum jam.

JAM, HARD AND SUGARY. Jam which has become hard and sugary can be put right again by placing it in a warm oven until the sugar has melted.

JAM, QUINCE. Cut the quinces in fine slices and cover them with water, allowing them to boil until they are soft. Then weigh the fruit and water together and allow ¾ lb. of sugar to each pound of fruit and water. Boil until the jam will set when tested. Skim well. Put into pots, tie down and store in the usual way.

JAM, RASPBERRY. Allow 1 lb. sugar to 1 lb. fruit. Boil the fruit half an hour, or till the seeds are soft. Strain one quarter of the fruit and throw away the seeds. Add the sugar, and boil the whole 10 minutes. A little currant juice gives it a pleasant flavour, and when that is used, an equal quantity of sugar must be added.

JAM, RHUBARB.

rhubarb   lemons   sugar

Weigh the rhubarb after stringing or peeling; allow 1 lb. of sugar to 1 lb. of fruit. Put the rhubarb into the preserving pan over the fire. When the juice flows add the sugar and the chopped rind of lemons (2 to every 6 lb. of rhubarb), boil until the jam is a good colour and thickness, skimming constantly. Pour into hot jars; cover the next day with paper dipped in whisky or brandy and then parchment.

Note.—Ginger added instead of lemons makes an excellent jam.

JAM, STRAWBERRY. Strew 6 lb. of sugar over same quantity of fruit and leave standing for 14 hours. Boil for 20 minutes.

JAMAICA PEPPER. *See* ALLSPICE.

JAMS AND PICKLES. These should not be stored on a top shelf as hot air rises and heat causes fermentation.

JASMINE. Increase by layers or cuttings of ripe wood, struck in a warm frame in a mixture of light soil and sand during the summer. Plant out from October to March and prune shoots after they have bloomed. The white species is spring flowering, the yellow in winter and January.

JAUNDICE. Signs of the trouble are sleepiness, yellow eyeballs, highly-coloured urine.

The diet should consist of milk and broth, and the bowels opened by a blue pill taken at night, and a seidlitz powder the following morning before breakfast. The bowels should be kept free, but violent purging should be avoided.

An easily prepared remedy: take 1 oz. each of senna, camomile flowers, ground ginger, and powdered jalap and pour boiling water upon the mixture. Take ½ teaspoonful of the decoction in a cup of tea once or twice daily.

Avoid premature getting about lest complications ensue.

JELLY, APPLE (for 6 or 7 people).

2 lb. apples	1 oz. gelatine
½ pint water	few pistachio nuts
8 oz. loaf sugar	carmine colouring
rind and juice of 2 lemons	½ pint cream

Peel, core and slice the apples, put them in a stewpan with water, sugar, lemon rind and juice; simmer gently until the apples are tender. Remove the lemon peel and rub the apples through a hair sieve, dissolve the gelatine in a little water, strain it into the apple purée, colour a nice pink with a few drops of carmine, pour into a wet border mould, and turn out when set on to a glass dish. Whip, sweeten and flavour the cream, and fill the centre; sprinkle with chopped pistachio nuts.

JELLY, ASPIC.

1½ pint stock or water	½ gill sherry
1 onion	2 tablespoonfuls vinegar
1 small carrot	2 tablespoonfuls tarragon
1 small turnip	vinegar
stick of celery	10 peppercorns
2 cloves	salt
bunch of herbs	2½ oz. gelatine
rind and juice of ½ lemon	whites and shells of 2 eggs

If stock is used remove the fat; put stock into a saucepan with all the ingredients except the whites and shells and the sherry; stir over the fire till the gelatine is dissolved. Whisk the whites slightly and add with the crushed shells. Whisk well until it comes to the boil, then stop whisking and let it boil gently for 10 minutes. Then set aside for a few minutes with the lid partly on. Strain through a hot teacloth: put the sherry through the cloth last.

Note.—More gelatine must be used in hot weather.

JELLY, BLACKBERRY. Boil 2 quarts blackberries in 2 quarts water, bruising the berries with a wooden spoon; strain through a fine linen bag and boil syrup for 5 minutes. Add to each pint of juice 1 lb. sugar. Boil for quarter of an hour, removing scum as it rises. Pour into jars and cover.

JELLY, BLACKCURRANT. Place the fruit in a preserving pan with a little water. Heat the currants, gradually pressing until all the juice is extracted. Mix 1 lb. sugar with every pint of juice, and boil for 10 minutes, stirring continually. Pour into moulds and cover.

JELLY, BRAMBLE. Place berries in a jar in a pan of boiling water. Allow to steam gently for 6 hours, then strain through a cheesecloth. Allow 1 lb. sugar to ½ pint juice and boil for 10 or 12 minutes.

JELLY, CALF'S FOOT. After cleaning and preparing two feet boil them for 8 hours in 1 gallon of water, removing scum as it rises. When tender, strain the liquor through a fine sieve and leave till the next day, then remove fat and wipe the jelly dry with a cloth. Dissolve jelly and stir into it a wineglassful of good old sherry or 2 tablespoonfuls of pale brandy. Beat up the whites and crush the shells of 3 eggs into ¾ pint of cold water. Stir this liquid into the jelly and simmer for 15 minutes. Let it settle for 5 minutes before straining.

JELLY, CRAB APPLE.

4 lb. crab apples
1 quart water
1½ lb. sugar to each quart of juice

There is no need to peel the apples; simply wash them and cut any large ones in halves. Put apples and water into preserving pan, bring to the boil, then simmer until all the juice has been extracted from the fruit. Strain, add the sugar, bring to the boil again and boil until the jelly sets when tested. Turn into jars, cover and store in the usual way.

JELLY, DAMSON.

damsons
very little water
8 oz. sugar to each pint of fruit juice

Place the fruit in either a double cooker or in a stone jar placed in a saucepan of boiling water. Add very little water to the fruit, cover and allow to cook slowly until the damsons are thoroughly cooked through and all the juice appears to have been extracted. Then strain and put the juice into a preserving pan with about 8 oz. of sugar to each pint of juice. Boil until the jelly sets when tested. Then turn into jars, cover when cold, and store in the usual way.

JELLY MOULD, AMERICAN (for 4 or 5 people).

1 pint milk	1 oz. castor sugar
2 eggs	vanilla essence
¾ oz. gelatine	

Dissolve the gelatine in the milk, but do not boil it; add the yolks of eggs and sugar, beat the whites to a stiff froth and add with the vanilla essence to taste. Put into a wet mould; turn out when set.

JELLY MOULD, FRUIT (for 8 or 10 people).

1 quarts lemon jelly	apples
bananas	glacé cherries
grapes	pistachio nuts
oranges	carmine colouring

Prepare the fruit very carefully; cut the bananas into slices, the oranges into quarters, removing the pips, cut the apples into fancy shapes and take out the seeds from the grapes. Decorate the bottom of a quart mould with cherries and chopped pistachio nuts, set it on ice with a little lemon jelly, arrange the fruit in layers, setting them with jelly, adding a little colouring getting darker each time, and allowing each layer to get firm before adding the next. Fill the mould quite full.

Note.—The lemon jelly for this must be made with more gelatine in proportion to support the fruit.

Fresh fruit such as strawberries, apricots, raspberries can be used.

JELLY, QUINCE.

1 dozen quinces
12 oz. sugar to each pound of juice

Slice quinces finely. Cover with cold water. Boil until quite tender. Strain through a clean cloth, wringing it well through—not merely running it through—weigh juice and return to pan with ¾ lb. of sugar to each pound of juice. Boil about 40 minutes, or until it jellies when tested. Put into pots, tie down and store in the usual way.

JELLY, RASPBERRY AND CURRANT.

Take 4 quarts of currants that are not over-ripe and pick them. Mash in preserving pan with 2 quarts raspberries and cook till almost white. Strain; take equal parts of sugar and juice. Boil juice 5 minutes; add heated sugar and boil for 3 minutes. Skim; pour into pots, and seal.

JELLY, RED CURRANT.

currants	sugar

Use the fruit when quite dry and clean. Put it in a preserving pan and boil until all the juice is set free; pour through a jelly bag. Add 1 lb. of sugar to every pound of juice; boil quickly. When quite clear remove the pan from the fire, pour the jelly into hot glasses or jars, fill to the brim, and cover down the day after it is made. This jelly is served with roast mutton and hare.

JERUSALEM ARTICHOKES. *See* ARTICHOKES.

JEWELLERY, to clean.

Dip the jewellery into clean soap-suds made from fine white soap. Dry by brushing with a soft badger brush. Then dip into a mixture of boxwood sawdust and jewellers' rouge.

JONQUIL. *See* NARCISSUS.

JUNKET.

½ pint milk	2 teaspoonfuls sugar
1 teaspoonful rennet	little cream
2 teaspoonfuls brandy	nutmeg and cinnamon

Warm the milk, add the sugar, brandy and pinch of cinnamon, mix in the rennet and pour into a glass dish or into custard cups. Leave until cold, pour a little cream on top and grate with nutmeg.

KALE. *See* BORECOLE.

KALE BROSE (for 6 or 7 people).

Scotch kale	1 turnip
2 quarts water or stock	2 oz. pearl barley
2 onions	salt and pepper
2 carrots	

Blanch the kale and cut into small pieces, boil the stock, add the barley and vegetables, cut into small pieces, simmer very gently from 2 to 3 hours, season and serve.

KAULFUSSIA (CAPE ASTER).

This hardy annual is only 6 inches high and so suited for edgings. The blue or rich crimson flowers are freely produced in about 4 months. Sow in early April in good garden soil, and a sunny position.

KEDGEREE (for 4 people).

1 cooked smoked haddock or any cold fish	3 oz. butter
¼ lb. boiled rice	salt and pepper
2 hard-boiled eggs	chopped parsley
	curry sauce

Flake the fish, carefully remove all bones and skin, add the butter, 1 egg chopped, salt and pepper, and the rice; get the mixture very hot, pile on a dish, scallop it round with a knife, garnish with chopped parsley and flaked yolk of egg. Place a cup of white of egg on the top with a sprig of parsley in it; serve with curry sauce.

KETCHUP, MUSHROOM.

6 lb. mushrooms	1 blade mace
to each pint of liquor allow:	¼ oz. allspice
4 cloves	¼ oz. ginger (well crushed)

Wash the mushrooms, cut off half the stalk of each and then break or cut the mushrooms in pieces and put them in an earthenware vessel in layers with salt sprinkled between. Place the vessel either in a cool part of the oven, or in a fairly warm place on the top of a range in order to draw off the juice from the mushrooms. Leave for a whole day. Strain, pressing out all the liquor, which must then be measured and boiled for about 30 minutes. Add the other ingredients tied in a piece of muslin and boil again for about 30 minutes. Remove the muslin and contents and allow the ketchup to cool. Strain again, bottle, cork and store in a cool place.

KETCHUP, TOMATO.

7 lb. tomatoes	1 heaped dessertspoonful salt
½ pint good vinegar	little less than ½ oz. celery seed
¼ lb. brown sugar	little less than ½ oz. mace
¼ oz. powdered cinnamon	little less than ½ oz. powdered
½ teaspoonful cayenne	allspice

Boil tomatoes until thoroughly cooked and then put through a colander. Do not use a sieve as this is too fine for this first operation. Stir the other ingredients into the resulting pulp and then put through a sieve. Put the mixture into a pan and boil gently until the quantity is reduced by half. Bottle, cork and keep in a cool dark place.

KETCHUP, TOMATO. (Another recipe.)

12 lb. tomatoes	3 gills vinegar
12 oz. onions (chopped)	¾ oz. allspice
1½ oz. ginger (cut into small pieces)	1½ oz. cloves
	salt

Cut the tomatoes into halves (large ones into quarters), place in a basin or pan and leave for 2 days. Then bring to the boil and cook until the skin and pulp come apart quite easily. Strain through a sieve (not too fine), return to the pan and add the other ingredients, bringing all to the boil once more and cooking until there is only two-thirds of the quantity left in the pan. Allow to cool, strain once more and bottle. Keep tightly corked and store in a cool place.

KETTLE, IRON, to free from fur. Fill the kettle with water; add 1 large spoonful sal-ammoniac and allow to boil for a few minutes. Empty it and stand over the fire to get red hot, when the fur will peel off. Boil in it some soda water for a short time. Then rinse well in cold water.

KETTLE-LID KNOB. If the knob comes off the kettle-lid place an ordinary cork over the hole, turn the lid upside down and insert a screw through the hole into the cork. This makes a fine knob that never gets hot.

KETTLES, to prevent fur coating in. Place in the kettle from the time it is first used after purchase either a stone marble or an oyster shell.

KIDNEY, DEVILLED (for 4 people).

4 kidneys	chutney
devil paste	buttered toast

Skin the kidneys, cut them open, spread with the devil paste and grill them over a clear fire; put them on rounds of buttered toast spread with chutney, and serve very hot.

Chops, steaks, cutlets, fish, etc., can be devilled in the same way.

KIDNEYS. Briskly fry kidneys for 15 minutes with a little butter. Remove from the pan when done, and stir into the gravy a spoonful of flour. When brown add water to make gravy.

KIDNEYS, INFLAMMATION OF.

Causes.—Cold, damp, scarlet fever, pregnancy.

Symptoms.—Fever, pain in the loins, headache, vomiting. Eyelids become puffy, and the face pale and swollen. The dropsy often extends to other parts of the body.

Treatment.—The person should be put to bed in a warm room and hot fomentations applied to the loins. The diet should consist of milk alone, or with soda water, home-made lemonade, or some such drink. Neither meat, fish nor eggs must be taken. During convalescence a meat diet should be returned to gradually and dry hot flannels, gradually reducing in temperature, wrapped round loins till pain has gone.

KIDNEY STEW.

1 oz. kidney	ketchup
½ teaspoonful mustard	salt and pepper
1 oz. butter	1 pint stock
1 onion	1 teaspoonful sugar
	1 oz. flour

Wash the kidney; dry and remove core. Cut in slices. Heat sugar till brown, add butter. Fry chopped onion and kidney till brown. Stir in flour and fry. Add liquid and seasoning. Stir till it boils. Cover and simmer slowly 3 hours. Add ketchup and serve.

KIDNEY TOAST (for 3 people).

3 kidneys	¼ oz. flour
1 teaspoonful chopped	1 tablespoonful Worcester
parsley	sauce
1 shallot	salt and pepper
¼ oz. butter	buttered toast

Mince the kidney finely; cook the chopped shallot in the butter for 5 minutes, add the flour and Worcester sauce, boil for 2 minutes; put in the minced kidney, season with salt and pepper. Put on the buttered toast, sprinkle with bread-crumbs, bake in a quick oven for 7 or 8 minutes and serve hot, sprinkled with the parsley.

KITCHEN INSECTS. To keep the kitchen free from pests every part must be clean and dry. Leave no uncovered food, soiled dishes, rubbish or crumbs about. Take two-thirds boracic acid, mix with one-third powdered sugar, sprinkle this round the sink, draining board, etc.; this will soon exterminate insect life; also a few drops of turpentine sprinkled in any cockroach haunt will drive them away.

KNIFE HANDLES, to remove stains. Dip a piece of damp flannel in table salt and rub the handles for a few moments with it.

KNIVES, to remove stains. Sprinkle a little bicarbonate of soda on the knife-board after the bath-brick has been applied, and this will speedily remove from knives all traces of stains.

Knives which have been used to peel onions can be cured of the smell immediately by plunging the blades into earth. Rust stains on knives can be loosened in the same way.

A reliable knife sharpener can now be bought at a very moderate cost. Half a dozen strokes with it give a lasting edge to any knife.

KNOBS AND KNOCKERS. When cleaning brass knobs or door-knockers, protect the paint by a piece of cardboard, out of which a hole has been cut just large enough to allow the brass edges to clear. For a brass door-knob slit the cardboard at the side, allowing the knob to pass through, and slip back firmly around the knob. You can then polish the brass without soiling the surrounding paint.

KNOCK KNEES, to straighten. The child should be put to bed and not allowed to walk, and the legs massaged for 15 minutes daily and straightened out. No force should be used to cause pain. Afterwards a pad of cotton-wool on a piece of doubled soft flannel should be put between the knees, and the legs bandaged together. The bandage should be taken off every day and readjusted. In older children whose bones are not so soft steel supports may be advisable, under advice from an orthopædic clinic.

LACE, to clean. Take some clean old white muslin and sew it round a large bottle full of cold water. Wrap the lace carefully around the bottle. To prevent wrinkles tack one end of the lace to the muslin. Take a clean sponge soaked with sweet oil, and saturate the lace thoroughly through the wrappings to the bottle which is to be fastened by strings in a wash kettle. Pour in a strong cold lather of white castile soap and boil the suds until lace is perfectly clean and white. The bottle should then be placed in the sun to dry. Remove the lace and wind it round a ribbon block or press.

LACQUER, to polish. Lacquered ornaments are apt to get dull and their gloss will return if they are washed in warm water and lemon juice, dried with a cloth, and polished with a leather.

LAMB, BREAST OF, to stuff and roast. *See* MUTTON, BREAST OF.

LAMB CHOPS, FRIED. Dip them in bread-crumbs, a little grated lemon, the yolk of an egg and chopped parsley. Fry to a light brown and serve with brown gravy.

LARDERS. Whether for dry or fresh goods, must always be cool, dry, well-ventilated and lighted, and not near any open drain or pipes. There should be a good supply of shelves and cupboards, so as not to be overcrowded. Jars and boxes must be covered and plainly labelled. Thoroughly clean and wash out the larder once every week. The shelves should be wiped with a damp cloth every day and the door and window, or windows, opened to give the larder a good airing. All wire, or muslin covers, bread-pan, etc., should be well washed each week.

Don't let damp in the larder spoil food. By keeping a small box of lime on one of the shelves any damp will be quickly absorbed, leaving food unharmed.

A few lumps of charcoal put in the corners will freshen the air, prevent food decomposition and drive away the flies.

LARKSPUR. Hardy annual, blue, white, pink, with graceful foliage, average 2 feet in height. Likes good soil and warm position, but will do well anywhere. Sow seed in January in open, as germination is slow, transplant when 1 inch high; give plenty of room.

LARYNGITIS.

Causes.—Exposure to cold is the most frequent cause. Other causes are inhaling irritating vapours, such as strong ammonia, breathing air full of particles of dust, drinking scalding fluids, acids or caustics.

Symptoms.—The throat is dry and sore, and the voice husky or completely lost. There is a short, dry cough, and small pellets of phlegm are expectorated. The breathing may be interfered with, but is not markedly so as a rule.

Treatment.—The person should refrain from talking. The room should be kept warm but not stuffy. A teaspoonful of Friar's balsam in a pint of very hot water may be inhaled, enveloping the head in a towel to secure utmost benefit. Keep eyes shut. Soothing drinks, such as gruel or barley water, may be taken. Dry, warm flannels applied to the throat give relief. Laryngitis in children is treated with a tea-spoonful of ipecacuanha wine, repeated, if necessary, until expectoration is produced. A hot sponge should be applied to the throat, and the air in the room kept warm and moist.

The throat should be rested and the use of tobacco and alcohol avoided. The clothing should be warm and the patient, if possible, should get out in crisp sunny weather though not in cold winds and damp days. A change to a milder climate is desirable. Gargles do not reach the seat of the mischief, but Glyco-Thermol lozenges gradually dissolved in the mouth are easing.

LAVATERA (TREE MALLOW). Growing 4 feet high on an average, these show up in the rear of the border. They are hardy annuals, sown in March to flower in July. Plant 18 inches apart and two or three in a group. The flowers have a satin-like appearance, some white, but the majority shades of pink.

159

LAVENDER. Plant slips in pots during March or April, and leave in a shady place till rooted. Then expose to the sun till strong enough for transplanting to permanent position.

LAVENDER SACHET. Mix together 75 parts powdered lavender, 20 parts powdered benzoin and 1 part oil of lavender.

LAVENDER WATER. *See* PERFUME.

LAWNS, to free from dandelions, docks and plantains. Cut the weeds to the ground in spring and immediately place gas tar or a little salt on them.

LAWNS, to kill worms. Add 2½ lb. freshly-slaked lime to about 8 gallons of water. Allow to settle and use the clear liquid on the lawn.

LAWNS, SOWING. Unless it is possible to obtain really good turf, free from weeds, for laying down a lawn, it is much better to make one from good seed. First of all prepare the ground by marking out the area of the plot, then dig all over, turning soil completely and breaking up finely, to a depth of 10 to 12 inches. Cover the whole surface with manure, forking to a depth of 3 or 4 inches. The next step is levelling. This is done by driving a stout wooden peg, about 2 feet long, sharp pointed at one end but with a flat head, into the centre of the plot, allowing the head of the peg to stand up from the ground at the height required for the level of the plot. From this centre, in radiating lines at distances of some 15 feet apart, similar pegs should be driven in, and by means of a spirit level and a level-edged board placed from peg to peg, the tops of all the pegs may be brought to an exact level. Next rake the surface of the plot to a uniform level, then, using a small roller, roll until even, as well as level, and so well consolidated that, when walked on, the imprints can scarcely be seen. The ground is now ready for sowing the seed. The amount of seed required will work out at about 1 lb. for every 4 square yards, or 10 bushels to the acre, and it is a good plan to mark out the plot accordingly. Sow the seed on a calm, dry day (not a windy nor wet one). The seed should be sown as evenly as possible and be lightly covered with soil—not deeper than ¼ of an inch—by carefully raking the surface in two directions, after which the whole should be rolled and cross-rolled with a light roller. Protect by crossing of black thread from birds. When the grass has grown to 2 inches above the ground it should be cut, either with a scythe, or sharp machine, and should be kept short. Roll frequently with a light roller.

LAYERING, to propagate plants by. Propagation by layering is usually done in July. Make an upward cut just below a joint in a lower shoot. The incision should pass halfway through the shoot and should be from 1 to 3 inches long according to the size of the plant. Peg the shoot securely into the soil, keeping the "tongue" as open as possible, but be careful not to break it. Place underneath a little grey sand, cover with earth and, after a couple of days, give plenty of water. Cut away from the parent plant when the layers are finely rooted—in soft-wooded, plants such as carnations this occurs in about six weeks.

LEADWORT. *See* PLUMBAGO.

LEAKAGE, GAS. *See* GAS PIPES, LEAKAGE.

LEATHER FURNITURE, to clean. A soft cloth dipped in boiling milk and rubbed gently over leather furniture will clean it excellently, and if rubbed afterwards with an old piece of velvet the leather will polish beautifully. Shabby dark leather after such cleaning will look like new if rubbed with a little well-beaten white of egg mixed with a little black marking-ink, before the final polish.

LEEKS.

leeks	½ pint white sauce
salt	toast

Wash the leeks thoroughly, trim into even lengths, tie them into bundles, put them into boiling water with salt and boil till quite tender; drain them, dish on a slice of toast in a hot vegetable dish, remove the tape, pour the white sauce over and serve.

LEEKS. Make successive sowings, February, March, April in open on deeply dug, well-matured ground. Do not sow thickly, nor cover with much soil; water well and thin out when about 3 inches high. Transplant into rows 1 foot apart. The bleaching can be done by nature if the young plants are dropped into deep dibbered holes, these holes not being filled, but only enough soil thrown to cover the roots, and then the hole filled with water. Do not allow to go dry.

For an early crop sow seed in boxes early in February on a moderate heat for an early crop. Prick out when about 2 inches high, transfer to a cold frame in April, and harden off and plant out in May.

LEMONADE, to make.

> 1 large lemon or 2 small ones
> 1 oz. sugar
> 1 pint water

Peel the lemon very thinly, squeeze out all the juice, put rind, juice and sugar in a jug and pour over the boiling water. Dissolve the sugar thoroughly in a small amount of boiling water and cool. Less sugar is needed; it mixes with the lemonade thoroughly and does not settle at the bottom of the jug. Cover the jug closely and strain when cold. Ice may be added.

LEMONADE, EGG, to make. Add 1 tablespoonful of water to 1 egg and beat well; then add the juice of a lemon and sugar to taste. Stir well and pour into a glass containing a little water.

LEMON CURD. Put ½ lb. fresh butter and 1 lb. fine white sugar in a saucepan. Place the saucepan in a larger one containing water and boil until the butter and sugar have melted together. Meanwhile grate the rind of 2 lemons into a cup and pour the strained juice of 3 lemons into another. Stir the lemon rind into the butter and sugar when they are quite melted. Add the lemon juice and finally 3 eggs well beaten and strained. Cook slowly until the curd thickens.

LEMON JUICE, uses of.   Lemon juice can be substituted for vinegar in any recipe except for pickling.

A little lemon juice and grated lemon rind give a flavour to stewed dried fruits.

A tough piece of meat can be made tender by adding a teaspoonful of lemon juice to the water in which it is to be cooked.

Add lemon juice to the water when boiling fish; this will help to keep it whole.

A few drops of lemon juice in the water in which old potatoes are cooked will keep them from discolouring, and in water in which eggs are poached will keep the eggs from separating.

When whipping cream add 3 or 4 drops of lemon juice to 1 cupful of cream to make it stiff and firm.

When aluminium kettles or pans have become dull or black, clean them with a cloth dipped in lemon juice and rinse in warm water.

A few drops of lemon juice in the rinsing water will give lustre to glass.

Wooden drain-boards or mixing-boards may be kept free from grease and cleaned by rubbing with half a lemon or lemon rind.

Dip the rind in salt to clean tarnished copper or brass.

LEMONS, to keep.   Cover with buttermilk or sour milk which should be changed each week.

Another way is to put your lemons in a jar filled with cold water which should be changed three or four times a week.   This will keep them fresh for quite a long time.

LEMONS.   A lemon heated in the oven before squeezing will yield twice as much juice.

LEMON SPONGE (for 5 or 6 people).

1 pint water	rind and juice of 3 lemons
1 oz. gelatine	3 whites of eggs
¼ lb. loaf sugar	

Peel the lemons thinly and put into a saucepan with lemon juice, sugar and gelatine; boil gently for 15 minutes. Allow to get cool, beat up the whites very stiffly, add the gelatine and water, etc., whisk well till it begins to stiffen, pour into a wet mould and turn out when set.

LENTEN ROSE,   *See* HELLEBORUS.

LENTIL CUTLETS.

½ lb. lentils	bread-crumbs
1 small onion	pinch of thyme
1 egg	1 small beetroot
1 dessertspoonful parsley	2 tablespoonfuls tomato ketchup
butter, size of a walnut	pinch of pepper and salt

Soak the lentils for at least 12 hours, then place in saucepan with enough water to cover, bring to the boil and then allow to simmer gently until thoroughly cooked. If unable to obtain beetroot already cooked, this must be cooked and then cut in small pieces. Next chop onion fairly small and dry. Chop parsley finely. Mix all ingredients and leave to get cold. Shape into cutlets, dip in egg and bread-crumbs and fry in oil.

LENTILS. Red lentils do not require soaking; simply wash and put into the saucepan with 1½ pints of water to each ½ pint of lentils, adding a small chopped onion and about 1 oz. of dripping. Stir all the time while bringing to the boil, then cover and simmer slowly for about 1½ to 2 hours, adding more water if necessary during this time.

LEO (THE LION). Fifth sign of the Zodiac, influencing persons born between 22nd July and 21st August. Such are leaders in life, knowing whence their ambitions lead and intent on success: they have artistic ability, astute in money-making, yet extravagant. They possess charm and dignity, though getting on brings a danger of arrogance and showiness in dress and social affairs.

LEOPARD'S BANE (DORONICUM). A family of showy, vigorous-growing plants, thriving in any soil. Useful as a covering for rough banks or for the wild garden, where its large, bright yellow flowers of daisy-like form are very effective in early spring. It can be easily propagated by division of the roots.

LETTERS OF INTRODUCTION. An introductory letter should be given unsealed to the bearer that he, or she, may read it if so inclined, but of course the bearer closes it before delivering to the addressee.

It should be remembered, both by the person who asks for an introductory letter and the one who writes it, that the writer is to a certain extent—according to the wording of the letter—making him or herself responsible for the person introduced.

The bearer of a social introductory letter should leave it, together with his or her own card, at the house of the person addressed, not asking then to see the recipient, but waiting for a return letter or call, making some arrangement for a meeting.

LETTER-WRITING. The most appreciated letter from a friend or relation is one written with an ease which breathes the writer's personality.

It is not at all polite to begin or end a letter with the information that you are too busy to write anything but a hurried scrawl.

Begin fresh pages in their proper order, so that the recipient does not have to twist and turn the letter about.

Never cross a written sheet with further writing or squeeze in cramped, illegible messages in the margin. It is now considered in bad taste to write the letters "P.S." before anything which has to be added to a letter after it has been finished.

To underline words and sentences in order to emphasize them is not necessary in a well-phrased letter.

Social correspondence should not be typewritten except where the sender knows the recipient will not feel slighted.

When penning a letter in the third person, great care must be taken to keep to the same mode right through. This form is reserved chiefly for briefly-worded formal notes between less intimate acquaintances or strangers, or orders for tradesmen and dependents.

When a letter asking a favour of a stranger requires a written reply, a stamp should be enclosed, a case in point being that of a request for a servant's reference.

Nothing of a personal or confidential nature should ever appear on a postcard.

LETTUCE. The tender crispness of these easily-raised salad plants can now be enjoyed nearly all the year round. For an early crop sow half-inch deep in February on a slight hot-bed, and transplant in April on a sheltered border; again in the middle of March, and in succession every fortnight. For winter and spring sow *All the Year Round* during the first week in August and in September, plant in good rich garden soil, 1 foot apart each way, and during dry weather give a liberal supply of water. The seedlings from the last sowing should be transplanted 4 inches each way under a south wall, for planting out early in spring. Frequent sowings in this way avoid a glut one month and none the next. Treat for quick growth and so that when ready they are still tender. The cabbage lettuce is mostly grown nowadays, thus doing away with the labour of tying up, as the cos lettuce demands.

LIBRA (THE SCALES). Seventh sign of the Zodiac, influencing persons born between 22nd September and 21st October. Such are sensitive and artistic, have personal charm, restless and of keen intuition. They are cautious, have a sense of humour, and have to guard against idleness and indifference.

LICE. Lice are of two kinds, one infests the head and the other the body.

Head Lice.—Head lice are small parasites that breed in the hair of the scalp. They lay whitish eggs called "nits", which attach themselves to the hair and give it a beaded appearance.

The presence of the parasites causes itching; this leads to scratching. The skin becomes inflamed and festers. The back of the head is the commonest place to be attacked. If the head is examined in a good light the "nits" can be seen glued to the hairs.

In bad cases, especially in children, the hair should be cut off and burnt, the head washed in warm soft soap and water. If this is not effective, olive oil should be applied at night and the head washed again the following morning, and white precipitate or sulphur ointment rubbed gently into the scalp. The "nits" can be removed by soaking the hair in vinegar and water—one part of vinegar to four of water—then washing the head, and afterwards combing out the hair with a fine-tooth comb.

Body Lice.—These are bigger than the head lice. They only occur on the parts covered by the clothes. The face, neck and hands are never attacked. The parts affected may fester and give rise to sores.

A warm bath should be taken and the body smeared with white precipitate ointment. The lice lay their eggs in the clothes, so the undergarments should be washed in soda water, and the other clothes baked in an oven.

LILIES. Lilies do best in deep, well-dug soil or in a fibrous loam which is well drained and contains decayed leaf-mould and gritty sand. Plant in October 4 to 5 inches deep, and do not take up oftener than once in three years. This in general applies to most varieties, which are numerous, except the hothouse types, which few have facilities to cultivate. A handy plan is to buy lilies in pots in the late spring, and sink the pots into the border in suitable groups according to ideas of colour. If the pots are small for the root growth, be very careful when repotting into larger size to use a soil without the addition of humus or lime. They do well in a loose compost of peat, leaf-mould and silver sand. *L. regale, L. longiflorum* (the Easter lily), *L. speciosum rubrum*, and *L. harrissi* are the most suitable sorts for bedding out.

LILY-OF-THE-VALLEY (CONVALLARIA MAJALIS). The prime necessity for the production of a good bed of lilies-of-the-valley is a well-manured soil, soft and loamy with plenty of sand, while a shaded south aspect, free from draughts, is the satisfactory position. The crowns should be planted in early autumn, singly and 2 or 3 inches apart, and the surface covered with a mulching of well-rotted manure. As soon as the new growth appears a weak solution of liquid manure should be applied occasionally, and for protection from spring frosts a light covering of fern litter is very useful. They will come up every year, and should be divided every three years.

LIME, to remove from new materials when washing. Soak article in a strong solution of salt and water for several hours, or overnight, before washing.

LINEN, to keep white. Wrap your linen in blue paper and put blue paper in between the folds.

LINEN, to mark. The following hints will be found of use in marking linen. Sheets are marked about 1 foot from the hem and in the centre; serviettes and towels in one corner; pillow-cases in one corner on the right side; and table-cloths in one corner, 2 inches above the hem. Nightdresses should be marked with the initials just below the opening of the neck. In the case of garments with a waistband mark on the band at the right side. To mark stockings sew on a piece of white tape.

LINEN, to remove mildew. Allow the stained article to soak for about half an hour in a weak solution of chloride of lime. Then rinse in a solution of ¼ oz. hyposulphite of soda in 1 quart water. Finally rinse in clear water.

LINEN, to remove iron-mould. Spread a thick paste of salt and lemon over the stain and put out in the sun to dry.

LINOLEUM, care of. After sweeping, wash with a cloth wrung out of soapy water to which has been added 1 tablespoonful of turpentine and 3 tablespoonfuls of linseed oil for every quart of water. Wipe with a clean cloth and polish.

LINOLEUM, FIREPLACE SURROUNDS. Linoleum round fireplaces soon gets stained owing to the heat. To protect it against heat, treat occasionally with equal parts of olive oil and vinegar. Remove stains with powdered pumice made into a paste with linseed oil and applied with a damp cloth.

LINOLEUM, to lay. Linoleum should always be seasoned in a warm room for at least 24 hours before it is laid; otherwise it will crack when unrolled. Wash and scrub the floor, and before it is quite dry slowly unroll the linoleum and place in position. The slight dampness renders it more pliable. When laying down new linoleum or floorcloth, do not fasten it down at once, but let a few days elapse before doing so. The floor-covering will then settle flatly. It can then be cut to fit perfectly and no wrinkles will result. *See also* FLOORS, DAMP.

LINOLEUM, to polish. Sour milk will give a non-slippery polish to linoleum.

LINSEED POULTICE. *See* POULTICE, LINSEED MEAL.

LINSEED TEA.

½ oz. linseed	¼ oz. licorice
1 pint water	¼ oz. sugar candy

Wash the linseed, put it into a saucepan with the cold water, simmer for half an hour; add licorice and sugar candy; strain before using.

LINT, BORACIC. *See* BORACIC LINT.

LINUM (FLAX). A family which includes several useful plants for the garden, some of them being perennial but better treated as annuals. A friable soil in a not too sunny plot suits them well. Average height, 18 inches. *L. grandiflorum* is both hardy and showy, and by sowing in autumn as well as spring a succession of bloom may be had throughout the summer; there are two varieties, one with deep scarlet and the other with bright rose flowers. *L. narbonnese* is also very good and gives a copious supply of large light-blue flowers, beautifully veined. *L. flavum* is a smaller but hardy plant with flowers of a peculiarly soft hue of yellow.

LIPS, to remove stains. Rub on a little diluted lemon juice or cold cream to remove fruit or nut stains.

LIQUOR STAINS, to remove. When white material is stained with wine, let it stand in boiled milk two or three minutes. Then rub the stains gently.

LIVER. To prevent liver from becoming hard when fried, when it is raw put each slice into a saucerful of milk and then straight out of the milk into boiling fat. It will cook deliciously tender and the milk can be used in the gravy.

LIVER À LA FRANÇAISE (for 5 or 6 people).

1 lb. calf's or sheep's liver	2 teaspoonfuls ketchup
¼ lb. bread-crumbs	1 teaspoonful Worcester sauce
½ lb. rashers	¼ teaspoonful herbs
3 or 4 mushrooms	1 teaspoonful chopped parsley
stock or water	salt and pepper

Well wash the liver and cut it into neat slices, lay these on a greased baking-tin; wash, dry and chop the mushrooms, mix them with the crumbs, parsley and season nicely. Lay a little of this mixture on each slice of liver, cover with a thin slice of bacon, pour round some stock or water, and bake in a moderate oven for three-quarters of an hour. Place the liver on a hot dish, add the sauces to the stock, boil up and pour round the liver; serve very hot.

LIVER AND BACON, FRIED (for 5 or 6 people).

1 lb. calf's liver	little flour
½ lb. rashers	salt and pepper

Prepare the rashers and fry lightly, well cleanse the liver, cut it in slices, coat well with flour and fry in the bacon fat, place on a hot dish with the bacon round, put the remainder of flour in the frying-pan, brown it carefully, add some stock or water gradually, boil up, season and strain over the liver.

LIVER, SLUGGISH, remedy for.

Boil 1 oz. freshly-sliced dandelion root in 1 pint of water, simmer until reduced to half the quantity, and add ½ oz. compound tincture of horse-radish. Use occasionally.

LOBELIA.

This dainty plant may be roughly divided into three classes—the compact or dwarf kind, the free-growing, spreading kind, and the tall perennials. It is the dwarf kind which is chiefly used for "bedding-out", being sown in winter under glass and transplanted into boxes until sufficiently established for "bedding-out". The spreading varieties are raised for filling hanging baskets and providing edging for window-boxes. Various shades of blue as well as white may be had in both these kinds—*Grandiflora* and *Magnifica*, *Prima Donna* (a red variety), *Speciosa*. Fine examples of the tall perennials are *L. syphilitica* (blue) and *L. cardinalis* (red) and they are very valuable for the garden as autumn flowers. But they are only fairly hardy and need some protection during the winter. Therefore lift them after flowering and store them in a dry place till spring. Lobelias need a rich, free soil and plenty of water during the summer.

LOBSTER, to boil.

Add 1 large handful of salt to boiling water and boil again. Throw in the lobster and boil from a quarter to three-quarters of an hour according to size.

LOBSTER AU GRATIN (for 4 people).

1 lobster or ½ a tin	1 egg
2 small shallots	1 tablespoonful chopped
1 oz. butter	parsley
1 oz. flour	little anchovy essence
½ pint milk	salt, cayenne

Chop lobster into small pieces, lightly fry the chopped shallot in the butter, add the flour and cook, then the milk, simmer for 5 minutes, put in lobster, parsley, anchovy essence, salt and cayenne. Stir till it boils, cool and add the well-beaten egg; grease some scallop shells, fill with the mixture, sprinkle over some bread-crumbs and pour over a little melted butter. Brown in the oven and serve very hot.

LOBSTER CUTLETS (for 6 people).

1 lobster or small tin	lemon juice
1 oz. flour	salt and pepper
1 oz. butter	egg and bread-crumbs
1 gill milk	parsley

167

Cut open lobster, crack the claws, take out the meat and chop it finely; make a roux with the flour and butter, add the milk in which the shells have been simmered, add the lobster meat, lemon juice, salt and pepper. Put the mixture on a wet plate, divide it into equal portions and allow to cool. Form into cutlet shapes, coat with egg and bread-crumbs; fry a golden brown in hot fat. Place a small piece of claw in each cutlet as a bone; place the head in the centre of the dish on a bed of fried parsley and place the cutlets round. If tinned lobster is used, a croûton of fried bread can take the place of the head, to support the cutlets.

LOBSTERS AND CRABS, to choose. The heavy medium-sized ones are the best. Fresh shell fish are never sticky or clammy. To test a lobster, the tail should be tightly pressed against the body; if it does not spring back sharply when pulled out straight with the fingers it should not be used.

LOCKJAW.

Symptoms.—These generally occur within ten days after microbic infection. The muscles of the neck and jaw become stiff and there is difficulty in opening the mouth and chewing food. Next the other muscles of the body gradually stiffen and the spine becomes arched backwards. By this time the jaws are firmly clenched and cannot be opened, the muscles of the chest are affected, and breathing becomes very difficult. Spasms occur more and more frequently as the diseases progresses and the patient finally dies of suffocation.

Treatment.—The treatment is entirely surgical and a doctor should be consulted immediately the first symptoms appear.

LOGANBERRY. Plant 5 feet apart in October in a deep, rich loam which is moist but well drained. Thin out the clumps in June, cutting away all but about half a dozen young shoots which should be fastened to supports such as trellis work or wire fencing. Cut away old branches after the fruit has been gathered and tie up the new shoots in their place.

LOGANBERRY JAM. *See* JAM, RASPBERRY.

LONDON PRIDE. A most useful perennial for border edgings with spikes of pink florets, making beautiful compact masses in the wild garden when grown in natural clumps. Will grow in almost any soil and needs little attention. It rapidly increases by offset suckers, and so should be reduced severely.

LOVE-IN-A-MIST. *See* NIGELLA.

LOVE-LIES-BLEEDING. *See* AMARANTHUS.

LOW FEVER. *See* AGUE.

LUCKY DAYS. Days of good fortune are considered to be connected with the month of birth. Thus:

Monday.—For those born during June, July.

Tuesday.—For those born during March, April, August, November.

Wednesday.—For those born during May, June.

Thursday.—For thos born during February, March, November, December.

Friday.—For those born during April, May, September, October.

Saturday.—For those born during January, February, December.

Sunday.—For those born during July, August.

LUMBAGO, to relieve.   Wring out a flannel dipped in scalding water, sprinkle it with spirits of turpentine and apply to the affected parts. It is also effective to apply a belladonna plaster.

LUMP OF SUGAR.   When you put away your best teapot put a lump of sugar in it—then it will never get musty.

LUNARIA (HONESTY).   A charming old-fashioned plant—a biennial—very useful for the wild garden or for rough banks, where its white or purple blossoms and flat silvery seed-pods may be made very effective; while if the branches bearing these seed-pods be cut at maturity and dried in the sun they form excellent indoor decoration.   Seed should be sown in spring or early summer and the seedlings thinned out so as to ensure strong plants for the following year.   Its natural soil is chalky ground, but is it perfectly hardy and will thrive almost anywhere.

LUPIN (LUPINUS).   As a hardy annual the lupin is a most useful flower, having a large range of colour and being quite easy of culture, while the perennial and tree kinds are valuable for the wild garden, and for rough, sandy banks, as they will thrive in a poor soil.   After blooming cut the stems down and mulch.   The *Russell* varieties have a wide range of delicate colours.

LYCHNIS (CAMPION).   A hardy perennial. *L. chalcedonica* is from 18 inches to 2 feet high and bearing large dense heads of bright-scarlet flowers; there is a white variety, but it is not so good.   *L. grandiflora* is a handsome plant (with several varieties) bearing fine clusters of large flowers with fringe-like edgings, and varying in colour through many shades of red to white.   All do well in a warm situation and on a light soil.   They may be raised either from seed or cuttings, and are improved by occasional transplanting.   In addition, is *L. lagascae*, a charming little plant for the Alpine garden, profuse in flowers of a bright-rose colour; it thrives best in a sandy soil and sunny position.   It is easily raised from seed.

MACARONI CHEESE (for 3 or 4 people).

2 oz. macaroni	2 oz. cheese
1½ oz. butter	few bread-crumbs
1 oz. flour	salt and cayenne
½ pint milk	

Cook the macaroni in fast-boiling water with some salt for 20 to 30 minutes.   Drain it and cut in inch lengths.   Make a sauce, using the ounce of butter, flour and the milk, add 1½ oz. of grated cheese, season well; add the macaroni and place in a greased dish; sprinkle over a few bread-crumbs, the remainder of the cheese, and put some small pieces of butter on top.   Brown nicely in the oven.

MACARONI, SAVOURY (for 3 or 4 people).

¼ lb. small macaroni	½ pint tomato sauce
¼ lb. cooked ham or tongue	brown bread-crumbs
1 oz. butter	salt and pepper

Boil the macaroni till tender in water with salt, drain and cut into inch lengths; melt the butter in a stewpan, add the ham or tongue cut in shreds, pour in the tomato sauce and put in the macaroni, season well. Put the mixture in a buttered fireproof dish, sprinkle over a few brown bread-crumbs, bake for 10 minutes in a hot oven and serve.

MACAROONS.

½ lb. ground almonds	whites of 3 eggs
½ lb. castor sugar	little vanilla essence

Whisk the whites of eggs very stiffly, add the almonds, sugar and a little vanilla essence. Put the mixture into a forcing-bag and force on to rice paper in small rounds. Put a piece of almond on each, sprinkle with sugar. Bake in a cool oven until set.

MACHINING. When machining georgette, chiffon, etc., the machine will behave much better if thin white paper is stitched under the work. It will not then draw up.

When machining materials which contain lime, such as calicoes, first rub the material with soap where the seams are to be formed. This will prevent mis-stitches.

MACKEREL, BOILED (for 6 or 7 people).

4 mackerel
salt
parsley or fennel sauce

Open the fish just enough to take out the roe, thoroughly cleanse the fish and the roe and replace it; remove the eyes. Place into salted water just below boiling point, simmer 8 to 10 minutes according to the size, taking care not to break the skin, which will happen if cooked too fast. Dish on a folded napkin, garnish with lemon and parsley and serve with parsley or fennel sauce.

MACKEREL, SOUSED. Lay fish in a dish lengthways; season with salt, whole pepper, allspice and chopped onion. Cover with vinegar and water and bake for about half an hour.

MACKEREL AU GRATIN. Cleanse fish well, dry in a cloth. Cut off heads and tails and open them down the back. Remove bones and take out dark brown portion near the head. Chop up small bunch of chives, add to it some chopped parsley, 1 dessertspoonful of bread-crumbs, 1 teaspoonful of mixed herbs, pepper and salt and a few drops of lemon juice. Sprinkle mixture on inner part of one mackerel and lay the other on it. Put the fish in a greased tin. Lay bits of dripping here and there upon them and bake in a moderate oven for half an hour basting occasionally with dripping. Lift carefully upon a hot dish and serve.

MACKINTOSHES. These should not be hung up when not in use, but after being dried should be brushed and folded and put in a drawer. They will last three times as long.

170

MADELINES (to fill 8 darioles).

2 eggs	jam
their weight in butter	2 oz. desiccated coconut
sugar	glacé cherries
flour	carmine colouring

Make mixture as for cup puddings; bake for 20 minutes in a quick oven. Make a tablespoonful of jam hot, add a drop or two of carmine to improve the colour, brush over the cakes and roll them in desiccated coconut; place a glacé cherry on the top. If served hot pour round some jam sauce, coloured nicely; if served cold, on a glass dish with a lace paper.

MAGNESIA, a remedy for acidity of the stomach.

Children.—Under twelve; 5 to 12 grains.

Adults.—20 to 30 grains.

Taken in a little milk or water.

MAHOGANY, to clean. The best liquids for cleaning mahogany are hot beer and hot tea. Either liquid will remove all signs of grease and leave the surface ready for polishing. *See also* STAINS, to remove from mahogany.

MAHOGANY, white spots on. Spread a thick coating of vaseline over the spots, leave it for 48 hours, and when you wipe it off you will find the spots are gone.

MAIDENHAIR. *See* ADIANTIFOLIUM.

MALLOW. *See* LAVATERA *also* MALOPE.

MALOPE. The annual variety of mallow is hardy and will flower freely in summer from a sowing in the open ground in April and May. Sow thinly in a sunny spot. The height is 1 to 3 feet, and the growth fairly upright. The flowers are violet, crimson or pink, or white. They prefer a heavy soil. The Tree Mallow is described under Lavatera.

MANNERS, or ETIQUETTE, when in a public place or vehicle. Frequent breaches of good manners are found in noisy laughter, exaggerated gesturing, loud talking, and the vulgar duscussion of private affairs in loud tones in bus or train; or in staring at passing pedestrians or fellow-passengers, perhaps drawing attention to some detail of their appearance or some peculiarity by nudging a companion, making whispered or audible remarks, giggling or directing obvious glances at the person who has been unfortunate enough to attract their ill-bred attention:

Amongst those guilty of breaches of etiquette in public we find;

1. Persons of both sexes who walk several abreast along the pavement so that other pedestrians are forced into the road when passing them, or who carry sticks and umbrellas so carelessly as to annoy other people.
2. Persons of both sexes who hustle unfairly to get on crowded public vehicles or push into them arrogantly while others are alighting.

3. People who will talk during concert, theatre and broadcasting performances, and those who at the cinema disclose the unfolding of the plot.

In these days of sex equality, let us leave it that it is a kindly, chivalrous act on a gentleman's part to vacate his seat, and the lady should accept it as such with a graceful word of thanks.

It is always correct for a gentleman to offer an unknown lady little courtesies as holding open a door for her to pass through, picking up an umbrella, parcel, bag or anything she may drop, merely saying, "Allow me," and raising his hat, not presuming on the action as a means to acquaintance. A word of thanks from the lady closes the incident.

When walking with a lady the gentleman's place is on the outside, also in pressing through a dense crowd where two cannot walk abreast, he takes the lead, she closely following, both out of doors or when entering a public place of entertainment.

Don't be niggardly over simple little words of apology if you know you have inadvertently caused annoyance to any other member of the public.

A gentleman should alight first from a vehicle, then offer his hand to the lady, or hand her into a vehicle before himself entering.

A gentleman always raises his hat when greeting or parting from ladies of his acquaintance, or when he is with either a lady or gentleman who offers recognition to another lady, though she be a stranger to him, or if he is greeted by a gentleman friend who raises his hat in respect of his own companion, but upon meeting a lady of his acquaintance he should wait for her to offer the first sign of recognition, especially upon a first meeting after being introduced to her, or when they are only slightly acquainted.

MANTELPIECES, MARBLE. Dissolve 1 oz. of soda in a ¼ pint of water, and add to it enough whiting to make a paste. Rub this compound well into the article to be cleaned, and when dry wash it off with clean water.

MANURING. On light and free working soil it is advisable to apply stable or farmyard manure in the spring in a partially-decayed condition, when it can be lightly dug in. On heavy and sticky soils, however, it is best to apply "strawy" manure at the autumn digging. When this is done the action of the weather makes the surface of the soil friable and suitable for seed-sowing in the spring.

"Strawy" manure improves the texture of heavy soils, increases the warmth, and makes them easier to work. It renders all soils more retentive of moisture.

Since the increase of mechanical transport stable manure is scarce and to some extent this is replaced by providing humus or decayed vegetable matter in the soil. All decayed vegetable matter except cabbage stalks and potato haulms should be kept in a heap or pit. Wood ash, soot and poultry, droppings are also valuable manures. *See* COMPOST.

Closely allied to manuring is the changing of positions for vegetable crops. Vegetables should be arranged in groups, and one crop, or group of crops, should be followed by another making somewhat different demands on the soil, and leaving the soil in best condition for the next crop. This will keep the soil in a better balanced condition, improve the quantity and quality of the crop. *See* ROTATION.

For artificial manures, *see* FERTILIZERS.

MARBLE, to remove smoke stains. Make a paste of equal parts of whiting, washing soda and chalk. Rub it well into the stained places and allow to dry. Afterwards wash over with cold water.

MARBLE, ARTIFICIAL, to make. Soak some plaster of Paris in a solution of alum. Bake it in an oven and then grind to a powder. When using, mix with water, and to produce the clouds and veins of marble stir in any dry colour you desire. The mixture will become very hard, and may be very highly polished.

MARGUERITE. The marguerite family is large and has many different names. The tall, large, white daisy with yellow centre is popularly known as the marguerite, and it grows freely making a grand show in the herbaceous border. Increase by shoots or cuttings in spring or autumn. It likes a sunny position and is not particular as to soil.

MARIGOLDS (CALENDULA). Marigolds love a sunny position, are well able to sustain drought, and will thrive in a poor soil. Sow under glass in March and plant out in the usual way.

MARJORAM. *See* HERBS.

MARKS ON POLISHED TABLE, to remove. If the table has white marks due to hot plates, etc., rub with camphorated oil. This will remove the marks.

MARKS, WHITEWASH, to remove from furniture, floors, windows, etc. Rub the marks with a soft cloth slightly damped with paraffin.

MARMALADE.

12 Seville oranges	2 lemons

Cut up the fruit into four parts, remove pips and slice finely. To each pound of pulp add 3 pints of water. Stand for 24 hours; then boil till clear and tender. Stand for a further 24 hours. To each pound of fruit and liquid add 1¼ lb. lump sugar. Boil (stirring constantly) until the syrup jellies.

MARMALADE, LEMON. Slice thinly any number of lemons and remove the seeds, but take care to leave in all the white pith as this helps to form the syrup. Add 3 pints of cold water to each pound of sliced fruit and stand for 24 hours. Boil until the chips are tender and then stand it in an earthenware jar until next day. Add 1½ lb. lump sugar to each pound of pulp and boil the whole together until the syrup jellies and the chips are almost transparent.

MARMALADE, ORANGE. Cut the rind of the oranges (Sevilles) into very thin strips, remove the pulp, take out the pips. To every pound of rind and pulp add 3 pints of cold water and allow to soak for 24 hours. Put it into a preserving pan and boil till tender. Then weigh it and to every pound add ³/₄ of a pound of sugar. Boil and skim.

To test when done put some on a saucer in a cool place. If it jellies, remove it. To 1 dozen oranges use 2 lemons, or 4 if preferred, cut in the same way.

MARRIAGE.

The Trousseau.—The provision of the trousseau is entirely the affair of the bride and her people.

A bridal gown is no longer necessarily all white, while the wearing of a veil or a more elaborate style of headdress is also optional.

The bride who is married in her going-away dress wears a hat.

Wedding Presents.—Presents are often given by intimate friends and relations from the time the engagement is an understood thing, but it is after receiving invitations to the wedding that the generality of people send their gifts.

Each gift should bear the sender's name and good wishes, and the cards upon which they are written should be saved in readiness for placing upon the various articles when they are displayed at the wedding reception.

The bride-elect must promptly acknowledge all presents sent to her home, whether sent to herself by her own friends or to herself and her fiancé, or received by her from friends of other members of her family, even though the donors are not personally known to her. She must not relegate this duty to anyone else.

Gifts for the bridegroom from his own friends are sent to his address, but afterwards removed to the bride's home to be shown with hers.

Presents should be sent as soon as possible after an invitation is received.

The Home.—Formerly it was an understood rule that the bride contributed all the linen for her new home, but that understanding no longer holds good. Strictly speaking, it is now the rule for the bridegroom to provide the entire home, complete in every detail, but it is often disregarded, bride and bridegroom both contributing their share of the household goods.

Expenses.—Doubt sometimes exists as to who pays the various expenses connected with a wedding.

The bride's parents provide the flowers for the church and house decorations; the car in which she drives to the church (and any which may be provided for guests or bridesmaids) and they bear the whole cost of the reception.

The bridegroom provides his own conveyance to the church, that in which he and his newly-made wife drive from the church to the reception, and the one in which they afterwards leave for the honeymoon.

He buys the wedding-ring, also the bouquets for the bride and her maids. Usually he gives each bridesmaid some little souvenir, such gifts being sent to their respective homes the evening before the wedding.

From his pocket come the fees for the clergyman and any other fees or "tips" connected with the ceremony.

The Bridegroom.—When the bride wears a bridal toilette, the correct dress for the groom is a morning coat, trousers with a pin stripe, grey tie, silk hat, white spats and grey gloves—and a white buttonhole—but in the event of a quiet wedding when the bride is married in her going-

174

away dress or an afternoon frock, a lounge suit and soft hat are quite suitable garb for the bridegroom.

The bridegroom should see beforehand, and in good time to comply with legal requirements, that all matters relating to notification of the marriage ceremony are complete and in order according to the form by which it is to be solemnized, especially in the case of a church wedding, making sure that the vicar or officiating minister and church officers are correctly informed as to the date and hour.

It is advisable, too, for the groom to arrive early at the church that he may go first to the vestry and give the clerk a note of all the particulars required for entry in the register, thus saving the delay occasioned if such details have to be discussed and submitted after the ceremony.

Amongst the necessary particulars are the bride's names in full, whether spinster or widow, and full names, and occupation of her father.

The bridegroom should of course go thoroughly into all the business details of the eventful day with his best man, giving him instructions concerning all arrangements to be made for the ceremony and afterwards, and also hand him a sufficient sum of money to cover the fees and tips, which he will pay for him, also train or car fares or anything else which the best man will disburse in his name.

One "best girl" may attend the bride, but of course it is very bad form for any friends and relations to show resentment if a bride is unable to single them out for the honour.

The Chief Bridesmaid.—The chief bridesmaid often helps the bride in various ways before the eventful day, but when that arrives her official duties begin and she should, if circumstances permit, be early with her friend to help her in dressing and in every possible way afterwards.

Later, in the church porch, she, with the other maids, awaits the bride's arrival, and they follow her up the aisle.

During the ceremony her place is behind the bride, on the left, the other bridal attendants grouped behind her, and she holds herself in readiness, to take the bride's gloves and bouquet, then later helps her, if necessary, to put her gloves on again, to adjust her veil, or render any other little service before the bridal party again faces the congregation after the visit to the vestry; then upon the bride's return home for the reception she remains watchful for any little attention her friend may need, finally going with her to assist in the change from bridal toilette to going-away frock.

The Bride's Mother.—An approaching wedding makes many demands on the time and attention of the bride's mother—the details of the trousseau and her own toilette, attending to correspondence and sending out the invitations, giving a dinner or other parties in celebration of the engagement, entertaining guests who are staying with her for the wedding, arranging for the music and floral decorations, catering for the wedding breakfast or reception and setting out the presents in the room where the reception will be held.

Sending out the invitations is by card, printed in the following manner:

Mr. and Mrs. Dash
request the pleasure of

. . . .

company on the occasion of
the marriage of their daughter
Elsa Mary
with
Major John Blank,
at St. Paul's, Knightsbridge,
on Thursday, 30th May,
at 2.30 o'clock,

and afterwards at

200 Portmyn Square, W.

R.S.V.P.

The bride's mother may either hand a number of the cards to the bridegroom's mother, so that she may invite his relations and friends, or a list of them may be given to the bride's mother that she may send these invitations out with her own. It is diplomatic so far as possible to post all invitations at the same time.

The Best Man.—The best man must take the bridegroom right under his wing, seeing that he does not forget anything.

He will see that he is irreproachably "turned out", to relieve him if need arises of any last-minute worries or the sending of messages, assist with the final details of packing; above all to make sure he has not mislaid the ring or forgotten any smallest matter connected with the day's arrangements, then see that they start off in good time for the church, where they will stand to the side of the chancel steps and await the coming of the bride.

During the ceremony the best man stands on the right of the bridegroom, a little to the rear, taking care of his hat and gloves, and also having charge of the ring, which he must produce without any fumbling at the right moment, and at the conclusion of the ceremony he goes with the bridal party into the vestry to sign the register, probably escorting the chief bridesmaid who is, by the way, regarded as his special partner during the festivities.

The best man takes all business details off his friend's shoulders, paying the clergyman's fees and giving any necessary tips.

He sees the bridal pair into their carriage or car when they leave the church, also the bride's parents, then drives off with the chief bridesmaid and any of her companions for whom there is room.

At the reception he should be helpful and agreeable to all and sundry, and if toasts are proposed he responds to that of the bridesmaids. He attends the bridegroom during his final preparations for going away, is responsible for the punctual arrival of the car, sees that the luggage is not forgotten and generally does his best to ensure the bridal pair a cheery send-off, without any hitches.

If they have a railway journey he may be asked to accompany them to the station to relieve them of all anxiety concerning the tickets (procured in advance) or the labelling and stowing away of luggage and finding the reserved seats for the journey, then he returns to the house and helps to speed the departing guests.

MARRIAGE FORMS. In the Church of England there are three forms of marriage: by publication of banns; by ordinary licence; by special licence.

Banns must be published prior to the marriage for three consecutive Sundays in the parish church of the parish in which the parties reside. If they live in different parishes, the banns must be published in each. The marriage must take place within three months or the banns have to be read again.

At least a week before the first Sunday on which it is wished that the banns should be read, written notice must be given to the incumbent of the parish, or of each parish, as the case may be. This notice must give the Christian and surnames of both parties, their address in the parish, or respective parishes, their age and condition (bachelor, spinster, and widower or widow).

Marriage by banns can only be solemnized in one of the churches at which the banns have been published and the ceremony must be performed between the hours of 8 a.m. and 6 p.m. The presence of two responsible witnesses is required.

An ordinary licence is an authority granted by a bishop for a marriage to be solemnized without publication of banns. Any vicar—if not himself a surrogate licensed to issue an ordinary licence—will give information where application should be made. Either prospective bride or groom must in person swear before the surrogate that there is no lawful cause for impediment of the marriage; that one of the contracting parties has for the fifteen days immediately preceding lived in the parish; that—should either of the parties be under age—the consent of parents or guardians has been obtained.

A licence obtained from the Faculty Office or the Vicar-General's office is available in any diocese.

A special—or Archbishop's—licence is an authority granted in special cases by the Archbishop of Canterbury only, and allows the marriage to be solemnized at any time or place.

In a Nonconformist Church.—A certificate of notice to marry—obtained from a superintendent-registrar of marriage—is the civil form which may be used instead of publication of banns or a bishop's licence.

Notice for obtaining the certificate must be given to the superintendent-registrar of the district in which the contracting parties have resided for at least seven days immediately before—or for at least fifteen days when a licence is required. In cases where the parties live in different districts and the marriage is not to be by licence, such notice must be given to the registrar of each district. A certificate of notice takes twenty-one clear days, not including Sundays and Bank Holidays, to obtain and a certificate with licence only one clear day after the notice.

The marriage may take place in any church—not Church of England —within the district of the superintendent-registrar issuing the certificate, in the same manner as after publication of banns, or in any building lawfully certified as a place of religious worship and registered for the solemnization of marriages.

Before a Registrar.—The marriage for which the certificate or licence has been obtained may, if wished, take place at the office of the superintendent-registrar before the registrar and two witnesses. This is an increasing custom as it dispenses with much formality.

MARRIAGE OF WIDOW. When a widow marries again she may have a full choral service, and church decorations, but she does not wear an all-white gown, a veil or orange blossoms. In any case a hat is worn. If a bouquet is carried it should not be an all-white one.

A widow may be married in church without anyone to give her away. She does not have bridesmaids, but may be attended by some friend or be accompanied by a small son or daughter.

A widow removes her first wedding-ring before going to the church. Whether she then discards it altogether or not is a matter for individual preference.

MARSHMALLOW.

whites of 2 eggs	4 oz. icing sugar

Thoroughly whisk the whites of the eggs for a few minutes, then gradually add the sugar, which should have been previously carefully sifted through a fine sieve. Continue whisking until the mixture is of a fairly firm consistency. This is usually flavoured with vanilla, or other essence before use.

MARZIPAN.

½ lb. ground almonds	1 lb. icing sugar
2 eggs	1 teaspoonful orange flower water

Rub the sugar through a sieve and add the almonds and orange water. Whip the whites of 2 fresh eggs to a froth with a pinch of salt and add to the mixture. Beat up with a wooden spoon until thoroughly mixed. Form into fruits as required next day. Other fruits may be made by using cloves, cochineal, angelica, etc.

MASCOTS. The word "mascot" is quite modern, at least in English, the older words with the same meanings being Talisman, Amulet and Sigil, the latter being a sentence or other writing which, generally written in red, warded off threatening trouble.

The rules governing the beliefs in mascots—to use the modern name—were written down when the world was young and in nearly every instance contain a great and lofty thought.

No mascot bought for one's own use can be a bringer of good fortune. To endow its possessor with happiness and health, a mascot must come as the gift of a friend or as token of gratitude or reward for a good deed. Seen in that light, even the most crude mascot possesses something of dignity and beauty.

No mascot will bring good fortune to one who is unworthy.

No mascot must be allowed to touch the ground. If it falls inadvertently, its virtue will have gone from it for a time.

Mascots, as a rule, have the greater power if worn on the left side.

Somewhat roughly all charms and mascots may be divided into three categories: those that concern love, those that bring health, and those which help to worldly success or guard against any evil.

There are mascots of all kinds, from the regimental mascot, the motorist's mascot, to the more personal one worn about the body. Of the last there are a great number, considered to possess special virtues and potency. The more popular are:

178

Bells.—Powerful against all forms of evil, particularly for the young, the helpless and weak. Until quite recent years the Chinese soldiers went into battle ringing bells. The wind bells which hang from their pagodas are another form of the same charm; while their priests rang bells at the time of an eclipse.

Cats.—If any cat, especially a black one, comes to the house, it will bring good fortune so long as it is fed and well treated. To hurt a cat or to drive away one that asks your help is a sure method of attracting disaster.

A cat with double claws is the greatest luck-bringer of all, and should be most carefully guarded and protected.

Coins.—Ancient coins bore mystic inscriptions and therefore were luck bringers. Thus the idea of the "lucky coin" began, and the spinning of a coin by opposing teams in sport is its survival. There is an old belief that good luck will be attracted to any house if a few copper coins are kept in the kitchen.

Frogs.—Small frogs in gold or gilt metal are charms worn to hasten recovery from any illness, or to win friendship.

Heather.—Perhaps because of its comparative rareness, a sprig of white heather is a symbol of good fortune, and if a wish is in the mind at the moment the heather is seen that wish will be granted.

Jochebed.—The name of the mother of Moses is a popular talisman in the East. The word written on a small scroll and hung round the neck averts ill fortune, while if the name is repeated aloud several times it brings back things that have been lost and reveals secrets.

Key.—The modern mascot in the shape of a key is given as a token of lasting love... symbolical of locking the door of the heart against other influences.

Merrythought.—The "wish bone" or "merrythought" of any fowl is a well-known mascot, and its use as a means of telling whether wishes will come true is a very ancient form of divination. Little "merrythoughts" in gold or silver are included in bunches of charms, though it is possible their virtue as luck bringers lies in their horseshoe-like shape.

Owl.—The owl is a greatly wronged bird, since its hooting is taken as an omen of misfortune in many parts of the country. Yet it was the bird of Minerva and the symbol of wisdom. Mascots made in its likeness give success in anything requiring study.

Pigs.—The idea that a pig is a mascot is widespread. The Chinese say little pigs made of either gold or silk bring good fortune in trade. In Ireland they tell you that a pig mascot is only fortunate after it has been slightly broken.

Robin.—Wherever a robin appears he is a sign of good fortune, which also applies to such a mascot.

Tortoise.—Mascots in this shape are worn on the East as protection from the Evil Eye and to assure long life.

MASSAGE. If properly carried out, massage is a valuable curative agent, it hastens the flow of blood and fluids, stimulates the muscle, skin and nerves, and thus restores muscular fitness.

A limb should be massaged at the part farthest away from the body and the manipulations extended upwards towards the trunk.

Friction consists of rubbing with the tip of the finger in an upward direction. The wasted muscles are grasped and rolled between the finger and thumb, small portions only being taken up at a time. The part may be stroked with the palm of the hand in an upward direction, each hand being used alternately. The muscles may be tapped with the fingers, or the little finger side of the half-closed hand. The dry hand should be used without any oil, ointment or other lubricants.

MATTRESS, RUSTY. *See* RUSTY MATTRESS.

MAYONNAISE DRESSING.

2 yolks of eggs	1 tablespoonful tarragon
1 gill salad oil	vinegar
½ teaspoonful mustard	1 tablespoonful cream
1 tablespoonful vinegar	salt and cayenne

Place two yolks in a basin, add salt and mustard, stir in the oil drop by drop to prevent curdling. When all the oil is in, stir in the vinegar in the same way; add the cream last of all. This sauce will keep some time if kept air-tight and in a cool place.

MEADOW SAFFRON. *See* COLCHICUM.

MEASLES. Measles is specially catching before the rash appears, and whilst the rash is out. Isolate the patient. It is a malady to watch, because of the possible after-effects.

Ten or eleven days after infection the child has fever, loses its appetite, is sleepy and out of sorts; sometimes it starts with vomiting and chill, or there may be convulsions. The eyes become inflamed and watery. There is a discharge from the nose and cough with expectoration. The fever goes down a little; on the third or fourth day the rash appears. The fever goes up again during the rash, but subsides as it goes away. The rash comes out first on the face, forehead and behind the ears. It consists of raised dark red spots in patches, which run together, and leave parts of the skin unaffected. The face is swollen and blotchy. The rash spreads irregularly to the body and limbs. In about three days it is at its height. It then commences to fade, leaving the skin mottled and brown, and later on the skin looks as if it had been dusted with fine bran.

The patient should be put to bed in a warm, ventilated room, and whilst the eyes are watering the blinds should be down, the bed being placed so that the light from the window does not fall on the face. The cough is the most troublesome symptom, and may turn into severe bronchitis. Two or three drops of ipecacuanha wine every four hours will relieve this. The diet should consist principally of milk whilst the fever lasts. The milk may be thickened with cornflour or arrowroot.

If the fever is high and the child restless the body may be sponged with tepid water. Pay particular attention to the eyes, which should be wiped periodically with a weak solution of boric acid. Bad cough and difficulty in breathing are bad signs and require special treatment. Discharge from the ear is best treated by gentle syringing with tepid Condy's fluid well diluted. The child may be allowed up three days after the fever has gone, but should not mix with other children for three weeks.

MEASLES, GERMAN. The rash appears on the first or second day instead of on the fourth as in the case of ordinary measles. The rash starts round the mouth, there may be slight sore throat, cold in the head and fever. ' Later the rash on the face resembles that of measles, but the body rash is like scarlatina (scarlet fever). It is therefore likely to give anxiety until the doctor has given his opinion. Isolate the patient and send for the doctor. *See* RASHES, to recognize diseases by.

MEASURES. Readers referring to recipes on this volume will find a table of simple equivalents and general measures under WEIGHTS AND MEASURES.

MEAT, to choose. Good meat is firm and not flabby; when pressed the mark quickly disappears. There is no disagreeable smell. It should be free from moisture. To test meat put in a skewer close to the bone and if it comes out clean and smells sweet the meat is in good condition. *See also* the respective meats: BEEF, MUTTON, PORK, etc.

MEAT, to keep fresh. To keep raw meat sweet run a little vinegar over a large dish, place two pieces of stick across, lay the joint on the sticks and the meat will keep fresh during the hottest weather. Flies are also prevented from attacking it as they dislike the smell of vinegar.

MEAT, BOILED, to make tender. Add a spoonful of vinegar to the water in which meat is boiled. This will help to make the meat tender.

MEAT CAKES (12).

½ lb. minced meat	salt and pepper
½ lb. cooked potatoes	egg and bread-crumbs
little stock	parsley

Mash the potatoes smoothly, add the minced meat and a little stock, mix well, season with salt and pepper, form into small flat cakes of even size, coat with egg and bread-crumbs, fry a golden brown in hot fat, drain on paper, dish in a circle on a hot dish with a fancy paper, and garnish with fried parsley. Serve with a good gravy.

MEAT, COLD, CURRIED. *See* CURRY.

MEAT, POTTED.

1½ lb. beef	2 cloves
½ lb. ham	blade of mace
2 oz. butter	salt and cayenne
pinch of cinnamon	½ pint stock

Cut up the beef and ham, removing all the skin, gristle and fat, put into a stewpan with the spices, cover with stock and stew very slowly till tender. Pass the meat through a mincing-machine twice, put it into a mortar, add the butter and season well and pound until smooth. Put into potted-meat jars and cover with clarified butter or mutton fat.

MEAT RISSOLES. *See* RISSOLES.

MEAT, TOUGH, to make tender. Soak tough meat for a few minutes in vinegar and water.

181

MEDICINE, hints as to giving. Read the label on the bottle. Shake the contents before pouring out. Measure the medicine in a marked glass. Medicines ordered three times a day should be given at 10 a.m., 2 p.m. and 6 p.m.; those to be given four times a day, at 8 a.m., at 12 noon, at 4 p.m. and 8 p.m. Take quinine before and iron after food. All poisonous mixtures must be kept in their original coloured bottles to prevent mistakes.

MEDICINE BOTTLES, to open. Many general medicines to-day are put up in bottles with screw caps which are often difficult to release. Dip the top of the bottle into hot water, or run hot water (not boiling) over the cap. It will then turn easily.

MEDICINE CHEST. A well-equipped medicine chest should contain the following: Boracic lint, medicated cotton-wool, bandages of various sizes, needle and cotton, antiseptic gauze, piece of oiled silk, adhesive tape or plaster in two sizes, medicine glass and measure, eye bath, glass syringe, clinical thermometer, 1 pair of scissors, 1 pair of forceps or tweezers, 1 bottle of iodine, a small supply of the most usual aperients, small quantity of ipecacuanha wine, sal volatile, sulphur, wintergreen, talcum powder, zinc and boracic ointments, any medicines which have been specially ordered by a doctor.

If any poisons are included in the contents of a medicine chest, these should be kept in a separate compartment, if at all possible, and clearly marked to warn anyone going to the chest of the fact that they are poisons. Liquid poisons are in coloured bottles and labelled "Poison." The chest should be kept locked when not in use, and the key should be hung either on the side of the chest itself, or on the wall quite near it.

MEDICINES, etc., the uses of the most common.

ALUM.—Piles, cuts, etc.
ACONITE OINTMENT.—Neuralgia.
ARNICA.—Bruises, sprains, rheumatism, etc.
BICARBONATE OF SODA.—Acidity, burns and scalds, flatulence, indigestion, palpitation of the heart, etc.
BORACIC ACID POWDER.—An antiseptic; for dusting wounds and for fomentations.
BRANDY.—A stimulant for faintness, etc.
CALOMEL.—An aperient.
CAMPHORATED OIL.—For external applications in chest colds, rheumatism of joints, sprains, etc.
CARBOLIC ACID.—A strong disinfectant (poison).
CARRON OIL.—Burns and scalds.
CASCARA.—An aperient.
CASTOR OIL.—An aperient.
CAMOMILE, INFUSION OF.—Tonic and stomachic. Emetic if taken warm.
EPSOM SALTS.—An aperient.
EUCALYPTUS OIL.—Colds and catarrh.
FRIAR'S BALSAM.—Colds, cuts, laryngitis, etc.
GLYCERINE.—Chapped hands, colds, coughs, sore throat, etc.
IODINE.—Antiseptic and for bruises, sprains, etc.

MEDICINES—*continued*

IPECACUANHA WINE.—A safe emetic.
MAGNESIA.—For acidity, constipation, etc.
MENTHOL.—For headaches.
OIL OF CLOVES.—For toothache or neuralgia.
OLIVE OIL.—For constipation.
PARAFFIN (MEDICATED or LIQUID).—For constipation.
PEPPERMINT.—For flatulence, colic, griping, etc.
QUININE.—For colds, fever, influenza, etc., and an excellent tonic.
QUININE, AMMONIATED TINCTURE OF.—For colds.
SAL VOLATILE.—A stimulant.
SEIDLITZ POWDER.—An aperient and for biliousness, etc.
SWEET OIL.—A safe antidote in cases of poisoning where cause
is unknown.
VASELINE.—For poultices, skin ailments, sores, etc.
VINEGAR.—For bruises, feverishness, etc.
WHITE OIL.—For sprains.
ZINC OINTMENT.—For skin complaints, sores, etc.

MEDICINE STAINS, to remove. When clothes are stained by the
contents of medicine bottles, a little ammonia will clean them.

MENINGITIS. *See* BRAIN, INFLAMMATION OF.

MENSTRUATION, SCANTY. A simple remedy is pennyroyal tea.
Plenty of exercise should be taken in the open air and hot rooms avoided.
Do not sleep too much. Just before the expected period place the feet
in warm water and take 2 cochiœ pills.

MENU, to arrange for a dinner. When giving a dinner the first
thing to be done is to arrange the menu. This requires both skill and
judgment, for upon this to some extent will depend the success of the
meal. For a complete dinner the courses are as follows:
Hors d'œuvres; Potages; Poissons; Entrées; Relevés; Rôti;
Entremets; Dessert; Café.
Sometimes one or more of the courses are omitted, as nowadays
long dinners are not the vogue, but the order of serving them remains
the same, and it is a good plan to have an alternative dish at one or
two of the courses. The service must be quick, but on no account
hurried.
In arranging a menu decide first what shall comprise the dinner
and then how it shall be dressed and served. Great care must always
be taken to avoid repetition, either with regard to material, colour,
garnishing or taste. Choose dishes which are in season, as they are
then at their best, and alternate the methods of cooking them. When
compiling a menu take note:
Hors d'oeuvres.—This is not, strictly speaking, a course. They are
usually served cold and should consist of highly-flavoured articles of
food, such as anchovies, olives, sardines, oysters, caviare, tiny salads,
marinaded herrings, etc.
Potages.—If two soups are served the clear should come before the
thick or purée. If only one is served a clear soup is preferable.
Poissons.—When two kinds of fish are included in the course one
may be plainly cooked (fried, grilled or broiled) and should be served

first. The second fish course may be dressed and should be in small portions, tastefully garnished. Great care should be taken to avoid sameness in composition and colour in the sauces.

Entrées.—The entrée is a "made" dish. It is invariably handed at the table, so that it is very necessary that it should be dished tastefully. If two entrées are served one should be brown and the other white. A light entrée should always precede a heavy and highly flavoured one, and hot entrées always be served before cold.

Relevés (or Removes).—This course constitutes the substantial part of the dinner and consists usually of a joint either boiled, roasted or braised. It is served from the sideboard or dinner wagon and the vegetables and correct accompaniments handed round. Two vegetables are sufficient. Sorbets (water ices) are served after this course.

Rôti or Roast.—This consists of poultry or game, either plainly roasted or otherwise prepared and dressed. The correct accompaniments should be sent to table with the dish, a salad is always served and usually potato chips.

Entremets.—This course is divided into three:

1. *A dressed vegetable,* which immediately follows the roast and is served as a separate course.

2. *Sweet entremets* served either hot or cold.

3. *A savoury.*—This precedes the dessert, is usually served hot and generally consists of cheese.

The dressed vegetable as a course is often omitted by English cooks, who know little as a rule of vegetable cookery, but it is a distinct feature in a French dinner, and is of more importance than the sweet course. It should consist of a choice vegetable in season, simply but well cooked and tastefully served so as to preserve its distinctive flavour. Great attention should be paid to the choice of sweets; they must be light and delicate, colour and taste well considered, and everything of a solid nature carefully avoided. They may be served hot or cold, but hot dishes should always precede cold ones. Ices may be included in this course or be served after with the dessert. The savoury which completes the dinner is generally served hot and more often than not includes cheese in its composition. It is invariably handed round and may be served in small portions, one for each guest, and should always be well flavoured and daintily dished.

MERINGUES.

4 whites of eggs	cream
8 oz. castor sugar	flavouring

Cut some strips of stiff white paper, rub them well with white wax, place them on a baking-sheet. Whip the whites of eggs very stiffly, then stir in the sugar as lightly as possible; put the mixture in a forcing-bag with a plain tube, force on to the prepared paper in egg shapes. Sift with icing sugar, bake in a slow oven till crisp; remove from the paper, scoop out carefully the soft part, place them the hollow side upwards and put back in the oven to dry. Fill with whipped and flavoured cream, joining two together.

184

MESSINA CROÛTES.

6 sardines	$\frac{1}{2}$ saltspoonful of dry mustard
yolks of 2 hard-boiled	2 tablespoonfuls chutney
eggs	$\frac{1}{2}$ teaspoonful lemon juice

Prepare some croûtes of fried bread. Skin sardines, pound them with the mustard, chutney, lemon juice, yolks and seasonings. Heap on the croûtes, cover with grated cheese, brown in the oven.

METAL POLISH. Steel, brass, and aluminium can be cleaned with the ashes from a burnt log. *See also* POLISH.

MICE AND RATS. The appearance of rats in a house is usually a sign of bad drainage, and this should receive immediate attention.

Ordinary poisons should not be placed in the holes because if the rats or mice die there, the result will be both unhealthy and unpleasant. Saturate some pieces of rag in pure carbolic acid and push them into the holes. The acid both kills the vermin by consuming the flesh and obviates the odours arising from decomposition. As a rule the presence of a cat in the house will be sufficient to prevent mice.

MICE AND RAT HOLES. Break some glass into small pieces, mix with plaster of Paris, and place it quickly in the holes. It must be used directly it is mixed into a paste, as it sets very quickly.

Hard soap may also be used for the same purpose.

MICE, WHITE, to feed. These animals may be fed upon nuts, wheat, oats, beans, peas and bread soaked in milk.

MICHAELMAS DAISY. Under this name is commonly known the perennial aster or starwort, a hardy, bush-like plant which may well find a place in our gardens not only because of the beauty of form and colour which the many varieties display, but also because of their blooming so late in the autumn. The best effect is achieved by allowing them to grow in masses and support each other. All varieties may be raised from seed in autumn for planting out in the spring. More often they are increased by division from outer shoots in spring.

MIGNONETTE. The delightful fragrance of this plant ensures its welcome. Of the various varieties, *Machet*, with its bold spikes of reddish-brown flowers, is a general favourite, especially as a pot-plant. For winter flowering indoors the seed should be sown about August in a compost of sandy loam and leaf-manure, taking care to sow thinly. For summer flowering sow in early May in a warm spot.

MILDEW, to remove. Rub the spots with soft soap mixed with powdered chalk. Lay in the sun to dry.

MILDEW, to remove from plants. Syringe either with a solution of 1 oz. nitre in 1 gallon water or with a mixture of sulphur and soap suds.

MILFOIL. *See* ACHILLEA.

MILK, HINTS AND HELPS. If milk looks like turning sour add to it a little bicarbonate of soda, enough to cover a sixpence for each pint of milk. Then boil the milk.

To keep milk sweet during the summer, add a little lime-water, about 2 teaspoonfuls to each pint of milk.

A lump of sugar in cream helps to keep it sweet.

When thunder is in the air, keep the milk in a bowl, and it will not turn so readily as in a taller vessel, such as a bottle or jug.

Make up sufficient waterglass as required to double strength (using only half the water stated on the tins). Place the mixture in a bowl and stand the milk jug in, taking care the mixture does not reach the top of the jug. The mixture will last through the summer and sweet milk can be assured on the hottest day.

To prevent milk boiling over, the edge of the saucepan should be rubbed with butter. Another means is to place an ordinary glass marble, thoroughly cleaned, in the pan along with the milk when being heated.

Boiling renders milk easier to digest, and kills the poisons of the various diseases that may have gained access to it. Milk should always be scalded; and if there is the slightest doubt with regard to its purity, it should be gently boiled for half an hour.

To test milk, place a bright steel knitting needle into the milk. If, on removal, the milk adheres and drips off slowly it is pure; but if it runs off leaving the needle bright, it is adulterated.

MILK, to use BURNT. *See* BURNT MILK.

MILK LEMONADE. Pour ½ pint boiling water over 1 tablespoonful of sugar, then add ½ gill each of sherry and lemon juice. Stir well until the sugar dissolves, adding ¾ pint cold milk. Again stir until the milk curdles. Strain through a cloth or jelly-bag.

MILK PUDDINGS. These cannot be cooked too slowly. If the milk boils the pudding spoils.

MILK SHORT AND COFFEE WANTED. Beat an egg very well and add to milk. Put into cups before coffee or it will curdle.

MIMOSA (ACACIA). The familiar mimosa of the florists is *Acacia dealbata*, and some of the rosy-flowered species are used for bedding-out for the backs of borders, or the tall-growing sorts which run to 10 to 16 feet are good for covering arches. They flower in summer, are planted out from pots and like a light, rich loam. The graceful, feathery foliage, of distinctive, grey-green colour, shows well, even if a cold summer prevents the golden blossom perfecting. Strike cuttings of half-matured wood with a "heel" in a hot-bed in July or August or sow the seed when ripe. Repot in September after blooming. The plants should be placed in a sheltered position in the open in summer. After flowering, cut back the straggling shoots.

MINCE, to prepare (for 5 or 6 people).

1 lb. cold meat	¾ pint stock
1 oz. butter or dripping	parsley
1 oz. flour	salt and pepper
1 shallot	

Pass the meat through a mincing-machine or chop it finely, make a sauce with the butter, flour and stock, adding the finely-chopped shallot or onion, boil it well, add the meat and seasoning; serve on a hot dish with a border of mashed potatoes, or sippets of toast or poached eggs, garnish with parsley.

MINCEMEAT.

1 lb. raisins	½ lb. Demerara sugar
1 lb. currants	1 teaspoonful cinnamon
1 lb. sultanas	¼ of a nutmeg
1 lb. apples	rind and juice of 2 lemons
½ lb. candied peel	2 tablespoonfuls orange mar-
½ lb. suet	malade
pinch of salt	¼ pint rum

Stone the raisins, chop the suet, peel and core the apples, wash the currants, chop all finely except the currants. Add these last with the sugar, spices, salt, marmalade and rum. Mix well together, put into jars, tie down and store in a dry place.

Note.—This quantity will make about 6 lb. mincemeat.

Brandy may be used instead of rum if preferred.

MINCE PIES.

mincemeat   flaky or puff pastry

Roll the pastry out to about a ¼ inch thickness, cut into rounds, line some patty tins with some of the rounds, brush round the edges with water, put in some mincemeat, place on a cover, press the edges together, work them up with a knife, brush with white of egg, sprinkle with castor sugar, and bake in a quick oven for about 20 minutes. Serve hot or cold.

MIRRORS, to clean. Add a little starch to the water when washing mirrors, windows and all kinds of glassware. It helps to remove the dirt and gives the glass a lasting polish.

A little spirits of camphor or alcohol rubbed on a mirror after the dust has been wiped off will brighten it, or you can rub the glass with a thin paste of powdered whiting and water; let it dry and wipe it off with a soft cloth or tissue paper.

Another method is to dip a clean duster in very little methylated spirits and rub thoroughly, taking care not to touch the frame. Polish with a soft dry cloth.

MONARDA DIDYMA (BEE BALM, SWEET BERGAMOT). A hardy perennial thriving in any soil, bearing whorls of deep red flowers which last a long time and attaining a height of about 2 feet; while *M. kalmania* is a still larger and more showy plant with flowers of brilliant crimson. In both cases the best effect is obtained by massing the plants together in bold groups.

MONTH BY MONTH IN GARDEN AND ALLOTMENT. Of the dozens of jobs always possible any day, at any time of the year in the garden or allotment, the following are the more imperative for the month indicated. *Note* that in northern districts and in bleak and exposed positions the work is better done a week or ten days later than in average temperatures, and that—so far as sowings are concerned—if cold winds persist it wastes no time to wait till it is a bit milder and heavy night frosts are over.

January. — Burn rubbish and vegetable stumps: wisdom in this prevents pests multiplying. Protect artichokes from frost. Prune fruit trees and top dress round about them. Protect roses with bunches of straw and bracken. Get on with digging, turn over if dug earlier, work in compost. Put in a few broad beans for early supply. Sow cauliflower in frame. Protect celery from frost. Plant out earliest cabbages. Examine stored potatoes, parsnips, carrots, etc.; throw out as needed.

February. —When not frosty do some deep digging, three spit trenching, and manure it in readiness for early peas and beans. Where soil is heavy, work in sand, wood ash, leaves (especially beech), fire ashes, to lighten in time for root crops. Prepare onion bed for sowing late in month. Plant shallots, divide chives; stir top soil of mint bed, trim runners to stop spreading unless more mint is wanted to grow. Make sowings of spinach, parsnips and early carrots if ground not too hard from frost. Start rhubarb under large pots. Get a hot-bed ready for hastening cauliflower seedlings. Spray roses and fruit tree buds. Sow sweet peas in warm corner for later transplanting. Look over seed potatoes. Clear up decayed rubbish; burn it. Make plans for garden lay-out and the rotation scheme for vegetables.

March. —Plant rose trees, make ground very firm. Sow tomatoes under glass. Pot rooted chrysanthemum cuttings. Trim up herbaceous border, pinching out weak new growth from perennials, stir and mulch ground around them. Plant out onion sets. Sow the hardier annuals and any new perennials. Get in early potatoes. Sow leeks. Give an eye to young peas, protect with ash, and put light twigs about to scare birds. Keep the weeds down or they will get you down. Slightly prune creepers, removing dead ends. Plant gladioli. Any new grass plot to be prepared and levelled, dug and raked to fine tilth for sowing as soon as frosts go. Strawberry runners should be laid for sprouting ends to root, cut off runners that show no new leaf. Raspberries that fruit in late summer should now be cut down to 6 inches, leaving a couple of buds; fresh shoots will grow in good time; canes planted in autumn will not fruit till following year. Pot on chrysanthemums, and where stock wants increasing take old clumps into greenhouse for hastening new shoots, which can be taken for cuttings. Roses should now be pruned if weather not bleak, the hybrid perpetuals not being cut too hard back.

April. —Plant out late-blooming lilies. Any fruit-tree grafting necessary ought to be done. Any new roses must not be planted later than first half of April, preferably first week. Sow most of vegetables now; if earlier sowings, put in more for succession. Put in a few more potatoes and make a sowing of carrots. Lawn mowing may now start or grass will get too long for easy work. Regular sowings of mustard and cress can start. Remember the value of the cold frame for sowings of annuals and half-hardy kinds, as well as for bringing along seedlings in protection from cold winds. The hardy annuals can be sown in open border where wanted to remain, thinning out later. Any repotting of perennials such as azaleas and other flowering shrubs ought to be done now. Do not forget to roll the lawn at intervals, the ground is not now too soft. Sow beetroot, globe and taper; also dwarf French beans. Keep the hoe going among the young plants before weeds get into vigour and stifle flowers or vegetables; as well keep the earth loose round new growth by using the hoe regularly. Plant out pansies and violas, trimming off dead growth from those which have survived the winter. Any lawn turving for renewals should be done not later than this mid-month. Main-crop vegetables can be sown and any thinning of earlier sowings should be kept in mind. Spray fruit trees and the larger shrubs. Paths can have attention for the summer tidiness, rolling, levelling, removing worked-up stones and regular weeding.

May.—The flower garden now demands close attention if fine plants are to develop. All annuals will be in vigorous growth, any weaklings can be sacrificed; allow plenty of growing space; tie up sappy shoots; watch out for insects; loosen soil round stems; give weak manure water; and where buds are showing pick off any showing blight or wither. The herbaceous border is in vigorous growth and some weaker shoots can be sacrificed, particularly the Michaelmas daisies; the flowering will be all the stronger. In the vegetable garden runner-beans can be put in, putting in the stakes at the same time, deeply enough to stand high winds. Sow vegetable marrow and cucumber in warm spots, seedlings of these raised earlier can be planted out if covered at nights to protect from frost, pots will do. Codlin-moth now starts to trouble; also American blight. Succession sowings of vegetables, roots and the lighter green stuff, as lettuce, can be made. Next year's perennials, wallflower, forget-me-nots, sweet-william and so on can now be sown and until mid-June, as well as biennials. Don't neglect the spraying of fruit trees. Spring flowering shrubs can be pruned when the blossom has died down. Manure rose trees.

June.—If the dahlias were not started last month do so now. Take the tubers from where stored for winter, put into good light soil mixed with sand, till the shoots are 4 inches high, lift gently, divide with a piece of tuber for each shoot, and plant in flowering quarters late in June, putting a few lettuce leaves about the spots to save them from slugs; they prefer the latter. Take advantage of a warm spell to clean out and fumigate the greenhouse. Herbaceous border plants could do with surface manuring, either liquid or one of the powder fertilizers. In the vegetable plot vigilance is needed to keep pests at bay with dustings of Derris powder or one of the special insecticides put up for particular plants or root crops. Do not overdo watering, but when done it should be thorough, a daily sprinkling is to be avoided; twice a week, well done, in average hot weather is better. Pinch out tomato shoots and, if in flower, shake blossom twice a week to aid pollination.

July.—Sow violas and pansies for next year, and a few more wall-flowers and some columbine to give a show for the spring. Layer carnations, pinning in with twigs, and do not allow to get dry. Particular attention must be given to pests both in flower borders and among the vegetables, destroying without mercy, or not only will this year's work be marred but the insects, etc., will increase beyond bounds next year. In the allotment there is plenty to do. Peas should be gathered as soon as the pods are full, else they toughen; picking also means a lengthening of the supply by allowing the late forming pods to mature. Plant out winter greens and sow for spring brassica. Celery and leeks should be planted out. Lift early potatoes. Make another sowing of perpetual spinach (spinach beet) for next year. Pick beans—runner and French

—as they become big enough, and so assure more from the same plants. All root crops need attention for loosening earth, watering, hoeing weeds and digging out weeds that are deep rooted; burn these latter.

August. —Chrysanthemums should now be budded and side shoots rubbed out. If red spider appears in the flower bed, syringe thoroughly. The earliest bulbs for next year, snowdrops and so on should be planted during this month; the larger bulbs can also be put in pots and kept in a warm corner in the open, otherwise keep in cool house. Cuttings of hydrangea can now be taken, heels, and firmly potted in sand till roots start, when repot into good, but not rich soil. Rose cuttings and evergreen shrub cuttings will root readily in the open, if sand is mixed in and watering not neglected. Cover cauliflower heads with leaves to hasten whitening, bend over onions, earth up celery and leeks. Make preparations on allotment or vegetable plot for next year, clear and dig where peas and beans are over, and remember your rotation plan in deciding what will go there for next year.

September. —Next year begins to loom large; the results of this season must be harvested, and make-ready the watchword for conditioning the plots for winter's sweetening. Beet, carrots, potatoes can be lifted and stored, the carrot and beet in boxes of sand or under mounds of earth in the open; the potatoes in clamps. Parsnips are better left in, the frost improves, and they can be pulled as required for the pot. Cauliflower should have a leaf put over each head for protection, and onions have the leafage bent over from close to the heads. Seedlings of spring cabbage can be planted into growing quarters. Young cauliflower can go into the frame (in pots) for safety during winter, and those still outside dusted around with soot. Cut back fruited raspberry canes to 1 foot above the ground. Plant the neet strawberry bed. Keep the ground loose by hoeing; turn over any ground cropped, watching out for insects and their eggs; burn rubbish as it accumulates. In the flower garden plant out what bulbs will flower in the early spring. Any transplanting of shrubs is done now. Prune rambler roses of old wood and tie up new runners. Take cuttings generally and have a second go at layering carnations if first lot have not provided enough new stock; roses can also be multiplied now by taking cuttings with a heel and thrusting deep into stiffish soil, ramblers and climbers take well but slowly, ordinary bush roses, etc., are difficult to strike.

October. —Those shrubs which are deciduous—leaf losing in winter —can be planted or shifted to other quarters: new roses can also be planted, making ground very firm. Put in pots another lot of bulbs to provide succession. Lift fuchsias and other summer bedding plants, such as lobelia, ivy-leaf geraniums, verbena. Take cuttings of shrubs, inserting them deeply, with sand well mixed in. They can go in open; do not disturb next year, they will make better root. Replanting and division of herbaceous perennials can now go ahead. Give the lawn a final mowing before winter sets in. Planting and cutting down is best done now, as also any lifting, such as dahlias, to keep during winter. Lift and store the rest of the root crops. Do some digging and manuring in the vegetable plots, turn over any already dug up. Any couch grass got out should be burned, and what potato haulms may be dry enough for the bonfire; decayed matter left about breeds disease and harbours pests.

November. —Lime-dress any dug plots, but clean of weeds first. Any leeks or celery still unearthed up should be so treated at once. Cut down artichokes and asparagus, cover rhubarb, gather green tomatoes for chutneying, cover seakale, heel over broccoli, plant horse-radish, blanch endive. Get ahead with more rough digging for frosts to break and purify; lime where sourness is suspected in lower spit, but liming must be done again in early spring for surface. Dress lawn with sand. Gather leaves for composting, particularly beech. Early flowering plants, such as wallflower, polyanthus, myosotis, daisies, if not already bedded out, should be put in at once and protected, till established, from frost. Plant fruit trees. Put in late flowering bulbs.

December. —If the privet hedge is gappy take cuttings below a joint and somewhere between 8 inches and 1 foot in length; insert deeply in stirred earth and let alone till wanted. Finish fruit and shrub pruning; prepare for next year by digging and turning; look over catalogues for interesting new floral adventures; burn rubbish, make out the rotation plan for vegetables; cut a good lot of wooden labels —18 inches high saves a lot of bending; clean and repair tools and, finally, remember there's always plenty of right-down useful work to be done this month, which, though not so interesting as in other months, is every bit as vital to success.

Note. —It will be observed that certain instructions are repeated in order to allow for the time differences of succession plantings and also as a last minute reminder.

MOSQUITO BITES. *See* STINGS AND BITES, INSECT.

MOTHS, to keep from clothes. A piece of linen damped with turpentine and put into the wardrobe or drawers for a day two or three times a year acts as a preventative against moth.

MOUTH WASH. Dissolve 60 g thymol in 3 oz. rectified spirit. Mix 10 or 12 drops in a tumbler of water and use as a mouth wash.

MUD-STAINS. Brushing mud-stains off soon makes a garment very shabby; so take a little lukewarm water in which 1 teaspoonful of salt has been dissolved. Dip a soft cloth in this and gently wipe the stains off. The material will not discolour, and will last much longer.

MULCHING. This means covering over the plot with a layer of compost or grass cuttings in order to save evaporation. It is merely laid on, not dug in, its purpose being to prevent the sun drying up the surface soil too rapidly. If left on, it also gradually manures the soil.

MUMPS. Mumps is a highly-infectious disease, in which the gland situated below the ear is enlarged and inflamed. It occurs mostly in children, who catch it one from the other.

Two or three weeks after infection the child complains of being ill, or the first sign may be pain and swelling under the ear; the jaw is stiff, and there is pain and difficulty in eating; the tonsils and throat may also be inflamed. In about two days the other side becomes affected. The complaint lasts from 4 to 6 days, and then commences to get better and, as a rule, 8 days from the first symptom the child is all right again.

The patient should be in a room by himself, and, if necessary, in bed. The bowels should be kept free. The mouth should be washed out with weak Condy's fluid and hot fomentations applied to the painful parts. The diet should be fluid. The patient is infectious for 3 weeks from the onset.

MUSCULAR RHEUMATISM. *See* RHEUMATISM, MUSCULAR.

MUSHROOM BEDS. The semi-darkness of a cellar or shed is favourable for growing mushrooms, but they can also be grown in the open. If no cellar or shed is available, make the bed out of doors from April to July. The bed does not differ whether in open or semi-darkness. It should be a firm ridge, about 4 feet high by 6 feet wide, composed of dung and loamy soil, and should be drained by a trench dug all round it. The spawn purchased in cakes should be put into shallow holes when the bed has attained a temperature of 80°; it should be covered with soil and then further covered with straw kept in place by mats. It will take about eight weeks to produce the crop, and the temperature of the bed should continue at not less than 60° during that time. Moisture is important, but when watering be careful that the temperature of the water is a little above that of the bed.

MUSHROOMS, to dry. After wiping with a dry cloth remove the skin and the brown part and place in a moderate oven on paper to dry. Then put them in paper bags and hang in a dry place until required for use.

MUSHROOMS, STEWED.

½ lb. mushrooms	chopped parsley
1 oz. butter	1 gill brown sauce
	salt and pepper

Peel and well wash the mushrooms, remove the stalks, melt the butter in a stewpan, put in the mushrooms and fry for a few minutes; add the brown sauce and simmer gently for 15 to 20 minutes till tender, season with salt and pepper, and serve sprinkled with chopped parsley.

MUSHROOMS, to test. To distinguish these from poisonous fungi sprinkle a little salt on the spongy part, or gills; if they turn yellow they are poisonous, if black wholesome.

MUSSELS, to test. Boil with the fish a silver fork or spoon. If the silver retains its brightness they are wholesome, but they are poisonous if the silver emerges black or of a dark colour.

MUSSELS MARINIÈRE, to cook. Well wash and scrape. Put in saucepan to which has been added chopped onion and a little chopped shallot. Add just sufficient water to cook them and a little cooking white wine. When cooked, take out the little black weed which is under the tongue. Now take a little of the stock, also some fish stock made from fish bones and peppercorns. Add a little butter and cream, strain off and add a pinch of chopped parsley, serve mussels in shells and pour sauce over them, and serve very hot. Mussels take 10 minutes to cook.

MUSTARD. By adding a pinch of table salt when mixing mustard you can help to keep it fresh for a longer period than usual and also prevent it from hardening.

Mustard mixed with milk instead of water will never turn dark and will keep fresh as long as required.

MUSTARD, as an emetic. *See* EMETICS.

MUSTARD AND CRESS. Sow the seed thickly; merely sprinkle on the soil, or cover lightly in March or April in a sunny spot. Cover with brown paper till germination begins; about four days in warm weather. The cress should be sown three days earlier than the mustard. Sow for succession at intervals of a fortnight until September in the open, and for winter use from October to March in boxes under glass. Many prefer to grow in boxes in summer also, as being cleaner and handier to crop. Gather by cutting with scissors, thus avoiding clinging earth.

MUSTARD BATH. A mustard bath is a good stimulant, especially for children who are in a state of collapse. Add 2 tablespoonfuls of mustard, previously mixed in a cup with cold water, to a gallon of hot water. The hand of the attendant should always try the water before a child is put into the bath. If a thermometer is used, the temperature should be 100° Fahrenheit.

MUSTARD, FRENCH. Take 1 oz. of best powdered mustard, 1 saltspoonful salt, a few tarragon leaves and 1 clove of garlic minced fine. Place on a plate, add ½ gill vinegar, and dilute to proper consistency. Mix with a wooden spoon and leave for a day.

MUSTARD, GERMAN. Mix with vinegar 2 tablespoonfuls of mustard, 1 tablespoonful of salt, 1 tablespoonful castor sugar, a pinch of cayenne pepper, the juice of 1 small onion and 1 tablesponful of melted butter.

MUSTARD PLASTER. Equal parts of flour and mustard spread on adhesive material or brown paper. A layer of gauze should be spread between the plaster and the skin.

If the mustard used for making a plaster is mixed with white of egg instead of water no blistering will result, even if the plaster is kept on for a long time.

MUSTARD POULTICE. *See* POULTICE, MUSTARD.

MUTTON. The flesh of mutton should be fine grained and firm, paler in colour than beef; the fat white and firm. Mutton is finest when it is between four and five years old; but it is seldom met with. Sheep are generally killed when between two and three years old. Mutton should be moderately fat. If very lean it will be poor in flavour and tough.

MUTTON, to keep. Wash with vinegar every day, and dry thoroughly before hanging. In hot weather rub it with sugar and sprinkle it all over with pepper and ground ginger to keep off the flies.

MUTTON, BREAST OF. Stew in good gravy until tender, bone, score, season with salt and cayenne pepper and boil. Serve with capers and melted butter or mushroom ketchup.

MUTTON, BREAST OF, ROAST AND STUFFED (for 3 or 4 people).

1 breast of mutton	1 oz. sage
4 oz. bread-crumbs	little milk
1 oz. fat	salt and pepper
3 or 4 onions	

Remove the bones and some of the superfluous fat, parboil the onions and chop them, add to the bread-crumbs chopped sage, butter or dripping, season and mix with a little milk, lay the stuffing on the breast, roll it up and bind with tape. Bake in the oven and serve with gravy made as for roast joints. Veal stuffing can be used instead of sage and onion stuffing if preferred.

MUTTON BROTH.

2 lb. scrag end neck of mutton	1 sprig parsley
1 quart water	1 onion
1 carrot	1 oz. pearl barley
	salt and pepper

Remove the meat from the bones, cut it up finely, chop the bones, soak in a basin with the water and a little salt for 1 hour. Put it into a saucepan with the vegetables and cook very slowly, removing the scum as it rises, blanch the pearl barley and add it. When the meat, bones and flavouring vegetables have been removed, the meat cut in tiny squares and the vegetables in dice may be put in if allowed, season and sprinkle chopped parsley over. Remove fat with kitchen paper if served at once.

MUTTON CUTLETS (6 or 7).

best end of neck of mutton	mashed potatoes
egg and bread-crumbs	vegetables for garnish
salt and pepper	brown or tomato sauce

Saw off the chine bone carefully and the end of the bones, allowing 2 inches below the eye of the cutlet; divide the cutlets, trim them, keeping the bone clean; dip in salt and pepper, then egg and bread-crumbs. Fry in a sauté pan till a nice brown, turning them occasionally; dish in a circle on a border of mashed potatoes, fill the centre with peas, sprouts or any suitable vegetable; strain a good brown or tomato sauce round.

MUTTON, Devonshire style.

	parsley
1 leg of mutton	2 onions
2 cupfuls cider	½ cupful red-currant jelly
2 cupfuls stock or water	12 cloves
2 tablespoonfuls lemon juice	apples and celery

Remove bone and skin from mutton, place in a stewpan with water or stock, onions each stuck with six cloves, cider and lemon juice. Cover closely, place over a quick fire; when boiling simmer slowly for 2½ hours; turn two or three times in cooking. Place on hot dish, add jelly to liquid in the pan, pour gravy over meat and garnish with chopped parsley. Serve with equal quantities of finely-chopped celery and grated apples in a salad bowl.

MUTTON, LOIN OF, STUFFED (for 8 or 9 people).

4 lb. loin of mutton	½ teaspoonful herbs
4 oz. bread-crumbs	little grated lemon peel
2 oz. suet	1 egg
1 teaspoonful chopped parsley	salt and pepper

Carefully bone the loin, taking away as little meat as possible; make a seasoning with the bread-crumbs, chopped suet flavouring; season well, bind with egg, place it in the loin where the bone was removed; tie up firmly with tape, roast in the oven, serve as other joints with gravy poured round.

MUTTON OLIVES.

slices of cold mutton	gravy
veal stuffing (*see* Forcemeat)	salt and pepper
allspice	mashed potato
	red-currant jelly

Take as many slices of cold mutton as required, of equal size, season with salt, pepper and a little allspice, place on each slice a little veal stuffing, roll up and secure with thread, place in a baking-dish, pour over some good gravy, cover with greased paper and cook for 30 minutes. Serve with mashed potato and red-currant jelly.

NAEVUS. *See* BIRTH MARKS.

NAIL HOLES, to fill in. Fill in with a mixture of glue and fine sawdust. Allow this to dry well, when it will take any kind of nail.

To prevent nails from bending when being hammered into hard wood, dip the points into lard or oil.

NAILS. The best way to drive nails into plaster is, after you have driven them in in the usual way, to withdraw them and fill up the hole with a paste made of plaster of Paris and alum water. Push the nails into this and leave it to set. The result will be perfectly neat.

NAMES AND NUMBERS. A branch of numerology uses names for omens. Each letter of the alphabet has a number associated with it, and the addition of these numbers indicates character. The following table shows the indicative numbers:

A—1	F—8	K—2	P—8	U—6
B—2	G—3	L—3	Q—1	V—6
C—2	H—8	M—4	R—2	W—6
D—4	I—1	N—5	S—3	X—6
E—5	J—1	O—7	T—4	Y—1
				Z—7

This calculation applies to the first or Christian name. Follow the same process as in "Birthdays" (which see) and the ultimate numeral refers to the table of characteristics there given. Thus "Joyce" gives 1—7—1—2—5, the total being 16, which, added, reveals 7 as the operative number. In this way the character of a new friend or suitor can be arrived at, the prospect of happiness be gauged from whether such characteristic would please you.

195

Further calculations can be made on surnames, and also where there are more than one first name, but the above will suffice to show the system.

NARCISSUS. These should be treated in the same way as hyacinths, but plant in a well-worked moist loam. Do not force daffodils.

NASTURTIUM. These may be grown in a light, poor soil. Sow the seed thinly about $\frac{1}{2}$ inch deep any time from March to June and thin out from 1 foot to 18 inches apart when large enough. Both dwarfs and trailers have a variety of colours and flower prolifically.

NASTURTIUMS, to pickle. *See* PICKLES.

NEMESIA. Of South African origin, this free-flowering half-hardy annual must be raised in heat and does best in a cool greenhouse. They do well in the open, however, if in a sunny position away from cold winds. Plant the short, shrubby sorts about 3 inches apart; the tall-growing, about 6 inches, for full effect in broad borders or large patches. The flower stems rise from tufts of leafage. Flowers are in a bewildering variety of shades and colours.

NEMOPHILA (CALIFORNIAN BLUEBELL). One of the hardiest of dwarf annuals and of compact growth, flowering freely, blue, white and variegated. Seed may be sown either in August, for spring flowering, or in April, and in the place where the plants are intended to bloom, though they will bear transplanting if it be carefully done. A light soil is desirable, in order that the seed may germinate freely and the plants be restricted from rank growth.

NERVOUSNESS. The best treatment for this disorder is early rising, plenty of exercise (especially out of doors), cheerful company and constant effort to induce confidence. Late meals should not be taken and overstudying and excitement should be avoided.

NET CURTAINS. If these are stretched between two rods close to window, always put up *wet* after washing. Do not iron.

NETTLE BEER. *See* BEER.

NETTLE RASH. This is usually caused by eating some kind of food which disagrees with the sufferer, and an emetic should be given if the food has recently been eaten. Then give an opening medicine. Take a warm bath each night in water which contains a large piece of common washing soda. A little boracic ointment or powder should be applied if the spots are broken and during the day they should be touched with a solution of 1 teaspoonful of carbonate of soda in $\frac{1}{2}$ pint of boiling water applied when only warm. The diet should be light, and include a calcium preparation.

NEURASTHENIA.

Causes.—Shock, severe injury, overwork or mental strain.

Symptoms.—Headache, sleeplessness, giddiness, languor, inability to concentrate on any particular thing or to exert the muscles even slightly without fatigue.

Treatment.—Change of air and surroundings, massage and electrical treatment. Firmness against self-pity is essential.

NEW BREAD, to cut. Let the bread-knife stand in boiling water for a few minutes before cutting; the bread can then be cut quite easily.

NEW OILCLOTH. Before putting this into use rub it with a little paraffin on a cloth. This will prevent the pattern and colours from wearing.

NEW POTATOES, to scrape. Buy a new wire pot-scourer and keep it for potatoes; it will take the skin off much more quickly and finely than scraping.

NEWSPAPER IN THE KITCHEN. Split your old newspapers through the middle and pile them in a neat heap; and every time you have to peel apples or potatoes, shell peas, etc., use one of the sheets which makes it easy to gather up the refuse and throw it in the rubbish pail.

The best way to clean glass is to use newspaper. Crumple it up and rub it round the inside of the glass, which should be damp.

NEW WOOLLENS, to wash. First soak them in cold rain water for 2 or 3 hours; this keeps the oil in the wool and after washing in soap flakes the garments will be beautifully soft and look like new.

NICOTIANA. *See* TOBACCO PLANT.

NIGELLA (LOVE-IN-A-MIST). A hardy annual which is attractive not only for its flowers but for its peculiar feathery and thorn-like growth, as indicated by its name of love-in-a-mist. Seed should be sown in March, in light soil and in the place where the plants are intended to bloom.

NIGHT-SCENTED STOCK (MATHIOLA BICORNIS). This hardy annual has inconspicuous greyish foliage, and single, straggly-looking lilac flowers. Its chief claim is the perfume it exudes freely at night. It will flower in sun or shade, is not particular as to soil, and blooms all the summer and autumn. Sow thinly.

NIGHT SWEATS. The patient should be dried and the night garments and the sheets, if necessary, changed. Sponging with lukewarm vinegar and water may diminish the perspiration. A slight powdering with talcum is helpful. In children if these sweats occur in the head, it may be a prelude to rickets.

NOSE, BLEEDING FROM THE. Slight bleeding may be beneficial, especially in full-blooded persons; it often gives relief to headache. If severe, cold water should be applied to the nose and nape of neck, and the nose held between the finger and thumb. If this does not arrest it, a handkerchief should be torn into strips and the nose plugged, continuing the bathing with cold water. Do not lie on the back.

NOUGAT.

whites of 2 eggs	vanilla flavouring
¾ lb. icing sugar	5 oz. almonds and pistachio nuts

Blanch the almonds and cut them into thin strips. Beat the whites of eggs and mix with the icing sugar to a firm paste. Add the almonds, pistachio nuts and the vanilla. Spread about ½ inch thick on wafer paper, put another sheet of wafer paper on top and press between two plates. Leave to dry in a warm place.

NUT CUTLETS.

6 oz. shelled hazel nuts	1 teaspoonful Worcester sauce
3 oz. vermicelli	1 egg
1 teaspoonful tomato sauce	bread-crumbs

Put the nuts and vermicelli through the nut-mill. Use the sauces to mix to a stiff consistency, then roll out until about ¼-inch thick. Shape into cutlets, dip in egg and bread-crumbs and fry in boiling oil.

NUTS. The kernels will come out whole from nuts if you have soaked them in salt water over night.

OAK, to make an oil for graining. Grind vandyke brown in turps; as much gold size as will set it, and enough soft soap to make it stand the comb. Add a little boiled oil if it sets too rapidly. Put a teaspoonful of gold size, ½ pint turps, and as much soap as will lay on a sixpence. Then mix a little soda with water and remove the veins.

OBESITY. Take regular exercise and eat in moderation. Potatoes, pastry, milk puddings, jams, sugar, fat and bread should be avoided or partaken of sparingly. Beer and sweet wines are harmful.

The diet should consist of lean meat, fish, green vegetables and fruit. Clear soup is preferable to thick, and toast to ordinary baker's bread. For drink use unsweetened fruit; particularly lemon or apple juice, and tea with lemon instead of milk or sugar. For general beverage Vichy water is good. A pint of hot water a quarter of an hour before food will, in some cases, considerably reduce the weight.

ODOURS, NOXIOUS. To get rid of the odours of tobacco, new paint, etc., place a large bowl of fresh cold water in the room at night. Remove all tobacco ash and cigar ends. In the morning all noxious odours will be removed.

OIL, BURNING. On no account must water be thrown on burning oil, because it causes the fire to spread. Earth, sand, flour or salt should be used as an extinguisher.

OIL, ESSENTIAL, to extract. Put herbs, roots or barks into a bottle and pour a spoonful of ether upon them. Cork well and keep in a cool place for a few hours; then fill the bottle with cold water. The oil will float upon the surface and may easily be skimmed off.

OILCLOTH. *See* NEW OILCLOTH.

OILCLOTH, to preserve. Wash with equal parts of skimmed milk and water every month. Every three months rub with a little linseed oil and polish with an old silk cloth.

OIL PAINTINGS, to clean. Rub over the picture with a slice of potato damped in cold water, wipe off with a damp sponge and finish with tepid water. Dry and polish with a piece of silk. Then rub the surface with a flannel moistened with linseed oil.

OLD PICTURE FRAMES. Large useless picture frames can be converted into curbs for bedrooms. Cut the two short sides exactly in the middle; place one on the top of the other and screw them together.

OLD RAZOR BLADES. These are very useful for opening up the seams of an old garment.

OLD WOOL, to use up. Take any wool that has been unravelled from jumpers and dresses, wind it round the back of a chair and tie in three or four places. Put the wool on a clean towel in a colander and stand it over a saucepan of boiling water. The steam will straighten it and when dried and wound it can be used as if it were new.

OLEANDERS. Treat as a greenhouse shrub. The plant will not bear cutting owing to its great tendency to bleed. A plentiful supply of water should always be given. Propagate by root-suckers, or by slips pulled from the stem and struck in a bottle of water, or in a light soil kept continually wet.

OLIVE OIL. Olive oil should be kept in an air-tight bottle, and this should not be stored in too cold a place.

OMELETTE. When beating eggs for an omelette or scrambled eggs only beat enough to break up yolk and white. Never froth as for cakes or batter.

OMELETTE, CAULIFLOWER. Take the white part of a boiled cauliflower after it is cold; chop it very small, and mix with it a sufficient quantity of well-beaten egg to make a very thick batter. Then fry it in fresh butter in a small pan and send it hot to table.

OMELETTE, CHEESE.

4 eggs	1 tablespoonful cream or milk
1 oz. butter	2 tablespoonfuls cheese
	salt and pepper

Beat the eggs in a basin, add the milk or cream, grated cheese (Parmesan or Gruyère) and seasoning; melt the butter in an omelette pan. When quite hot pour in the mixture, stir until it begins to thicken, cook until a golden brown; put the pan in the oven for a minute or so to brown, fold over, turn on to a hot dish, sprinkle with grated cheese and serve immediately.

OMELETTE, KIDNEY.

4 eggs	1 kidney
1½ oz. butter	1 shallot
	salt and pepper

Skin the kidney and chop finely, put ½ oz. of butter into a small saucepan, add the finely-chopped shallot and fry for a few minutes, then add the kidney and cook for 3 or 4 minutes, season well with salt and pepper. Beat the eggs, melt the remainder of the butter in an omelette pan, pour in the eggs and stir till the mixture begins to set. When cooked sufficiently put the kidney in the centre and fold over in the usual way, serve on a hot dish with a little gravy poured round if liked.

OMELETTE, SAVOURY.

3 eggs	pinch of herbs
1 teaspoonful parsley	garlic or shallot
¾ oz. butter	salt and pepper

Well whisk the eggs, add the chopped parsley, herbs, salt and pepper; rub the omelette pan with a head of garlic or a piece of shallot, melt the butter in the pan. When hot pour in the eggs, stir till the mixture begins to set. When cooked sufficiently (it should be of a creamy consistency inside) fold over into an oval shape and serve immediately.

OMELETTE, SPINACH.

some cooked spinach	1 oz. butter
3 eggs	little cream
	salt and pepper

Warm the spinach, season and add a little cream, beat the eggs thoroughly, add the seasoning, heat the butter in an omelette pan, pour in the eggs, stir lightly, and then allow it to set. When cooked sufficiently place the omelette pan in a quick oven or under the gas to set the top, shake to the side of the pan, lay on the spinach, fold over and serve immediately.

OMELETTE, SWEET.

3 eggs	¾ oz. butter
little jam	1 teaspoonful castor sugar

Separate the whites and yolks of eggs, beat the whites to a stiff froth with the teaspoonful of sugar, mix lightly with the well-beaten yolks; melt the butter in an omelette pan, pour in the eggs, stir quickly till the mixture begins to set; put the omelette pan in the oven for a minute or two to brown slightly. Shape the omelette, put the warmed jam in the centre, fold over and turn on to a hot dish and serve immediately.

OMELETTES. *See also* Fish.

OMELETTES. Instead of turning the omelette when one side is done simply put the pan under the hot grill for a few seconds. The omelette will not only be beautifully browned but much lighter and can be easily rolled.

ONIONS. This important crop needs careful cultivation, but the results repay diligence. Although the onion itself matures on the surface, the fibrous roots go deep and consequently, well drained soil is required, deeply trenched and well manured the previous autumn. A fortnight before sowing, give the ground a good dusting with soot. Sow the seed for the main crop in March in drills 12 inches apart, making the ground very firm both before and after sowing. Six weeks after sowing, thin out the plants to 2 inches; in another 6 weeks, to 6 inches. Give manure water twice a week. Just before the tips turn yellow, bend down the stems flat upon the bed from 2 inches up the neck, this prevents running to seed, and increases the size of the bulbs. Should any of the onions start for seed, pinch off the seed shoot; the bulb will then continue to grow. Onions are ready for lifting at the end of August or early in September.

For spring onions make a sowing of *Lisbon* in August, and protect from frost. The ordinary thinnings from general sowings are also quite tasty as spring onions. For pickling onions sow any time up to June.

ONIONS, BOILED.

Spanish onions
salt
½ pint white sauce

Skin the onions, put them into boiling water with salt and cook for 2 or 3 hours, according to the size. Drain them, place them in a hot dish and pour the white sauce over and serve. Another method is to put about an ounce of butter in the pan when the water is poured off, allow it to get quite hot, season with salt and pepper and serve in a hot vegetable dish.

ONIONS, to counteract the smell of after eating. A cup of black coffee or a little parsley eaten with vinegar will remove the odour from the breath.

ONIONS, to peel. Dip in warm water during the process and no smell will be left on the hands. Peeling before a fire prevents the spirit of the onion getting into the eyes.

ONIONS, to remove smell of when washing up. The smell of onions, fish, or cabbage can be quickly removed from pans if a little vinegar is added to the washing-up water.

ONIONS, to store. After having dried them in the sun, onions should be hung by the stalks or strung on ropes. Shallots, chives and garlic may be stored in the same way.

ONIONS, STUFFED.

4 or 6 onions
minced meat
brown sauce
salt and pepper

Choose large onions, peel very carefully, cut off a slice at the top, scoop out as much as possible from the inside, fill with minced meat well seasoned and mixed with a little sauce. Replace the top, and stew very slowly for as long as possible. Serve with brown sauce. The onions can be parboiled, the inside removed and stuffed in the same way and baked in the oven, basting them well. Serve with brown sauce. Any cold meat, game or poultry will be suitable for the stuffing.

ORANGEADE. Take the juice of 4 oranges and the thin peel of 1 orange, ¼ lb. lump sugar and mix with 3 pints of boiling water.

ORANGE CREAM FILLING.

4 oranges
2½ cupfuls water
yoolks of 3 eggs
1 lemon
1 cupful castor sugar
4½ tablespoonfuls cornflour
1 tablespoonful butter

Put 2 cupfuls of the water into a saucepan, add the grated rind of 2 of the oranges and put the pan on the fire. Dissolve the cornflour in the ½ cupful of water and stir into the boiling water with a wooden spoon. Simmer for 10 minutes stirring all the time, beat sugar and

201

yolks together and add. Cook another 2 minutes, still stirring. Remove from fire, add butter, orange and lemon juice and set to cool. Use as filling.

ORANGE CRUSH. Slice the oranges across the centre and remove the core. Pare away from the peel, removing all the white skin. Place the pulp and any juice remaining in skins in a basin. Add sugar and 2 tablespoonfuls of boiling water to each orange. Allow to stand overnight.

ORANGE PEEL. A piece of orange peel in the water in which a pudding is boiling not only improves the flavour of the pudding but collects the grease, and the pudding cloth will be no trouble to wash afterwards.

Place this in a jar containing soft sugar from time to time and you will always have a supply of tasty sugar for cakes, puddings, etc.

Dry all lemon and orange peel in oven and use for sauces, etc.

ORANGE SAVARINS.

¼ pint milk	½ lb. flour
¾ oz. yeast	3 oz. butter
4 egg yolks	2 oz. sugar
8 almonds	2 oz. margarine
cream	orange syrup

Dissolve the yeast in milk at blood heat. Rub sugar and margarine into flour and mix to a soft dough with the milk. Set to rise in a warm place for 1¼ hours, then spread it out on a board and heat the butter and egg yolks into it. Knead well, dust with flour and put to rise for about 1 hour. Grease 16 small deep pans, set half a blanched almond in the bottom of each and half fill with dough. Allow to rise to double their size, bake in a moderate oven. When cold dip each into a hot orange syrup. Drain on a wire tray. When convenient to handle split them open at the side and pipe in whipped cream with a forcing-bag. Serve in greaseproof paper cups.

ORANGE TODDY. Squeeze the juice of a large orange into a glass and add 2 tablespoonfuls of sugar. Half fill the glass with boiling water, and stir well.

ORANGE TONIC. Steep in 1 pint of boiling water 1 oz. orange peel, 1 oz. camomile flowers and a few cloves.

ORNAMENTS, to clean. Half fill wooden bowl with warm water in which a teaspoonful of ammonia has been stirred and enough white soap dissolved to make a good lather. Each article should be plunged quickly into the water. A fine nail brush and camel hair brush are necessary. Rinse ornaments in cooler water.

ORNITHOGALUM. *See* STAR OF BETHLEHEM.

OVER-SALTED SOUPS. When soups or stews have been over-salted a single potato cooked in them will absorb the surplus salt. It must be removed before it crumbles.

OX KIDNEY, STEWED (for 4 people).

½ lb. kidney	1 small onion
1 oz. butter or dripping	1 teaspoonful ketchup
1 oz. flour	1 teaspoonful Worcester sauce
½ pint stock	salt and pepper

Scald the kidney and cut it in neat slices, melt the butter or dripping and fry the onion, also the kidney; remove and brown the flour carefully, add the stock gradually. Stir till it boils. Replace the onion and kidney, add the flavourings and seasoning. Simmer very gently for two hours, the kidney will be hardened if it boils; dish with a border of boiled rice or macaroni or mashed potatoes.

OX TONGUE, BOILED (for 8 or 9 people).

1 ox tongue	2 sticks celery
1 carrot	bunch of herbs
1 turnip	brown or piquante sauce
1 onion	

Wash the tongue in cold water, if it is pickled let it soak for some hours, put it in a saucepan with tepid water to cover, bring it to the boil, remove the scum, add the vegetables and herbs, and simmer gently from 3 to 4 hours. When tender remove the skin, brush over with glaze and put it in the oven for a few minutes; serve with a good brown or piquante sauce. Spinach is a suitable vegetable to serve with the tongue, and can be used to garnish the dish. If the tongue is to be served cold it must be trimmed and fastened on a board in an upright position with skewers. When cold and firm glaze it and decorate with butter put through a forcing-bag with a fancy tube, and aspic jelly.

OYSTER COCKTAIL À LA TABOR.

1 dozen oysters	2 tablespoonfuls tomato
1 teaspoonful lemon juice	catsup
1 teaspoonful Worcester	salt
sauce	sugar

Cook oysters 15 minutes, serve in glasses covered with lemon juice, Worcester sauce, tomato catsup, a little tobacco, salt and sugar.

OYSTERS, to choose.

The healthier the fish the more difficult is the shell to open. If the shell opens immediately on touching, the fish is dead and unfit for eating.

OYSTERS, BAKED.

To bake oysters effectively, first scrub their shells with a brush. Then place them with the deep shells down in a baking-pan in a very hot oven; the shells will soon open. Then remove the upper shells, add a little butter, salt and pepper and serve on the under shells.

To fry oysters, use eggs to dip the oysters in before frying. Each egg should have 1 tablespoonful of water to 2 of milk.

OYSTERS, SCALLOPED (for 6 or 7 people).

2 dozen oysters	1 oz. butter
½ pint white sauce	bread-crumbs

Open the oysters, wash them in their own liquor, put them in a white-lined saucepan, strain the liquor over them, slowly heat but do not let them boil, take them out and remove their beards; make the white sauce hot, put in the oysters, strain in the liquor, stand at the side of the fire for a few minutes. Butter some scallop shells, put some of the mixture in each, dividing the oysters equally, sprinkle over the bread-crumbs, put on some small pieces of butter, bake in a moderate oven and serve hot.

OYSTERS AU CITRON. Open the oysters and leave them in their bottom shells. Squeeze some fresh lemon juice and a little soluble cayenne over them.

PACKING PLEATS. To pack pleated skirts cut off the feet of old stockings and draw the skirts through. They will arrive in perfect condition.

PAEONY. This requires a well-manured soil and plenty of water during the summer, and being of slow growth, it does not flower fully until the third year, when it produces bushy flowers of pink, red or white. September and October are the best months for planting. Increase by cuttings detached at their junction with the stem, by slips of the root, or by layers half cut through behind each bud.

The herbaceous variety of paeony needs a rich soil, is grateful for a little shade, and planting should be done in September, and each plant should have plenty of space. They are easily propagated by root division.

PAIL PRAM. Mount a square board, 4 inches bigger each way than the bucket bottom, on four little wheels. On this "pram" can go the pail, and when scrubbing floors, cleaning walls, or any job that requires a bucket, and as work proceeds, the whole can be pushed along, saving much bending. On it the soap and brush and wiping-cloths can also be placed.

PAINT, to remove the smell. Place a bowl or pail of water in the room all day. This will be even more effective if you can place a handful or so of hay in the water. Change the water every three hours.

PAINT-BRUSHES, care of. *See* BRUSHES, PAINT.

PAINT FOR FENCES. Mix tar and yellow ochre together. This will make a good green colour and is excellent for painting rough woodwork or iron.

PAINT-MARKS, ON CLOTHING. Mix equal parts of turpentine and ammonia and apply to the marks with a piece of cloth the same colour as the garment. Rub the way of the nap very gently until all stains have disappeared; then sponge the place with warm water and a little white soap.

PAINT-WORK. When the front door or paint-work gets bleached with the sun, cover with boiled linseed oil. Leave to soak for one day the rub off the surplus. This restores the colour and gives a nice finish.

PAINT, WHITE, to clean. Onion water is a splendid cleanser for white paint. Boil the onions till all goodness is removed and use the water with or without soap.

Another method is to make a paste of soap powder and paraffin and apply the paste with a bit of flannel.

PAINTER'S COLIC, to relieve. This is a dangerous disease and medical advice should be obtained, but in the interval aperient salts should be given and hot salt or bran bags applied to the stomach to relieve the pain. The diet should be light.

PALPITATION OF THE HEART. *See* HEART, PALPITATION OF THE.

PANADA, or THICK SAUCE.

2 oz. flour	2 oz. butter	½ pint liquid

Melt the butter, add the flour, mix smoothly and cook for a few minutes; add the liquid and cook well until the mixture leaves the sides of the saucepan. This mixture is used for binding the ingredients in cutlets, croquettes, rissoles, etc.

PANCAKES (10 or 12).

¼ lb. flour	1½ oz. lard
1 pint milk	1 lemon
2 eggs	castor sugar

Make a batter with the milk, flour and eggs, beating well before all the milk is added, and allow it to stand for 1 hour or more if possible. Put the batter into a jug, melt the lard in a saucepan, pour a little into the frying-pan—enough to cover the bottom of the pan. When brown on one side toss and brown the other side. Turn on to a piece of paper sprinkled with sugar, sift with castor sugar and squeeze over some lemon juice, roll up and put on a dish with a fancy paper. Serve very hot.

PANCAKES, SAVOURY. Make as above, but omit sugar. Place hot mince of either meat, game, or poultry on the pancake and roll up. Other fillings for savoury pancakes or omelettes can be made from tomatoes, cooked mushrooms, or onion, or a mixture of these three. Cooked celery and tomatoes will also be found to give an excellent filling for savoury pancakes.

PANSY, HEARTSEASE AND VIOLA. The pansy may readily be raised from seed (in heat), or, if it is desired to perpetuate a particular variety, by cuttings taken early in April and kept under glass in a shady border until well rooted. Transplant in September to bloom early the following year. Take cuttings from the ends of the shoots, snipping them off just below a joint. Propagation is also by root division. Pansies require a light, rich soil, well drained but not too dry, and do well in cool but not shady spots. Even if in bud and flower they suffer very little check from being bedded-out, and may be used massed, in beds and borders of selected types and colours. Do not plant pansies that are drooping, but immerse roots in soft water till they stiffen; then water in well when planting and always water pansies freely in dry spells to get good blossom. Snipping off seed pods ensures a continuance of flowering.

PAPER, to remove grease spots from. Put blotting-paper over the stain and rub it with a hot iron. Repeat this several times. Apply to both sides of the paper a little oil of turpentine with a soft brush, and afterwards some rectified spirits of wine.

PAPER-HANGING. Prepare the paper the day before you start work by (a) cutting off the margin on the left-hand side of each roll; (b) measuring the exact height of your walls and cutting off several lengths of paper in readiness, making sure you cut them so that the pattern will match. Use one of the cold-water paste powders sold by decorators, as the old-fashioned flour paste may mark the paper if you get any on the front of it. Use a whitewash brush for pasting the paper, a deal table for pasting on, and wipe the table between each piece. Have a clean sweeping brush ready for smoothing the paper on to the wall. When patching or joining on small pieces of the paper do not cut these pieces with straight edges but tear the paper with jagged edges and then the joins will not show.

Amateurs will find their task a much easier one if they apply the paste to the wall instead of the paper, which is apt to tear and give trouble.

PARKIN.

½ lb. fine oatmeal	4 oz. butter
4 oz. flour	1 teaspoonful baking-powder
½ lb. golden syrup	½ teaspoonful ground ginger
2 oz. sugar	about 1 gill milk

Mix dry ingredients, rub in the butter, gradually add the treacle or golden syrup and then sufficient of the milk to make the whole into a soft dough. Place in a shallow cake-tin lined with buttered paper and bake about 1 hour in a moderate oven.

PARSLEY. Sow thickly in a rich soil, from March to April, ½ inch deep in rows. It is slow in starting. To assist its coming up quicker, soak the seed a few hours in warm water. Thin out to 6 inches apart, when large enough, and then leave to mature. For winter use, sow in July and protect in a frame.

PARSLEY, to dry. Pick the parsley in dry weather, spread it on a plate and bake in a moderate oven, turning frequently. Rub between the palms of the hands when dry and pick out all the stalks. Keep in a closely corked bottle in a dry place.

PARSLEY SAUCE. When making this do not add chopped parsley until the sauce has boiled. The parsley will then retain its colour and freshness. *See also* SAUCE, PARSLEY.

206

PARSNIPS. Peel the parsnips, cut into quarters, place in boiling water with salt, cook till tender; drain them and dish in a hot vegetable dish with a little butter. Parsnips can be served with boiled meat and salt cod.

PARSNIPS. Sow in a rich and somewhat sandy loam, in drills 15 inches apart. Put the seed in successions February to April; push a dibber well down, fill the hole with loose earth; press a couple of seeds in to about 1 inch and water. This takes time but results in good tapering parsnips without forked roots. When big enough, gradually thin out if needed to 9 inches apart but do no transplanting. Remove all weeds by frequent hoeing. Parsnips are much sweeter if left in till frosted.

PARSNIPS, to keep. Dig up the roots with the tops on late in autumn and carefully heel in thickly together in rows. Cover with litter. If after a few days the tops grow on, slice off but do not cut the actual parsnip.

PARTRIDGE, ROAST (for 3 or 4 people).

1 brace of partridges	watercress
a little fat bacon	fried crumbs
gravy	croûtons of toast
bread sauce	

Pluck, singe and draw the birds, truss firmly, making them look plump, roast for 30 minutes, basting frequently. A slice of fat bacon can be tied on to the breast to keep them moist; remove it and flour and froth them well a few minutes before dishing. Dish on croûtons of toast, garnish with watercress, serve with bread sauce and fried bread-crumbs. *See also* PHEASANT, to roast.

PASTIES, CORNISH.

¼ lb. meat	1 small potato
small piece of onion	pepper and salt

For Pastry:

½ lb. flour	water to mix
3 oz. fat	pinch of salt
½ teaspoonful baking-powder	

Put the flour in a basin, rub in the fat, add baking-powder and salt, mix to a stiff dough with the water, knead lightly, put on a board, cut into six pieces, roll into rounds; chop the meat, potato and onion into small pieces, season and put some of the mixture on each piece of pastry; moisten the edges, draw them together, pinch into a frill. Bake in a quick oven for three-quarters of an hour.

PASTRY, LIGHT. To ensure pastry being light and digestible it is better to use the yolk of an egg and 1 tablespoonful of lemon juice instead of baking-powder. The yolk of an egg contains mineral matter, which takes the place of the soda in the baking-powder, and the lemon juice that of tartaric acid. The pastry can stand for a time without baking, whereas pastry with baking-powder must go into the oven as quickly as possible.

PASTRY, BISCUIT CRUST.

½ lb. flour	yolk of 1 egg
4¼ oz. butter	pinch of salt
1 oz. sugar	little water

Rub the butter into the flour, add sugar, salt, mix with the beaten yolk and a little water, knead until smooth, roll out and use.

PASTRY, CHOUX.

6 oz. flour	½ pint water
2 oz. butter	4 eggs

Put the water and butter in a saucepan and bring to the boil, sift the flour and add to the water and butter, cook well until it leaves the sides of the saucepan; allow the mixture to cool slightly, then beat the eggs in one at a time very thoroughly, sweeten and flavour and use as required.

PASTRY, FLAKY CRUST.

½ lb. flour	pinch of salt
5 oz. butter or butter and lard	water to mix

Sift the flour, add the salt, divide the fat into four portions, rub one into the flour, mix to a paste with water, roll out on a floured board to an oblong shape; put one portion of fat on in flakes two-thirds of the way down, fold into three, press the edges together; roll out again, keeping the edges square, flake on another portion of fat and repeat until all the fat is rolled in; roll out to shape required and use.

Note.—This crust can be made some time before it is wanted if kept in a cool place.

PASTRY, GENOESE.

5 eggs	3 oz. butter
6 oz. sugar	flavouring
4 oz. flour	colouring if required

Whisk the eggs and sugar together over hot water for about 20 minutes until thick and creamy, stir the sifted flour in very lightly and add lastly the butter, which must be melted. Pour the mixture into a flat baking-tin lined with buttered paper, and bake in a moderate oven for about half an hour.

Note.—This mixture is suitable for the foundation of all kinds of fancy cakes.

PASTRY, PUFF.

	1 teaspoonful lemon juice
½ lb. flour	pinch of salt
½ lb butter (fresh)	water to mix

Rub 1 oz. of the butter into the flour, make a well in the centre, pour in the salt, juice and water, gradually working the flour into a stiff paste. Press the butter in a clean cloth to squeeze out all the water, knead the pastry until quite smooth, roll out on a floured board to an oblong shape, keeping the corners square; place the butter on in a layer two-thirds of the way down the paste, fold in three, press the edges together, set aside for 20 minutes, roll out to the same shape, fold as before, press the edges; repeat this and set aside again in a cool place for 20 minutes, roll out the pastry again, repeating the process twice more; set aside for the third time for 20 minutes, roll out and use. The pastry has in all seven rolls and is set aside three times. Always after folding remember to keep the rough edges turned the same way each time.

Note.—A marble slab is best to make puff pastry on, and a hot kitchen must be avoided to make it successfully. It can be made two or three days before it is used if kept in a cool place. Less butter can be used to make a cheaper pastry.

PASTRY, RAISED PIE-CRUST.

1 lb. flour	1 gill water
4 oz. lard	pinch of salt

Boil the water and lard together, make a well in the centre of the flour, pour in the liquid, add salt, mix to a stiff dough as quickly as possible, and knead until smooth, keeping it warm.

Note.—A yolk of egg may be added to make the crust richer and milk used instead of water.

PASTRY, ROUGH PUFF.

	salt
½ lb. flour	lemon juice
6 oz. butter or butter and lard	water to mix

Add the salt to the flour, cut the butter into large pieces and mix with the flour, make a well in the centre, moisten with the lemon juice and water and mix carefully until it is a stiff paste; roll out to an oblong shape, fold in three, roll out again; repeat the process, keeping the rough edges in the same direction till it has been rolled four times and does not look streaky. It is then ready to use for covering meat pies, patties or for sausage rolls, etc.

PASTRY, SHORT CRUST (No. 1.)

½ lb. flour	pinch of salt
¼ lb. butter, lard or dripping	water to mix

Sift the flour, add the salt, rub in the butter or lard finely with the tips of the fingers, mix to a stiff paste with cold water, turn on to a floured board, roll out lightly, and it is ready for use.

Note.—The flour for rolling out the pastry should be taken out of quantity weighed for use or the proportions will be altered.

PASTRY, SHORT CRUST (Very Plain) (No. 2).

10 oz. self-raising flour	pinch of salt
3½ oz. lard or dripping	water to mix

Make as for Short Crust No. 1.

PASTRY, SUET CRUST.

½ lb. self-raising flour	pinch of salt
4 oz. suet	water to mix

Chop the suet finely, mix all the dry ingredients together, mix to a stiff paste with cold water, turn on to a floured board, roll out to size required and use.

Note.—If a cheap crust is required use less suet and add ½ teaspoonful baking-powder.

PASTRY, TREACLE.

golden syrup
bread-crumbs
lemon juice
pastry short crust

Roll the pastry out to a square shape, mix the bread-crumbs into the syrup, add some lemon juice, spread the mixture on the pastry not too near the edge; roll out the rest of the pastry to the same shape, place it on the top, fold over the edges, brush the pastry with white of egg, sprinkle with castor sugar, and bake on a greased tin in a quick oven. When done, cut across in neat sections; serve hot or cold.

Note.—Flaky or rough puff pastry can be used.

PASTRY TABLE. The marble top of an old-fashioned wash-stand if laid on the kitchen table will make a cool table for pastry-making and is easily kept clean. Its weight will keep it rigid.

PATENT LEATHER, to renew. When patent leather shoes begin to look dull and lose their freshness, a few drops of spirit of turpentine applied with a soft cloth will brighten them up so that they look almost like new. If your shoes chafe at the heels a tiny piece of chamois leather sewn round the inside of the back of the shoe will prevent it from rubbing the heel and delay appearance of holes in stockings.

PATENT LEATHER SHOES, to keep soft. Rub them occasionally with a little vaseline when they are not in use. This will keep them soft and prevent them from cracking.

PEACH LAYER CAKE.

weight of 2 eggs in butter
weight of 4 eggs in flour
½ cupful crushed peaches
weight of 4 eggs in castor sugar
1 teaspoonful lemon juice
2 teaspoonfuls baking-powder
1 cupful cream
4 eggs
vanilla
6 oz. icing sugar
1 white of egg

Beat butter and castor sugar to a cream. Stir in gradually 4 eggs well beaten alternately with half flour. Stir in rest of flour with baking-powder. Pour into two buttered layer cake-tins and bake in moderate oven till firm and golden. Put on cake rack. Whip cream stiff; add ½ cupful castor sugar, stiffly frothed, white of 1 egg and peaches. Flavour with vanilla and spread between layers. Put together and ice top with sugar moistened with water and lemon juice.

PEACHES AND CREAM.

6 peaches
2 oz. almonds
cream
¾ pint custard
3 oz. almond essence
1 tablespoonful chopped walnuts
¼ cupful sugar

If you use ripe peaches place them in glass dish and sprinkle them with the sugar. Cover closely and stand in a cool place for two hours, then pour over the custard already chilled. When required, cover with lightly-whipped cream, mixed with walnuts and sweetened and flavoured. Prick each peach with split roasted almonds. If tinned peaches are used, prepare for table at once.

PEARL NECKLACES, to clean. Submerge in a small tin of powdered magnesia; leave for a night and gently brush the powder off in the morning.

PEARLS, to remove external stains from. Wash in ground rice and salt, or starch and powdered blue.

PEAR FLAN. As for APPLE FLAN.

PEARS, bottling of. *See* FRUIT.

PEARS, STEWED (for 6 or 7 people).

2 lb. pears	4 cloves
6 oz. sugar	1 inch cinnamon
1 pint water	strip of lemon peel
little claret	carmine colouring

Peel the pears, cut them in half, take out the core, put them in a stewing jar with the water, sugar, lemon rind and spices, add the claret and some drops of carmine, cover with the peelings and stew gently in the oven for 3 or 4 hours. When cool put into a glass dish and pour the syrup over.

PEARS, to store. Pears may either be hung by their stalks or placed separately on shelves.

PEAR TREES. The pear, especially when grown as a wall-trained tree, requires root pruning more frequently than any other fruit tree, or the tree becomes unfruitful. Summer nipping is imperative in pruning the pear, as if all the wood-buds be allowed to remain they will so drain the strength of the tree that fruit-buds will not form, excessive wood growth being characteristic of the pear. For pests *see* APPLE, *also* PESTS.

PEAS. Sow in double rows 6 to 8 inches apart, the rows 2 feet apart. In heavy soil put seed 3 inches deep; in light soil 2 inches deep. Peas mature earliest in light, rich soil; for general crop, a rich, deep loam or inclining to clay, is the best. Sow the extra early varieties in February or March and every fortnight for succession until May or June as required. The plants should be kept clean and earthed up twice during growth. The wrinkled varieties have the nicest flavour but are not so hardy as the round sorts, and if planted early should have a dry soil. The dwarf varieties are best suited for small gardens or for forcing, planted in rows 1 foot apart. The taller kind should be well supported by branched twigs high enough to take full height. Keep the hoe going between rows. Some take the risk of a November sowing to secure an early crop, but frost and birds often combine to defeat the effort.

PEAS, EVERLASTING. Propagate by root division in a well-drained hazel loam.

PEAS, GREEN, to keep till Christmas. Shell the peas and put them in a pan of boiling water. Warm them four or five times. Pour the peas into a colander. Dry them in a cloth and then place in dry bottles. Pour over them melted mutton-fat and cork tightly. Put into boiling water with a spoonful of sugar when cooking.

PEAS, SWEET. *See* SWEET PEA.

PEASE PUDDING.

1 pint split peas   pepper and salt

Soak peas for 24 hours, then drain off water and place the peas in a cloth. Tie up cloth, taking care to leave sufficient room for the peas to expand. Boil for 2 hours with the pork with which they are to be served. Add the pepper and salt just before serving.

PELARGONIUM. Although considered a bit old-fashioned, these free-flowering and attractive perennials make a grand pot display or in the border, if put out after the frosts are over. As bedders they will flower out of doors from early May till autumn, if seeding heads are carefully removed.

There are double, as well as single flowered sorts, and variegated, dark-leaved, ivy-leaved, and other handsomely-foliaged varieties. As a rule, however, the best sorts, bearing fine trusses of bloom, have quite ordinary green foliage. Knock out of pots carefully and plant firmly in loose soil in the positions they are to occupy for the season, in light soil and sunny position. They have a bold effect and when all of one variety and colour are grouped together, they are seen at their best.

PENCIL WRITING, to fix. Pencil writing or drawings may be fixed by brushing over with a little skimmed milk.

PENTSTEMON. Both for the border and the rock garden the pentstemon, in one or other of its many varieties, is admirable; a tall and handsome plant with spikes of bell-like flowers of charming pink or deep scarlet. They thrive best in a warm soil with some protection during winter. For the rock garden there are various dwarf varieties. Pentstemons may be grown either from cuttings or seed, but they are a little tricky in culture and need a good friable soil, well drained.

PEPPERMINT CORDIAL. Pour 1 pint boiling water on to ¼ lb. loaf sugar; stir till sugar dissolves; add 12 drops oil of peppermint and bottle while warm.

PEPPERMINT, INFUSION OF. Steep 6 drams peppermint in 1 pint boiling water for 15 minutes and then strain. Useful for flatulence, colic, gripes, etc.

PERCOLATOR, to clean. To clean your percolator put 1 table-spoonful of borax and 1 of soap flakes in the coffee pot, fill it with hot water and let it percolate as when making coffee.

PERFUME, COLOGNE WATER. (A simple recipe.) One dram each of oil of lavender, oil of lemon, oil of rosemary, and oil of cinnamon. Add 2 drams oil of bergamot. Mix in a bottle, and add 1 pint of alcohol. Or:

Mix together 2 drams each of oils of lemon and cedrat, 1 oz. oil of bergamot, 1 dram oil of rosemary, 2 fluid oz. spirits of neroli and 5 fluid oz. pure alcohol.

PERFUME, LAVENDER WATER. Mix the following thoroughly together, and the longer the perfume is kept before using the better it will be: 3 drams each oils of lavender and bergamot, 6 drops each oil of cloves and attar of roses, ¾ dram each oil of rosemary and essence of musk, 1 oz. honey, ½ dram benzoic acid, 1 pint alcohol and 2 oz. esprit de roses.

PERSPIRATION, EXCESSIVE. The feet should be washed twice a day with soap and lukewarm water, and then dusted all over with boracic acid, and boracic acid sprinkled in the boots. The socks should be changed at least twice a day; cork socks should be worn in the boots. They should be removed at night and dipped in fairly strong Condy's fluid, and dried before being replaced the following morning. Old socks should be burnt when tainted and new ones procured.

PERUVIAN LILY. *See* ALSTROMERIAS.

PESTS ON PLANTS. For destroying pests among flowers or vegetables, a good all-round medium is Derris, either dusted on young plants or through a syringe with a fine spray. For particular species, special treatments are applied, among which are the following, as recommended by the Ministry of Agriculture:

Black Fly on Beans.—Pinch out the growing points and burn them. In bad attacks plants should be treated with nicotine dusts or preparations sold for the control of green-fly and used as directed on the packet.

Cabbage Caterpillars.—Cabbages and related vegetables are regularly attacked by the caterpillars. Hand pick the young caterpillars and crush the egg clusters. Derris dust is satisfactory.

Flea Beetle.—Attacks radishes, turnips and green crops both above and below ground. Dust the young seedling with Derris. In bad attacks the treatment may have to be repeated at intervals of three or four days. If the seedlings are kept growing with plenty of moisture, less damage occurs.

Potato Blight.—To prevent blight, spray the foliage with Burgundy or Bordeaux mixture in mid-July and again at intervals. There are also on the market proprietary copper fungicides which are similar in their effects.

Slugs.—Place small heaps of a mixture of "Meta" and bran or tea leaves (1 brick of crushed Meta to 1 pint of bran) around the attacked crop on a warm evening when the soil is moist. Cover the heaps with wood or glass.

Green-fly and caterpillars are instantly killed by immersion in water heated to 45° C. (113° F.), while beetles perish in water of 50° C.

Here is an excellent insecticide for black-fly, green-fly, hop aphis, red spider and woolly aphis;

Steep ½ lb. quassia chips in ½ gallon water for 12 hours and add ¼ lb. melted soft soap. Make up with water to 4 gallons and use after showers in warm weather. Or:

A thin mixture of oil of turpentine and soap may be applied to the stems and branches.

PETUNIA. A showy, half-hardy plant with large, rich blossoms, embracing a great variety in shades of colour, marking and form. The single-flowered kind are useful for borders, producing a charming effect when properly massed, and may be raised from seed sown in heat in February or March. They are not now so widely grown as the stems are fragile.

PEWTER, to clean. Rub the pewter with powdered rottenstone moistened with equal parts linseed oil and turpentine; then wash in warm soapy water and polish as usual. If the pewter is very badly stained this may have to be repeated several times before its brightness is quite restored.

PHEASANT, ROAST.

1 brace of pheasants
fat bacon
little butter
gravy
bread sauce
fried bread-crumbs
watercress

Pluck, singe and draw the pheasants, scald and skin the legs, removing the claws, wipe with a damp cloth: put a small piece of butter with pepper inside, truss, for roasting: tie some pieces of fat bacon over the breasts, cook for about 1 hour, basting frequently. Remove the bacon, dredge with flour and cook again till brown and frothy. Remove the string, place on a hot dish, garnish with watercress. Serve with bread sauce, fried bread-crumbs and some good gravy.

For the Fried Bread-crumbs.—Melt some butter in an enamelled frying-pan, put in some white bread-crumbs, stir them carefully over the fire until they are nicely browned, drain them on paper, place in the oven for a few minutes. Serve on a lace paper.

PHEASANT, SALMIS OF.

remains of pheasant
1 oz. butter
½ oz. flour
1 shallot or small onion
1 bay leaf
pinch of herbs
1 teaspoonful red-currant jelly
½ pint stock made from
    pheasant bones
salt and pepper
glass of port wine

Remove the bones from the pheasant and cook them in stock. Cut the meat into neat pieces, melt the butter in stewpan, brown the flour, add the stock and stir till it boils. Add the chopped shallot, herbs, jelly, wine and bay leaf, and simmer slowly for 20 minutes. Then strain and put in the pieces of pheasant, season and reheat. Serve garnished with triangles of fried bread.

PHEASANT'S EYE. *See* ADONIS.

PHLOX. Grow from seed sown not earlier than May. Where roots are obtained, of the perennial kinds, April will not be too late to plant to bloom from July to August in all shades of red, from palest pink to deep carmine, lilacs, lavender and whites, many showing an "eye" of deeper tint. Phlox are excellent plants for the herbaceous border, being tall and requiring little attention after planting beyond watering in dry seasons. A light, friable garden soil and a sunny position are most congenial.

PHLOX DRUMMONDI. Will grow to nearly 36 inches, in full sturdy habit and fine floral clusters, and may be sown in boxes of fine compost indoors, in a sunny frame in March or April, bedding out the seedlings early in May. They will flower profusely the most of the summer. Sown outdoors in May these annuals may flower by July. Flowers are now in a variety of colours and shades, usually with a dark centre. They like a sunny position and a fairly rich, light soil. The height is about 3 feet, and the root clumps should be divided every second

214

year. It is advisable to plant half a dozen young roots, a little apart each way, to form a clump, but take care that they are of one colour and variety.

PIANO. To keep this in good condition, place a shallow tin filled with unslaked lime inside it at the bottom. This will attract the damp, keep the wires clean and bright and prevent the keys from sticking.

PIANO KEYS, to clean. Take an old piece of muslin and dip it in alcohol.

For very yellow keys use flannel moistened with eau-de-cologne. Fine powdered French chalk mixed with benzine is also good. Lemon juice is also effective. Another bleaching method for ivory keys which have turned yellow: make a saturated solution of potash and enough whiting to answer your purpose. Mix the whiting into a paste with the solution of potash, making it as thick as putty. Put it on the keys, and let it remain overnight. In the morning remove it. Polish the keys with prepared chalk. Take care to prevent paste falling between the keys.

PIANOS, position. If possible, keep well away from any wall, out of draughts and not too near a fire, as all these things have a detrimental effect on the tone. Keep closed up when not in use. Have it reguarly tuned.

PICCALILLI.

2 cauliflowers	1 tablespoonful flour
2 cucumbers	1 oz. whole spice
2 lb. shallots	¼ lb. sugar
1 marrow (medium)	½ oz. ground ginger
1 quart vinegar	1 oz. mustard powder
	½ oz. turmeric powder

Prepare and salt the vegetables overnight. Boil the whole spices in a covered saucepan (not brass, copper or iron) with most of the vinegar for a few minutes. Mix the other ingredients with the remaining cold vinegar into a smooth paste, then add the strained spiced vinegar and boil for 15 minutes before pouring over the vegetables and bottling.

PICKLES, to detect copper in. Mix a little ammonia liquid with an equal amount of water. Put a few of the pickles into a glass vessel and add the mixture. Stir well together. The presence of copper is indicated if the liquid turns blue.

PICKLES, BEETROOT. Gently boil the roots from 1½ to 2 hours or until nearly done; then drain. When partly cool, peel and cut in slices ½ inch thick. Place in a pickle of 1 oz. black pepper, 1 oz. allspice, ¼ oz. each pounded ginger, sliced horse-radish, salt and 1 quart strong vinegar. To every quart of vinegar 1 dram of cayenne pepper or 2 capsicums may be added.

PICKLES, CABBAGE. Shred red and white cabbage, spread it in layers in a stone jar, with salt over each layer. Put 2 spoonfuls of whole black pepper and the same quantity of allspice, cloves and cinnamon in a bag, and scald them in 2 quarts of vinegar, pour the vinegar over the cabbage and cover it tight. Use it after two days. For red cabbage only see p. 216.

PICKLES, CAULIFLOWER or BROCCOLI. Keep for 24 hours in strong brine. Then remove. Heat the brine and pour it on scalding hot. Stand till next day, drain and throw into spiced vinegar.

PICKLES, CHERRIES. Take large red cherries, perfectly ripe, and put them into jars with layers of powdered sugar between each layer of fruit, interspersing them with thin muslin bags of broken cinnamon, mace and nutmeg. The jars should be three-quarters full of cherries and sugar. Fill up with cold vinegar and cover them closely.

PICKLES, CUCUMBER. Put some spiced vinegar in a jar with a little salt in it. Every time you gather cucumbers pour boiling vinegar on them, with a little alum in it. Then put them in the spiced vinegar. Keep the same vinegar for scalding all. When you have enough, take all from the spiced vinegar, and scald in the alum vinegar 2 or 3 minutes till green, and then put them back in the spiced vinegar.

PICKLES, GHERKIN. Keep them in strong brine till they are yellow, then take them out and pour on hot spiced vinegar. Keep in a warm place till they turn green. Then pour off the vinegar and add a fresh supply of hot spiced vinegar.

PICKLES, MIXED. Whatever vegetables, etc., may be preferred or available, should be prepared by washing and slicing. Cauliflowers should be broken into small pieces; beetroot should be boiled, peeled and cut into cubes.

The prepared vegetables are put in a basin and covered with brine (1 lb. salt to 1 gallon water) or sprinkled with salt. After leaving overnight, the vegetables are removed, washed and drained, put into jars, and covered with cold spiced vinegar.

PICKLES, MUSHROOMS. Stew them in salted water—just enough to keep them from sticking. When tender pour off the water and add hot spiced vinegar. Then cork them tightly if you wish to keep them a long time. Poisonous ones will turn black if an onion is stewed with them, and then all must be thrown away.

PICKLES, NASTURTIUMS. Gather the seeds as soon as the blossoms fall. Put them in cold water and salt for 30 minutes. Then place in boiling salt and water and boil for 2 minutes. Place in a jar and cover with good vinegar; flavour with spice and keep covered for at least 7 days. They may be eaten as capers.

PICKLES, ONION. Peel and boil in milk and water 10 minutes, drain off the milk and water, and pour scalding spiced vinegar on to them.

PICKLES, PEACHES. Take ripe but hard peaches, wipe off the down, stick a few cloves into them and lay in cold spiced vinegar. In three months they will be sufficiently pickled, and also retain much of their natural flavour.

PICKLES, RED CABBAGE. The cabbage should be firm and of good colour. Remove outer leaves, wash the cabbage and cut into shreds. Place in layers in a basin, sprinkling salt between each layer, and leave for 24 hours. Drain thoroughly, pack into jars and cover with cold spiced vinegar (which see).

PICKLES, WALNUTS. To every quart of vinegar use 2 oz. pepper-corns, 1 oz. each allspice, ginger and 2 shallots. Boil together for 10 minutes. The walnuts must be young. Rub with a cloth, prick them with a fork, put them in brine (1 lb. salt to 1 quart water), leave them for 8 to 10 days, drain and leave in the sun for 2 or 3 days until quite black. Put them in jars, pour over the spiced vinegar while hot, tie down with bladder or parchment and keep in a dry place.

PICKLING. Use vegetables gathered on a dry day and only those which are quite sound.

Add 1 tablespoonful of alum and 1 teacupful of salt to each 3 gallons of vinegar, and tie up a bag with pepper, ginger-root and spices of all sorts in it, and you have vinegar prepared for any kind of common pickling.

Use enamelled iron pans rather than those made of copper or brass, as the vinegar used has a harmful effect on these metals.

Always use the best vinegar, whether it is the white wine kind or malt, and do not boil it too long as it evaporates and loses its strength. White wine gives pickles a better appearance, but malt a better flavour.

Anything that has held grease will spoil pickles. Do not keep pickles in common earthenware, as the glazing contains lead and combines with the vinegar.

Stir pickles occasionally, and if there are soft ones, take them out and scald the vinegar, and pour it hot over the pickles. Keep enough vinegar to cover them well. If it is weak, take fresh vinegar and pour on hot.

PICTURE FRAMES, GILT, to clean. Remove all dust from the frame. Then make a solution of 1 gill of vinegar and 1 pint of soft cold water. Dip into the liquid a large camel hair brush, squeeze it almost dry, and brush gently up and down the frame, doing only a small portion at a time until the gilding looks bright and clean. Wash the brush frequently and renew liquid when dirty. To dry, squeeze the brush out tightly; then rub over gilding until all moisture has been removed. Dust with a soft brush to renew burnish.

PICTURES, covering backs. When backing pictures with brown paper, moisten the paper with water before sticking it. This will ensure a taut surface when dry.

PIE, BEEFSTEAK (for 6 or 7 people).

1 lb. steak	little flour
¼ lb. kidney	salt and pepper
stock or water	

Flaky Crust:

10 oz. flour	water
6 oz. butter and lard	salt

Cut the steak in thin slices, roll a small piece of kidney in each slice, dip in flour with salt and pepper added, pile in a pie-dish, high in centre. Do not pack the dish tightly, but leave enough space to add some stock or water. Make the pastry; wet the edges of the dish, line with pastry; egg the edge of pastry and place on the top. Do not touch the cut edges; make some leaves from the trimmings, arrange them round a hole made in the centre, brush over the top with egg; make a rose, place in the centre of the leaves. Bake in a hot oven for 2 hours. The hole under the rose must be kept open during baking to allow the steam to escape.

PIE, COTTAGE. *See* PIE, SHEPHERD'S.

PIE, GAME. Separate the game into joints or pieces, and place into a pie-dish with some fat ham or streaky bacon. Season highly, cover with puff paste and bake in the oven. Raise the crust when half cooked and pour in 4 or 5 tablespoonfuls of melted butter, a glass of light wine and the juice of a lemon.

PIE, PIGEON (for 7 or 8 people).

3 or 4 pigeons	2 oz. ham
1 lb. beefsteak	stock
3 hard-boiled eggs	salt and pepper
flour	flaky or puff pastry

Prepare, singe and draw the pigeons, cut them in halves or quarters. Cut the steak in small pieces, dip them into seasoned flour; put the steak, pigeons, ham and slices of hard-boiled eggs in a pie-dish in layers, pour over enough good gravy or stock to half fill the dish, cover with pastry, trim edges, glaze and decorate in the usual way. Bake from 2 to 2½ hours; scald and skin the feet and put in the centre when the pie is cooked, to show what the pie is made of. If the pie is to be eaten cold, when it is cooked pour in some more good gravy or stock to which some gelatine has been added.

PIE, PORK.

	½ pint water
1½ lb. flour	2 lb. pork
6 oz. lard	salt and pepper

Skin the pork and cut into large dice, boil the water and lard together, pour into the centre of the flour and mix to a stiff dough, keeping it as warm as possible. Knead it to get it smooth; well grease a pork-pie mould, line it with the pastry, keeping one-third for the top. Dip the pork in water and pack in neatly; add plenty of seasoning, place on the top, decorate edges and the top with leaves, leaving a hole in the centre. Bake for about 5 hours.

PIE, SEA (for 5 or 6 people).

½ lb. lean meat	1 lb. potatoes
2 or 3 tomatoes	water
2 onions	salt and pepper

Suet Crust:

6 oz. self-raising flour	salt
2½ oz. suet	

Cut up the meat, peel and slice the potatoes, and slice tomatoes and onions. Put in layers in a saucepan with a little water for gravy, add salt and pepper; make a suet crust, roll out to the size of the top of the pan, lay it on the meat and cook gently for 2 hours. To serve either lift out the crust whole and place the stew under or cut into sections and place round the stew.

PIE, SHEPHERD'S (for 4 people).

½ lb. cooked meat	½ oz. butter or dripping
½ lb. boiled potatoes	little milk
1 small onion	salt and pepper
stock or gravy	

Mince the meat, season, add onion, put in a pie-dish with gravy or stock; mash the potatoes, add the butter and milk, cover the meat with the potatoes, smooth the top with a knife, mark round the edge, brush over with milk, and bake in a hot oven till a nice brown.

PIE, VEAL AND HAM (for 5 or 6 people).

1 lb. veal (fillet)	½ teaspoonful herbs
¼ lb. ham	little grated lemon peel
2 hard-boiled eggs	salt and pepper
1 teaspoonful chopped parsley	onion, stock

For Pastry:

10 oz. flour	water to mix
6 oz. butter and lard	egg to glaze

Cook the veal in enough cold water to cover, with an onion stuck with cloves; when cold cut into thin slices, put a pinch of seasoning (parsley, herbs, lemon peel, salt and pepper) on each slice and roll up, pack the rolls in a pie-dish not too tightly, with the ham and hardboiled eggs cut in slices; reduce the stock, add a leaf of gelatine if necessary, pour it into the pie-dish. Cover with pastry, decorate with leaves and a rose, brush over with egg, bake for 1½ hours, remove the rose and pour in the remainder of the stock. Rough puff or flaky pastry can be used for this dish.

PIES. *See also* FRUIT PIES.

PIGEONS, ROAST.

pigeons	butter
larding bacon	bread sauce
toast	gravy

Draw, singe and truss the pigeons, lard the breasts, roast in a hot oven, basting frequently from 20 to 30 minutes; serve on squares of toast with bread sauce and gravy. A plain French salad of lettuce dressed with oil and vinegar can also be served.

PILES. Constipation or the constant taking of strong purgatives, especially those containing aloes, are common causes of piles, as also is chill from sitting on damp surfaces.

The treatment consists of avoiding constipation and taking a proper amount of exercise, ith care as to the diet, which should contain liberal allowances of fruit, green vegetables and butter. If the piles bleed they should be treated with witch-hazel applied on cotton-wool. When the bleeding has ceased an ointment containing the herb called Pilewort (the Lesser Celandine) perhaps is the best that can be used. Regulate the bowels by taking liquid paraffin, which acts as a lubricating agent on the lower end of the bowel. Hot fomentations will relieve acute pain.

PILLOWS, to restuff. Rub a little beeswax over an iron and press the inner surface of the ticking with it, to prevent the feathers from working through.

PIMENTO. *See* ALLSPICE.

PIMPLES, to remove. Mix 1 oz. each of barley meal and powdered bitter almonds with enough honey to make a smooth paste and apply. Wash off after an interval by swabbing the area with boracic water or calamine lotion.

PINEAPPLE SNOW (for 5 or 6 people).

½ tin pineapple
3 oz. loaf sugar
1 oz. loaf gelatine

whites of 3 eggs
wineglassful of sherry

Dissolve the gelatine in some of the pineapple syrup and a little water, cut the pineapple into small pieces, add to the syrup with the sugar and simmer for 10 minutes, add the sherry and allow the mixture to cool. Whisk the whites of eggs to a stiff froth and add the mixture and whisk till nearly set. Pile roughly in a shallow glass dish, decorate with some pieces of pineapple and serve.

PINK. *See* CARNATION.

PIPES, TOBACCO, to clean. To clean and sweeten tobacco pipes alcohol should be poured in the bowl and allowed to run out through the stem.

PISCES (THE FISHES). Twelfth sign of the Zodiac, influencing persons born between 22nd February and 21st March. Such are rather like Gemini folk (May to June); their own sign, however, imparts adaptability, a sort of second-sight, courageous, sympathetic; yet a tendency to an inferiority-complex mars progress.

PISTACHIO NUTS, to skin. Put the pistachios into a small saucepan with a pinch of carbonate of soda; bring to the boil, remove and drain. Take off the skins, wash in cold water, and dry in a cloth.

PLAICE, FILLETS OF, FRIED (for 3 or 4 people).

fillets of plaice
a little flour

salt and pepper
egg and bread-crumbs

Wash and thoroughly dry the fillets, dip them in flour seasoned with salt and pepper. Beat up the eggs, dip in the fillets, drain and roll them in the crumbs, shaking off any loose ones; fry a golden brown in hot fat, drain well, and serve garnished with lemon and parsley.

PLAICE, FILLETS OF, STUFFED and BAKED (for 3 or 4 people).

1 plaice
½ oz. butter
½ oz. flour
1 gill milk
little lemon juice

salt and pepper
chopped parsley
coraline pepper
veal stuffing

Fillet the plaice, skin the fillets; if large, cut in half lengthways, place a little stuffing on each half fillet, roll up, place on a greased tin, squeeze over each a little lemon juice and bake slowly for 15 to 20 minutes. Serve on a hot dish. Make a sauce with the butter, flour and milk, coat the fillets with it; garnish with coraline pepper and chopped parsley.

PLANT-LICE, APHIDES. Make a solution of tobacco or line-water and repeatedly syringe the leaves and stems of the plants. Ladybirds destroy aphides. *See also* INSECTS ON PLANTS, to destroy.

PLASTER, ADHESIVE, to make. Melt together $\frac{1}{4}$ lb. yellow resin and 2 oz. Burgundy pitch. Spread upon linen. Apply when cool after rubbing a little cold cream well into the affected parts.

PLASTER, MUSTARD. *See* MUSTARD PLASTER.

PLASTER STATUETTES, to clean. Take some finely-powdered starch and make it into a thick paste with hot water. Apply thickly all over the statuette by means of a brush. Allow to dry very slowly and, as the starch falls away, it will take the dirt with it.

PLATES, to heat. Do not put these into the oven as they become discoloured. The correct way is to dip them quickly into hot water and dry them just before they are wanted.

PLEURISY. This is inflammation of the covering of the lungs, and unless a very mild attack demands medical attention.
Causes.—Exposure to cold is by far the most frequent cause. Pleurisy occurring in a young person without any obvious reason is generally the first sign of consumption. It may complicate scarlet or rheumatic fever, measles or Bright's disease.
Symptoms.—Chills and shivering fits may commence the attack. The tongue is furred and the appetite lost. There is pain in the side of the chest, which is made worse by breathing, coughing, sneezing, or any kind of muscular exercise. The person takes short breaths to avoid the pain, and seems to be easier lying on his back or on the healthy side. A short cough is generally present. In bad cases practically only one lung is in use. In favourable cases the fluid in the chest goes away gradually, the lung expands and breathing becomes normal again. If the fluid fills one side of the chest, the action of the heart and the other lung is interfered with, the person becomes livid and the position becomes serious.
Complications.—Congestion of the lungs may occur, or the fluid may turn into matter and form a big abscess in the chest.
Treatment.—The person should be put to bed and fluid diet given. The pain in the side may be relieved by applying linseed-meal or mustard poultices.

PLUMBAGO (LEADWORT). A graceful perennial, of which the two varieties, *P. capensis* and *P. larpentoe*, are of value for the greenhouse and the rock garden respectively. The former, with its delicate blue blossoms, makes a charming training plant for the greenhouse, while the latter is perfectly hardy and forms dense tufts of wiry stems, some 6 inches high, bearing trusses of deep-blue flowers early in September, which last until the frost cuts them off. It is easily propagated by division in spring.

PLUM CAKE. *See* CAKE, PLUM.

PLUM DUFF (for 6 or 7 people).

8 oz. flour	6 oz. raisins
4 oz. suet	1 egg
1 oz. sugar	little milk
pinch of salt	½ teaspoonful baking-powder

Add the chopped suet and stoned raisins to the flour, with sugar, salt and baking-powder. Mix with the egg and milk; tie in a cloth and boil for 2 or 3 hours. Serve with Demerara sugar.

PLUM JAM. *See* JAM, DAMSON or PLUM.

PLUM PUDDING. *See* PUDDING, PLAIN PLUM.

PLUM TART. *See* TART, FRUIT.

PLUMS, to bottle. *See* FRUIT, to bottle.

PLUM TREES. The plum (of which the greengage is, perhaps, the most delicious variety) does not do well on a cold or clay subsoil, nor in a moist-laden climate. A poor soil really suits it best so long as it has good drainage, for it has a tendency to make a superabundance of wood if the soil be at all rich. As a consequence, frequent rootpruning is generally necessary, and it should not be planted deep—a covering of 6 inches of soil is sufficient.

PNEUMONIA. *See* CONGESTION OF THE LUNGS.

POISONS, antidotes for. In all cases send for a doctor at once. If cause is unknown give 1 pint sweet oil as an antidote. Poisons are divided into four classes: (1) Corrosive poisons, which produce intense agony with swelling of the mouth and throat. (2) Irritant poisons, of which the symptoms are sickness, purging and abdominal pains. (3) Narcotic poisons, which give no pain but induce giddiness, loss of sight, stupor and sleep ending in death, with perhaps convulsions. (4) Narcotico-Irritants, poisons of which the first symptoms are the vomiting and purging of the irritants, though stupor and death follow.

When any poison has been taken it is of the greatest importance that treatment should be given without delay. The first thing to be done is to empty the stomach by means of an EMETIC (which see), but *only if the lips and mouth are not corroded (burnt)*. Do not give an emetic for burning poisons such as vitriol, spirits of salts, nitric acid, strong ammonia, caustic soda, carbolic acid, creosote. Then give the right antidote to neutralize the poison, which remains in the system; make the atient lie still if possible, apply hot-water bottles, give stimulant such as strong coffee or brandy if there is a sign of collapse. For acid-poisoning generally, a neutralizing antidote, quickly at hand in most households, is baking-powder or bicarbonate of soda, either of which should be given immediately in milk, or in water if milk is not available.

ACETIC ACID.—Chalk and water or white of an egg.

ACONITE, MONKSHOOD OR BLUE ROCKET.—Emetic; castor oil. Apply hot bottles to feet. Strong coffee.

ALCOHOL.—Give emetic; cold water to the head and strong ammonia to the nose.

ALKALIS (POTASH, SODA, AMMONIA), etc.).—Give drinks containing vinegar or lemonade or lemon juice or olive oil.

ARSENIC.—Emetic; and whites of eggs and milk in large quantities.

BITTER ALMONDS.—Emetic, followed by large quantities of hot water. Pour cold water on head and face. Keep the patient warm.

CARBOLIC ACID.—Flour and water or glutinous drinks (as barley water)—whites of egg and milk.

CHLORAL.—An emetic and an enema of a pint of strong hot coffee. Wrap in hot blankets; rub and apply hot bottle.

CHLOROFORM.—An emetic of soda with water. Do everything possible to keep patient awake.

COAL GAS.—Remove into the fresh air; cold water to the head and artificial respiration.

COPPER.—An emetic, followed by hot water and barley and water or arrowroot and water.

DEADLY NIGHTSHADE (BELLADONNA).—Emetic; water and big drinks of stewed tea; then strong coffee.

FISH POISONING.—Emetic; warm water, castor oil and stimulants.

FOXGLOVE.—Emetic, followed by castor oil and strong tea.

FUNGI.—Emetic, followed by castor oil.

HEMLOCK.—Emetic; castor oil or Epsom salts.

HYDROCHLORIC ACID.—*See* SULPHURIC ACID.

LABURNUM.—Mustard and water followed by warm water.

LAUDANUM.—*See* MORPHIA.

LEAD.—Emetic; then 2 teaspoonfuls of Epsom or Glauber salts every 2 hours till bowels are moved. Then give salts in smaller doses.

MERCURY.—Emetic; large draughts of warm water; and egg and milk frequently repeated.

MORPHIA, OPIUM, LAUDANUM.—Emetics. If the patient can swallow a solution of permanganate of potash, a pinch to a pint of water should be given and repeated. Condy's fluid in water has the same effect as an antidote. Flick the patient with a towel dipped in cold water, put strong ammonia under the nose, and do everything to rouse him and keep him awake. He should be shaken by the shoulders, pinched and compelled to walk about; as he becomes more sensible give hot strong tea or coffee.

MUSHROOMS.—Emetic; and a big dose of castor oil or salts.

NICOTINE.—Emetic; douche head and face with cold water, and give tea, coffee or alcohol.

NITRIC ACID.—Force down some chalk and water, and afterwards large draughts of plain or barley water given.

OPIUM.—*See* MORPHIA.

OXALIC ACID (ACID OF SUGAR).—Magnesia or chalk and water. Then castor oil.

PARAFFIN OIL.—Emetic; tea and coffee.

PHOSPHORUS.—Emetic, to which is added, if available, a teaspoonful of oil of turpentine. A weak solution of Condy's fluid should be given. Epsom salts. Castor oil should be avoided, as it causes the poison to act more quickly.

POTASH.—*See* ALKALIS.

PRUSSIC ACID.—Emetic. Cold water in a jug should be poured over the head and chest. Give a teaspoonful of sal volatile in water. The rapidity with which the poison acts renders treatment difficult. The patient becomes insensible at once, and nothing can be done but remove him to the open air and pour cold water over his head and chest.

PTOMAINE.—Emetics, followed by purgatives. Brandy if necessary.

SALTS OF LEMON.—Encourage vomiting by tickling the back of the throat. Water should not be given as it dissolves the acid and makes the poison act more quickly. Whiting (the thickness of gruel) should be taken, or failing this, chalk and water. If the patient collapses he should be well covered and hot-water bottles put to the feet and sides of the body.

SPANISH FLY—BLISTERING FLUIDS.—Emetic; warm water; oil should not be given as it hastens the action of the poison.

SPIRITS OF SALT.—Chalk mixed with water; barley water.

STRYCHNINE.—Emetics and strong tea, the tannin of which acts as an antidote.

SUGAR OF LEAD.—Emetic; and a big dose of Epsom salts; egg and milk.

SULPHURIC ACID (OIL OF VITRIOL).—Chalk mixed with water; barley water or linseed tea.

TURPENTINE.—Emetic; Epsom salts, eggs and milk, barley water.

YEW TWIGS AND FRUIT.—Emetic. Epsom salts or castor oil.

POLISH, FOR STOVES. Here is an economical stove polish which is cleaner to apply than ordinary blacklead. Mix plumbago with a little water as required and use in the usual way. ½ lb. plumbago should be enough for a year.

POLISH, FRENCH. Dissolve 6 oz. finest orange shellac in 1 quart methylated spirits and strain before using. A thin coating of French polish on brass keeps the air from the brass for a considerable period and tarnishing is avoided.

POLISH, NON-SLIP, FOR FLOORS. Mix together equal parts of turpentine, linseed oil, vinegar and coach varnish. Rub the mixture on to the floor and do not polish.

POLYANTHUS. The strain has lately been greatly improved in variety and beauty of colours, many blossoms being in pastel shades. Its cultivation is perfectly simple, for it will thrive in any garden soil, though it prefers one which is rich and moist, and flourishes best in a sheltered and somewhat shady situation. It can easily be raised from seed sown in the open during the summer months, and being perennial may be increased by division in autumn or early spring.

POPPY. Among the annual poppies the Shirley takes foremost place, by reason of its great variety of delicate colours and profusion of blossom, while the taller Mikado varieties, which grow to 2 feet and are larger and more decided in their colours are also a favourite in the border. They are not particular as to soil if not sown too early, say in May. The Shirleys should be thinned out to 1 foot apart. The French ranunculus annual species is also in many colours. Of the perennial sorts, the Oriental grows to 3 feet, with orange, pink and scarlet flowers, while the Iceland is only 1 foot high: both flower profusely in their second year, but make a good show in their first season. The perennial varieties have the same cultural rules as the annuals. Poppy seed is very tiny: mix with fine earth and sand and spread this thinly on seed bed and cover slightly.

PORES, ENLARGED, to treat. When bathing the face add a little borax to the water. This tends to contract as well as cleanse the pores.

PORK, to choose. Pork must be more carefully chosen than any other butcher-meat, and should never be bought in warm weather. It is only wholesome in the winter. The lean of good pork is pale pink and firm; the fat white and clear; the skin thin and smooth and cool to the touch. Any signs of knots or kernels in the flesh indicate disease, and it should be rejected as unwholesome.

PORK, to pickle. Rub all over with saltpetre and drain for a day. Then rub with a brine of 1 lb. salt, ½ lb. coarse sugar and 2 oz. saltpetre. Place in a tub, cover with common salt, and lay a weight on it to keep down and keep out the air. Scrape off the salt and soak the meat for half an hour in clear water before using. Place in a saucepan of cold water and boil till the rind is tender.

PORK, CROWN OF.

2 lb. neck of pork	apple sauce
sage and onion stuffing	mashed potatoes

This is made with cutlets from the best end of the neck of pork. Have the cutlets chined but not separated and tie the end two together. Bake in the oven standing up until the meat is cooked, then fill the centre with a layer of sage and onion stuffing, on this place a layer of apple sauce and last some mashed potatoes. Put in the oven for a minute or two and serve very hot. Put cutlet frills on each bone.

PORK, LOIN, ROAST.

	apple sauce
5 lb. loin of pork	sage and onion stuffing
gravy	salad oil

Choose the pork with thin skin, score it at equal distances with a sharp knife, brush it over with salad oil, bake in the oven, basting frequently. It must be well done; make the gravy in the dripping pan, pour round the meat, serve with apple sauce and baked sage and onion stuffing. If preferred, the loin can be stuffed by making an incision under the skin and putting in the stuffing.

Roast pork should be cooked in a slow oven allowing about 25 minutes to a pound.

PORK PIE.

1 lb. pork sausages	3 tomatoes
chopped parsley	3 oz. macaroni
salt, pepper	pastry

Skin and cut sausages in halves. Slice tomatoes. Butter a pie-dish, fill with sausage, sliced tomato, seasoning and boiled macaroni. Add a little stock, cover with puff pastry and bake 1 hour.

PORRIDGE, OATMEAL. Put 4 tablespoonfuls coarse oatmeal into a basin, gradually adding 1 quart milk. Stir briskly into 1 quart boiling water, add a little salt and boil until it thickens. Stir constantly.

POTASH, PERMANGANATE OF. This is a very useful deodorant for sinks, etc. Proportion, 1 dessertspoonful in each 2 gallons of water used.

POTATO BALLS.

2 cupfuls mashed potatoes	½ cupful chopped cooked meat
butter	buttered peas

Melt a lump of butter in a saucepan, add potatoes, stir well, season and add a little hot milk. Roll into balls. Make a hollow in top of each with a teaspoon and fill hollow with seasoned meat. Put in a buttered tin with a pat of butter on top of each. Brown and serve hot in a circle on a round hot dish with buttered peas or cauliflower au gratin in centre.

POTATO CHIPS. Peel the potatoes thinly and cut into thin slices, dry well in a folded cloth, and keep covered with the cloth till wanted. Put the slices a few at a time in a frying-basket and plunge them in hot fat for a few minutes to cook; drain them and put them in another pan of smoking hot fat to crisp. Drain well on paper, sprinkle with salt and serve at once on a folded napkin or fancy paper. If one pan of frying fat only is available, it must be left to get several degrees hotter for the second cooking. Straws can be cooked in the same way, and should be cut in even lengths about ¼ inch thick.

POTATO CROQUETTES. Put the cold potatoes through a sieve or a potato masher, make them hot and add butter, little milk, chopped parsley and season well with salt and pepper. Divide into equal portions, form into balls, coat *twice* with egg and bread-crumbs, and fry a golden brown in hot fat. Put a small piece of parsley stalk in each. Dish on a hot vegetable dish on folded napkin or a fancy paper.

POTATO OMELETTE.

	1 egg
3 cupfuls mashed potatoes	¼ teaspoonful salt
½ cupful hot milk	pepper

Mix all together. Season and cook in tablespoonfuls on a greased girdle turning each omelette when brown till it is brown on the other side. Fold and serve with chops or steaks.

POTATO SCONES.

10 oz. cooked potatoes	3 oz. butter
6 oz. flour	pinch of salt

Pass the potatoes through a sieve, mix in the butter and flour while warm, add the salt, roll out, cut into rounds with a pastry cutter, bake about 15 minutes either on a girdle or in the oven, split open, spread with butter and serve hot on a napkin.

POTATO SOUP. *See* SOUP, POTATO.

POTATOES. Early potatoes can be grown on an exhausted hotbed. A covering of light soil must be given before putting a frame over them, and they must be carefully protected from frost. If started in the middle of January, the potatoes will be ready for use well ahead of the usual time. Potatoes grown for usual crops require rather deep, light sandy soil, well drained and of a dry nature. It is best to plant them in ground that has been well manured or used for a green crop the previous year. They are a good first crop, too, on virgin soil. Seed potatoes are medium tubers that have been placed in shallow wooden trays under cover for about a month before they are to be planted. Exposure to light, at the temperature of 60° F. causes the "eyes" to sprout, and if the tuber is planted so as to avoid damage to these tender green shoots, leaving the tip of it just level with the surface soil, the young potato plant will start into growth almost at once and much time be saved; otherwise cut the tuber into two vertically so that each piece of the potato has one or two eyes, and plant them for main crop in March or April in rows of 2 feet apart, 12 to 15 inches distant in the row and 3 or 4 inches deep. Make further plantings till June. Earth them up as soon as the leaves are well above ground. Not only does it help on the growth in the early stages, but when the tubers begin to swell, and those on the top rise through the soil, prevents becoming greened and spoilt in flavour, unless earthing up has been attended to. Often several earthings are necessary between the first and when the plant begins to flower. The best way of earthing is to draw it up around the leaves with a hoe or spade. If the soil is in a heavy, sticky condition, mix up a light compost with silver sand, and use two or three handfuls of this around each young plant, forming a little mound to protect from the frost.

As the leaves grow upwards, and the haulm begins to show, place short, twiggy pea-sticks along both sides of the row, to keep in position some clean, dry straw loosely twisted around each plant. The main crop matures October or November.

POTATOES, to keep. Potatoes will keep if they are piled on the ground and covered with earth and straw; do not expose them to the light. Otherwise it is best to keep potatoes in a dark place, preferably in a cellar. Heap them up and cover with straw.

POTATOES, to mash. When thoroughly cooked, strain off water and allow the potatoes to dry off for about 2 minutes. Mash with a fork, while dry, until there are no lumps left. Then add one or two small pieces of butter and mash again until the butter is all absorbed. Do not add any milk. It will be found that the addition of butter instead of milk will considerably improve the flavour of the potatoes.

POTATOES, BAKED. If these are baked with a joint they are much nicer parboiled and merely browned in fat.

227

POTATOES, BAKED AND STUFFED.

6 baked potatoes	3 tablespoonfuls hot milk
1 tablespoonful butter	salt and pepper

Cut off the tops of potatoes lengthways and scoop out all the insides. Stir in the milk, butter, salt and pepper and beat till creamy. Put back into the baked skins and into the oven to brown. An egg might be slipped into a slight hollow in the centre of the mixture with a dab of butter on top and bake until the egg is set.

POTATOES, BAKED IN THEIR SKINS.

Take some large potatoes, scrub in cold water. Dry and place in a fairly hot oven, turning occasionally. When ready the potatoes should be soft; make a cut in each to allow steam to escape. Shake in salt and pepper and serve with a pat of butter on top, on a paper mat in a hot dish.

When baked potatoes are wanted in a hurry, boil for 15 minutes before baking.

POTATOES, BOILED IN THEIR SKINS.

Scrub potatoes, put them with a teaspoonful of salt in boiling water. Boil until tender. Drain off the water. Let them stand for a minute or two in the covered saucepan, then peel. Serve sprinkled with chopped parsley and a little butter in a hot vegetable dish.

POTATOES, FRIED.

Parboil the potatoes—they can be fried whole or in slices—make the dripping hot in a frying-pan, put in the potatoes, brown them well all over, drain on paper and serve hot on a fancy paper. Cold potatoes can be mashed, seasoned well and fried in the same way, and turned out into a hot vegetable dish.

POTATOES, LYONNAISE (for 4 people).

cold boiled potatoes	juice of ½ lemon
2 small onions	1 tablespoonful chopped parsley
3 oz. butter	salt and pepper

Heat the butter in a sauté pan, slice the onions and toss them in the butter, add the cold potatoes cut in slices and cook both till a nice brown colour, then add the parsley, salt, pepper and lemon juice, mix well and serve hot.

POTATOES, NEW, to boil.

Scrape the potatoes gently, putting them at once into cold water. Put them into a saucepan of boiling water with salt and mint, and cook gently from 20 to 30 minutes. Drain off the water, add 1 oz. butter, shake gently to coat them, turn into a hot vegetable dish and sprinkle over some finely-chopped parsley.

POTATOES, NEW. *See* NEW POTATOES.

POTATOES, OLD, to boil.

2 lb. potatoes	salt	cold water

Peel the potatoes thinly, put them in a saucepan with cold water, add the salt, cook very gently with the lid on till tender; test with a skewer. Pour off the water, put them back on the stove with the lid half on the pan to dry; place a folded clean cloth over them. Serve in a hot vegetable dish.

POTATOES, SAUTÉ.

1 lb. potatoes   2 oz. butter
salt   chopped parsley

Cut the potatoes into neat shapes, parboil them with a little salt, melt the butter and let it get hot, put in the potatoes, toss them over the fire until they are a nice golden colour, sprinkle with chopped parsley and serve at once.

Cold potatoes can be sautéed in the same way, cut into slices.

POTATOES, what to do with. Cold boiled potatoes sliced, dipped in seasoned flour and fried are nice with grilled bacon. They can be added to a mixed vegetable salad or made into hors d'œuvres if minced with spring onion, cucumber and pimento.

POULTICE, BRAN. Make a flannel bag the size required. Fill with bran and place in the oven till thoroughly hot through. Then apply. It will be seen this is a "dry" poultice.

POULTICE, BREAD. Put into a basin a slice of bread without the crust and pour boiling water over it. Cover with a plate and stand the basin near the fire. Then strain pulp with a fork, and spread.

POULTICE, JACKET. (Used in Cases of Pneumonia.) Two large linseed poultices, of which one is applied to the back and one to the chest. They must be large enough to meet on the shoulders and under the arms.

POULTICE, LINSEED MEAL. To ½ pint boiling water gradually add, constantly stirring, 4½ oz. linseed meal or enough to make a thick, stodgy poultice. This may be used to promote the ripening of boils, tumours, etc.

POULTICE, MUSTARD. One part of mustard to seven of linseed meal; mix the two with white of egg—which prevents blisters—add only enough hot water, if any, to make the mixture spread on muslin. The parts where the poultice is applied should be examined after two hours in case of irritation. Four hours is long enough to keep it on.

POULTRY. Always buy poultry when young, except for soup and stock. If young the breast-bone and the tips of the pinions will be soft, the beak brittle, the spurs short, legs smooth, the feathers downy and long coarse hairs absent. If in good condition the flesh should be firm, the breast plump, and there should be some fat. If too fat the flavour is rank and the flesh greasy. Poultry should always be cooked while fresh, staleness being very objectionable and easily detected by a faint unpleasant odour. When freshly killed there is no smell, the feet are limp and moist, and the eyes full.

When the flesh is discoloured or has begun to turn green it should be rejected, and it is not advisable to purchase fowls with the skin torn in plucking or the breast-bone broken. This spoils the appearance when served.

White-legged fowls should be chosen for boiling, as they have the whitest flesh. Those with black or yellow legs are suitable for roasting, as the flavour is richer. When buying poultry already trussed from a poulterer it is advisable to wipe the birds carefully, pick them over and retruss them, replacing steel skewers or using a trussing needle and string for the wooden skewers used by the poulterer. These often impart a flavour to the flesh and are difficult to remove when the birds are cooked.

POULTRY, to keep fresh. Pluck off the feathers, remove the crop and draw the inside. Wash them well in a couple of waters, rubbing all over with salt. Then place them in a saucepan of boiling water, drawing them up and down by the legs several times. After remaining in the pot for 5 minutes, hang them to drain in a cool place. When dry, well salt and pepper the insides and hang them up till required. Well wash in cold water before roasting.

PRAWNS, CURRIED (for 3 or 4 people).

2 or 3 dozen prawns	3 oz. Patna rice
½ pint curry sauce	lemon and parsley

Head, tail and shell prawns, make the curry sauce very hot, put in the prawns and heat them very slowly at the side of the fire. Serve very hot with a border of rice; garnish with cut lemon and parsley.

PRESERVING. Fruit for jam-making should be dry, sound and ripe; damp or over-ripe fruit causes jam to ferment or become mouldy.

As a rule use a pound of sugar with each pound of fruit, though less may be used if the jam is for immediate use. *See also* JAM.

For *Stone Fruit* use a pound of sugar with a pound of fruit.

For *Juicy Fruit* do not use water. In the case of hard fruits, add from ½ to 1 gill water. Add some kernels from the stones to plum jam. A gill of red-currant juice added to each pound of fruit greatly improves raspberry and cherry jams.

The pan should be not more than three-quarters full and the jam should boil steadily and quickly. Skim well when the jam boils and when it appears thick and reduced in quantity, test by pouring a little in a saucer and allowing to cool. The jam is ready when it jellies. Allow it to simmer whilst testing.

JARS.—Should be quite dry and clean. Heat before filling them with jam, and either seal immediately or when cold.

PAN.—It is best to use a thick pan either of copper or iron lined with enamel.

SUGAR.—Use good cane sugar—cheap sugar causes considerable loss of jam owing to the large amount of scum that arises from it, in addition to spoiling the quality of the jam.

Long boiling hardens the fruit. If the jam "catches" at the bottom of the saucepan, immediately stand the pan in cold water, leave for a few minutes, and then place jam in another pan. After cleaning the original pan, replace the jam with a little more sugar. A little lemon juice will often remove any taste of burning. In making jelly do not squeeze when straining through jelly-bags.

PRIMULAS. These are of the same family as primroses and thrive under the same cultural treatment, for the hardy outdoor kinds. Of late years they have been greatly improved in flowering, now comprising many different colours and shades and make a grand show in the fronts of borders or the rockery. Primulas of hardy species —the tall *Primula florindae* (The Giant Himalayan Cowslip), 3 feet high; *Primula microdonta*, with violet flowers, 18 inches high, and *Primula Beesiana*, violet-purple with golden eye—and their cultivated varieties are among the newer sorts. There is a greenhouse strain which also has delicate varieties of colour and which can be raised from spring-sown seed. Care in handling is advised as the leaves bring out a rash on hands if contact is made, though not all varieties do this, nor are all persons susceptible.

PROPORTIONS IN COOKING, general suggestions.

BATTER, *Pancake Batter.*
> 8 oz. flour, 1 pint milk, 2 eggs.
> More eggs and less milk for richer batter.

BREAD.
> 1. *Fermented*—
>> ½ oz. yeast to 1 lb. flour.
>> 1 oz. yeast to 3½ lb. flour.
> 2. *Baking-Powder Bread, Unfermented*—
>> 2 teaspoonfuls baking-powder to 1 lb. flour.

CREAMS.
> 1. *Whole Creams*—
>> ½ oz. gelatine to 1 pint cream.
> 2. *Custard and Fruit Creams*—
>> ¾ oz. gelatine to 1 pint cream.

CUSTARDS.
> 1. *Plain*—
>> 2 yolks of eggs and 1 oz. cornflour to 1 pint milk.
> 2. *Rich*—
>> 4 yolks of eggs to ¾ pint milk.

JELLIES.
> 2 oz. gelatine to 1 quart liquid.
> *Aspic Jelly*—2½ oz. gelatine to 1 quart liquid. Increase the proportion in hot weather.

MILK PUDDINGS.
> 2 oz. cereals to 1 pint milk.
> 1 oz. semolina to 1 pint milk.

MOULDS.
> 3 oz. whole cereals to 1 pint milk.
> 2 oz. ground cereals to 1 pint milk.

PASTRY.
> 1. *Suet Crust*—
>> 8 oz. suet to 1 lb. flour (good)
>> 6 oz. suet to 1 lb. flour and a teaspoonful baking-powder (cheaper).
> 2. *Short Crust*—
>> 8 oz. fat to 1 lb. flour.
>> 6 oz. fat to 1 lb. flour and 1 teaspoonful baking-powder.

PROPORTIONS—*continued.*

   3. *Flaky*—
      10 oz. shortening to 1 lb. flour.
   4. *Puff Pastry*—
      1 lb. shortening to 1 lb. flour.

Note.—Where self-raising flour is preferred, omit baking-powder and add its equivalent to the amount of se'f-raising flour.

SAUCES.

   1. *Foundation Sauces*—
      2 oz. butter, 2 oz. flour to 1 pint liquid.
   2. *Thickened Gravies*—
      1 oz. butter, 1 oz. flour to 1 pint liquid.
   3. *Stiff Binding Mixtures (Panada)*—
      1 oz. butter, 1 oz. flour to 1 gill liquid.

SOUPS.

   1. *Stock*—
      1 lb. bones or bones and meat to 1 quart cold water and 1 quart over for evaporation.
   2. *Thick Soups*—
      1 oz. flour to 1 quart soup.
      1 oz. sago, rice, etc., to 1 quart soup.
   3. *Purées*—
      2 oz. butter and 2 oz. flour to 1 quart purée.

PRUNES. When cooking prunes add half a wineglassful of port wine and a few cloves. The flavour will be greatly enhanced.

PRUNING. The pruning of shrubs, roses and trees is a necessary operation and one which the less experienced usually do insufficiently. Pruning strengthens, improves appearance and results in freer flowering. Old branches which will no longer bear flowers, weak shoots which will only yield poor blossoms, and where the growth is rampant a percentage of good growth can with benefit to future flowering be pruned away.

Roses should be pruned in March or early April, cutting down the growth severely to leave only a couple of shoots on each branch, and cutting out branches which turn inward. This applies to bush roses or standards. Climbers and ramblers need less drastic treatment, but all weak shoots, whether long or not should be cut right down and only three or four sturdy runners left. Note that climbers and ramblers are best pruned in autumn after flowering.

With shrubs, the pruning is to keep shapely and to save weakening by too rank growth. Old wood should also be pruned away as it harbours insects. Spring flowering shrubs are best pruned in May or June, or if late in flowering, in July. Summer-flowering shrubs, prune from March to June, or immediately after flowering. Autumn flowering, mostly prune in March or April, but some are better pruned in autumn after flowering. Winter-flowering shrubs are best pruned in late April or May.

Trees are pruned occasionally both the branches and, less frequently, the roots. It is wiser to ask expert advice as individual treatment is necessary, particularly in regard to fruit trees, but to those who feel competent the following will be useful:

Root pruning of fruit trees is essential to a good crop of fruit. Root pruning may be effected by digging away the soil from the roots until the strong feeders are disclosed, when they may be severed either with a sharp chisel or with a fine-toothed saw, leaving the weaker roots untouched.

In cutting away the branches of wall-trained, espalier or cordon fruit trees, care should be taken to use a thin, sharp knife, sufficiently keen to make a clean cut. If the cut be left with a rough, fractured edge, the branch is liable to split, with disastrous results.

For cutting thick branches, the fine-toothed pruning saw should be used, afterwards smoothing the saw-cut with the pruning knife and smearing it over with grafting paste, so as to prevent decay. This paste may be made by melting, over a slow fire, equal quantities of mutton fat and beeswax with about four times the quantity of pitch. It should be applied warm, while it is sufficiently liquid to be spread with a brush.

PRUNING FRUIT TREES. *See* FRUIT TREES, *also* APPLE TREES.

PUDDING, APPLE.

½ lb. flour	1 tablespoonful sugar
4 oz. beef suet	1 tablespoonful water
pinch of salt	little grated lemon rind
1 lb. good cooking apples	little butter

Chop the suet finely and roll in flour, then mix with the flour and pinch of salt. Make into a dough with water, knead and roll out thinly. Butter a basin and line it with this paste. Peel and core the apples and slice into thin slices until the basin is filled. Add the sugar, lemon rind and water and a small piece of butter. Cover the top of the basin with paste, cover with a cloth and boil for 3 hours. When cooked turn out of basin and serve with cream or custard.

PUDDING, APPLE AMBER (for 6 or 7 people).

2 lb. apples	3 eggs
1 lemon	short or flaky pastry
3 oz. sugar	

Peel, core and slice the apples, put them in a stewpan with the grated lemon rind, juice and sugar, cook till quite tender, then pass it through a sieve; add the well-beaten yolks of eggs. Line the edges of a pie-dish and decorate them with pastry, pour in the apple mixture and bake in a quick oven for about half an hour. Whip the whites to a stiff froth with a little sugar, pile roughly on the top of the pudding, sift over some sugar and bake till crisp.

PUDDING, APPLE AND BROWN BREAD.

2 cupfuls brown bread-crumbs	1 tablespoonful flour
1 egg	⅔ cupful minced suet
2 cupfuls chopped apples	½ teaspoonful salt
1 cupful raisins	1 cupful milk

Mix apples and bread-crumbs. Add suet, stoned and chopped raisins, egg beaten with the milk, flour and salt. Mix well and steam in buttered mould for 2 hours. Serve with lemon sauce.

PUDDING, ARROWROOT.

1 dessertspoonful arrowroot	1 egg
½ pint milk	sugar
	flavouring

Mix the arrowroot smoothly with a little of the cold milk, put the rest of the milk into a saucepan and when boiling pour it on the arrowroot. Return to the saucepan and cook for 3 minutes, stirring all the time. Turn it into a basin, let it cool, add sugar and the yolk of the egg and the white beaten to a stiff froth. Stir lightly and pour into a buttered pie-dish and bake for about 10 minutes. It must not boil.

PUDDING, BAKEWELL (for 7 or 8 people).

rough puff pastry	self-raising flour
egg	2 tablespoonfuls jam
its weight in butter	1 white of egg
sugar	

Line a plate with the pastry, work up the edges and decorate them, put the jam in the middle; cream the butter and sugar together, add the egg and a little of the flour and beat well, stir in the rest of the flour; spread this over the jam. Bake in a quick oven for 30 minutes, whip the white of egg stiffly with some castor sugar, pile it roughly on the top and bake till crisp.

PUDDING BATTER.
This can be made lighter by adding 2 teaspoonfuls of ground rice to the flour before mixing.

PUDDING, BEEFSTEAK (for 7 or 8 people).

2 lb. steak	flour
¼ lb. ox kidney	salt and pepper
Pastry:	6 oz. suet
¾ lb. self-raising flour	water to mix

Wipe and cut the meat into thin slices, roll a small piece of kidney in each and dip into seasoned flour.

Mix the finely-chopped suet with the flour; mix to a stiff dough, knead lightly. Place on a board, cut off a piece for the top, roll out and line a greased pudding basin; put in the meat with some stock or water, lay on the top, press the edges together, tie on a scalded and floured cloth and boil for 3 hours. Serve in the basin with a napkin pinned round it.

PUDDING, BOILED FRUIT (for 6 people).

½ lb. suet crust	water
any fruit	sugar

Well grease a pudding basin with butter or dripping, line with suet crust, put in some fruit, add the sugar and a little water, put in the rest of the fruit, cover with the rest of the pastry, tie on a scalded and floured cloth and boil for 2 hours.

PUDDING, BREAD (for 2 or 3 people).

¼ lb. stale bread	1 gill milk
1 oz. suet or dripping	1 egg
currants	nutmeg
½ oz. sugar	pinch of salt

Soak the bread in cold water, squeeze it dry, put a layer into a greased pie-dish, then a little chopped suet and some sugar and a few currants. Repeat tnis until the dish is nearly full, grate on a little nutmeg, beat the egg, mix with the milk, add a pinch of salt and pour over the bread. Bake in the oven for about three-quarters of an hour.

PUDDING, CABINET (for 5 or 6 people).

4 sponge cakes	1 oz. sugar
some ratafias	1 oz. glacé cherries
1 pint milk	1 oz. sultanas
3 eggs	1 oz. peel
essence of almond or vanilla	jam sauce

Well grease a mould; decorate with cherries; cut the sponge cakes into dice, put in the mould in layers with chopped peel, sultanas and ratafias. Boil the milk, pour on to the well-beaten eggs; add the sugar and flavouring; pour in the mould. Allow it to soak, place over a greased paper and steam from 1 to 1½ hours. Let it stand for a few minutes before turning out. Serve with jam sauce.

PUDDING, CHEESE. *See* CHEESE PUDDING.

PUDDING, CHOCOLATE, to make (for 5 or 6 people).

2 eggs	2 bars of grated chocolate
their weight in butter	vanilla essence
sugar	pinch of salt
self-raising flour	

Cream the butter and sugar, add the sifted flour and eggs alternately, beating well; add grated chocolate and vanilla essence. Decorate the mould with blanched almonds or cherries and angelica. Steam for 2 hours.

Sauce:

2 oz. chocolate	½ oz. crême de riz
½ pint water	vanilla essence
sugar	little brandy

Dissolve chocolate in the water, thicken with crême de riz, boil and add flavourings.

PUDDING, CHRISTMAS.

1 lb. flour	1 lb. sultanas
1 lb. bread-crumbs	1 nutmeg
2 lb. suet	¼ lb. almonds
2 lb. currants	½ oz. mixed spice
2 lb. raisins	¼ teaspoonful salt
1 lb. sugar	1 gill brandy
¼ lb. candied peel	1 gill porter
juice and rind of 2 lemons	8 to 10 eggs
	milk if required

Prepare all ingredients carefully, mix thoroughly, put into buttered basins and boil for 9 hours.

235

PUDDING, CHRISTMAS (Very Plain).

1 lb. potatoes	¾ lb. sugar
½ lb. boiled and mashed carrots	2 oz. mixed peel
	1 grated apple
½ lb. flour	1 teaspoonful spice
½ lb. bread-crumbs	2 tablespoonfuls treacle
1 lb. raisins	2 or 3 eggs
1 lb. currants	milk
½ lb. suet	salt

Prepare ingredients and mix all thoroughly with eggs and as much milk as required. Boil in well-greased basins for 12 hours.

PUDDING, COBURG (for 6 or 7 people).

6 or 8 apples	strip of lemon rind
marmalade	3 eggs
2 oz. cornflour	sugar
1 pint milk	short or flaky crust

Stew the apples till tender; line and decorate the edges of a pie-dish with pastry, put in a layer of stewed apples. Cover this with a little marmalade, then put another layer of apples. Mix the cornflour smoothly with some of the milk, put on the remainder to boil with the lemon rind, add the cornflour, stir till it thickens and cook thoroughly. Add the beaten yolks of eggs, pour over the apples in the pie-dish and bake in a moderate oven till pastry is cooked. Whip the whites stiffly, pile on the top, sprinkle with sugar and crisp in the oven.

PUDDING, COLD LEMON (for 5 or 6 people).

4 sponge cakes	½ pint cold water
2 oz. sugar	some blanched almonds
juice of 2 oranges	custard sauce or whipped
juice of 2 lemons	cream

Add the juice of the oranges and lemons to the water with the sugar; put the sponge cakes in a glass dish and soak well with the liquid. When quite moist, stick with blanched almonds, cut in strips and pour over a thick custard or whipped cream.

PUDDING, FIG (for 6 or 7 people).

4 oz. flour	½ lb. figs
4 oz. bread-crumbs	2 eggs
6 oz. suet	½ pint milk
4 oz. sugar	a little nutmeg
pinch of salt	

Chop the suet and figs finely, mix with the dry ingredients; add the eggs well beaten and the milk, mix all thoroughly together; put into a greased basin, cover with prepared cloth and boil for 3 or 4 hours. Dates may be used instead of figs.

PUDDING, GINGER (for 6 or 7 people).

4 oz. self-raising flour	pinch of salt
4 oz. bread-crumbs	2 tablespoonfuls treacle
4 oz. suet	2 eggs
2 oz. sugar	1 dessertspoonful ground ginger

Mix all the dry ingredients together, stir in the beaten eggs and treacle—if too stiff add a little milk; pour into a greased mould, cover with greased paper and steam for 2½ hours. Serve with treacle sauce.

PUDDING, HALF-PAY (for 8 to 10 people).

¼ lb. flour	2 oz. candied peel
½ lb. suet	1 teaspoonful spice
½ lb. raisins	pinch of salt
½ lb. currants	½ cupful treacle
½ lb. bread-crumbs	1 cupful milk

Chop the suet finely, stone and chop raisins, mix all the ingredients well together and boil for at least 4 hours.

PUDDING, JAM ROLY-POLY (for 6 or 7 people).

½ lb. suet crust
jam

Make the pastry, roll out to an oblong shape, spread with jam, moisten the edges, roll up, fold in a scalded and floured cloth and tie up the ends with string. Boil for 1½ hours; turn out carefully.

When making this sprinkle a few bread-crumbs over the paste before the jam is spread; this will prevent the jam from boiling out.

A treacle roll can be made in the same way, using golden syrup, some bread-crumbs and lemon juice instead of jam.

PUDDING, LEMON (for 6 or 7 people).

6 oz. bread-crumbs	3 oz. suet
3 oz. brown sugar	2 lemons
3 oz. self-raising flour	pinch of salt
1 egg and a little milk	

Chop the suet finely, mix with the flour, crumbs, sugar, grated lemon rind and salt; beat the egg and add with enough milk to make into a stiff mixture; add the juice of the 2 lemons; steam in a greased mould covered with greased paper for 1½ hours.

Sauce:

½ pint milk	½ oz. castor sugar
1 dessertspoonful cornflour	rind of ½ and juice of 1 lemon

Boil milk with lemon rind, pour it on the cornflour smoothly mixed, and cook for 10 minutes; add lemon juice and sugar.

PUDDING, MACARONI (for 2 or 3 people).

2 oz. macaroni	1 egg
1 pint milk	flavouring
1 oz. sugar	nutmeg

Break the macaroni into short lengths and soak in the milk for some time. Put it in a saucepan and cook till tender; add the sugar, beaten egg and flavouring. Put into a greased pie-dish, grate over a little nutmeg and bake for about 20 minutes.

PUDDING, MARMALADE (for 6 or 7 people).

4 oz. self-raising flour	2 oz. sugar
4 oz. bread-crumbs	4 tablespoonfuls marmalade
4 oz. suet	2 eggs and little milk

Chop suet finely; mix all dry ingredients together; mix marmalade with beaten eggs and add, using a little milk if necessary; put into a greased basin or mould, cover with greased paper and steam for 2½ hours. Serve with sauce.

PUDDING, ORANGE (for 5 or 6 people).

3 oz. butter	pinch of salt
4 oz. sugar	grated rind of 2 oranges
4 oz. self-raising flour	juice of 1 orange
2 eggs	

Cream the butter and sugar together, add the eggs and flour alternately, beating well between each; add grated orange rind and juice. Well butter a mould, decorate with quarters of orange, pour in the mixture, cover with buttered paper and steam for 1½ to 2 hours. Serve with orange sauce.

PUDDING, PLAIN PLUM (for 6 or 7 people).

½ lb. flour	2 tablespoonfuls golden syrup
3 oz. suet	½ teaspoonful carbonate of soda
1 oz. raisins	pinch of salt
1 oz. currants	water to mix

Chop the suet and mix with the flour; stone and chop the raisins, clean the currants, dissolve the soda in a little water, mix in with the syrup; make into a light dough with water; steam in a prepared basin covered with a greased paper for 1½ to 2 hours. This mixture can be cooked in the oven in a pie-dish.

PUDDING, PRESERVED GINGER (for 5 or 6 people).

2 eggs	self-raising flour
their weight in butter	3 oz. preserved ginger
sugar	pinch of salt

Cream the butter and sugar, add the sifted flour and eggs alternately, beating well between each addition; add finely-chopped ginger, Put in a well-greased mould, cover with greased paper and steam for 2 hours.

Sauce:

1 gill water	strip of lemon rind
1 stick ginger	1 tablespoonful brandy
juice of 1 lemon	2 oz. sugar
	1 glass sherry

Boil and strain.

PUDDING, RICE (for 2 or 3 people).

2 oz. rice	1 teaspoonful chopped suet
1 pint milk	nutmeg
sugar to taste	

Wash the rice, put into a pie-dish with the sugar and milk, sprinkle over the finely-chopped suet and a grate of nutmeg. Bake in a slow oven for 2 hours.

Note.—Sago and tapioca can be cooked in the same way, using same quantities.

PUDDING, SAGO (for 2 or 3 people).

2 oz. sago	½ oz. sugar
1 pint milk	any flavouring

Wash the sago, put into a saucepan with the milk, cook till transparent, add the sugar and flavouring, put in a greased pie-dish and bake in a quick oven. Serve hot or cold.

Note.—Rice and tapioca can be cooked as above.

PUDDING, SEMOLINA (for 1 or 2 people).

½ oz. semolina	1 teaspoonful sugar
½ pint milk	1 egg

Boil the milk, shake in the semolina, cook till it thickens; add the sugar, remove from the fire; add the beaten yolk of egg. Beat the white to a stiff froth with a pinch of salt, stir in lightly; flavour with vanilla or lemon; put into a greased pie-dish and bake in a moderately quick oven. Serve hot or cold.

PUDDING, SPONGE (for 4 or 5 people).

2 eggs	2 tablespoonfuls water
2 oz. butter	pinch of salt
1 teacupful self-raising flour	jam
½ teacupful sugar	

Mix the eggs, butter (melted) and sugar together and beat well, sift in the flour and add the water; pour into a well-greased pie-dish and bake in a moderate oven. When cooked, turn out and spread a layer of jam on top. Serve hot or cold.

PUDDING, SUET. If the flour and suet be mixed with warm water instead of cold, the pudding will be lighter.

PUDDING, SUMMER.

any suitable fruit	bread
sugar	custard sauce

Stew the fruit with sugar; line a pudding basin with thin slices of stale bread, fitting to a round at the bottom, pour in the stewed fruit gradually, allowing the bread to get well slaked with the syrup; place on a round of bread, cover with a plate and allow to stand till quite cold and set. Turn out and serve with thick custard sauce or cream.

Note.—The best fruits to use for this pudding are raspberries, red currants and black currants.

PUDDING, TAPIOCA. *See* PUDDING, SAGO, and PUDDING, RICE.

PUDDING, TREACLE (for 6 or 7 people).

½ lb. flour	3 tablespoonfuls treacle
3 oz. suet	1 dessertspoonful ground ginger
½ oz. candied peel	½ teaspoonful carbonate of soda
1 gill milk	

Put flour into a basin, shred and chop the suet, add all the dry ingredients; dissolve the soda in some of the milk, add with the treacle and the rest of the milk, mix thoroughly; put into a greased basin, boil for 2 hours and serve with following sauce:

Sauce:

½ oz. butter   1 gill milk
½ oz. flour   little lemon juice
little sugar

PUDDING, YORKSHIRE.

½ lb. flour   2 eggs
1 pint milk   1 oz. dripping
                            salt

Add the salt to the flour; make a well in the centre and drop in the eggs; add a little milk and mix smoothly; beat until it bubbles; add the remainder of the milk and, if possible, stand aside for an hour or two. Melt the dripping in the tin; make it quite hot and pour in the batter. Bake in a quick oven for 25 minutes; serve on a hot dish; cut in neat sections.

PUDDINGS, to steam. The water over which puddings are steamed should never be allowed to boil away. From 1½ to 4 hours is required for steaming, according to the amount of fruit being used.

Always allow for the swelling of a steamed or boiled pudding. Make a pleat in cloth or paper when tying down or you will have a disaster.

PUDDINGS, BOILED. Instead of cloth, use a double piece of grease-proof paper over the basin; tie down with string. This prevents grease boiling out or water getting in.

PUDDINGS, QUEEN OF (for 3 or 4 people).

1 pint milk   lemon flavouring
5 oz. bread-crumbs   2 oz. sugar
2 eggs   jam
1 oz. butter

Boil the milk with some strips of lemon peel, strain it over the bread-crumbs and cook them for a few minutes. Allow the mixture to cool slightly, add the butter, sugar and yolks of eggs, pour it into a buttered pie-dish, and bake in the oven for about half an hour. Spread the jam over. Make a meringue with the stiffly-beaten whites and sugar, pile it on top of the pudding and bake till crisp.

PULSE. To take the pulse, put the three middle fingers lightly on the patient's wrist on the radial artery, which is just beneath the thumb. Get the feel of the beat before counting.

An irregular pulse is a sign of exhaustion.

A full and quick pulse, a sign of fever.

A hard pulse, one which is not easily stopped by pressure.

A soft pulse, one which is stopped easily.

A thread-like pulse is a pulse that is very small and weak.

The pulse of a woman beats more rapidly than that of a man and during sleep it is slower than when awake.

Age						Pulsation per Minute
Baby up to 1 year	.	.	.	.	.	130 to 140
At 2 years	.	.	.	.	.	100 to 110
„ 3 years	.	.	.	.	.	90 to 100
„ 7 years	.	.	.	.	.	85 to 90
„ 14 years	.	.	.	.	.	80 to 85
Adult	.	.	.	.	.	75 to 80
Aged person	.	.	.	.	.	about 60

PUMPKIN. Sow seed in April in a hotbed. Transplant to any open, sunny spot in May on good stable manure.

PURÉE, GREEN PEA (for 4 people).

2 pints peas	1 small onion
sprig of mint	1 teaspoonful castor sugar
sprig of parsley	salt and pepper
1 quart white stock	1 gill cream

Boil the stock, add the peas and the shell, mint, parsley and onion; boil till peas are tender, pass through a hair sieve, return to the saucepan; add the cream, sugar and seasoning, reheat it, but do not allow to boil. Serve with croûtons of fried bread.

PURGATIVES. The common purgatives in use are: Taxol, Epsom salts, Carlsbad salt, confection of senna, senna tea. They should be used only as needed. Purgatives must be given with caution to children, delicate people and the aged. In ulcerated conditions of the bowels, and with people suffering from piles, they should be avoided. If the bowels require unloading, senna at night, followed by a Seidlitz powder the next morning before breakfast, will answer the purpose in most cases.

PUTTY, to remove. Old putty has to be removed when a new glass is put in. A good way to accomplish that is to heat a poker red hot, and pass it slowly over the hard putty; the heat will soften it for removal.

PUTTY, GLAZIERS'. Mix together to a thick paste whiting and linseed oil.

QUEEN OF PUDDINGS. *See* PUDDINGS, QUEEN OF.

QUENELLES, BEEF.

4 oz. lean beef	stock
1 oz. bread-crumbs	salt and pepper
1 egg	gravy

Slightly grill the meat, trim off all the fat and skin, mince it and then pound it in a mortar; pass it through a wire sieve, add the bread-crumbs, beaten egg, salt and pepper, and about 1 tablespoonful of stock. Form into egg shapes with two dessertspoons, place them in a buttered sauté pan, pour round some hot stock and poach very slowly from 10 to 15 minutes. They should be covered with greased paper. Drain them on a clean cloth. Serve them with a good gravy.

Note.—Chicken quenelles can be made in the same way by using chicken instead of beef.

QUININE. This is recommended as an excellent tonic in cases of debility and can be purchased in powder (quinine sulphate) as pills, or liquid, as orange and quinine wine. It will also help greatly in relieving neuralgia, whilst ammoniated tincture of quinine is splendid for warding off colds.

QUINSY (ABSCESS IN THE TONSIL). The patient should be in bed, and take fluid diet, mutton broth, beef tea and milk; and given small pieces of ice to suck. Hot fomentations should be applied to the neck, and the throat steamed over hot water; the bowels should be well opened and kept free. If the abscess does not burst naturally it may have to be opened by a surgeon.

RADISH. Sow for early use in hot beds during the winter and early spring, or later on in sheltered borders, in well-manured, deeply-dug and finely-raked soil to promote quick growth. Sow thinly 1 inch deep, broadcast or in drills, 10 inches apart, and thin to 2 inches in the rows. Protect from birds. Sow at intervals of 2 or 3 weeks until September for a succession. Sow winter varieties in July and August, but lift before severe frost and store in a cool cellar in sand or a pit.

RAINCOATS, to wash.

The following recipe may safely be used for washing raincoats without the slightest fear of damaging the rainproof qualities. Dissolve 1 lb. alum in 3 gallons of cold water. Use the solution for washing the coat. Do not use soap.

RAIN SPOTS, to remove.

Rain spots on georgette may be removed by ironing the article under an evenly-damped cloth. The iron should be only warm.

RANCID BUTTER. To make rancid butter sweet put it to soak for a couple of hours in cold water with a good pinch of carbonate of soda. The rancid taste will disappear and the butter be as good as ever.

RANUNCULUS. Among the cultivated spices the Alpine buttercup makes a good plant for the rock garden if set in a moist, sandy and porous soil. Plant bulbs in the latter half of February, claw downwards, about 2 inches deep, and as soon as the leaves fade, after flowering, lift and store till following year.

RASHES, to recognize certain diseases by. ("I" after the name of the disease indicates infectious and "N" that it is notifiable. See page opposite.)

RASPBERRIES, to preserve. *See* STRAWBERRIES.

RASPBERRY. The soil for raspberry canes should be light and of sandy substance, while a yearly dressing of manure is necessary to induce vigorous growth. Every autumn, before manuring is done, the stray suckers should be removed and the pruning of the canes attended to. Cut down close to the ground all but four canes, but should they be weak leave only three, two or even one. None of the canes should exceed 5 feet in height; if so cut off. Pruning is required each year, as canes which have borne fruit never do so a second time. Do not crowd; free access of sun and air is vital. Allow 3 or 4 feet between each plant.

RASHES.

Disease	Where the rash *first* appears	Its appearance	Day when rash appears
Chicken-pox (I)	Face, head, back	Small red, raised spots, rather resembling flea bites	1st or 2nd
German Measles (I)	Face	Similar to measles but smaller and paler. Oftenvery irritating	2nd
Measles (I)	Face, arms, behind ears	Dark, crimson pin-point spots	4th
Nettle Rash	Any part of the body	Raised white lumps on a red surface. Very much like "heat-spots." Very irritating	1st
Scarlet Fever (Scarlatina) (I) (N)	Neck, back, chest	Small, bright red dots close together	2nd
Septic Poisoning.	— — —	Very similar to Scarlet Fever	— —
Smallpox (I) (N)	Face and wrists	Somewhat resembling Chicken-pox	3rd
Typhoid Fever (I)	Abdomen, back and chest	A few small, pale pink spots	10th

RASPBERRY CORDIAL. Pour over 6 lb. ripe raspberries, 3 oz. tartaric acid dissolved in 1 quart water. Strain through a jelly-bag after remaining standing for 3 days; do not press the fruit. To each pint of juice allow 1¼ lb. loaf sugar. Stir till dissolved, and bottle. Keep in a warm place, but do not cork for a fortnight. Then remove to a cool, dark cellar or pantry. Add a little to cold water to make a delicious drink.

RASPBERRY VINEGAR. Use freshly gathered raspberries and pick them from the stalks. Pour 3 pints of best vinegar over every 1½ pints raspberries in a stone jar and leave for 24 hours. Strain the liquor over another 1½ pints raspberries, leave for another 24 hours and repeat the process. Drain off the liquor without pressing and pass it through a jelly-bag (previously moistened with vinegar) into a stone jar. To every pint of liquor add 1 lb. of pounded loaf sugar, stir until sugar is dissolved, then cover the jar. Boil for 1 hour in a saucepan of boiling water, removing the scum as it rises. To every pint add a glass of brandy; bottle and seal the corks.

RATS AND MICE. Chloride of lime is very effective in driving these out, but it must be put in a metal container as it destroys almost anything it touches. Lime is also effective in getting rid of silver fish.

RED MULLET (for 4 people).

4 mullet
1 oz. butter
lemon juice

1 glass port or claret
anchovy essence
½ pint white sauce
salt and cayenne

Wash the fish and dry thoroughly in a cloth; do not open it, only remove the gills and small intestine, which will come out with them; squeeze over some lemon juice, sprinkle with salt and pepper, wrap each fish in thickly-buttered paper, place on a baking-tin and bake in a moderate oven for 20 minutes. Serve in the paper cases. Add to the white sauce some lemon juice, anchovy essence, cayenne and a glass of port or claret, and the liquid which has flowed from the fish; serve this sauce with the fish.

RED-TILE DOORSTEPS, to clean. It is a great saving of labour to polish these with floor polish instead of washing. It requires doing only once or twice a week with a rub up on other days. The tiles soon acquire an attractive deep colour.

REGISTRATION OF BIRTHS, DEATHS, MARRIAGE. *See* under respective headings.

RELAXED THROAT.

Causes.—Excessive use of the voice; over-indulgence in tobacco— especially cigarettes—and alcohol.

Symptoms.—The throat is sore, and the person is always clearing his throat. The glands in the neck may enlarge.

Treatment.—Rest of the voice and moderation in smoking and drinking. The throat should be gargled with lukewarm Condy's fluid night and morning and chlorate of potash lozenges sucked during the daytime. Parrish's food—a teaspoonful three times a day—will act as a tonic. Change of air to the seaside is beneficial.

REMOVING "SHINE". Navy-blue clothes can be freed from "shine" by sponging with a little vinegar and warm water. The same results can be obtained with petrol or ammonia.

RHEUMATIC GOUT, treatment. The diet should be good and easily digested, and beer avoided. The joints should be wrapped in flannel, and protected from injury. Massage, liniments and gentle movements may do good. Liniment of iodine painted over the joint till it produces slight blistering is beneficial.

RHEUMATIC PAINS. *See* LUMBAGO.

RHEUMATISM, liniment for. Mix equal parts of oil of wintergreen and olive oil.

RHEUMATISM, medicine for. A tried and excellent remedy for rheumatism: sulphur, 1 oz.; cream of tartar, 1 oz.; rhubarb, 1 oz.; gum guiacum, 1 dram; honey, 16 oz. A teaspoonful or more is taken night and morning.

RHEUMATISM, MUSCULAR.
Causes.—Cold and damp, strain, excessive muscular exertion.
Symptoms.—One set of muscles is affected as a rule. It may be the back, sides of the chest, neck, shoulder, or scalp.
Treatment.—Rest and the application of hot flannels. The part may be covered with a cloth and a hot iron run over. Massage, Turkish baths and electricity afford relief, but great care must be taken not to catch cold after a bath, as this will make the affliction worse. Ten grains of salicylate of soda should be taken at bedtime when the pain is very troublesome.

RHODANTHE. A half-hardy annual, one of the brightest of "Everlasting" flowers. *R. manglesi* has rose-coloured blossoms with yellow centres, while *R. maculata* may be had with either white or carmine flowers. *R. atrosanguinea* is more branched, of dwarfer growth and bears flowers of bright magenta. Sown in heat in February or March. Seedlings do not transplant successfully except when quite small.

RHUBARB. Rhubarb may be forced in a pit, cellar, or a shed if the light is excluded and the plants are protected from rain. Lift the stools with the surrounding soil and pack them closely together in the place prepared. A good dressing of well-rotted manure should be dug in about the roots after pulling the leaves.

RHUBARB, to make fresh plantations. In February or March divide part of the rhubarb bed into plants having one eye apiece, and replant a yard apart in good soil. These new plants should be left until next season before gathering sticks.

RHUBARB TART.

rhubarb
½ lb. self-raising flour
¼ lb. butter
1 teaspoonful castor sugar
pinch salt

Remove skin of rhubarb. Cut into pieces and half fill pie-dish. Sprinkle with sugar and pile dish high. Rub butter into flour, add sugar and salt and enough water to make a firm paste. Roll out $\frac{1}{4}$ inch thick. Line edge of pie-dish and cover. Notch edges, brush with egg, sprinkle with sugar. Bake in quick oven 40 minutes.

RICE BLANCMANGE or MOULD.

2 level tablespoonfuls	sugar to taste
ground rice	little lemon rind to flavour
1 pint milk	

Make the ground rice into a smooth paste with 2 or 3 tablespoonfuls of cold milk. Place the rest of the pint of milk in a saucepan with the lemon rind and sugar. After bringing to the boil, allow to simmer very gently for about 20 minutes and then remove the lemon rind. Pour the hot milk gradually over the ground rice, stirring all the time to keep it smooth, and then return to the saucepan and boil for a further 10 minutes, stirring all the time to prevent burning. To set, turn into a mould which has been well rinsed out with cold water.

RICE HEDGEHOG.

1 cupful rice	salt
$\frac{1}{2}$ pint custard	3 oz. sugar
nutmeg	1 gill cream
2 oz. almonds	3 pints milk
lemon rind	3 oz. crystallized cherries

Pour milk into saucepan; flavour with grated nutmeg and rind of lemon. Wash rice and simmer in milk till thoroughly cooked; stir in sugar and salt and turn into basin. When cold, add cream, custard, chopped cherries and almonds. Pile in glass dish and top with more cherries.

RICE, LEMON (for 3 or 4 people).

3 oz. rice	1 lemon
2 eggs	little apricot jam
1 pint milk	1 oz. sugar

Cook the rice in the milk with the grated lemon rind. When quite tender, add the well-beaten yolks of eggs, sugar and lemon juice, put it in a buttered pie-dish and cook in the oven till firm. Spread over a thin layer of apricot jam. Make a meringue with the whipped white of egg, pile on the top and crisp in the oven.

RICE, PATNA, BOILED.

rice	lemon juice	salt

Have a large white-lined pan with plenty of boiling water, wash the rice, plunge it into the water, to which lemon juice and salt have been added. Boil fast, stirring occasionally. Test by breaking a grain between finger and thumb. When tender, pour in a cupful of cold water to stop the boiling, drain in a sieve, pour cold water over to separate the grains. Dry on a greased paper in a cool oven or in the saucepan covered with a clean cloth.

RING, TIGHT, to remove. Pass a needle and cotton under the ring. Pull the cotton up towards the hand and twist the rest of the cotton several times round the finger until it reaches the nail. Take hold of the end nearest the hand and it will be an easy matter to slip the ring off the finger. Or, wash the hands in warm soapy water.

RINGWORM. This is very contagious; the sufferer should sleep alone and use separate towels, etc. Wash the affected place with iodine or antiseptic lotion after cutting off the hair round the sore. Keep clean and apply precipitate ointment at intervals.

RISOTTO À L'ITALIENNE.

2 oz. butter	½ pint tomato sauce
½ lb. rice	2 oz. Parmesan cheese
1 shallot	little nutmeg
1 pint stock	salt and pepper

Chop the shallot finely and cook in the butter; wash, drain and dry the rice and fry lightly; add the stock by degrees as the rice swells, stir in the tomato sauce, season well, and add a grate of nutmeg. When rice is tender add the grated cheese. Serve very hot.

RISSOLES.

¼ lb. cold meat	egg and bread-crumbs
4 tablespoonfuls bread-crumbs	½ pint stock
	1 teaspoonful chopped parsley
1 oz. butter	½ teaspoonful anchovy sauce
1 oz. flour	salt and pepper

Mince the meat finely, mix in the bread-crumbs, parsley and flavourings; cook the butter and flour together, add the stock, boil well, mix in the anchovy sauce and add to the meat; allow it to cool, form into balls with a little flour, coat with egg and bread-crumbs and fry in hot fat. Serve on hot dish with fancy paper; garnish with fried parsley.

RISSOLES À LA POMPADOUR.

4 tablespoonfuls minced chicken, rabbit or veal	¼ pint stock
	3 mushrooms
4 tablespoonfuls ham or tongue	¼ lb. short crust
	salt and pepper
½ oz. flour	egg and bread-crumbs
½ oz. butter	

Make a thick sauce with the butter, flour and stock, cook well, add the minced chicken, mushrooms, ham and seasoning, allow it to cool; make the pastry, roll out very thin and cut into rounds; put a little of the mixture on one round and cover with another, pinch the edges together, coat with egg and bread-crumbs and fry a golden brown in hot fat. Dish in a circle with fried parsley in the centre.

RITZ CREAM.

2 bananas	raspberry jam
cream	1 breakfastcupful vanilla
grated chocolate	custard

Put a teaspoonful of jam in custard glasses. Fill up with custard, till half full. Pile up with sliced bananas and cover with cream. Grate chocolate over. Serve cold with sponge fingers.

RIVER ETIQUETTE. The rule of the river is that small craft should, when travelling against the stream, keep in near the banks, but those coming down with the stream should be in the middle.

In the former case another boat—meaning any small craft—travelling the same way and wishing to pass one in front, must not push between it and the bank, but make a detour to pass it on the outer side of the river.

A sailing-boat, tacking about, has certain rights, and other types of craft should give is as much room as possible, never, if avoidable, cutting across its tacking radius.

Do not interfere with an angler's line.

Large and power-propelled craft, such as barges, or steam, electric and petrol launches, are privileged to take whatever part of the river is expedient for them, and smaller craft must give way.

Upon reaching a lock, never try to get in ahead of others who are before you. Keep in your place quietly and ship oars or poles without splashing or annoying occupants of other craft. When much traffic has to pass through the lock, it may be impossible to avoid a little bumping and pushing, but every care should be taken and an apology made if occasion calls for one. It is unpardonably rude to force your way into a better position by pushing, pulling or hanging on to another boat, and both risky and ill-timed to attempt any changing of seats while waiting or while in the lock. Launches and other large craft have precedence in passing through a lock.

ROCKERY, to make. To be a success a rockery needs to have adequate drainage. Dig out the site to a couple of feet and fill with rubble, small stones and rough earth. On this build gradually, layer by layer, with good earth having a percentage of sand and loam and grit worked in, so as not to leave spaces. Gradually reduce width and breadth of layers so as to get a good angle of slope, and arrange all surface rocks so that the pockets have an outward angle for the rain to get into the soil-filling instead of draining down the surface. Do the job thoroughly, for if rocks are piled anyhow and soil well packed, in the weathering will silt the earth down beyond the roots and also roots will come across cavities without earth. Granite is the best material, but sandstone and limestone are easier to obtain and do quite well, though not so lasting. Vary size of pockets and also of the rocky chunks. There are many dwarf border plants that are suitable, such as the aubretia, saxifrages, alyssum, heuchera, London pride, dianthus, arabis, campanula and ageratum. The more ambitious should consult a florist for the rarer suitable rockery plants, including Alpine (which see). Always plant firmly and make sure pockets are filled at base.

ROCKET (HESPERIS). Hardy perennial with sweet-scented spikes of purple or white flowers. It blooms freely; height about 18 inches. It needs a rich, moist soil, and even then is the better for division and transplanting into fresh ground. Seeds should be sown in spring in a sunny situation.

ROES, SOFT, on toast.

anchovy paste	herring roes
cayenne pepper	salt

Cut buttered toast into finger-lengths after removing the crusts and spread thinly with anchovy paste. Rinse soft roes in cold water, dry with a cloth and cook lightly in a little butter in a frying-pan. Put a roe on each piece of toast and serve hot, sprinkled with salt and cayenne.

ROLY-POLY, COLD MEAT (for 4 or 5 people).

6 oz. flour	cold meat
2½ oz. suet	onion
water	¼ teaspoonful herbs
salt	salt and pepper

Make a suet crust with the flour and chopped suet, roll out to an oblong shape; chop the meat finely, add the onion, finely-chopped herbs and seasoning, mix well and lay it on the suet crust; wet the edges, roll it up, roll it in a scalded and floured cloth, tie it and boil for 2 hours. Serve hot with a good gravy.

ROMAN FIGURES. The ordinary numbers in common use are know as Arabic numerals, but as in the Bible, the Roman style is often used for chapter numbers in ordinary books, and in numbering paragraphs in official and professional documents.

The Roman numerals can soon be memorized. The one is obviously I, with II and III for 2 and 3. Then 4 is IV and 5 is V, with VI as 6. For 7 is VII, for 8 is VIII and for 9 is IX. Ten is X, 20 is XX, 30 is XXX, while 40 is XL, because L is 50.

It will be seen, therefore, that the 4s, of whatever value are expressed by the I in front of the V (5) and the 6s by the I following the V. In the same way with X (10), IX is 9 and XI is 11. So XIX will be 19.

Bearing this in mind as the Roman system, note that:

X stands for the tens
L	„	„ fifty
C	„	„ hundred
D	„	„ five hundred
M	„	„ thousand

If therefore the year 1957 had to be expressed in Roman numerals it would be—MCMLVII: that is to say—M=1000, CM=900, L=50, VII=7.

ROSE LEAVES, to preserve. Gather leaves when dry and place in a jar with common salt.

ROSES. Any good soil will be found satisfactory for roses, though a rich, leafy loam with a clay subsoil is best. Cleanliness, sunshine, plenty of air and keeping clear of greenfly and blight are essential. Autumn is the best season for planting, which should be done in mild, moist weather. Prune early in March, cutting away the previous year's growth and any dead wood, but for climbing roses cut back only a few inches of the previous summer's growth and prune to the ground the older growths. The annual pruning of roses other than climbers may be supplemented by thinning the shoots in May, and to obtain fine specimens it is usually necessary to pick some, or all, of the side buds of a cluster.

Do not use strong crude fertilizers, specially suitable ones are on sale. Keep the soil loose 5 or 6 inches from the surface, using a small, thin-pronged fork for the purpose. Give plenty of soft water in June if May happens to be very dry. Examine daily for greenfly and cater-pillars.

When planting roses give the roots plenty of room; place decayed compost at foot of hole, cover with a little soil, then spread roots and fill up, treading soil very firmly round. Do not bury the stock; it should just be showing on the surface. Cuttings can be taken in August of climbers and ramblers and struck in sand; but bush roses seldom strike from cuttings.

ROSE TREES, to clear from blight. Sprinkle the trees when still damp with the morning dew with a mixture of equal quantities of sulphur and tobacco dust. After a few days the insects will disappear and the trees should then be syringed with decoction of elder leaves. A dusting of Derris is an effective precaution. *See* INSECTS ON PLANTS, to destroy.

ROSE WATER. Take a glass bottle with a wide mouth and ground glass stopper. Fill two-thirds full with deodorized alcohol, add rose leaves (preferably white) until no more can be forced into the bottle. Allow to stand several months keeping bottle air-tight. Then strain.

ROTATION. In vegetable gardening, the system of rotation of crops materially assists production. Simply explained it means that the same crop is not grown year after year on the same plot, as that would exhaust from the soil the chemicals that crop needs and yet for crops of another sort the soil would be good. Therefore an allotment, or part, is divided into three sections and what is grown on No. 1 the first year, is grown on the second section next year, and on the remaining section for the third year. On the first section for the second year another kind of crop is grown, moving to the second and third sections on succeeding years. A third variety fills the first section for the third year, and passes to the other two in due course. Then the whole process is repeated, as the soil has renewed the chemical quality required.

The following table will act as a guide in carrying out a system of rotation, and also in applying artificial manures to particular plots in order to supplement dung:

Group 1.—Crops requiring chiefly phosphates and potash: potatoes, peas and beans.

Group 2.—Crops requiring chiefly nitrogen and phosphates: cabbage, cauliflower, sprouts, broccoli, etc.

Group 3.—Crops requiring nitrogen and potash; beet, carrot, parsnip, radish.

Certain crops requiring the three elements in more equal proportions, onions, leeks, turnips, celery and fruits do not benefit by rotation. They need ground that is manured every season.

ROUX.

2 oz. butter   2 oz. flour

Melt the butter in a saucepan, stir in the flour and cook well. A *white* roux should not colour: a *brown* roux should cook till a good dark brown.

RUBBER, to preserve. Make a mixture of 2 parts water and 1 part liquid ammonia and dip the articles into it until they are soft, smooth and elastic as at first. This will prevent rubber articles from cracking.

RUBBER BOOTS. To preserve these fill a pair of old socks with bran and keep them inside the boots when not in use. This dries up the dampness inside the boots.

RUBBER HOT-WATER BOTTLES. To preserve these when not in use, inflate bottle with air by blowing into nozzle, replace stopper and smear the outside of the bottle with a little vaseline. Hang up till required.

RUGS, SKIN. To clean a light skin rug, thoroughly brush it and then rub in plenty of warm bran for about quarter of an hour. When the rug has been well shaken it will look as good as new.

White skin rugs can be satisfactorily cleaned at home with powdered magnesia. Sprinkle it on generously, work it well into the fur with the tips of the fingers; leave it for half a day and then shake and brush the rug vigorously out of doors.

Never allow good rugs to be beaten. Merely brush both sides and rub over quickly with a cloth wrung out of hot salted water.

RUPTURE.

Causes.—Violent exercise and straining, lifting of heavy weights, violent coughing, stricture. Lifting of heavy weights and straining to hang up clothes, etc., should be particularly avoided during pregnancy, as this is very liable to give rise to either single or double rupture. Occasionally a child is born ruptured.

Symptoms.—There is a rounded tumour in the groin, which increases in size when the person coughs or strains. A rupture may, through a sudden strain, become strangulated, which means that it cannot be returned to the abdomen. This is a very serious condition and a risk which a person with a rupture always runs.

Treatment.—A surgeon should always be consulted.

RUSKS, HOME-MADE. Rusks, of which children are so fond, can be made very cheaply at home. Remove the crusts from odd pieces of bread, cut the bread into fingers and bake thoroughly. Serve with butter.

RUST, to keep iron and steel articles free from. Take 1 lb. of pig's lard and dissolve in it $\frac{1}{2}$ an oz. of camphor. Remove the scum and mix enough blacklead to give an iron colour. After rubbing the mixture over the article, it should be allowed to remain for 24 hours. Then wipe off with a clean cloth. This will keep the article in excellent condition for months.

If curtain pins be dipped in white enamel before using, rust will be prevented. All hooks and nails for hanging damp towels, etc., should be similarly treated to avoid unsightly marks.

Polished steel should be treated with pure paraffin wax. The wax should be warmed, rubbed on and then removed with a piece of woollen rag.

Another excellent mixture may be made from white lead, tallow and linseed oil. Mix to the consistency of a thick paint.

RUST, to prevent on grates. Smear as thickly as possible a strong paste of fresh lime and water over the polished surface. This will keep grates not in use free from rust for many months, and is particularly useful where a house is to be unoccupied for some time.

RUST, to remove. Mix 1 part of muriatic acid with 4 parts of water and allow the rusty article to soak in this mixture for 24 hours. Now rub vigorously with a scrubbing brush and wash in plain water. Allow the article to dry before a fire and then polish with oil and emery powder or emery cloth.

Another method is to cover the metal with sweet oil. Allow it to remain for two days. Then rub with finely-powdered, unslaked lime until the rust disappears.

Kerosene or benzine are probably the best cleaning liquids for iron and steel. But if articles have become pitted by rust they must be scoured with very fine emery paper. If steel is rubbed with a mixture of lime and oil or with mercurial ointment it will not easily rust.

RUST, to remove. To remove from marble rub with lemon juice. Tinware should be treated with salad oil and whitening. Rusty vessels should be boiled with borax and water and then scoured.

RUSTY MATTRESS. If your spring mattress gets rusty give it a coat of aluminium paint which you can obtain from your ironmonger, putting it on with a stiff brush. It will never rust again.

RUSTY NEEDLES (KNITTING). Rub briskly with cinders and they will become smooth as glass.

SAGE. *See* SALVIA and HERBS.

SAGITTARIUS (THE ARCHER). Ninth sign of the Zodiac, influencing persons born between 22nd November and 21st December. Such are energetic and determined, quick-witted yet impulsive. They resent interference, work better as their own masters, but need to guard against changeability. Qualities they need to watch are fault-finding, selfishness and easily taking offence.

SALAD, BEETROOT.

1 beetroot	watercress
white of egg	salad dressing No. 1

Scrub the beetroot, do not cut it, boil gently till tender. When cold peel and slice it, place the slices in a salad bowl, pour over the salad dressing and garnish with cress and the white of egg finely chopped or rubbed through a sieve.

SALAD, CHICKEN.

cold boiled fowl	boiled green peas
lettuce	beetroot or tomato
cucumber	hard-boiled egg
watercress	mayonnaise dressing

Cut the meat from the bones of the fowl; wash, tear into pieces and thoroughly dry the lettuce, arrange in a salad bowl with slices of cucumber, a few cooked green peas, slices of beetroot or tomato and the chicken cut into neat pieces. Just before serving pour over some good mayonnaise sauce and garnish with quarters of hard-boiled egg and watercress.

SALAD, CRAB.

1 crab	1 lettuce
3 or 4 tomatoes	mustard and cress, or water-
1 egg	cress
pepper and salt	mayonnaise sauce

Shred the meat of the crab up finely and mix with it a little mayonnaise sauce. Thoroughly wash the lettuce and arrange the leaves around the sides of and at the bottom of the salad bowl. Place the crab mixture in the centre and then add the pepper and salt, sliced tomatoes and slices of hard-boiled egg and garnish with the mustard and cress, or watercress.

SALAD CREAM. Beat the yolks of 3 fresh eggs with 10 grains cayenne pepper. Mix together 1½ drams of salt, 1 oz. mustard, ½ pint vinegar and 2 oz. salad oil. Add the eggs, shake well and bottle.

SALAD, CUCUMBER.

cucumber   oil
vinegar   salt and pepper

Peel and slice the cucumber very thinly, place on a dish, sprinkle with salt and let them remain from 10 to 15 minutes; pour off the liquid, mix the dressing, using 1 part of oil to 2 parts of vinegar, season with salt and pepper and pour over the cucumber. This salad is served with cold salmon.

SALAD DRESSING (1).

1 teaspoonful salt   3 tablespoonfuls salad oil
¼ teaspoonful pepper   1 tablespoonful vinegar
1 teaspoonful mustard   pinch of sugar

Put the salt, pepper, sugar and mustard in a basin, add the oil (always in the proportion of 3 parts oil to 1 part vinegar), stir in the vinegar slowly with a wooden spoon until all the ingredients are thoroughly mixed. Use as directed.

SALAD DRESSING (2).

1 raw egg   1 gill vinegar
1 dessertspoonful sugar   ½ gill cream
1 teaspoonful mixed mustard   salt and pepper

Put the salt, mustard, pepper and sugar in a basin, add the beaten egg, vinegar and cream. Use as directed.

SALAD DRESSING (3).

1 tablespoonful mustard   1 teaspoonful salt
1 saltspoonful pepper   1 tablespoonful sugar
pinch cayenne   1 tablespoonful salad oil
¼ pint vinegar   1 tin Swiss milk

Mix dry ingredients, add salad oil, then vinegar and lastly Swiss milk very slowly.

SALAD DRESSING, FRENCH.

4 tablespoonfuls olive oil   2 teaspoonfuls sugar
1 tablespoonful catsup   salt, paprika
1 tablespoonful vinegar   1 tablespoonful cream

Mix the oil, vinegar and sugar. Season with salt and paprika, stir in catsup. Beat up with egg-beater and add cream just before serving. Cheese can be added to this dressing and beaten till smooth.

SALAD, EGG.

6 hard-boiled eggs	coraline pepper
aspic jelly	green salad
chopped parsley	mayonnaise dressing

Boil the eggs until quite hard, cut into slices; rinse out a border mould with cold water, pour in a little liquid aspic, decorate the bottom of the mould alternately with chopped parsley, coraline pepper and yolk of egg passed through a sieve, pour in a little more aspic and allow it to set on ice; fill the mould with layers of hard-boiled egg and aspic. When set, turn out on a bed of green salad, fill the centre with chopped egg mixed with mayonnaise, and decorate with cress and chopped aspic.

SALAD, FISH.

cold white fish	watercress
lettuce	a few shrimps
hard-boiled egg	aspic jelly
capers, gherkin	mayonnaise dressing

Flake the cooked fish, taking great care to remove all bones; mix in a bowl with the picked shrimps, chopped white of egg, a few capers, shreds of gherkin; pour over some mayonnaise sauce. Make a border of lettuce (torn into pieces and well dried) on a dish, place the fish salad in the centre and garnish with watercress, chopped aspic and yolk of egg passed through a sieve.

SALAD, FOR COLD MEAT.

1 head of celery	cream
1 beetroot	vinegar
some capers	salt and cayenne
hard-boiled egg	

Wash and trim the celery, cut into fine shreds, chop the beetroot into small dice, mix together with about 1 tablespoonful of capers and the chopped white of the egg; whip the cream, flavour carefully with a little vinegar, salt and cayenne; mix with the other ingredients just before serving and sprinkle over finely-grated yolk of egg.

SALAD, FRUIT (for 10 or 12 people).

For Summer:	*For Winter:*
¼ lb. strawberries	2 tangerines
2 oz. white grapes	3 bananas
2 oz. black grapes	2 apples
raspberries	few pineapple chunks
currants (red and white)	¼ tin apricots
1 orange	¼ lb. prunes
juice of 1 lemon	juice of 1 lemon
wine or liqueur	wine or liqueur
½ pint water	½ pint water
¼ lb. loaf sugar	¼ lb. loaf sugar
almonds and pistachio nuts	almonds and pistachio nuts

Prepare all the fruit very carefully, removing all stems, seeds, pips and skin, cut in convenient-sized pieces, place in a bowl, pour over some syrup made by boiling the sugar and water together for 10 to 15 minutes, add the wine or liqueur flavouring, and allow to steep for several hours. Place in a salad bowl: decorate with almonds blanched and shredded and chopped pistachios. Keep on ice if possible.

Note.—The fruits used can be varied according to taste and season, but as many kinds as possible should be used.

SALAD, LOBSTER.

1 lobster	hard-boiled egg
lettuce	chopped parsley
watercress	aspic jelly
mayonnaise sauce	

Split the lobster lengthways and remove the meat from the shell and claws. Rinse out a border mould with cold water, pour in a little liquid aspic and allow it to set; decorate the bottom of the mould with the meat from the claws, chopped parsley, etc., pour over a little more aspic and allow it to set, then fill the mould with lobster and aspic. Turn out when cold on a bed of lettuce, mix the remainder of the lobster and egg with mayonnaise sauce and place in the centre and garnish with chopped aspic and cress.

SALAD, POTATO.

cooked potatoes	chervil
shallot	tarragon
parsley	salad dressing No. 1

The potatoes must not be over-cooked; cut them in neat slices. Mix the dressing, pour over the potatoes; sprinkle over some finely-chopped shallot, parsley, chervil and tarragon.

SALAD, SARDINE.

	mayonnaise
1 tin sardines	1 chopped pickle
2 hard-boiled eggs	lettuce

Remove bones from sardines. Chop egg whites and add pickle. Mix all together; arrange on lettuce. Cover with mayonnaise; crumble yolks over top.

SALAD, TOMATO.

tomatoes	shallot
parsley	tarragon
3 tablespoonfuls salad oil	salt and pepper
1 tablespoonful vinegar	1 teaspoonful mustard

Place the tomatoes in boiling water for a minute or so, drain them and remove the skin, cut them in slices and place in a salad bowl. Mix the dressing, put the salt and pepper in a basin with the mixed mustard, pour in the oil, stir in the vinegar thoroughly with a wooden spoon; pour over the tomatoes and sprinkle over the finely-chopped shallot, parsley and tarragon.

SALAD, WINTER.

$\frac{1}{4}$ lb. Brussels sprouts	1 head celery
2 carrots	mustard and cress
1 beetroot	1 shallot
$\frac{1}{4}$ lb. potatoes	mayonnaise dressing

Cook all the vegetables carefully. They must not be *over*-cooked. Cut into fancy shapes a vegetable cutter. Chop the trimmings roughly, mix with mayonnaise sauce, pile in the centre of a salad bowl; arrange the fancy shapes of the vegetables round in layers, garnish with mustard and cress and celery tops and pour over a little more mayonnaise sauce.

SALADS. An upturned saucer placed in the bottom of the bowl will receive any moisture that may come from the ingredients and ensure the salad being crisp throughout.

All salads are greatly improved by adding chopped apple.

SALLY LUNN.

¾ lb. flour	1 teaspoonful sugar
2 oz. butter	¼ teaspoonful salt
1 egg	1 gill milk
½ oz. yeast	

Cream the yeast and the sugar together. Warm the butter and milk together, add the beaten egg. Sift the flour into a basin with the salt, mix to a light dough with the milk and yeast. Knead the dough, then divide it into two, and put into two small well-buttered cake-tins and allow it to prove for 1 hour in a warm place, brush over with beaten egg and bake in a hot oven for 20 minutes.

SALMON, BOILED (for 8 people).

4 lb. salmon
salt
cucumber

Well wash the fish, put it in boiling water with salt, allow it to boil for a few minutes, then simmer very slowly till cooked; if a large thick piece allow 8 minutes to the pound and 8 minutes over, if a thin piece 6 minutes. Drain well, put on a hot dish with a folded napkin, garnish with sliced cucumber and parsley and serve with dressed cucumber and a suitable sauce, such as hollandaise, mayonnaise or tartare.

SALMON CROQUETTES.

1 tin salmon	1 pint mashed potatoes
1 teaspoonful butter	½ cupful hot milk
1 egg	parsley
pepper, salt	paprika

Mix together in basin the flaked salmon free from skin and bone, potatoes, butter, milk, well-beaten egg and seasoning. Leave till cool. Make into balls. Dip in beaten egg mixed with tablespoonful milk, then into crumbs and fry in smoking hot fat. Serve piled up in dish and surrounded by green peas drained from a tin and heated in a little well-seasoned butter.

SALMON, FILLETS À LA TARTARE (for 4 people).

3 or 4 slices of salmon	some chopped tarragon and
½ pint mayonnaise	chervil
1 teaspoonful French	anchovies
mustard	olives
1 teaspoonful anchovy	gherkins
essence	

Grill the salmon slices and set aside to get cold, add to the mayonnaise sauce the mustard, anchovy essence and chopped tarragon and chervil. Arrange the fish on a dish, pour the sauce over garnish with stoned olives, filleted anchovies and sliced gherkin. If preferred hot, add all flavourings to some good brown sauce instead of mayonnaise, adding a little tarragon vinegar.

SALMON, MAYONNAISE (for 9 or 10 people).

cold salmon (2 or 3 lb.)	capers, gherkin
cucumber	anchovy fillets
lettuce	aspic jelly
cress	mayonnaise sauce

Remove the skin from the salmon, arrange a bed of lettuce on a dish, coat the salmon well with thick mayonnaise sauce with a little liquid aspic added, place it on the salad and garnish tastefully with cucumber slices, little heaps of capers, shredded gherkin, cress and chopped aspic. Lay across two anchovy fillets or if liked they can be rolled.

SALMON SALAD.

1 tin salmon or 1 lb. boiled salmon	vinegar
	2 hard-boiled eggs
shredded cabbage	salt, pepper
sliced cucumber	parsley
	juice of 1 lemon

Flake salmon, mix with cabbage and cucumber. Add eggs finely chopped, lemon juice, salt and pepper and vinegar. Garnish with chopped parsley.

SALMON, SMOKED. This is usually served as an hors-d'œuvre.
Drain off the oil in which it is preserved, cut into small thin slices and garnish with chopped parsley. Serve fresh oil and vinegar with it.

SALMON STEAKS, BAKED (for 4 or 5 people).

2 or 3 salmon steaks	lemon juice
chopped parsley	salt and pepper
butter	caper sauce
shallot	

Place the steaks in a buttered baking-dish, season with chopped parsley, shallot, salt, pepper and lemon juice, cover with buttered paper and cook in a quick oven from 10 to 15 minutes, dish and serve with caper sauce or, if preferred, a rich brown sauce.

SALSIFY, to boil.

salsify	lemon juice
salt	½ pint white sauce

Wash and peel the salsify roots, keeping them under water as much as possible during the process; place them at once into cold water with salt and lemon juice to prevent them from becoming discoloured. Put them into boiling water with salt and lemon juice and boil till quite tender; drain them. Dish in a hot vegetable dish and pour the white sauce over and serve.

SALSIFY, to scallop.

some cooked salsify	grated cheese
½ pint white sauce	butter
bread-crumbs	salt, cayenne, lemon

Cut the cooked salsify into neat pieces, warm in the white sauce, which must be well seasoned with salt, cayenne and a little lemon juice. Place in some well-buttered scallop shells. Sprinkle over some fresh bread-crumbs, then a little grated cheese and a few small pieces of butter on top, brown in a hot oven and serve.

SALT, an ironing hint. Add a pinch when making the starch; it will prevent sticking.

SALT, to keep dry (1). A little cornflour added to the salt in the salt-cellar will prevent it hardening. Proportions are, ½ teaspoonful of cornflour to 2 tablespoonfuls of salt.

SALT, to keep dry (2). During damp weather it is a good plan to put a small piece of blotting-paper at the bottom of each salt-cellar; it absorbs the moisture and keeps the salt dry.

SALTS, EPSOM. *See* PURGATIVES.

SALVIA (SAGE). This family includes perennial and annual, hardy and half-hardy sorts. *S. splendens* has clear green foliage and brilliant scarlet flowers, *S. patens*, flowers of intense blue. *S. roemeriana*, flowers of deep crimson, is of compact dwarf growth. All these may be treated as half-hardy annuals. Other varieties are *S. azurea*, a perennial which will thrive in the open in mild districts, with fine spikes of pale blue flowers, and *S. cacaliaefolia,* also perennial in warm situations, with grey-green downy foliage and erect stems bearing flowers of deep blue.

SAL VOLATILE. This is sometimes known as aromatic spirit of ammonia. For children suffering with pains from flatulence give 2 drops in a little water. For adults it acts as a stimulant in cases of fainting, or hysteria, if a teaspoonful is taken in a wineglassful of water.

SANDWICHES, COUNTRY CLUB.

toast	cooked chicken or tongue
lettuce	bacon
mayonnaise	sliced tomato

Butter 12 slices of toast; on 6 place thin slices of chicken, sprinkle with salt and pepper and place on top of each two rashers of broiled bacon, cover with lettuce and mayonnaise and sliced tomato, then place other half of toast on top. Cut crosswise and serve with a knife and fork.

SANDWICHES, TOASTED CHEESE.

6 thin slices cheese	1 teaspoonful mustard
12 slices bread	pimento

Spread 6 slices with butter. Lay the cheese on the other slices. Sprinkle with mustard and chopped pimento. Spread buttered slices over the cheese and toast slowly on both sides until the cheese melts. Cut crosswise.

SARDINE CANAPÉS (for 5 or 6 people).

4 or 5 sardines	salt and pepper
1 oz. grated cheese	6 rounds of toast
1 oz. butter	

Rub the sardines through a sieve, mix with the butter, grated cheese, salt and pepper, pile some of the mixture on the rounds of toast, sprinkle with grated cheese, put under the grill to heat and brown the cheese and serve hot.

SARDINE PYRAMIDS (for 6 or 7 people).

6 sardines	salt and cayenne
1 oz. butter	lemon juice
chopped parsley	buttered toast

Take the skin and bones from the sardines, pound them in a mortar with the butter, season well with salt, cayenne and a squeeze of lemon juice; cut the toast into fingers, put the mixture on pyramid shape, sprinkle over a little chopped parsley and coraline pepper and serve with watercress as a garnish.

SARDINES À LA ROYAL (for 6 or 8 people).

6 or 8 sardines	gherkin
lettuce	beetroot
salad oil	hard-boiled egg
vinegar (tarragon)	

Skin and remove bones of sardines, close them up again; wash, dry and shred the letuce, season it with oil and a few drops of tarragon vinegar, place on a small dish and arrange sardines on the lettuce; decorate the sardines with strips of gherkin and white of egg, crossways, and finely-chopped beetroot down the sides. Serve as hors-d'œuvre or savoury.

SARSAPARILLA DRINK.
Take 2 oz. decoction of sarsaparilla compound, 1¼ oz. bruised sassafras root, 12 oz. honey, 1 lb. cane sugar, 4 oz. fresh yeast and 1 gallon distilled water (boiling). Dissolve the sugar and honey in the water; add the sassafras and, when cool, the sarsaparilla and yeast. Leave a warm place for a few days, and then strain and bottle. Take a small wineglassful every morning.

SAUCE, ANCHOVY.

1 oz. butter	pinch each of salt and pepper
1 tablespoonful flour	½ pint new milk, or milk and
1 or 2 teaspoonfuls of	water, or milk and fish stock
anchovy essence	

Melt the butter and stir in the flour, taking care to keep smooth. Then gradually add the milk, stirring well until the mixture boils. Add pepper, salt and anchovy essence and simmer for 5 minutes. This sauce is used with various fish dishes.

SAUCE, APPLE.

1 lb. cooking apples	little water
1 oz. butter	sugar

Peel, core and slice the apples, put into a saucepan with a little water and cook to a pulp, beat smooth, add the butter and sugar to taste. Served with roast pork, duck and goose.

SAUCE, APRICOT.

2 tablespoonfuls apricot jam
1 gill water

a squeeze of lemon juice
carmine

Boil together for 5 minutes, strain and colour with a drop or two of carmine.

SAUCE BÉCHAMEL.

2 oz. butter
2 oz. flour
1 small shallot
6 peppercorns
blade of mace

strip of lemon rind
small bunch of herbs
½ pint white stock
½ pint milk
little cream
salt and pepper

Put the milk or stock into a saucepan with the shallot and the peppercorns, mace, lemon peel and herbs tied in muslin, simmer for 15 minutes and strain. Melt the butter in a saucepan, cook the flour in it, add the flavoured stock and milk gradually and allow it to cook well; add salt and pepper and a little cream last. Strain if not smooth.

SAUCE. BREAD.

1 pint milk
4 oz. bread-crumbs
2 oz. butter
blade of mace

1 onion
2 cloves
2 tablespoonfuls cream
salt and pepper

Boil the milk with the onion stuck with the cloves and the mace, rub the bread-crumbs through a wire sieve, pour the seasoned milk over them, return to the saucepan and cook well; add the butter, salt and pepper and the cream just before serving. Served with roast game and poultry.

SAUCE, CAPER.

½ pint white sauce (using
half milk and half stock)

1 tablespoonful capers
salt and pepper

Add the capers chopped to the white sauce and season. Served with boiled mutton.

SAUCE, CELERY.

½ pint white sauce
1 head celery

pinch of mace
lemon juice
salt and pepper

Cook the celery till tender, chop and add to the white sauce, season with a squeeze of lemon juice, pinch of mace, salt and pepper. Served with boiled turkey and fowl.

SAUCE, CHOCOLATE.

2 oz. chocolate
½ pint water
½ oz. crême de riz

sugar
vanilla
branty

Melt the chocolate in the water, thicken with the crême de riz, add sugar, vanilla and brandy to taste.

SAUCE, CRANBERRY. Wash fruit and pick off any stalks. Put fruit in saucepan after brusing well and add water in the proportion of 1 gill to each pint of cranberries used. Bring to the boil and then simmer gently until the fruit is thoroughly cooked, after which put it through a fine sieve. Return to the saucepan and add 1½ oz. of sugar for each pint of fruit used. Bring to the boil again and serve. Makes an excellent sauce for serving with roast turkey.

SAUCE, CURRY.

1 oz. butter
1 sour apple
1 or 2 shallots
½ oz. flour

½ oz. curry powder
½ pint stock
1 dessertspoonful chutney
lemon juice
pinch of sugar and salt

Chop the apple and shallot finely, melt the butter and fry them a pale brown, add the flour and curry powder and cook well, stirring occasionally; stir in the stock smoothly and simmer for 25 to 30 minutes, skimming off the fat as it rises; strain and add the chutney, lemon juice and seasonings. Served with meat and fish.

SAUCE, CUSTARD

½ pint milk
1 egg

½ oz. cornflour
½ oz. sugar

Mix the cornflour with a little of the milk; put the rest on to boil. When boiling, stir in the cornflour and cook for 3 minutes; add the sugar. When a little cool add the beaten egg, stir till it thickens—but it must not boil again—add flavouring if required.

SAUCE, EGG.

½ pint white sauce
2 hard-boiled eggs

salt and pepper
lemon juice

Chop the hard-boiled eggs roughly, add to the sauce and season with salt and pepper and add a little lemon juice. Served with boiled salt cod and other kinds of boiled fish and boiled fowl.

SAUCE ESPAGNOLE.

2 oz. butter
2 oz. flour
1 shallot
1 carrot

1 or 2 tomatoes
1 oz. ham
2 or 3 mushrooms
1 pint brown stock
salt and pepper

Melt the butter, fry the chopped shallot, carrot and mushrooms until a golden brown. Add the flour and brown it. Add the stock gradually, stirring all the time. Bring to the boil, add the chopped ham and tomato, boil gently from half to three-quarters of an hour, skimming and stirring occasionally, season and strain and it is ready to use.

Note.—This is the foundation brown sauce. A great variety of brown sauces can be made by adding various ingredients to this foundation.

SAUCE, GERMAN.

2 yolks of eggs
1 gill sherry
1 oz. sugar

Put the ingredients into a double saucepan and whisk until the sauce becomes thick and frothy. It must not boil or it will curdle.

SAUCE, GUARDS'. (For Christmas Pudding.)

2 oz. good fresh butter
4 oz. icing sugar
brandy

Cream the butter and sugar together until quite smooth, beat in slowly the brandy to flavour—about a tablespoonful or a little more.

SAUCE HOLLANDAISE.

4 oz. butter	1 bay leaf
4 yolks of eggs	sprig of thyme
1 shallot	1 tablespoonful vinegar
	salt and pepper

Simmer the flavouring in the vinegar; melt the butter in a saucepan and mix in the yolks, stir till the sauce thickens; strain the vinegar and add to the yolks and butter; season with salt and pepper. This sauce is best made in a double saucepan. It must not boil or the eggs will curdle.

SAUCE, HORSE-RADISH.

1 root horse-radish	½ gill milk
½ teaspoonful mustard	½ gill cream
(mixed)	½ gill vinegar
1 teaspoonful castor sugar	salt and pepper

Grate the horse-radish finely, mix with mustard, sugar, salt and pepper, add the milk, cream and vinegar and mix all together.

SAUCE, LEMON.

1 gill water	½ teaspoonful cornflour
2 oz. sugar	rind and juice of 1 lemon

Boil the sugar, water and lemon rind together, add the lemon juice and thicken with the cornflour.

SAUCE, MAÎTRE D'HÔTEL.

½ pint white sauce	juice of ½ lemon
½ tablespoonful chopped	salt and cayenne
parsley	

Chop and blanch the parsley, add to the sauce with the strained lemon juice, season with salt and cayenne. Served with fish, boiled meat and with vegetables.

SAUCE, MAYONNAISE.

	salt and pepper
2 yolks of egg	1 tablespoonful vinegar
1½ gills salad oil	1 tablespoonful tarragon vinegar
1 tablespoonful castor sugar	1 tablespoonful cream

Stir the oil into the yolks, drop by drop, mixing well all the time, add the vinegar slowly, then the sugar and salt, cayenne and cream. This is served as a salad dressing and as a sauce for salmon and cold fish, etc.

SAUCE, MELTED BUTTER. *See* BUTTER, MELTED.

SAUCE, MINT.

2 tablespoonfuls mint
1 oz. castor sugar
½ gill boiling water
1 gill vinegar
salt

Wash the mint and chop very finely, dissolve the sugar in the boiling water, add the vinegar and mint. Stir before serving. Served with roast lamb.

Sprinkle well with sugar before chopping. Mint sauce should be thick with mint and really sweet.

SAUCE, MUSHROOM.

mushrooms   butter   espagnole sauce

Peel mushrooms—using for preference the small button-size mushrooms—and fry them in the butter. Then add them to some espagnole sauce and thoroughly beat.

SAUCE, MUSTARD.

½ pint white sauce
1 dessertspoonful made mustard
salt and pepper

Add the made mustard to the sauce and season. Served with grilled herrings.

SAUCE, ONION.

½ pint white sauce
3 or 4 onions
salt and pepper

Boil the onions till tender, chop and add them to the white sauce and season. Served with roast shoulder of mutton and boiled rabbit.

SAUCE, ORANGE.

½ pint water
rind and juice of 2 oranges
juice of 1 lemon
2 oz. sugar
1 teaspoonful cornflour

Boil the water, sugar and orange rind together for 10 minutes, strain and thicken with the cornflour.

SAUCE. PARSLEY.

½ pint white sauce
½ tablespoonful chopped parsley
pepper and salt

Chop and blanch the parsley, add to the sauce and season. Served with boiled fish, boiled mutton, rabbit, fowl, calf's head, etc.

SAUCE, REFORM.

½ pint brown sauce
juice of ½ lemon
wineglassful port
bouquet garni
2 teaspoonfuls red-currant jelly
salt and cayenne

Add the herbs, lemon juice, port and jelly to the brown sauce, simmer and skim till reduced to two-thirds, season and pass through a tammy cloth. Suitable to serve with cutlets and any meat.

SAUCE, SHRIMP.

½ pint white sauce
1 oz. shelled shrimps
cayenne

lemon juice
salt and pepper
colouring

Add shrimps to the sauce, season with salt, cayenne pepper and lemon juice. Colour a drop of carmine. Served with turbot and other fish.

SAUCE, SWEET PUDDING.

½ pint milk
1 oz. butter
½ oz. flour

½ oz. castor sugar
any flavouring

Melt the butter, add the flour and cook it for a minute, stir in the milk and sugar; boil gently for 5 minutes. Any flavouring can be added, such as vanilla, lemon or almond essence, brandy or sherry.

SAUCE TARTARE.

mayonnaise sauce
lemon juice

chopped parsley
chopped gherkin, capers

Add the capers, gherkin and parsley to the mayonnaise, with a little lemon juice.

SAUCE, THICK.

2 oz. flour   2 oz. butter   ½ pint liquid

Melt the butter, add the flour, mix smoothly and cook for a few minutes, add the liquid and cook well until the mixture leaves the sides of the saucepan. This mixture is used for binding the ingredients in cutlets, croquettes, rissoles, etc.

SAUCE, TOMATO.

3 or 4 tomatoes
2 oz. butter
1 oz. flour

1 gill milk
salt and pepper

Slice the tomatoes and cook them in the butter, pass through a sieve; make a white sauce, using 1 gill of milk and 1 gill of the tomato purée, boil the sauce and season with salt and pepper. Suitable to serve with fish.

SAUCE, TREACLE.

2 tablespoonfuls treacle or
golden syrup

1 gill water
lemon juice

Put all together in a saucepan and boil for 5 minutes.

SAUCE, WHITE.

2 oz. flour
2 oz. butter

1 pint milk
salt and pepper

Melt the butter, stir in the flour, allow it to cook without taking any colour; add the milk gradually, mixing smoothly, stir till it boils; boil for 5 minutes and add the seasoning.

Note.—This is the foundation white sauce. By adding various ingredients to this a great variety of sauces can be easily made.

SAUCEPANS, cleaning and care of. As soon as the contents of a saucepan have been dished up, the saucepan should be filled up with cold water. Clean both the inside and outside of all saucepans after use. Iron, brass, copper, enamel or tin saucepans should all be washed thoroughly with the aid of a pot scourer and hot soda water, but soda should never be used when washing aluminium saucepans. After washing, rinse saucepans, then dry both outside as well as inside and, in the case of aluminium, or light enamel saucepans, hang them up, but in the case of the heavier saucepans, these should be placed bottom uppermost on the shelf. Saucepan lids should be treated in the same way as the saucepans themselves, except that the use of a pot scourer is usually unnecessary. After washing, rinse, wipe well and place in saucepan lid rack if you have one.

SAUSAGE ROLLS (8).

½ lb. sausages
½ lb. flour
6 oz. butter or butter and lard

lemon juice
salt
water to mix
1 egg

Boil the sausages for 10 minutes, skin and cut them in half; make the pastry, roll it into a square shape, divide it into as many squares as there are pieces of sausage; put a piece on each square, brush round the edge with egg, fold over, letting the fold come on top, mark with a knife, brush over with egg, put on a baking-sheet and bake in a hot oven for 20 minutes.

SAUSAGES.

Sausages should be boiled for about 5 minutes before being fried. This will save shrinkage.

SAUSAGES AND POTATOES (for 3 or 4 people).

1 lb. sausages
cooked potatoes
½ oz. butter

little milk
salt and pepper

Mash the potatoes, adding the butter, milk, salt and pepper, put them in the centre of a hot dish; prick the sausages, put them into a hot pan with a little dripping, fry till a crisp brown, place them round the potatoes and serve.

SAVOY.

Sow early in March. The large varieties require a space of 2 feet when transplanted, and the dwarfer kinds about 1½ feet. For use in late spring make a further sowing in August. General treatment as for cabbage.

SCALDS.

In small scalds the parts should be anointed with vaseline or dusted over with powdered starch and boracic acid should be added in equal proportions and covered with lint. If blisters form, they should be punctured with a clean needle, and the area dusted with boracic acid powder and wrapped in cotton-wool.

If the patient is suffering from shock, he should be wrapped in blankets, and hot-water bottles put to the extremities and a hot drink of whisky or brandy and water given. *See also* BURNS AND SCALDS.

SCALLOPS EN COQUILLES.

some scallops
white sauce
butter

lemon juice
bread-crumbs
salt and pepper

Trim the scallops, removing the black portion, wash them in vinegar, cut them up, place in some buttered shells mixed with some thick white sauce and some of the bread-crumbs. Season and squeeze over some lemon juice, sprinkle over some more bread-crumbs, put some small bits of butter on top, brown nicely in a quick oven.

SCARLET FEVER (SCARLATINA). These two names indicate the same disease. It usually begins with headache and vomiting and is frequently accompanied by sore throat, diarrhœa and a high temperature. The skin is dry, the tongue furred and the face is frequently flushed. The rash appears after 24 hours. It begins on the sides of the neck and chest, spreads quickly all over except about the mouth, which is usually pale. (*See* RASHES, to recognize diseases by.) Isolate and send immediately for the doctor.

SCIATICA. Bathe the affected parts with hot water. Then add to 2 oz. camphorated oil 1 oz. ammonia dissolved in ¼ pint turpentine. Shake well and use for rubbing into the affected parts.

SCILLA. *See* SQUILL.

SCISSORS, to sharpen (1). Sharpen each blade with a fine file, carefully keeping the original angle. Oil the edges.

SCISSORS, to sharpen (2). To sharpen scissors, open them and gently draw the cutting edges backwards and forwards on a piece of glass or on the neck of a bottle as though you were going to cut it off.
Cutting sandpaper with scissors will also sharpen them.

SCONES (1).

½ lb. flour	1 teaspoonful cream of tartare
1 oz. butter or lard	pinch of salt
½ teaspoonful carbonate of soda	1 teaspoonful sugar
	1 oz. sultanas
	1 gill sour milk

Rub the butter into the flour, add the cream of tartar, salt, sugar, and sultanas, dissolve the carbonate of soda in the milk and mix all to a soft dough; form into two rounds; cut them across to form three-cornered scones. Bake on a greased tin in a quick oven for 10 to 15 minutes. When half baked, brush over with milk.

SCONES (2).

½ lb. self-raising flour	pinch of salt
1 oz. sugar	1 dessertspoonful butter
	1 tablespoonful sultanas

Make into a soft dough and bake in a very hot oven for 10 to 15 minutes.

SCONES, DROP.

½ lb. flour	½ oz. sugar
pinch of salt	½ teaspoonful cream of tartar
1 egg	½ teaspoonful carbonate of soda
½ pint milk	

Sift the flour into a basin, add the salt, make a well in the centre, put in the well-beaten egg and mix to a smooth batter with the milk and add the sugar. Dissolve the cream of tartar and carbonate of soda in separate cups with a little milk, add them to the batter and mix well. Get the girdle hot, rub it with a piece of suet; put a spoonful of batter on the girdle. When it is set on one side, turn and brown on the other. Butter and serve hot.

SCONES, GIRDLE or GRIDDLE.

¾ lb. flour	¼ teaspoonful carbonate of soda
1 gill milk	pinch of salt

Add the salt to the flour, dissolve the soda in the milk and mix into a soft light dough; roll out at once and cut into rounds. Heat the girdle, rub it with a piece of suet, place on the scones; when set and cooked on one side, turn and cook on the other. These scones are best split open, buttered and served hot.

SCONES, WHOLEMEAL.

4 oz. wholemeal	1 oz. butter or lard
4 oz. white self-raising flour	pinch of salt
	1 gill milk

Rub the butter into the flours, add the salt and mix to a soft dough with the milk; roll out and cut into rounds or three-cornered shapes and bake from 10 to 15 minutes. When half baked brush over with milk.

SCORCHED FLANNEL. Steep the affected part in milk; then cover it with salt and leave if for half an hour before rinsing in clear water. Glycerine will also take scorched marks from flannel if it is used without delay.

SCORCHES. The best method for removing scorch marks from material is to moisten the damaged part with lemon juice and then leave the article exposed to strong sunlight.

SCORPIO (THE SCORPION). Eighth sign of the Zodiac, influencing persons born between 22nd October and 21st November. Such are of strong character—good friends but bad enemies—successful teachers, wise advisers, and in speaking have the power to sway others. There is a danger of cunning habits and hurting feelings, while jealousy is easily aroused.

SCOTCH KEDGEREE.

1½ cupfuls cold cooked fish	½ cupful rice
2 hard-boiled eggs	1 tablespoonful chopped parsley
4 tablespoonfuls butter or margarine	

Skin and bone the fish, flake into a basin, wash and boil rice, drain and dry it in the oven. Melt butter in a saucepan, add chopped whites of eggs, fish and rice and stir over fire till quite hot but do not brown. Season with salt and pepper and heap on a hot dish. Decorate with hard-boiled yolk of egg and parsley.

SCOTCH SHORTBREAD.

½ lb. flour	2 oz. castor sugar
6 oz. butter	pinch of salt

Sift the flour and salt into a basin, add the sugar and rub in the butter, turn it on to a pastry board or marble slab and knead until quite smooth; shape it into a round, pinch the edges with the thumb and first finger, put it on a buttered baking-sheet with several layers of buttered paper under it, prick the top and tie round the outside of the cake a band of stiff buttered paper. Bake in a slow oven for about three-quarters of an hour. A piece of citron may be put on the top if liked.

SCREW TOPS, to loosen. A small piece of sandpaper is a great help in loosening stubborn screw tops. It gives a grip.

SCREWS, to loosen rusted. One of the easiest ways of loosening a rusted screw is to apply heat to its head. A small bar or rod of iron, flat at the end, if reddened in the fire and applied for 2 or 3 minutes to the head will, as soon as it heats the screw, render its withdrawal as easy by the screwdriver as if it had only recently been put in.

SCRUBBING BRUSHES. To prolong the life of these, wash them from time to time in a strong solution of salt water. Dry them in the open air with the bristles pointing down.

SCULLERY WOODWORK. Discoloured draining-boards, tables, etc., may be cleaned by scrubbing with cold water and salt.

SCURF IN THE HEAD. Apply gentle friction with a flannel dipped in olive or almond oil, and when the oil has well soaked in and loosened the scurf, the head should be washed with soft soap and warm water. This may require repeating several times before the head is quite free. Sulphur ointment should be rubbed in.

SCURVY. Eat plenty of vegetables and fresh meat and drink 3 or 4 oz. of lime juice daily. Children require a plentiful supply of fresh milk, raw meat juice, and the juice of lemons, diluted with water and sweetened with sugar.

SEA-KALE.

sea-kale	½ pint white sauce
salt	toast

Well wash, trim and tie the sea-kale in bundles, put into boiling salted water and boil from 20 to 30 minutes. When tender drain it, dish on a slice of toast and pour the white sauce over and serve.

SEEDS, to protect from birds. Seeds of plants such as spruce, fir, larch and Scotch fir, should be rolled in red lead just before sowing.

SENNA. *See* APERIENTS.

SENNA, INFUSION OF.

1. One oz. senna, 30 grains sliced ginger, 10 oz. boiled water; infuse for 1 hour and strain. Dose 1 to 2 oz.

2. One oz. senna, 6 fluid oz. boiling water; infuse, strain, add 12 oz. treacle and evaporate till it thickens. This is an aperient. Dose 1 to 4 drachms.

SEWING MACHINE.

When a sewing machine refuses to run smoothly, take out the screw that holds the footplate and lift the plate out. The probable cause of the trouble is an accumulation of fluff. Clean out the parts with a penknife, first however removing the needle.

SHALLOTS. Plant the separate offsets in spring, or in October or November. They should be 2 inches deep and 6 to 8 inches apart. Gather in July or August. If dried and stored they will keep till next year. Cultivation on same lines as onions.

SHEEP'S HEAD, AND BROTH (for 5 or 6 people).

1 sheep's head	1 oz. butter
2 carrots	1 gill milk
2 turnips	3 oz. rice
1 onion	chopped parsley
1 oz. flour	salt and pepper

Thoroughly cleanse the head, take out the splinters, wash in salt and water, put the head in cold water and bring to the boil; pour away the water, add fresh water and boil, removing the scum; cut up the vegetables and add with the rice, simmer gently for 3 hours or till the meat will leave the bones. Put the brains into a small piece of muslin and drop into the stewpan about 15 minutes before the head is done. Cut the meat from the head, place in the centre of a hot dish, put a border of rice and vegetables round; slice the tongue and chop the brains; make a sauce with the butter, flour and milk, adding some of the liquor; season well and add chopped parsley. Coat the head with this sauce and garnish with sliced tongue and chopped brains.

SHEEP'S HEART, ROAST (for 1 or 2 people).

1 sheep's heart	1 small onion
2 oz. bread-crumbs	½ teaspoonful herbs
1 oz. chopped suet	1 egg or little milk
1 teaspoonful parsley	salt and pepper

Thoroughly cleanse the heart in salt and water; cut off the muscle, mix the stuffing, fill the heart with it; skewer or sew up the openings. Bake in the oven, basting frequently; place on a hot dish. Pour off the fat, put a little flour in the tin, brown it, add water; boil up, season it and pour round the heart. The heart can be cooked in a saucepan if more convenient.

SHEET IRON. A piece of sheet iron, 10 or 12 inches square placed over a gas ring will, when hot, keep three or four pots boiling at once.

SHEETS, to save wear. Run a tape for about 2 inches along the hem at each corner. This will save frayed or torn corners caused through the wind when pegged on the line, no matter how long they have been in wear.

SHERBET, LEMON. Dissolve ¾ lb. loaf sugar in 1 pint water, add the juice of 5 lemons, and press them so as to extract not only the juice but the oil of the rind, and let the skins remain awhile in the water and sugar. Strain through a sieve and then freeze it like ice cream.

SHERBET, ORANGE. Take the juice of 6 oranges and pour ½ pint boiling water on the peel and let it stand covered half an hour. Boil ½ lb. loaf sugar in ½ pint water, skim, and then add the juice and the water in the peel to the sugar. Strain it and cool with ice, or freeze it. The juice of a lemon and a little more sugar improves it.

SHERBET, STRAWBERRY. Crush 1 quart ripe strawberries and add the juice of 1 lemon, 2 tablespoonfuls orange flower water and 3 pints water. Allow to stand for several hours and strain over ¾ lb. sugar. Stand in ice 1 hour before using.

SHINGLES. Shingles is generally the result of a chill. It may occur anywhere on the body. The most usual places are around the corners of the mouth, on the neck, arm, chest and waist.

Symptoms.—The eruption consists of small blisters on an inflamed base, and always follow the course of a nerve. The eruption is painful, tingles and smarts. The attack usually lasts from four to fourteen days. In the ordinary course of events the blisters dry up and the inflamed spots disappear. If the blisters break and become infected, or the patient irritates them by scratching, alarming sores may develop and take weeks to heal.

Treatment.—Zinc ointment or powdered starch and zinc oxide should be constantly applied. If the blisters break and leave a raw surface, the area should be at once dusted with the powder or the ointment applied. A raw surface should never be allowed to be exposed to the air, neither should clothes be allowed to touch it. Keep covered with the powder or ointment and bandaged. A 10-grain dose of antipyrin will relieve the pain and smarting.

SHOES, to repair. Old cycle tyres can be utilized for soling children's shoes. Cut to the necessary size for shoe soles and heels and nail on with sprigs. These will last well and one tyre will do many shoes.

SHOES, to restore wet. Remove immediately, wash off all mud, and wipe thoroughly. Then rub in plenty of vaseline and set aside, away from the fire, for several days. When quite dry the grease will have restored the natural oil, and the shoes will be almost as good as new.

SHOES, BADLY FITTING, to remedy. Sew a piece of garter elastic—about 6 inches—at the inside of the back of the shoe. Taper it off gradually towards the instep at either end.

SHOES, DAMP, to polish. A little paraffin should be added to the shoe polish when cleaning damp shoes. When shoes are to be laid aside for some time, it is advisable, to prevent them becoming mildewed or mouldy, to sponge them very lightly with some essential oil, like cloves, lavender or almond.

SHOES, SUÈDE, to clean. The shoes should first be stuffed with soft paper. Then apply some spirits of turpentine to them by means of a clean rag. Continue to rub until clean, constantly turning the rag. Hang up to dry in a draughty place to remove all smell of turpentine.

SHOPPING LIST. Use an old diary for keeping note during the week of various housekeeping and kitchen commodities of which supplies are running low, so as not to forget them when ordering from tradesmen.

SHORTBREAD. *See* SCOTCH SHORTBREAD.

SICK-ROOM TEMPERATURE. In illness it is most important to keep the room sweet and fresh without draughts and at an equable temperature. About 66° in the daytime and 50° during the night is a healthy atmosphere. Nothing hinders the progress of a patient more than a stuffy room.

SILK, SHANTUNG, to iron. Usually Shantung silk is ironed whilst still damp, but a better and a quicker way is to iron with a fairly hot iron when quite dry.

SILK, TUSSORE, to wash. The garment should be soaked in cold water, squeezed out of a soapy lukewarm lather, and then rinsed in water of the same temperature in which a little salt has been dissolved. Hang in the shade and iron when quite dry on the right side.

SILVER, to clean. In order to clean silver, place a good-sized enamelled saucepan on the stove and pour 1 quart of water in it with 2 heaped tablespoonfuls of soda. Let it come to a slow boil and then put the silver in it. It will come out clean and shining.

Silver will retain its polish longer if it is rinsed in boiling water after being used.

SILVER, to keep bright. Silver in constant use should be washed every day in soap and warm water, drying with old soft linen cloths. Twice a week (after this washing) give it a thorough brightening with finely-powdered whiting, mixed to a thin paste with alcohol; rubbing longer and harder where there are stains. Then wipe this off and polish with clean soft old linen.

Another way to keep silver bright without constant cleaning is to dissolve a small handful of borax in a panful of hot water with a little soap. Put the silver in, let it stand for several hours, then pour off the suds; rinse with clean cold water and wipe with soft cloth before polishing with a clean leather.

Unused silver will keep bright if laid away in a box of flour.

SILVER, to save tarnishing. A piece of camphor where silver is stored will keep it from tarnishing.

SILVER WEDDINGS. The Silver Wedding, twenty-fifth anniversary of a marriage, is often marked by some special celebration, such as a dinner-party followed by a dance.

Invitation cards printed in silver are in either case sent out about a fortnight or three weeks in advance. The ordinary form for invitations is used, with the additional words "To celebrate their Silver Wedding." If a dance is to follow, "Dancing" should be printed in one corner of the card.

It is a charming idea to secure the presence of as many as possible of those friends and relations who attended the marriage.

Each guest invited sends a gift, which should be of silver.

A silver-ornamented wedding-cake should occupy a prominent place amongst the refreshments.

When a toast is drunk the husband replies for his wife and himself, and she cuts the cake, when the dessert course is reached.

If a dinner-party is given the usual etiquette for such occasions is observed, except that husband and wife together lead the way into the dining-room.

If a dance follows, husband and wife again lead the way and dance the first dance together.

SILVER-PLATED WARE, to resilver.   Place in a glass vessel 1 oz. nitrate of silver, 2 oz. cyanuret potassa, 4 oz. prepared Spanish whiting and 10 oz. pure rain water.   The article to be replated should first be thoroughly cleansed in strong hot soda water.   Apply mixture with a soft brush and finish with a chamois skin.

SINKS, to clean.   Mix together a pennyworth each of pearl-ash, soft soap and Fuller's earth, gradually adding a quart of boiling water. Keep this mixture in an old tin and rub the sink each day with a flannel dipped in it, rinsing thoroughly.

Dissolve 1 oz. of permanganate of potash in 3 pints of boiling water and pour a little of the solution down all sinks, baths and basins once a week.

Spirits of salt removes stains from sinks, but it is a highly dangerous poison.

SLEEPLESSNESS.   The diet should be regulated if indigestion is the cause.   A walk or anything that takes the thoughts off the subject or business that the patient has been studying will often enable him to spend a good night.   Over-fatigue should be avoided.   A biscuit and a glass of hot milk or home-made lemonade is an excellent sleeping draught.   Hot-water bottle to the feet and a tepid bath are sufficient in some cases to induce sleep.   Drugs of any sort are dangerous; sleeping draughts are not advised.

SLIPPERS FROM HATS.   Ladies' old felt hats can be made into bedroom slippers for children.   The pattern can be taken by undoing an old pair and they can be run up on the machine with a larger stitch.

SLOE GIN.

4 lb. sloes	½ oz. bitter almonds, finely
1½ lb. sugar candy	minced
½ gallon gin	½ lb. sugar

Well bruise the sloes, crush the sugar candy and put all together into a small cask, stirring thoroughly.   Leave for three months and then strain through fine muslin, bottle and securely cork.

SLUGS AND SNAILS.   Particularly in moist gardens, slugs and snails do much mischief.   Fresh lime, dusted on the ground, is a common remedy, but not in rainy weather.   Bonfire ash, if kept dry and mixed with a little soot and coal ash, are invaluable for dusting over seedlings and young vegetable crops to ward off the attacks of slugs and also enrich the soil.   This method is also a protection from the ravages of snails.   A good plan to prevent snails crawling up a wall is to daub the bottom of the wall with a paste compounded of oil and soot, over which they will not pass.

SMALLPOX.

Causes.—It arises by contagion: is highly infectious, and therefore must be notified. It is conveyed by clothes, bedding, or anything which has come into contact with an infected person. Breathing the air that surrounds a case of smallpox is considered sufficient to convey the disease. All ages and both sexes are liable to it.

Symptoms.—As a rule, the disease first makes its appearance twelve days after infection. It starts suddenly with a shivering fit, severe pain in the loins, vomiting, headache, fever, loss of appetite, thirst and furred tongue. If on the third day from the onset the eruption appears—small, red, raised pimples on the forehead, face and scalp—it is certain that the illness is smallpox, and if not already done, a doctor must be called in and the patient isolated.

If an epidemic of smallpox breaks out, everyone should be vaccinated, regardless of when they were last operated on.

SMELL OF BOILING GREENS. This unpleasant smell can be avoided by putting a bit of dry toast in a muslin bag into the saucepan with the greens.

SMELTS (for 4 people).

1 dozen smelts	egg and bread-crumbs
flour	lemon
salt and pepper	parsley

Wash the smelts—they require gentle handling in cleaning—trim with scissors, dip in seasoned flour, coat with egg and bread-crumbs, roll on board to make them a nice shape and fry a golden brown in hot fat. Arrange on a hot dish with fancy paper; garnish with quarters of lemon and fried parsley. Serve with tartare or tomato sauce.

SMOKING LAMP, to prevent. Soak the wick in very strong vinegar and dry it well before you use it. The flame will be clear and bright.

SNAKE ROOT. *See* ARUM.

SNAPDRAGON (ANTIRRHINUM). These hardy perennials are most useful border plants as they are easy of cultivation and thrive almost anywhere, though a free sandy soil is that congenial to them. They are best treated as annuals, sowing the seed in the open in April and thinning out to about a foot apart. Take cuttings of the best colours in July and protect from frost during winter.

SNOWDROP. A few bulbs to start with, put 2 inches deep and 6 inches apart, will soon increase to fine clumps. Plant offsets in a moist, shady place in autumn at a depth of about 3 inches. Take up once every three or four years after the leaves have withered.

SOAP SCRAPS, how to use up. Buy a "shaker" for a few pence to take odd bits which can be "shaken" in washing up water, etc. If you have many scraps, soap jelly is worth making. Simply simmer in an old pan with enough water to cover. Here is the proportion: 1 cupful of boiling water to $\frac{1}{2}$ cupful of the soap scraps cut into small pieces. When melted, add powdered borax enough to make a paste. Then let dry and harden before using.

SOILED ARMS OF CHAIRS. These can be cleaned with a piece of flannel and petrol: use a circular movement and do it in the open air if possible; in any case not in a room with gas or a fire going.

SOILED COAT COLLARS, to clean. To clean the collar of a coat which has touched the neck rub a little powdered magnesia on it with a clean cloth and leave it on until the coat is needed again when it can be brushed off. The most delicate fabrics can be treated in this way.

SOLE, FRIED. Skin and trim the fish and cut them open. Dip them in egg and bread-crumbs and fry in boiling lard to a light brown. Serve with whole lemons.

SOLE À LA CRÈME (for 2 people).

1 filleted sole	½ pint milk
1 oz. butter	lemon juice
1 oz. flour	salt and pepper

Wash and dry the fillets, roll up the skinned side inside, cook in the milk till soft, then remove and place on a hot dish, make a sauce with the butter, flour and flavoured milk, season well and add lemon juice, pour over the sole, garnish with lemon and parsley and serve hot.

SOLE À LA PORTUGAISE (for 4 people).

1 sole	1 oz. butter
1 Spanish onion	1 oz. grated cheese
2 or 3 tomatoes	salt and pepper

Skin the sole, place it in a greased fireproof dish, slice the onion very thinly, place on the top of the sole with the tomatoes sliced, sprinkle over salt and pepper and the grated cheese, put the butter in small pieces on the top and bake from 20 to 30 minutes. The sole can be filleted if preferred and tomato sauce used instead of sliced tomato; fillets of any fish can be "à la Portugaise."

SOLE AU GRATIN (for 4 people).

1 sole	some Italian sauce
4 mushrooms	little sherry or white wine
lemon juice	½ oz. butter
parsley	brown bread-crumbs
1 small shallot	salt and pepper

Chop the shallot, parsley and mushrooms finely; grease a fireproof dish, lay in some of the seasoning, skin and score the sole, place it in the dish, moisten with lemon juice and a little sherry or white wine, place on the rest of the seasoning and cover with Italian sauce, sprinkle over a few brown crumbs and put some small pieces of butter on top and bake for 20 minutes; sprinkle over a little finely-chopped parsley and serve.

SOLE FRITTERS.

3 soles	1 teaspoonful chopped chives
1 tablespoonful olive oil	and parsley
salt and pepper	3 tablespoonfuls vinegar

Fillet the soles, cut them in halves crosswise, place them in a deep dish with vinegar, oil, chives, parsley, pepper and salt. Leave them for 1 hour turning frequently. Ten minutes before serving drain fillets, dip them in frying batter, then into hot fat and fry for 5 or 6 minutes. Drain, serve on a hot dish on a fish paper and accompany with tartare sauce.

SOOT (1). If soot falls from the chimney on the carpet this should be sprinkled with salt before the soot is swept up; no disfiguring mark or stain will then be left.

SOOT (2). To clear the chimney of soot, put ½ lb. saltpetre on the fire once a month.

SOUFFLÉ, CHEEESE. *See* CHEESE SOUFFLÉ.

SOUFFLÉ, CHOCOLATE (for 4 or 5 people).

1 oz. butter	½ oz. sugar
1 oz. flour	yolks of 2 and whites of 3 eggs
1 gill milk	vanilla essence
3 oz. chocolate	chocolate sauce

Make a panada or thick sauce with the butter, flour and milk in which the chocolate has been dissolved and mix smoothly; cook for a few minutes; allow the mixture to cool and add the sugar, yolks of eggs and vanilla essence; whip the whites stiffly and stir in lightly. Pour into a buttered soufflé dish, tie round a band of buttered paper and bake in the oven for 35 minutes. Serve with chocolate sauce.

Note.—This soufflé may be steamed like vanilla or sago soufflés. It will take 45 to 50 minutes.

SOUFFLÉ, VANILLA (for 4 or 5 people).

1½ oz. butter	4 yolks and 4 whites of eggs
1½ oz. flour	vanilla essence
1 gill milk	cherries and angelica
½ oz. sugar	jam sauce

Cook the flour in the butter and add the milk, cook for a few minutes; allow the mixture to cool, add the sugar and beat in the yolks of eggs, flavour well with vanilla; whip the whites to a very stiff froth, stir in very lightly. Pour the mixture into a well-buttered soufflé-tin decorated with cherries and angelica; tie a band of buttered paper round outside the tin, place a piece of paper on the top and steam gently for 35 to 40 minutes. Serve at once with jam sauce poured round.

SOUP. To avoid the dangers of bone splinters when cooking soup bones, do them up in a muslin sack.

A fine flavour can be imparted to an ordinary soup by adding a few cloves to the meat stock.

A piece of cheese the size of a walnut added to potato or onion soup gives it a nice creamy taste.

For soup that is too salt, slice a raw potato and drop it in the soup. Bring the whole thing to the boil for a few minutes and the salt flavour will disappear. Then remove the potato and serve the soup.

To remove fat from soup pour the soup through a cloth that has been rinsed in cold water. Most of the fat will remain in the cloth.

A fine soup can be made of left-over peas, beans or carrots. Cook them slowly for 20 minutes and then add them mashed to a thin white sauce highly seasoned.

SOUP, BROWN VEGETABLE (for 4 people).

1 quart water	bunch of herbs
1 carrot	1 oz. flour
1 turnip	1 oz. dripping or butter
1 onion	salt and pepper
1 stick celery	

Melt the dripping in a stewpan, prepare and chop the vegetables and brown them carefully in the fat, remove them, add the flour to the fat and brown it, taking care it does not burn; add the water gradually, stir till it boils, return the vegetables and the herbs to the stewpan and simmer gently for an hour; strain, season well and serve with squares of toast.

SOUP, CARROT (for 4 people).

4 carrots	1 quart stock
2 or 3 sticks celery	1 slice ham or ham bone
2 onions	2 lumps sugar
1 turnip	salt and pepper
1 oz. butter	

Prepare and slice the vegetables, put them into a saucepan with the butter and cook 10 minutes with the lid on; pour over the stock, add the ham, a bouquet garni and the sugar; simmer for 2 hours. Pass the soup through a sieve, season and serve with fried croûtons of bread.

SOUP, CELERY.

1 head celery	a little salt and white pepper
1 piece butter (size of 1 egg)	yolk of 1 egg
2 pints water	1 gill milk or cream

Melt the butter in a pan, then add the celery and stir till covered with butter. Pour on the water, add salt and pepper, and boil (without a lid on the pan) till celery is quite soft. Skim constantly as the froth rises. When celery is soft, rub through a sieve. Pour soup back into pan and stir till boiling. Mix the egg and cream and add to the boiling soup.

SOUP, COCK-A-LEEKIE.
Boil a young fowl for 1 hour in stock or water and remove from saucepan. Well wash 6 or 8 leeks and cut the heads into 1 inch lengths and add to soup. Then add 3 tablespoonfuls rice (cooked and well dried) and a little seasoning to taste. Place this mixture into the liquid and boil for half an hour, then add the fowl cut into small pieces. Serve very hot.

SOUP, CREAM OF CORN.

	chopped parsley
1 small tin of corn	1 oz. margarine
¾ pint water	½ oz. flour
¾ pint milk	½ teaspoonful salt
1 slice onion	pepper

Add corn and onion to the milk and water. Cook for half an hour and rub through coarse wire sieve. Melt margarine, cook flour in it but do not brown and slowly add the corn. Season and boil for 10 minutes. Sprinkle parsley on top.

SOUP, HARICOT (for 4 people).

1½ pints water	1 onion
½ pint milk	½ oz. dripping
½ pint haricot beans	salt and pepper

Soak the beans for 12 hours in cold water with a pinch of carbonate of soda; melt the dripping in a saucepan, add onion and beans, cook for 5 minutes with the lid on, add the water and simmer for 3 or 4 hours until the beans are tender. Pass through a sieve, add the milk, season well, reheat and serve with croûtons of fried bread.

SOUP, IMITATION HARE (for 4 people).

1 quart stock or water	bouquet garni (which see)
¼ lb. gravy beef	1 dessertspoonful mushroom
1 carrot	ketchup
1 onion	1 dessertspoonful Worcester sauce
1 small turnip	1 wineglassful port
1 oz. flour	½ teaspoonful red-currant jelly
1½ oz. butter	salt and pepper

Cut up the meat, dip in flour and brown in the butter with the onion whole stuck with cloves; remove the meat and onion and carefully brown the flour; add the water or stock gradually, allow to boil. Put back the meat and onion, the vegetables cut up, and the flavourings. Simmer for 1½ or 2 hours, strain and return to the stewpan; add the forcemeat balls, cook gently for 10 minutes, season well and add last the port and red-currant jelly.

SOUP, KIDNEY (for 5 or 6 people).

1 oz. kidney	1 oz. dripping
1 carrot	3 pints water
½ turnip	1 teaspoonful vinegar
1 onion	½ tablespoonful ketchup
3 small potatoes	salt
1 oz. flour	pepper

Wash and cut up the kidney into pieces, prepare and slice the vegetables, melt the dripping in the saucepan and fry the onion; dip the pieces of kidney in the flour and fry lightly, add the water and vegetables, simmer for 3 hours; rub all through a sieve and reheat and add the seasoning and flavourings. Some of the pieces of kidney may be kept back before sieving and served in the soup as a garnish.

SOUP, LEEK.

	cayenne
1 bunch leeks	1 pint stock
3 sticks celery	¾ lb. potatoes
2 oz. margarine	½ oz. flour
½ pint milk	salt, pepper

Wash leeks and celery and cut in small pieces. Fry in the margarine, add stock and cook about 20 minutes. Cut potatoes in small pieces and cook till soft (20 to 30 minutes). Add flour and milk and boil 10 minutes. Season and serve.

SOUP, LENTIL (for 4 people).

½ pint lentils	1 small turnip
1 quart water	1 oz. dripping
3 onions	2 potatoes
2 small carrots	bunch of herbs
	salt and pepper

Wash the lentils and soak for 12 hours with a little carbonate of soda in the water. Cut the vegetables into small pieces, put the dripping into the pan with them and cook for 5 minutes with the lid on. Add the lentils, water and flavourings, boil gently till reduced to a pulp, pass through a sieve, season and serve with small squares of toast or croûtons of fried bread.

SOUP, MOCK TURTLE (for 12 or 14 people).

4 quarts water	½ lb. ham (raw)
½ calf's head	bunch of herbs
1 shallot	blade of mace
1 onion	6 cloves
1 carrot	3 oz. butter
1 turnip	3 oz. flour
2 sticks celery	2 wineglassfuls sherry
6 mushrooms	salt and pepper

Wash the head thoroughly, cut the flesh from the bones and tie in a cloth, place in a stewpan with the bones and simmer gently for 3½ hours; take out the head, strain the stock, and when it is cold remove the fat. Melt the butter in a stewpan and fry the vegetables and ham, add the flour and brown it carefully; add all the flavourings, pour in the stock and simmer for 2 hours, removing the fat as it rises; strain, return to the stewpan, add some of the calf's head cut into neat pieces, with the sherry; season well and serve with small forcemeat balls made with veal stuffing and previously fried, or with egg balls.

SOUP, ONION (for 4 or 5 people).

3 Spanish onions	2½ pints water
2 small onions	¼ pint milk
1 oz. dripping	salt
2½ oz. flour	pepper

Peel and cut up the onions, put into a saucepan with the dripping and cook for 5 minutes with the lid on. Add the water and salt. Boil until the onion is quite tender, mix the flour smoothly with the milk, add to the soup and boil well. Season to taste.

SOUP, OX-TAIL (for 6 or 7 people).

1 ox-tail	bouquet garni (which see)
2 quarts water	2 oz. butter
2 onions	2 oz. flour
2 carrots	salt and pepper
1 turnip	wineglassful port

Joint the tail, fry it with the vegetables in a little butter; add the water and herbs, bring to the boil and skim well; simmer from 3 to

4 hours and strain it. Cook the butter and flour together, carefully browning the flour, add the stock and boil; put back some of the best pieces of the ox-tail, season well, add the port and serve.

SOUP, PALESTINE (for 3 or 4 people).

1½ pints white stock	1 oz. butter
1 lb. artichokes	1 oz. flour
1 onion	2 tablespoonfuls cream
½ pint milk	salt and pepper
bouquet garni	

Peel the artichokes under water with a little lemon juice or vinegar added; put the stock in a saucepan, add the chopped onion and sliced artichokes, simmer till tender; pass through a hair sieve. Make a roux with the butter and flour, add the purée and stir till it boils; add the milk and season well. Put the cream in the tureen, pour the soup over and stir gently; serve with croûtons of fried bread.

SOUP, PEA.

1 quart water	small piece of carrot
½ pint split peas	small piece turnip
1 onion	stick of celery
	salt and pepper

Soak the peas for 12 hours with a pinch of carbonate of soda added to the water, put them in a saucepan with the water and vegetables cut up in small pieces. Simmer for 2 or 3 hours till tender, pass through a sieve, season and serve with croûtons of toast or fried bread; sprinkle dried mint over just before serving.

SOUP, POTATO (for 3 people).

	½ pint milk
1 lb. potatoes	1 oz. fat
2 onions	½ oz. sago
1 pint water	salt and pepper

Peel and cut the potatoes into slices, chop the onions, melt the fat in a saucepan, add potatoes and onions and cook for 5 minutes with the lid on; add the water and boil gently till reduced to a pulp; add the washed sago and the milk. Cook till the sago is transparent. Season and serve.

SOUP, RICE AND TOMATO (for 4 people).

4 large tomatoes	1½ oz. rice
1 oz. dripping	salt
1 onion	pepper
1 quart water	

Melt the dripping in the saucepan. Lightly brown the chopped onion, add the tomatoes cut into slices, also the water and rice. Boil gently until cooked. Add the seasoning and serve.

SOUP, SAVOURY BEAN.

4 oz. butter	1 dessertspoonful tomato chutney
½ pint water	½ lb. or small tin tomatoes
1¼ pints stock	½ oz. margarine
2 sticks celery	¼ oz. flour
¼ onion	salt and pepper

279

Soak the beans overnight; place in covered pie-dish with water and bake in moderate oven 1½ to 2 hours. Add stock and vegetables; simmer half an hour. Rub through a sieve. Melt margarine, stir in flour, add vegetables. Season and boil 10 minutes.

SOUP, TOMATO (for 3 or 4 people).

1½ pints white stock	1 gill cream
1 lb. tomatoes	1 small onion
1½ oz. butter	small piece of carrot
1 oz. flour	salt and pepper
1 teaspoonful sugar	

Put the sliced tomatoes, chopped onion, sugar and carrot in a saucepan with the stock and simmer until tender, then pass through a hair sieve. Make a roux with the flour and butter, add the soup, stirring well until it boils. Then season, put in the cream, stir gently, pour into the tureen. Serve with croûtons of fried bread. If liked, a little tomato ketchup added will improve the colour.

SOUP, WHITE VEGETABLE (for 4 or 5 people).

2 carrots	1 oz. butter or dripping
2 turnips	1 quart water (boiling)
1 leek	1 oz. flour
1 onion	½ pint milk
1 stick celery	½ teaspoonful sugar
1 bay leaf	salt and pepper

Clean, prepare and cut vegetables into strips, put them into a pan with the butter or dripping and cook for 5 minutes with the lid on, shaking occasionally; add the boiling water, bay leaf and sugar; boil gently until the carrot is tender. Mix the flour smoothly with the milk, stir into the soup, boil well and season.

SOUR MILK. This is very good for polishing linoleum. It will remove iron rust from white fabrics.

SOWING. Sow at depth according to size of seed. Small seed only needs covering; sweet-pea can be put 1 inch deep, and so on. Have seed plot of sieved earth mixed with sand, water an hour or so before sowing, make slight drills with a wooden plant label or an old fork, drop the seed in sparsely, cover, pat down and water. Then let them alone, save watering twice weekly or, if hot weather, every evening. In general, vegetable seed are sown where they are to be grown.

SPAGHETTI. Can be cooked according to any recipe for macaroni.

SPILT GREASE. If a jar of hot fat is turned over on the kitchen table or floor, fling on cold water at once. It saves the fat soaking in and hard fat on surface can easily be scraped away.

SPINACH. This is of easy culture and valuable for promoting health. It can be stripped of its tender leaves and in a week or so more will be ready. For spring and summer use, sow thinly either broadcast or in drills, 1 foot apart and 1 inch deep, as early as the ground can be worked, and every two weeks for a succession. Thin out to 6 inches and use the thinned-out plants for the pot. For winter and early spring use sow in September, in well-manured ground; cover with straw on the approach of severe cold weather. The richer the ground the more delicate and succulent will be the leaves. For Perpetual (Beet) Spinach, *see* BEET.

SPINACH.

spinach	hard-boiled egg
salt	croûtons of fried bread
soda	salt and pepper and butter

Pick the spinach over and remove the stalks and mid ribs of the leaves, wash thoroughly in several waters to remove the grit, put in a saucepan with no water except that which adheres to the leaves; add a little salt and pinch of carbonate of soda; stir occasionally. When tender drain it and pass it through a sieve, return to the pan, add a little butter or cream, season it, dish in a pyramid shape in a hot vegetable dish; garnish with quarters of hard-boiled egg and triangles of fried bread.

SPIRIT LAMP. If upset, pour a little milk on the flame.

SPLASH ON WALLPAPER. If grease, put on plenty of French chalk, leave for a day, brush off with clean brush and, if necessary, repeat process.

SPLINTERS. To extract splinters, put affected part in very hot water or hold over steaming water, press from farthest point of splinter and then extract with tweezers.

SPONGES. A sponge, when first purchased, is frequently hard, stiff and gritty. To soften it (having first soaked and squeezed it through several cold waters), put the sponge into a clean saucepan, set it over the fire, and boil it a quarter of an hour. Then take it out, put it into a bowl of cold water and squeeze it well. Wash out the saucepan, and return the sponge to it, filling up with clean cold water and boil it another quarter of an hour. Repeat the process, giving it three boils in fresh water; or more than three if you find it still gritty. Take care not to boil it too long, or it will become tender and drop to pieces. You may bleach it by adding to the watter a few drops of oil of vitriol.

After using a sponge, always wash it immediately in clean water, squeeze it out and put it to dry.

SPONGES, to wash.

1. Wash sponges in warm water with either vinegar or tartaric acid added. Then rinse in plenty of cold water and hang in the air to dry.

2. Or dissolve 1 tablespoonful of sea salt in 1 quart of hot water. Soak the sponge in this mixture until it is quite cold, then rinse it out in several clean waters.

3. Or they can be cleaned with a solution of ammonia and hot water. Leave the sponge in this solution for about 12 hours, then rinse and squeeze in running hot water and the sponge will then be quite clean.

SPONGES, RUBBER, to clean. Dissolve ¾ oz. bicarbonate of soda in ½ pint tepid water and place the sponge in the solution. Leave it for a time and then thoroughly rinse in cold water.

SPOONS. Egg stains can be cleaned off with damp salt.

SPRAINED ANKLE, to relieve. Wash the ankle very frequently with *cold* salted water. Dry lightly but thoroughly. Keep your foot as cool as possible to prevent inflammation, and sit with it elevated on a cushion. Massage gently with liniment at intervals.

SPRING MEADOW SAFFRON, to cultivate. *See* BULBOCO-DIUM.

SPRUCE BEER. *See* BEER.

SQUILL (SCILLA). These beautiful spring flowers demand only the simplest culture. The bulbs are planted in early autumn, will bloom in spring—from February to May, according to kind—and need no attention for years beyond a yearly top-dressing of manure.

SQUINTING.

Causes.—Injury to the head, paralysis, or more commonly defective sight. Near objects cannot be seen without straining the eyes. If this is allowed to continue a squint develops—generally at about the age of three to six years, when children begin their lessons.

Treatment.—An oculist should be consulted. In the early stages glasses will correct this condition.

STAIN, IMITATION OLD OAK, to make. Mix together equal parts of turpentine and black cycle enamel and give one or two coats. It is not necessary to apply any varnish as this is contained in the cycle enamel.

STAINING THE FLOOR. When you are re-staining the floor scrub it first very thoroughly with hot strong soda water and allow to dry for 24 hours.

STAINS (1). To remove the greasy marks on leather chairs caused by the arms and head resting on leather chairs put a few drops of the following mixture on a flannel and rub into the leather:
Boil ½ pint linseed oil and when almost cold, add ½ pint vinegar. Mix thoroughly and bottle. After applying the oil, polish off with a soft cloth.

STAINS (2). To remove stains from mahogany, rub the stained part with a cork dipped in a little oxalic acid or aqua-fortis and then thoroughly wash with water. Dry and polish.
If a white mark has been left on a mahogany table by carelessly setting down on it a vessel of hot water, rub the place hard with a rag dipped in lamp oil; and afterwards pour on a little Cologne water, or a little alcohol and rub it dry with a clean rag.
The dish-marks left on a dining-table can of course be taken off in the same manner.
If brandy is spilt on mahogany, and leaves a whitish mark, that mark can be removed by rubbing it hard with a rag dipped in more brandy. Try it.

STAINS, a precaution in using petrol, etc., for removing. Before starting to remove a stain with petrol or any other liquid cleaner, first damp the material with the cleansing agent round the outside of the stain and work inwards. Otherwise the stain will spread as the damp part grows bigger, and when dry the soiled edge will be almost as unsightly as the original stain. Any operations with petrol should be done in the open.

STAINS for wood. *See* WOOD.

STAINS on leather. Remove by rubbing the leather with a cloth dipped in spirits of wine.

STAINS, BLOOD. A little starch should be mixed and spread on the stains. Allow to remain for a few hours; then wash, and the stains will come out quite easily.

STAINS, COAL OIL. Cover the stain with cornmeal or finely-powdered chalk; place a paper over this and rub over with a warm iron. It is necessary to apply two or three times.

STAINS, COCOA. These should immediately by sponged with cold water. Hot water should not be employed.

STAINS, COFFEE. A little glycerine should be gently rubbed on the stain. Rinse in tepid water and iron on the wrong side with a moderate iron until dry. Or:

Mix the yolk of an egg with a little warm water and use it as soap on the stain. For stains that have been on the material for some time add a few drops of alcohol to the egg and water.

STAINS, DYE, on silk and cotton. Damp the stained article, thoroughly soap the soiled parts in a basin or plate. Repeat several times, rinsing well each time.

STAINS, GREASE. To remove grease from silk, take a lump of magnesia and rub it wet on the grease spot. When dry, wash off and the mark will have disappeared.

STAINS, INK. Ink stains can be removed by soaking them in tinned tomato juice for about 10 minutes and then washing. They may also be removed by washing them in warm milk and them sprinkling them with cornflour, which should be brushed off after 24 hours. To remove ink from woollen materials place a pad beneath the spot and rub the upper surface with a cloth dipped in turpentine.

STAINS, INK. To remove an ink stain from a light carpet or woolen material, rub the spot with some ordinary fruit salts mixed in a little methylated spirits.

STAINS, INK.
From Linen.—Melt a piece of tallow and dip the stained part in it. The wash the linen and all marks will have disappeared without injury to the material.

From Mahogany.—Touch the stains with a feather dipped in a mixture of a few drops of spirits of nitre in a teaspoonful of water. When the ink has disappeared, rub the place over with a rag moistened in cold water.

From Paper.—Make a mixture of 2 dr. solution of muriate of tin and 4 dr. water. Apply to the stains with a camel's-hair brush and pass the paper through water after the ink has disappeared. Then dry.

From Silver.—A little chloride of lime mixed with water will remove ink stains from silver articles.

STAINS, IODINE.

From White Material.—Rub the stains with a freshly-cut lemon. *See also* IODINE STAINS.

STAINS, IRONMOULD. Cover the stain with salt and then squeeze a few drops of lemon juice on top. Leave for half an hour, rinse in a weak solution of ammonia and wash in clean water.

STAINS, MARKING INK. Dip the linen in a solution of chloride of lime. When the stain has turned white quickly place the linen in solution of ammonia and let it remain for a few minutes. Then rinse in clean water.

STAINS, MEDICINE. Medicine stains on clothes may usually be removed with Fuller's earth or ammonia. From silver or electro-plated spoons, wipe with a rag moistened with a drop of sulphuric acid. Protect hands. Then wash in warm soapy water and rinse thoroughly in clean water.

STAINS, MILK, to remove. Soak the clothing in a saucer of methylated spirits; keep all lights away from this dangerous liquid.

STAINS, on metal teapot. Put a teaspoonful of baking-soda into the teapot, fill with cold water, put on the range and let it boil for 3 minutes; pour out the water and wash with clean suds, then rinse with clear water. The soda removes all stains and sweetens the pot.

STAINS, PAINT. Wet paint stains will always yield to turpentine, but dry paint stains need to be treated with a mixture of turpentine and ammonia. Rub this on a piece of flannel and let the article dry in the open air.

STAINS, PERSPIRATION. Place the garment in warm water containing a little ammonia. Do not use soap. Allow to soak for half an hour. Wring out; then, if the stain has not entirely disappeared, squeeze a little lemon juice on it and rinse in clean, warm water. Then wash in the usual way.

STAINS, SALT WATER. These stains may be removed from black serge by soaking the garment in clean, soft water slightly blued for 10 minutes. Hang on line to dry with hem down. If creased, press well on the inside.

STAINS, SEALING WAX. Dissolve the spots with naphtha or alcohol applied with a camel-hair brush.

STAINS, TAR, to remove from carpet. Make a paste of powdered Fuller's earth and turpentine. Rub well into the stains and allow to dry. Then brush vigorously.

STAINS, TAR. Lard will remove tar stains from all kinds of materials. Rub it into the stains and let it stay for an hour or so and then wash the material in the usual way.

STAINS, TEA, on china. Tea stains on china can be removed by salt rubbed on the china when damp. One vigorous treatment will be sufficient.

STAINS, TEA, to remove from table linen. Put 2 tablespoonfuls of chloride of lime into a basin, adding a tiny morsel of soda, pouring on gradually 1 pint of boiling water. Mix until quite smooth and allow to remain all night. Remove any scum and drain off the clear solution. Strain through muslin; bottle and cork for use. Rub the stain with a soft rag saturated in the solution, or allow the stained part to soak for an hour in 1 tablespoonful of the solution added to 1 pint of cold water. Then rinse thoroughly in cold water.

STAINS, WAX, to remove from cloth. Place two thicknesses of blotting-paper over the stains and press with a moderately hot iron. As the wax melts it will be absorbed by the two layers of paper and the stains will be entirely removed.

STAINS, WINE, to remove from linen. Place the stain in some boiling milk. This will remove sufficiently to cause it to disappear when washed with soap and water. Apply some salt and a few drops of lemon juice if this should not prove effective.

STAIR FELT. Ordinary corrugated paper, cut to size and placed beneath the stair carpet, makes an excellent substitute for felt and is very soft to the tread.

STALE BREAD. Brush the loaf all over with milk. Bake in a moderate oven about 15 minutes. The crust will be crisp and the bread much nicer than when fresh from the baker.

STALE CAKE, to freshen. Put it in a pudding basin, cover with a lid or plate and steam for half an hour. The cake will be like one newly baked.

STALE TOBACCO. To remove the odour of stale tobacco from a room, place a lupm of rock ammonia in a jar with 3 or 4 drops of oil of lavender. Add a few tablespoonfuls of boiling water and let the jar stand uncovered in the room.

STAR OF BETHLEHEM (ORNITHOGALUM). Plant about 3½ inches deep, and at distances of 3 inches, from September to October. Give protection against frost. Propagation is by offsets.

STARCH. There are certain materials that will not stand starch and for these melt a lupm of sugar in boiling water and add it to the rinsing water to get the starched effect.

When starched clothes get wet while hanging on the line let them dry there and the stiffness will remain.

STARCH BATH. Two tablespoonfuls of starch dissolved in a bath will act as an excellent tonic for the skin.

STEAK, BROILED. A rump steak cut about 1 inch thick is very good when broiled in a pan. Pound the steak on both sides while waiting for the pan to heat and be sure the pan is hot enough to sear the steak very quickly. Do not salt the meat until it has been cooking at least 5 minutes. It should be turned once or twice during the cooking. It must not be cooked too much and the juice in the pan will do for gravy.

STEAK, GRILLED (for 3 or 4 people).

1 lb. rump steak	lemon juice
butter	salt and pepper
1 teaspoonful chopped parsley	

Grease the bars of the griller, brush the steak over with butter, put on the steak and grill over a clear fire from 6 to 8 minutes, according to the thickness, turning every 2 or 3 minutes. Serve on a hot dish with a piece of maître d'hôtel butter on the top. This is made by mixing the chopped parsley and lemon juice into the butter on a plate, forming it into a nice shape.

STEAK, IMPROVING. To make the toughest steak tender when fried, place on a dish and make the gravy in the frying-pan. Put the steak back in the gravy, cover with a saucepan lid to fit the pan and simmer slowly for 20 minutes. This also applies to chops.

STEAK, STEWED (for 4 or 5 people).

1 lb. beefsteak	1 oz. butter
1 onion	1 oz. flour
1 carrot	¾ pint stock or water
1 turnip	salt and pepper
bouquet garni	

Wipe and trim the steak, chop the onion, melt the butter in a saucepan, brown the steak, remove it and brown the onion; add the stock, herbs and vegetable trimmings; simmer very gently till tender, from 2 to 2½ hours. Place the steak on a hot dish. Strain and thicken the gravy with the flour, stir till it boils, season it well and pour it over the meat. Garnish with vegetables, cut in fancy shapes and cooked separately.

STEAK, STUFFED AND STEWED (for 6 or 7 people).

1½ lb. steak	veal stuffing
2 oz. butter or bacon	1 pint stock or water
2 oz. flour	salt and pepper

Beat the steak well with a rolling pin, spread with veal stuffing, roll up and tie with tape. Melt the butter or fat in a stewpan; when hot put in the steak and brown nicely all over, cover with the stock or water and let it simmer gently till quite tender. Take out the steak, remove the tape, lay it on a hot dish, thicken the gravy and season it; strain over the steak and serve.

STEAKS, VIENNA (for 3 or 4 people).

1 lb. lean beef (raw)	1 oz. flour
1 onion or shallot	little stock
1 egg	salt and pepper

Pass the meat through a mincing-machine, add the finely-chopped shallot or onion, season well and bind with well-beaten egg. Divide into small round steaks, using a little flour or bread-crumbs, fry in butter or dripping in a frying-pan, turning occasionally. When cooked place on a hot dish, put the flour in the frying-pan, and allow it to brown; add the stock, boil up, season and pour round the steaks. Garnished with fried onions if liked.

STEAMING. Steaming is a method of cooking by moist heat, or heated vapour rising from boiling water. It is a slower process than boiling, and is especially useful in invalid cookery, because the cooking although slow, is thorough, and the loss of nutritive properties of the food, as well as the flavour, is less than by either boiling or roasting.

Steaming can be done in various ways. A proper steamer (with holes to admit the steam) can be fitted to a saucepan. A saucepan can be converted into a steamer by placing in it only sufficient water to come about half-way up the vessel containing the food which is to be steamed. In both cases the pan must be closely covered to keep the steam in. This method requires care as the water evaporates. In such a case more must be added. It is an economical way of cooking, because two things can be cooked at the same time in the same sauce-pan; for instance, a pudding can be boiled in the lower part and potatoes steamed on the top.

Meat, fish, vegetables and puddings can all be cooked by steam. As a rule, the flavour is better than that got by boiling.

STEEL. A good way to clean scratches off steel is to use a liquid metal polish alternately with an emery cloth. Finally polish with a soft cloth and you will get a perfect surface.

STEEL, to preserve. *See* RUST.

STEEL, to remove rust. *See* RUST.

STEP CLEANING. Use red ochre, a little milk mixed with the powder; it prevents the colour coming off when stepped on.

STEPS AND HEARTHS. When applying white hearthstone or red ochre to steps, hearths and window-sills, use thin starch instead of water and you will find that the mixture goes on more easily, stays on better and is less easily affected by rain.

STEW, IRISH. *See* IRISH STEW.

STEW, SUMMER (for 4 or 5 people).

2 lb. neck of lamb	spring onions
6 young potatoes	peas
6 young carrots	water or stock
6 young turnips	salt and pepper

Cut the lamb into neat chops, put in a stewpan with enough stock or water to cover, bring to the boil, and remove the scum. Carefully prepare the vegetables, which should be small and of equal size, put them in the stewpan whole and simmer gently; season and dish up the stew, the meat in the centre and the vegetables arranged nicely round.

STEWED FRUIT. A pinch of carbonate of soda added to stewed fruit reduces the quantity of sugar needed.

STEWING. Stewing is cooking in a small quantity of liquid in a closed vessel for a long time. It is an economical method because by it the toughest meat can be rendered tender, digestible and savoury, but success cannot be attained without long, slow cooking. Another advantage to the busy housewife is that a stew requires little attention.

There are two ways of stewing: (1) On the stove or fire; (2) In the oven.

In both cases the vessel in which the stew is cooked must be covered closely.

Contrary to boiling, where the meat is plunged into boiling water to close the pores and retain the juices, a stew is made with cold or tepid liquid in order to draw out some of the juices, which form, with the added gravy, the liquid which is served with the stew. Meat is often lightly fried, or seared, before it is stewed. This prevents all the juices going into the gravy, besides making the stew more savoury and a better colour. Meat can be stewed either in a thick or a thin liquid. If good meat is used, it is better to put it into an already thickened gravy. The colour of the stew will be better, as the thickening medium or liaison is flour and that is browned. If tough or inferior meat is used, it is better to stew it in a thin liquid. It penetrates and softens the meat better than a thick gravy. A little vinegar added softens the fibres of tough meat. The liquid of a stew should never boil during the whole process—merely simmer very gently. The disadvantage of a stew is that it is rich and cannot be digested by some people. Meat, fish, vegetables and fruit can be cooked by this method.

STEWS, BOUQUET GARNI FOR. *See* BOUQUET GARNI.

STIFF NECK.

Causes.—Sitting in a draught, rheumatism, injury during birth, overstrain, hysteria, spinal disease, swollen glands. It occurs more often in females than in males.

Symptoms.—The onset is gradual, pain and discomfort in the neck. The muscles on the affected side pull the head over to that side.

Treatment.—In the early stages hot flannels to the neck; afterwards massage and manipulation. If it persists, the cause may be rheumatism or swollen glands, in which case advice should be taken.

STINGS AND BITES, INSECT.

To prevent.—After the morning bath, the body should be sponged with a solution of about 1 dessertspoonful of Epsom salts in 3 pints of water. Just before going out of doors put a drop or two of oil of citronella on to an old handkerchief to pin on hat, or coat, when insects are about.

To treat.—Rub on the bitten parts either camphorated oil or a solution of 1 part carbolic acid in 10 parts oil. Other simple remedies that may be carried about are soda or carbonate of ammonia, finely crushed.

When there is a good deal of inflammation after a bite the part should be bathed with warm boracic acid lotion. Starch powder often effectively allays irritation.

Gnat and Mosquito bites should be immediately painted with a paste made of violet powder moistened with equal parts of chloroform and eau-de-Cologne.

In all cases if there is pain and great inflammation a doctor should be immediately consulted.

Wasp and Bee Stings.—The sting in these cases is generally embedded in the flesh. It may protrude above the surface of the skin, and if so should be removed immediately with a pair of tweezers. If it does not protrude, the best method of making it do so is to place over the spot a hollow key, or something of that nature, and press it to force the sting sufficiently out to be able to remove it with tweezers. Dab the wound with either iodine, sal volatile, vinegar, juice of an onion or a little soda solution. By this means not only will the pain be reduced but the swelling also.

STINGS, NETTLE. Rub the affected part with dock, rosemary, sage or mint leaves.

STOCK FOR SOUP. Never throw away water from fish or vegetables. Use as stock.

STOCK (1).

2 lb. bones	1 stick celery
2 lb. shin of beef	bunch of herbs
2 carrots	peppercorns
2 onions	1 oz. fat
1 turnip	2 teaspoonfuls salt
	6 pints water

Melt the fat in a large saucepan and brown the bones, cut the meat into small pieces and allow to soak for half an hour or longer. Put the meat, bones, water and salt into the pan, and bring slowly to boiling-point; skim well, add vegetables cut in large pieces and herbs and peppercorns tied in muslin. Simmer for 5 hours; strain.

STOCK (2).

bones as available	1 bay leaf
any trimmings from fresh	bunch of herbs
meat or poultry	12 peppercorns
1 carrot	2 cloves
2 onions	2 oz. fat
stick of celery	2 teaspoonfuls salt
ham or bacon bones	water

Chop and wash the bones, fry a nice brown in a little fat, add the trimmings of meat or poultry, ham bone or bacon bones, salt and water. Bring to the boiling-point, then add the vegetables, well cleaned, the herbs, spices, and peppercorns tied in muslin. Boil gently from 4 to 5 hours, skim well, strain, and remove the fat when cold.

STOCK, WHITE.

2 lb. veal bones	stick of celery
1 lb. lean veal	salt
1 turnip	2 quarts water
1 onion	bouquet garni

Put bones chopped and washed in a white-lined pan with meat cut in small pieces. Bring to the boil, add salt, vegetables, bouquet garni, and skim well. Boil gently for 3 to 4 hours and strain. This stock is suitable for white soups, purées and sauces.

STOCKINGS, saving wear. Rubbing a candle over the heels before putting them on saves them from going into holes.

Directly you take off your stockings rinse them out under tepid running water. This not only preserves the life of the stockings but keeps them fresh looking as though they had never been worn.

You can save wear and tear on silk stockings by rubbing beeswax on the heel and toe which strengthen the delicate threads.

It is always.an economy to buy several pairs of stockings of the same colour and kind, for then there is no necessity to discard a good stocking when its mate is unwearable.

STOCKINGS, SILK, invisible mending. When these ladder you can mend them invisibly with a very fine steel crochet hook. Begin where the ladder ends in a loop, pick this up carefully with the hook. Then pick up the first step of the ladder next to the loop and pull this gently through so that the loop is slipped off and you have a new loop on the needle and continue this right up the ladder. Catch the last thread securely with needle and cotton.

STOCKINGS, SILK, to prevent laddering. Here is a sure way of preventing ladders in silk stockings. Three or four rows of machine stitching should be run around the top of the new stockings before they are worn. The stitching should be just below the place where the suspender is fastened and the rows must be fairly close together. Do not drag on your silk stockings as this not only pulls them out of shape, but also weakens the fabric. After washing stockings turn the leg back over the foot, and when putting them on, slip the foot in first and then work the stockings up the leg.

STOCKINGS, SILK, to wash. To wash silk stockings turn them inside out, and wash the colours that are inclined to streak or fade separately and in cool water. After you have rinsed them squeeze the stockings in a soft cloth to absorb the excess water.

STOCKS. The difficulty about stocks is that all seed contains a percentage of singles. In consequence sow thickly and plant closer than needed so that the singles—which are straggly—can be thinned out before blooming. The Ten Week should be sown under glass in early spring and planted out in April and May to flower in July to September. Or they may be sown in the open from late April onwards to flower a week or two later. The taller Bromptons if sown in July and August and planted in sheltered positions will flower from autumn till the frosts. The Intermediates also bloom outdoors during or near winter. A rich moist sandy loam, containing lime, suits them and they thrive best in a sunny position, growing neat and compact, to a height of from 9 to 24 inches with laden flower spikes of charming colours, including rose, scarlet, lavender, mauve, white and yellow. The doubles may usually be recognized by their long concave, pale-green leaves; the single ones have a deeper green foliage which is convex and firmer.

STOMACH-ACHE. *See* COLIC.

STOMACH ACIDITY. *See* ACIDITY.

STOMACH, inflammation of.
Treatment.—The bowels should first be emptied by means of an enema. No food should be taken in solid form. The only food which should be given is gruel, milk and water, or tea made with milk. For an ordinary drink, cold water, iced if possible, should be given. Fomentations should be applied to the stomach. Beyond these measures do nothing except under medical advice.

STRAWBERRIES, to preserve. Select the largest and finest strawberries. To each pound allow 1 lb. (powdered) sugar. Divide the sugar into two equal portions. Put the strawberries into a preserving pan and one portion of sugar. Boil slowly till all the sugar is melted. Then put in, gradually, the remainder of the sugar; and after it is all in let it boil hard for 5 minutes, taking off the scum. Heat a number of small jars and pour in the fruit boiling hot. Lay at the top a round piece of white paper dipped in brandy and close tightly.

Raspberries and large ripe gooseberries may be preserved as above. To each pound of gooseberries allow 1½ lb. of sugar.

STRAWBERRIES, to preserve whole. Take equal quantities of fruit and sugar. Place the fruit in a large dish and sprinkle half the sugar over. Next day make a thin syrup with the rest of the sugar, using 1 pint of red-currant juice instead of water to every pound of strawberries. Simmer them in this till sufficiently jellied.

STRAWBERRY BEDS. Runners, selected from the plump, healthy crowns in February or March, may be planted about 18 inches apart and well mulched in manure. Clear old beds in April and give a good dressing of decayed leaves and soot. In August the first runners may be selected to make new beds, when the weather is favourable.

STRAWBERRY MERINGUE PIE.

1 quart strawberries	pastry case
castor sugar	whipped cream or meringue

Roll plain shortcrust out to ¼ inch thick. Bake on layer cake-tin. When cool, fill with strawberries. Sprinkle with sugar. Cover with whipped sweetened cream or a meringue made from 3 eggs. Bake in slow oven till crisp.

STRAWBERRY MOUSE (for 5 or 6 people).

2 lb. strawberries	juice of ½ lemon
1 gill water	3 whites of eggs
¾ oz. leaf gelatine	carmine colouring
2 oz. castor sugar	

Rub the strawberries through a sieve and use half a pint of the resulting purée. Dissolve the gelatine in the water, strain it into the purée and add the sugar and lemon juice and carmine colouring. Whip the whites of eggs very stiffly; stir lightly into the mixture when it is cool. Turn into a fancy mould and decorate with some whole strawberries. Turn out when set.

Note.—Almost any ripe fruit can be used in this way, such as raspberries, apricots, etc.

STRAWBERRY WORM. Spray the plants with a solution of 1 lb. white hellebore in 20 gallons water.

STRAW ENVELOPES. The straw envelopes of wine bottles when strung together make a good mat to place outside the door in bad weather.

STUFFING, CHESTNUT. *See* FORCEMEAT, CHESTNUT.

STUFFING, FOR DUCKS. Take 1 apple, 1 onion, and 1 oz. sage leaves and chop very finely. Add 6 oz. bread-crumbs, 1 oz. butter, 1 egg and a little pepper and salt.

STUFFING, SAGE AND ONION.

6 or 8 onions	1 oz. butter or dripping
½ lb. bread-crumbs	little milk
1 teaspoonful sage	salt and pepper

Peel the onions, put them in a saucepan with cold water and a little salt and boil them until half done; chop them and add to the other ingredients, moisten with a little milk, season well and use as directed.

STUFFING, VEAL. *See* FORCEMEAT, VEAL.

STYES. Bathe the eye with warm water during the day or with salt and water each morning and evening. Use 1 small teaspoonful of salt to 1 pint lukewarm water. The eye should also be bathed with a lotion of boracic powder. The general health should be attended to; take plenty of open-air exercise and a quinine and iron tonic. If the patient be full-blooded and fat he should be kept for a few days on a farinaceous diet.

SUET PUDDINGS. Mix flour and suet with warm water instead of cold; this will make them much lighter.

SUGAR, some uses of. The flavour of carrots and turnips will be greatly improved if a pinch of sugar is added to them while cooking.

Mint can be chopped much more easily if a little sugar is sprinkled over it before chopping.

Try sugar instead of salt for bringing out the flavour of tomatoes that are to be used as sandwiches.

SULPHUR CONFECTION. *See* APERIENTS.

SUMMER PUDDING. *See* PUDDING, SUMMER.

SUNBURNT SKIN. To restore the natural colour to sunburnt skin, hydrogen peroxide is the quickest remedy. It is an excellent substance for bleaching the skin. It also stimulates the functional activity of the skin glands, thus helping materially in rejuvenating it.

For delicate skin the wash should be diluted with an equal volume of water.

SUNFLOWER. *See* HELIANTHUS.

SUNSTROKE. The patient should be removed to a cool place, the clothes loosened and cold water douched on the surface of the body and a doctor called. Stimulants may be necessary to restore the action of the heart.

SUNSTROKE. *See* HEAT-STROKE.

SWEATERS, to wash. All coloured sweaters and jerseys should be soaked in cold water to which a handful of salt has been added, then washed in warm soapy water, hung on a coat hanger in the open air but not in the sun and they will look like new when dry.

SWEDES, to prevent destruction by "fly" in dry weather. *See* TURNIPS.

SWEEPING A ROOM. When sweeping out a room first sprinkle damp screwed-up newspaper about; this will keep the dust from rising.

SWEET ALYSSUM. *See* ALYSSUM.

SWEETBREADS, FRIED (for 3 or 4 people).

2 calf's sweetbreads	salt and pepper
1 teaspoonful chopped parsley	egg and bread-crumbs
little grated lemon peel	little flour
1 dessertspoonful chopped ham	

Soak the sweetbreads in salted water, put on in cold water and bring to the boil; throw it away, put on again with fresh water and simmer gently for 1 hour; drain and press between two plates with a weight on top. When firm, dip in seasoned flour, brush over with egg, coat with a mixture of parsley, ham and lemon peel, then again with egg and crumbs; fry a golden brown in hot fat, dish on hot dish with fancy paper and garnish with fried parsley. The sweetbreads can be cut in slices if preferred.

SWEETBREADS, STEWED (for 3 or 4 people).

calf's or sheep's sweetbreads	1 oz. butter
1 onion	1 oz. flour
blade of mace	little cream
½ pint milk	salt and pepper

Soak the sweetbreads in salted water, put them in a stewpan with cold water, bring to the boil; throw it away, put the sweetbreads on again with the milk, onion and mace and simmer very gently till tender; drain them, press them between two plates and trim them when firm. Make a sauce with the butter, flour and milk the sweetbreads were cooked in, add a little cream, season well, reheat the sweetbreads and serve garnished with cut lemon and parsley.

SWEET-PEA. The culture of the sweet-pea requires care but no special knowledge; it seems ever ready to do its best under any circumstances—even in a prolonged drought. An ordinary garden soil, well and deeply dug in the autumn and enriched below with a fair amount of manure, an average forking and pulverizing of the ground in the spring, and with some protection against slugs and snails and birds, a bounteous crop may be relied upon; while to maintain a continuance of bloom it is only necessary to cut the flowers day by day and never permit a single seed-pod to be formed. A wide choice of colours is available nowadays. Grow either in groups of three or four plants, or in rows, and stake rows early with well-branched sticks of good height—say 6 to 8 feet. For obtaining early bloom make an autumn sowing, but otherwise sow about mid-February, gradually hardening the young seedlings and planting them out as early in April as the weather permits. Keep peas well watered at every stage of growth.

SWEET SULTAN. A hardy annual of unusual thistledownish flower in many delicate colours, mainly whites, light blues and pinks, with mauves and yellows in the newer varieties. They flower freely on stems about 18 inches high, and are easy to grow by sowing in a sunny spot in the late spring and growing them on in well-drained soil with loam mixed in. They prefer a warm situation.

SWEET VERBENA. *See* ALOYSIA.

SWEET-WILLIAM. Sow in the open in June or July for flowering in the following summer. The seed should be sown in a shady spot in drills of finely-sifted soil, and covered very lightly, and the seedlings should be transferred to their final positions as soon as they will bear removal. The colours are white, red, pink, maroon and speckled. The most suitable soil is a sandy loam, and an open, sunshiny position is necessary. Newer varieties include doubles, as also a hybrid class, Sweet Wilvelsfield, which flowers freely during the summer months.

SWISS ROLL (for 5 or 6 people). 3 oz. sugar
    2 eggs (3 if small)   castor sugar
    2 oz. self-raising flour   jam

Whisk the eggs and sugar well in a warm place, sift the flour in gradually and stir lightly, add baking-powder, turn quickly in a prepared baking-tin and bake in a quick oven for about 6 minutes. Turn on to a sheet of paper sprinkled with castor sugar, cut down the edges, spread with warm jam, roll up, sprinkle with sugar, serve with jam sauce if hot and on a glass dish with lace paper if cold.

Note.—Apricot and raspberry are the most suitable jams to use.

SWISS ROLL, CHOCOLATE. 1½ oz. chocolate powder
    2 eggs   ½ teaspoonful baking-powder
    their weight in butter,   little vanilla
       sugar and flour   apricot jam

Cream the butter and sugar until soft, add the sifted flour and chocolate powder alternately with the eggs, beating well; stir in the baking-powder and a drop or two of vanilla essence. Pour into a flat baking-tin lined with well-buttered paper. Bake in a quick oven for 8 to 10 minutes. Turn on to a sheet of paper sprinkled with sugar, spread with jam, cut down the edges and roll up quickly. Place on a cake rack to cool.

SYRUP, BLACKCURRANT. Dissolve $\frac{3}{4}$ lb. white sugar in 1 pint water and boil to a syrup with the addition of $\frac{1}{2}$ pint stained blackcurrant juice.

Note.—The same recipe may be used for making raspberry syrup by substituting raspberry juice for blackcurrant juice.

SYRUP, FOR SWEETMEATS, to clarify. For each pound of sugar allow $\frac{1}{4}$ pint water. For every 3 lb. of sugar allow the white of 1 egg. Mix when cold, boil a few minutes and skim it. Let it stand 10 minutes. Then skim and strain.

TABLE, to clean. Marks on a polished table, caused by hot plates, disappear when rubbed with camphorated oil.

TABLE-LINEN, to preserve. When this has become very worn tack a piece of fine new muslin on the back of the part to be mended; then darn the surface. The muslin will make the darn much stronger and after laundering it should be quite invisible.

TABLE MANNERS.

DO NOT:

Break lumps of bread into a plate to soak up surplus gravy or sauce.

Bite or cut the bread or roll served with other courses. Convenient-sized pieces should be broken off as required on the plate, with the left hand.

Lay your knife down while eating with the fork, or rest the knife blade and fork prongs on respective sides of the plate with their handles on the table, or lay the knife and fork down crossed on the plate, or hold one in either hand, pointing upwards.

Remove and hold spoon, fork, or knife from a plate when sending it for a second helping.

Drink when you have any food in your mouth, or with greasy lips that will leave a mark round the rim of the glass, or omit to wipe your lips after drinking.

Tilt your plate ostentatiously to spoon up the last drop of soup, fruit juice or custard.

Make any undue clatter on the plate with silver or cutlery or scrape a plate round with the knife.

Critically examine any dish offered, ask questions or touch it and then refuse it.

Push your plate away upon finishing a course.

Continue stolidly eating your own meal if there are no servants waiting upon those present, but look round to see if you should pass anything to other people.

Collect condiments, butter, cakes, biscuits, etc., round your own plate, but after helping yourself put them where they may be reached by others.

Ask for a second helping of anything at a formal lunch or dinner, though at simple family meals of only two or three courses an offer of a second helping of any dish may be accepted.

Take spoons or other serving implements on to your own plate when trained servants or waiters are removing vegetable or other dishes or plates from the table.

Make any attempt to stack up plates, clear away crumbs or tidy any tagle appointments. Is it incorrect, though perhaps meant kindly.

Leave a teaspoon in a cup or pour any spilt liquid in the saucer back into the cup.

Eat with the fingers stickly fancy cakes and pastries, such as those containing jam, cream or custard, when a fork is provided. A whole slice of cake should not be bitten into, but first cut through, thus handled more daintily.

Let nervousness make you appear awkward if unused to lunching or dining out. Other people may not notice mistakes if you are quietly self-possessed.

Make voluble apologies or explanations if you use the wrong fork or spill your wine, but pass the mishap off as quietly as possible.

Take such a large portion of anything that other guests must go short, or an absurdly small one, but just help yourself moderately.

TAPESTRY, to clean. Apply petrol with a small brush or piece of flannel and allow to dry in the open air. Or rub in powdered magnesia thoroughly and evenly with a cloth and remove it a few hours later with a stiff brush.

TAPEWORM. Two teaspoonfuls of powdered kamala should be taken on an empty stomach. If the bowels are not moved within about $2\frac{1}{2}$ hours a further teaspoonful should be taken. Two hours later this should be followed by between $\frac{1}{2}$ oz. and 1 oz. castor oil. This is a certain cure for tapeworm and does not cause a sickness. (Note that kamala is like red brick dust in appearance.)

TAPIOCA PUDDING. *See* PUDDING, SAGO.

TAR, to remove. First scrape off as much as possible, then thoroughly damp the place with salad oil or melted lard and allow this to remain for 24 hours. If the article be of cotton or linen it should be washed in strong warm soap-suds. If it is of wool or silk, remove the grease with ether or spirits of wine.

TART, APPLE AND DATE.

$1\frac{3}{4}$ lb. cooking apples	$2\frac{1}{2}$ teaspoonful ground cinnamon
$\frac{1}{2}$ lb. dates	$\frac{1}{2}$ lb. flour
$\frac{1}{4}$ lb. Demerara sugar	$\frac{1}{2}$ teaspoonful baking-powder
1 tablespoonful butter	6 oz. icing sugar

Peel, core and cut apples, melt butter, mix sugar and cinnamon together and add to the fruit with 2 tablespoonfuls water. Cover pan and stew slowly till quite cooked. Turn out and cool. Grease tin.

Mix flour with baking-powder and 1½ teaspoonfuls cinnamon. Rub in butter, stir in sugar (2 oz.). Mix to a paste with cold water, lay on tin, line sides, put in fruit, cover and bake for 35 minutes. When cooked, cool and ice with 6 oz. icing sugar, moistened with white of egg.

TART, FRUIT.

any fruit (apples. cherries,	sugar
gooseberries, etc.)	water
	short crust

Prepare the fruit, half fill the pie-dish, add sugar and water and fill up with fruit. Roll out the pastry, place the pie-dish in it and cut out the top; brush the edges of the dish with water and line them with strips of pastry, moisten them and place on the top, press the edges together and cut round sharply; work the edges up with a knife and decorate them. Brush over the tart with water or whipped white of egg, sift with sugar and bake for about half an hour; serve hot or cold.

TART, FRUIT, to prevent juice from boiling.

Two or three lumps of sugar placed under the pie chimney will prevent the juice in fruit tarts from boiling.

TARTLETS.

jam   short crust

Roll out the pastry, line some patty tins with it, put some jam in each and bake in a quick oven for about 15 minutes.

Note.—A crust of bread can be put in instead of the jam, and removed when the pastry is cooked and warmed jam put in after.

Flaky, rough puff or puff pastry can be used for tartlets.

TARTLETS, CHERRY.

	¼ lb. sugar
8 oz. self-raising flour	¼ teaspoonful salt
3 oz. dripping or lard	½ lb. cherries

Put the flour and salt in basin, rub in dripping, lard or butter, mix to a stiff paste with water. Roll out and line some patty-pans. Bake in quick oven 15 minutes. Boil sugar and water, add cherries, simmer till tender. Put a few cherries in each tartlet and fill up with syrup.

TARTLETS, CUSTARD (10 or 12).

½ pint milk	sugar to taste
2 eggs	nutmeg
½ oz. cornflour	short crust

Line some patty tins with the pastry; mix the cornflour smoothly with some of the milk, add it with the well-beaten eggs to the remainder of the milk; sweeten to taste. Put some of the mixture into each tartlet and bake in a moderate oven about 30 minutes. Any flavouring, such as vanilla or almond, can be used. The nutmeg should be grated on the top.

TARTS, MACAROON (14 to 16).

¼ lb. ground almonds	whites of 3 eggs
¼ lb. castor sugar	½ lb. puff or flaky pastry
some raspberry jam	

Line some patty tins with the pastry, cut some strips to go across the top, put a little jam in each. Whip the whites to a stiff froth, stir in the sugar and ground almonds lightly. Put a spoonful of this mixture in each tart and cross with two strips of pastry; bake in a quick oven from 15 to 20 minutes.

TAURUS (THE BULL). Second sign of the Zodiac, influencing persons born between 22nd April and 21st May. Such are methodical, go-ahead, realists, good musicians, careful in work, but will not launch out on uncertainties nor be hurried.

TEA. Tea keeps better in a glass jar with a stopper than in a tin. To make tea, pour freshly-boiled water over the tea-leaves and let it stand for two or three minutes.

TEA. Before using, spread the dry tea on a sheet of paper and place in a warm oven for 10 minutes. The flavour will be greatly improved and the tea go much further.

TEACAKES. *See* CAKES.

TEACUPS, reading the leaves. One of the most ancient methods of peering into the future: it flourished in the early Chinese Dynasties, and still survives. The signs and interpretations would fill a book, and will probably be generally familiar. The right way to test out the fortune of the leaves is not so fully understood, however, and therefore is given below:

It is better to use a proper teacup, not one of the coffee shape. The real teacup is shallow and wide compared to its depth.

Do not use a cup that has any pattern on the inside and avoid fluted china. A plain white cup—white on the inside at least—is what you want and the shallower it is the better.

Drink the contents of the cup, leaving about a teaspoonful at the bottom as dregs. That done, take the cup in the left hand—this is important—and turn it three times to the left, so as to make the few drops remaining in the cup swing round and round. Then turn the cup upside down in the saucer, doing it gently so that the leaves may fall naturally into their places. Leave for a few minutes to allow it to drain. Then lift and examine the leaves.

All readings should begin at the left side of the handle and travel round the cup.

Those leaves which lie high up the side of the cup near the rim tell what is going to happen quickly. Those half-way down denote what will happen shortly, those at the bottom concern the far future.

Do not be disheartened if at first nothing can be made out of what is seen. Gradually, after concentration, one figure after another will emerge, and each attempt at reading will be more easy than the last.

Tea dust or very small leaves forming lines are signs of a journey. If the line is wavy it suggests doubt and difficulty.

The wish should be kept in the mind and all thoughts concentrated upon it while the tea is being drunk and the cup whirled round. When it is taken from the saucer after draining it should be looked at intently and the first symbol on which the eyes rest is an answer to the question.

TEA-LEAVES, some uses. Don't throw tea-leaves away. Collect them for a week in a pail, then pour over them 1 quart of boiling water. Leave for 1 hour. Strain and bottle the brown liquid; it is a splendid gloss-maker. If used on mirrors, glasses or windows it makes them shine like crystal. It is also a good cleaner for doors, furniture and linoleums. Polish afterwards with soft duster.

Always wash leaves well before sprinkling on carpet. Many a good carpet has been hopelessly stained by carelessness about this.

The practice of draining tea-leaves in the sink quickly causes discoloration.

Stains on tiles made by tea leaves, lavatory basins, can be removed in the same way, which is: Mix a twopenny packet of chloride of lime with 1 lb. of soda, then pour on 1½ pints of boiling water and stir. When the lime and soda are dissolved, bottle the liquid for use. It should be rubbed on with a flannel and then rinsed away with clean water. The bottle should be well shaken before use.

TEA TOWELS. If these leave fluff on your china, pass them through a solution of weak starch water.

TEETH, a simple powder for. Take 8 oz. fine precipitated chalk and mix into it a crushed peppermint. Use with a soft toothbrush.

TEETH, to whiten. Pour hot water on a few dry sage leaves and use as a lotion when cold. Rub the gums and teeth with sage.

TEETH, MILK. Baby should complete his first set of teeth by the time he is two and a half years. They should appear more or less at regular intervals as shown in the following table:

Age	Number of Teeth	Kind
6 to 9 months . .		Central incisors (lower)
8 to 12 months . :	4	Central incisors (upper)
12 to 15 months . {	2 4	{Lateral incisors (lower) {Anterior molars
18 to 24 months . .	4	Canines (Eye Teeth)
24 to 30 months . .	4	Posterior molars

TEETHING FEVER. If the tooth is half through and the gum over it is swollen and tender, much pain and discomfort will be spared if the doctor lances the gum and allows the tooth to emerge freely. Mostly, however, rubbing the gums and letting the infant have a rubber teething ring to bite on, will be sufficient. The child should be given a dose of castor oil.

TEMPERATURE, to read on different thermometers.

	Fahrenheit	Centigrade	Réaumur
Freezing Point . . .	32°	0°	0°
Boiling Point . . .	212°	100°	80°
Normal Temperature of the Human Body . . .	98·4°	36·9°	29·5°

TEMPERATURE, to take.   The normal temperature of the body is 98.4 degrees; it is best taken by the thermometer being held under the tongue and the lips closed.   It may also be taken under the arm or in the groin.   If taken in these parts it always registers a little lower than if taken in the mouth.

TENANCIES.   Apart from the operation of the Rent Restriction act, tenancies vary in length and, in consequence, the requisite notice of termination.   Houses taken for a definite period, or on sufferance, need no notice, but must be vacated exactly at the arranged time. A monthly or weekly tenancy require notice of a month or a week respectively.   A yearly tenancy is subject to six months' notice, to expire at the end of any twelve months' tenancy.   A three years' agreement requires three months' notice, to expire at the end of the three years, and thereafter a quarter's notice.   Tenant's fixtures which can be removed without damage to the structure, or, as sheds and greenhouses, are not built into the ground, can now be taken away at the end of the notice by the tenant.   A tenant need not move till midnight of the day the notice expires.

THERMOS FLASKS.   Never leave the cork in when not in use. To save the cork going astray use a rubber band large enough to go round the cork and the flask and so keep it attached where it can always be found.   After using a thermos, even if only for hot water, never fail to rinse out, and after other liquids add a pinch of carbonate of soda to the rinsing water.   If, however, this has been overlooked, and the flask soured, half fill with warm water to which an eggshell and a tablespoonful of vinegar have been added.   Shake well and the result will be perfect cleanliness.

THINNING OUT.   The process of reducing the number of seedlings resulting from sowing seed in drills or groups is known as thinning out. This rather wasteful way has long been, mostly in rural districts, of putting in more seed than necessary and then, when seedlings are too close together, pulling up most of them, preferably the weaker, so as to leave one in every 6 inches to grow on.   The slower way of putting in just enough seed, spaced to what room plants need to mature properly, is a much greater economy of seed, but seldom adopted, the argument being that, if seed does not fructify, time is lost and there are unsightly gaps. The time element has some value in vegetables, which take long to mature, hence the persistence of the custom. The Brassica, that is green vegetables generally—cabbage, cauliflower, broccoli and so on—are allowed to grow to 4 inches in height, then thinned out and when six inches high transplanted to their growing quarters, adequately spaced, as directed in the entries for particular vegetables. Root crops, such as carrot, turnip, parsnip, beet, shallots and such should never have their seedlings transplanted, but must grow where sown, hence more sparse sowing is recommended, with thinning out to full growing space, which see under particular entries, or the seed down to the full spacing for maturing and the risk taken of coming up—onions do not mind transplanting. With flowers, the quantity of seed is usually so small as to be of no great concern or expense, hence thinning out is usual. Hardy and half-hardy annuals should be thinned out as soon as in the fourth leaf, thereby giving the plants a chance to develop into fine flowering specimens.

THREAD WORMS. These infest the lower part of the bowels and give rise to heat and irritation round the anus. The parts should be kept very clean and washed in warm water and soap. The diet should be regulated and sweets avoided. A dose of castor oil or magnesia should be given, and after it has acted, a solution of salt and water should be injected into the bowels with a syringe. One teaspoonful of salt to 12 teaspoonfuls of tepid water. The chemist can supply effective "worm tablets."

THROAT, RELAXED. *See* RELAXED THROAT.

THRUSH. Very weakly infants or persons who are suffering from extreme debility develop thrush, recognized by small raised patches of white upon tongue, gums and roof of mouth. Treat with a mixture of borax, ¼ teaspoonful worked into 2 tablespoonfuls of honey.

THUMBS, what shape indicates. The shape of the thumb indicates those influences which are inherited from our parents or earlier ancestors. A firm thumb with some stiffness in the joints, shows great determination which may degenerate into obstinacy. Often there is a narrowness of outlook and always a tendency to secretiveness. One with a supple thumb is more adventurous, more careless of popular opinion, more ready to spend his money or to give thought to others.

The length of the thumb is of importance also. A long thumb belongs to a person who has dominant will power but uses it with judgment.

The short thick thumb shows sheer obstinacy. It belongs to the type of people who will face danger or discomfort simply because they have been told not to take a certain line of action. If you want them to do a thing you must tell them not to do it.

When a thumb lies close to the palm it shows a character which will pay whatever is owing with scrupulous care, yet is quite ready to take such advantage of the folly of others.

The more clearly a thumb forms a right-angle with the palm when it is outstretched, the stronger the sense of justice indicated. These people are emphatically just in all things, not only in money matters but in their thoughts.

If the angle is wider still and the thumb droops when outstretched, it shows tenderness amounting to weakness.

The divisions of the thumb and fingers by their joints form the Phalanges, and these have the same meanings in all cases. The upper Phalange, where the nail is, indicates the will; the second Phalange (between the top and middle knuckle) stands for reason, and the lowest one for love. With the thumb that Phalange runs down the side of the palm.

When the first and second Phalanges of the thumb are of equal length it is an excellent sign. There is a sane and equitable balance kept between the will and the judgment. When the first Phalange is much the longer of the two, it shows a determination to get what is wanted no matter what the cost may be. The worst cases are when the Phalange is very thick, which indicates a fierce and ungovernable temper which rises to dangerous fury if its owner's will is crossed.

Should the second Phalange be longer than the first, it suggests unhappiness and discontent; also a lack of concentration necessary to carry plans through. Thus they let all opportunities slip.

Sometimes the second Phalange has a cut-away appearance, with the result the thumb is of the type known as waisted. This indicates tact and understanding.

THYME. *See* HERBS.

TIGHT SCREW. A red-hot poker held for a minute or two on the head of a tight screw will loosen it so that it can be quite easily withdrawn.

TIN, to polish. Use soapy water (hot) and rub over with whitening.

TINCTURE OF IODINE. *See* IODINE.

TIN LIDS, to open. Some tins give trouble every time they are opened. To avoid this lip a tab of tape underneath the lid before closing it down. The lid can always easily be removed by lifting this tab.

TINNED FRUIT, to test. The soundness of tinned fruit can be tested by an ordinary steel knife as soon as the tin is opened and the top removed. Hold it there for a few minutes, and if there is any copper present the knife will show traces of it when withdrawn.

TINWARE. Tins will not rust when put in water if when they are new they are well rubbed with lard and thoroughly heated in the oven.

TIRED FEET. Bathe them in 2 quarts of hot water to which a handful of salt has been added. This will stimulate the circulation and remove the waste products which are responsible for the fatigue. Two handfuls of salt to a basin of hot water.

TOAD-IN-THE-HOLE (for 3 people).

$\frac{1}{2}$ lb. sausages	1 egg
$\frac{1}{4}$ lb. self-raising flour	salt and pepper
$\frac{1}{2}$ pint milk	

Skin the sausages, place in a greased pie-dish. Mix the flour smoothly with the egg and milk, beat well, season and pour over the sausages. Bake in a quick oven for about 1 hour.

TOBACCO, HERB. Mix and press together 2 oz. each of hyssop, marjoram and thyme, 3 oz. coltsfoot, 4 oz. each of betony and eyebright, 8 oz. each of rosemary and lavender. Cut up finely.

TOBACCO PLANT (NICOTIANA). Half-hardy annual, plant out in warm borders. Seed should be sown early in the year in a warm frame, and the seedlings pricked off into pots and placed in a temperature of about 60°, when about the end of May they ought to be well grown and ready for putting out. As well as white, there are also magenta flowers.

TOBACCO WASH, FOR PLANTS. Boil in ½ pint water 1 oz. shag tobacco. Apply to the leaves and stems of infected plants (with a brush), then syringe with water. This acts as a deadly poison to insects.

TOE NAIL, INGROWING. Properly fitting boots should be worn and the part frequently washed and kept clean. The nail should be cut level at the top and the angles left and not trimmed away or rounded off, and a piece of cotton-wool packed between the nail and fold of overhanging skin. The wool should be frequently changed.

TOFFEE (1). Toffee should never be stirred. It must be gradually heated and not be permitted to boil till all the sugar melts, then boil quickly. Ingredients:

½ lb. brown sugar | ½ teaspoonful flour
4 oz. fresh butter | 1 dessertspoonful treacle

Melt the butter, add the sugar, flour and treacle, boil furiously for about 20 minutes, stirring all the time till it sets when dropped into cold water. Spread in a buttered flat tin. When beginning to set mark into divisions, and when partly set cut into slabs and put in a tin to keep.

TOFFEE (2).

¼ lb. butter | ½ lb. golden syrup
1 lb. brown sugar | flavouring or lemon juice

Melt the butter, add the syrup and sugar and boil quickly for 20 minutes. It is ready when a little will harden in cold water. Then remove from the fire, add the flavouring and pour into a greased dish.

TOFFEE, EVERTON. Melt ½ lb. butter in a saucepan and then add 1 lb. moist sugar and 1 lb. treacle and boil together for 10 minutes. Pour into a well-greased flat dish.

TOFFEE, TREACLE. First rub the saucepan with butter and pour in the required amount of treacle. Boil gently until it will break between the teeth when tested after being thrown into cold water. Then immediately take the pan off the fire and pour the toffee on a buttered dish. When cool, roll it into sticks. Essence of peppermint, lemon or almond may be used for flavouring if desired, whilst a little cayenne pepper added to treacle toffee gives a splendid cough cure.

TOMATO AND CHEESE TOAST.

½ oz. butter	1 tablespoonful tomato sauce
1 oz. cheese	or ketchup
lemon juice	cayenne

Put butter and sauce into a saucepan and heat. Add cheese grated, a few drops of lemon juice and cayenne. Stir over a gentle heat until the cheese is melted and serve at once on hot buttered toast.

TOMATO CHUTNEY. *See* CHUTNEY, TOMATO.

TOMATO PURÉE (for 3 or 4 people).

1½ pints white stock	1 gill cream
1 lb. tomatoes	1 small onion
1½ oz. butter	small piece of carrot
1 oz. flour	salt and pepper
1 teaspoonful sugar	

Put the sliced tomatoes, chopped onion, sugar and carrot in a saucepan with the stock and simmer till tender, pass through a hair sieve; make a roux with the flour and butter, add the purée, stirring well till it boils, season. Put the cream in the tureen, pour the soup over and stir gently; serve with croûtons of fried bread; if necessary, a little tomato ketchup added improves the colour.

TOMATO SOUP. *See* SOUP, TOMATO.

TOMATOES. Tomato seed may be thinly sown in November to get early supplies in May or at the end of January for July tomatoes. Put one seed each in well-drained pots filled with light soil. Cover with glass and keep at an even temperature of not less than 60° till germination starts, then transfer and keep near the glass until well established. The transferred seedlings should be put singly into 4-inch pots, drain the pots with one "crock," and a little rough soil, and plant the seedlings up to their seed-leaves. Any good loamy soil will be suitable for this operation, but it should be *warmed* before use, placed in a warm position, carefully watered, and shaded from bright sunshine. Keep near the glass, so as to make sturdy plants; when rooted through, transfer the plants to their fruiting quarters. If to be grown in pots, 9½ inches is a suitable size, and in these the plants should be planted deeply, so as to admit of subsequent top dressing. For outdoor cultivation sow in a hot-bed in March, and when the seedlings are a few inches high, pot them singly into 3-inch pots; carefully harden off, snad finally plant out at the end of May under a south wall allowing plenty of room. The plants must be plentifully supplied with water during the period of growth. Tomato plants will need the support of sticks when they are in their final position. If grown in beds, plenty of room must be given. The best soil for tomatoes is a fibrous loam mixed with a little sharp sand, leaf-mould and well-decayed manure. Add more soil as the roots grow and do not use manure which has not fully fermented. Give a pinch or two of nitrate of potash or kainite occasionally. Nip off all side-shoots, allowing only the flower trusses to grow from the main stem, and where robust keep only three trusses.

TOMATOES, to fry. Wipe the tomatoes and cut them into halves crosswise. Fry them gently in dripping for 10 minutes or a quarter of an hour.

TOMATOES, to keep. Green tomatoes should be picked off before the plants die and stored in a cool, dry, airy place where they will be protected from the frost.

TOMATOES À LA BRESLAU.

3 tomatoes
1 oz. butter

1 teaspoonful chopped parsley
little lemon juice
6 croûtons of fried bread

Cut the tomatoes in halves and bake in a moderate oven on a greased tin. Mix the butter with parsley and lemon juice into six small pats. Place each piece of tomato on a hot croûton of fried bread and place a pat of butter on the tomato. Serve on a fancy paper and garnish with parsley.

TOMATOES, SAUTÉ.

1 lb. tomatoes
2 oz. butter

chopped parsley
salt and pepper

Cut the tomatoes in slices and fry in butter, put in a hot dish, season and sprinkle with chopped parsley. Tomatoes cooked in this way are suitable to serve with bacon as a breakfast dish.

TOMATOES, STUFFED.

4 or 6 tomatoes
2 tablespoonfuls bread-
    crumbs

1 tablespoonful cheese
little butter
chopped parsley
salt and pepper

Choose tomatoes of equal size, make a small hole in the top, scoop out the pulp, mix the stuffing, moisten with the pulp and season. Refill the tomatoes, sprinkle on a few crumbs and place a small piece of butter on each. Put on a greased baking-tin and bake in a moderate oven for about 20 minutes. Serve on croûtons of toast or fried bread and garnish with parsley.

TONGUE, to examine for symptoms. Brown or black tongue indicates blood-poisoning; dry tongue indicates-feverishness; strawberry-coloured tongue indicates scarlet fever; white-coated tongue indicates disordered stomach; yellow-coated tongue indicates disordered liver.

It is a good sign when tongue cleans gradually from the edge.

TONSILS, ENLARGED.

Causes.—Repeated attacks of sore throat. It occurs very frequently in consumptive children.

Symptoms.—There is a heavy look about the face; the mouth is kept half open; the child snores at night, waking up in the morning with a very dry mouth. Deafness may be present. The voice is metallic.

Treatment.—Once the tonsils are enlarged in a child, an operation is advisable.

After the tonsils have been removed, the child ceases to snore, gets rid of the attacks of sore throat, the speaking becomes clear and the general health is better in every way.

TOOTHACHE, to relieve. A couple of drops of oil of cloves on cottonwool, inserted into the cavity, if the tooth is hollow. If not, rinse the mouth with strong salt and water, holding it in the mouth as long as possible, and repeat two or three times.

TRANSPLANTING. Lift without damaging roots and get out all the roots. Have the hole plenty big enough to spread the roots in its new situation. Well water before putting in, fil soil, press firmly all round, water again, put a stake to save loosening in the wind, then let it alone to recover and make good on its own. Coddling is the great fault of the beginner.

TRAVELLING, etiquette for. If talking with strangers leads to further conversation, it should still remain impersonal.

A lady may certainly accept from a stranger any little polite attentions—the loan of a rug or cushion on a long journey, opening or closing a window, help with the luggage or securing the services of a porter.

The Window Question.—A much debated travel question is which of several passengers in a train carriage has the right to decree whether a window shall be open or closed. It is generally conceded that the window-seat passenger facing the engine has that right, but should not excercise it in an arbitrary manner.

It is excessively rude for anyone to reach across window-seat passengers to raise or lower the window without at least a polite question or apology.

Any refreshments taken in the train should be of a nature, and consumed in a way, that cannot cause offence to others. Little children, too, should be properly looked after.

TRIFLE (for 8 ot 10 people).

6 or 8 sponge cakes	¼ lb. ratafias
2 eggs and 2 yolks	1 gill sherry
1 oz. castor sugar	2 tablespoonfuls brandy
apricot jam	1 oz. almonds
½ pint milk	2 oz. preserved fruits
½ pint cream	essence of vanilla

Cut the sponge cakes in slices and spread with jam, put them together again and arrange in a glass dish with the ratafias; soak well with the sherry and brandy. Make a custard with two whole eggs and two yolks extra; stir till it thickens, sweeten and flavour with vanilla and let in become quite cold. Just before serving pour the custard over the cakes, whip the cream, add sugar and flavouring. Force it over the mould and decorate with the preserved fruits and blanched and shredded almonds.

TRIFLES, flavouring for. *See* FLAVOURING.

TRIPE AND ONIONS (for 4 people).

1 lb. tripe	½ pint milk
2 onions	salt and pepper
1 oz. flour	

Wash the tripe, place it in a stewpan, cover with cold water and bring to the boil. Put it on a board, scrape it if necessary, cut into neat pieces, return it to the pan with about $\frac{3}{4}$ of a pint of water and the onions finely chopped; simmer till the tripe is tender. Mix the flour smoothly with the milk, add it, stir till it boils, season well and serve.

TROPAEOLUM. *See* NASTURTIUM.

TROUSER HEMS, to prevent fraying. Before new trousers are worn cut two strips half an inch wide from old kid gloves and neatly hem inside where the material comes in frequent contact with the shoes.

TROUSERS, BAGGY, to avoid. When tousers are new, future bagging at the knees can be prevented by tacking a 6-inch piece of lining with a hem either side, at the bend of the knee, fixing securely at either side seam. Press well with a damp cloth on the right side.

TROUT À LA MEUNIÈRE.

6 fresh trout	juice of 1 lemon
flour	2 tablespoonfuls butter
pepper, salt	1 teaspoonful chopped parsley

Whiting, plaice and soles can also be fried by this method. Sprinkle both sides of fish with pepper and salt, melt butter in frying-pan and fry well-floured fish for 5 minutes on either side. Lift carefully on to hot dish, add lemon juice and parsley to butter, cook for a second and pour over.

TROUT, FRIED.

trout	egg and bread-crumbs
lemon	parsley

Wash and cleanse the trout and dry them in a clean cloth; dip them in seasoned flour, then coat them with egg and bread-crumbs, fry a golden brown in hot fat, drain thoroughly and dish them on a hot dish on a serviette; garnish with cut lemon and fried parsley. Send cut lemon to table with them.

TROUT, GRILLED.

trout	butter	salt

Well clean the fish, sprinkle a little salt inside, wrap it in well-buttered paper and grill over a quick clear fire, turning it occasionally and taking care that it does not burn. The time will depend on the size of the fish. Serve very hot.

TRUNKS. Attach "domes of silence," so that the trunks slide into luggage vans.

TULIPS. Tulips thrive in any good soil, though succeeding best in that which is sandy and well drained. Plant bulbs in October or November, about 6 inches apart and 4 or 5 inches deep. Either lift as soon as the stems begin to fade and store for the summer, or as they multiply freely leave them in the ground (unless the soil is cold and wet) for two or three years, after which they should be lifted. The tulip has recently been developed considerably both in variety, colour and period of flowering. Results in pot culture are not so fine as in plots.

TUMBLERS, to prevent from cracking. If new glass tumblers are placed in cold water and gradually brought to the boil it will prevent them from cracking when used.

TUMOURS. A tumour is a swelling, caused by a formation under the skin which tends to grow.

Tumours often arise, especially in the breast, from blows or squeezes. If a growth is observed in the breast it should never be neglected. Treatment of a cancerous tumour is often left too late: a doctor should be consulted at onset. Even a non-cancerous tumour is best removed. The operation is not complicated.

TURBOT, BOILED (for 8 people).

4 lb. turbot	parsley
vinegar or lemon juice	lobster coral
1 lemon	

Well wash the fish but do not remove the fins, these are considered a great delicacy; place in a fish-kettle of warm water with salt and vinegar added, bring to the boil and simmer very gently until cooked, allowing 6 to 8 minutes to the pound and 6 to 8 minutes over, according to size and thickness. Drain the fish, dish on a folded napkin on a hot dish and garnish with lobster coral and lemon and parsley; serve with lobster or shrimp sauce.

TURKEY, to choose. A greenish colour about the vent indicates staleness, as does a high smell. The legs of a young bird ate smooth and black, those of an old one are rough and red. Newly-killed birds have full, bright eyes and supple, moist feet.

TURKEY, ROAST.

1 turkey	sausages
forcemeat	bread sauce
gravy	bacon or ham

Draw, singe and wipe the inside with a clean wet cloth, cut off the feet and draw the sinews from the thighs, put the liver and gizzard in the wings, stuff the breast where the crop was with forcemeat, either veal stuffing with sausage meat added or chestnut stuffing, truss for roasting, place in a baking-tin with some dripping and put in hot oven. After the first 15 minutes cook very gently, basting frequently. When nearly cooked dredge with flour, put it back in the oven and baste well till brown and frothy. Remove the skewers and string, put it on a hot dish; make the gravy as for a joint of roast meat, using the stock the giblets (neck, heart, liver, gizzard and feet) have been boiled in; strain some round the turkey and garnish with the sausages previously fried. Serve with bread sauce and boiled ham or bacon and the rest of the gravy in a tureen.

TURKISH DELIGHT.

¾ teaspoonful tartaric acid	1 oz. leaf gelatine
2 breakfastcupfuls castor sugar	½ teacupful cold water
¾ cupful boiling water	1 teaspoonful essence of vanilla
juice of 1 lemon	a little carmine or colour

Soak the gelatine in cold water for 2 hours. Dissolve the sugar in the boiling water. Boil for 7 minutes with the tartaric acid, then add lemon and pour over gelatine. Stir well and add the vanilla. Pour into a shallow tin and, when set, cut into blocks and dip in icing sugar.

TURNIP TOPS. Wash well, remove damaged leaves and any very hard stalks. Old leaves should not be used. Place in boiling water to which has been added the usual amount of salt and boil quickly for 20 to 25 minutes. Drain, squeeze out all water possible and then chop finely. Add salt, pepper, and a piece of butter about the size of a walnut, if from 1 to 2 lb. of turnip tops have been used. If more than this quantity of the vegetable is cooked, then the amount of butter to be added must be increased accordingly. Return all to the pan and stir continuously until it is heated through again. Serve on hot dish.

TURNIPS. These can be grown for the turnips or for the turnip-tops. A good plan is to use the thinnings for the pot, though the tops off older plants bulk more. Turnips want well-manured ground and a moist situation as they should be grown quickly to be at their best. Sow in March immediately after good rains for first crops, make later sowings and in August for the winter supply. Sow in rows, $\frac{1}{2}$ inch deep and thin out to two to the foot. Do not let grow big, those about 2 inches across are best for the pot.

TURNIPS, MASHED.

turnips	cream
1 oz. butter	salt and pepper

Peel the turnip thickly, put into boiling water with salt, cook gently with lid on the pan and skim. When tender drain them well and mash them; add butter, cream, salt and pepper; serve in a hot vegetable dish. If very moist shake in a little flour and cook. This also improves colour.

TURNIPS or SWEDES, to prevent destruction by "fly" in dry weather. Sow in a well-prepared bed and use superphosphate to force the plant quickly into the rough leaf, when it is not so liable to be attacked.

TUSSORE, to iron. When ironing tussore or shantung have the articles bone dry. Use a very hot iron. It will only take a few minutes to iron them. When finished they will look like new.

ULCER.

Treatment.—If due to any constitutional disease, suitable remedies must be taken internally. For a simple ulcer, such as after injury on the bursting of a boil, the part should be kept at rest in a sling, or kept elevated. If yellow shreds are about the ulcer, hot antiseptic fomentations should be applied frequently till the part looks clean and a healthy red colour. The bowels should be attended to and salts or castor oil taken. As long as the ulcer is open it should be protected by suitable dressing and a bandage. If the ulcer looks an unhealthy bluish red, or small masses of proud flesh spring up, it is better to take advice.

ULCERS in the mouth. Ulcers in the mouth or canker may be extremely painful and difficult to cure, yet not really serious. Their causes are a state of general ill-health or some local cause of irritation such as smoking a foul pipe, drinking too much alcohol, the presence of a decayed or jagged tooth, an ill-fitting palate or where children are concerned, the cutting of teeth.

All highly spiced food should be avoided, borax and honey applied to the ulcer, and a mouth-wash containing tincture of myrrh used.

UMBRELLAS, to renovate. Take ½ a cupful of strong tea and 2 tablespoonfuls of sugar. Open umbrella and sponge well. Tea revives the colour and sugar stiffens. Leave the umbrella open until it is dry.

UNINVITED GUEST. An unexpected visitor would not be taken to a dinner or luncheon, a whist drive or bridge party or to any other affair where it is obvious that certain arrangements have to be made beforehand for a given number of guests; or to a house where there is illness or trouble, or where the facilities for offering hospitality are limited, or at such times as when an extra guest might just mean the overcrowding of a boat, a car, or a box at the theatre.

It goes without saying that it is a breach of good breeding for a lady to take with her an uninvited guest when accepting an invitation at another friend's expense; for instance, when being entertained to a restaurant lunch or dinner, a theatre or a concert, yet instances do occur when an uninvited guest will coolly turn up with some friend or relation whose expenses will have to be paid by the dispenser of the hospitality. An offer to pay for the interloper would not right the error of taste.

UPHOLSTERED FURNITURE, to beat. To prevent the dust flying over the room place a damp cloth over the articles and beat with a light cane. The dust all gathers on one side of the cloth, which can be washed and used over and over again.

VACCINATION OF INFANTS. *See* INFANTS.

VARICOSE VEINS. A vein is said to be varicose when it is enlarged and becomes twisted: it has corrugations like a rope, a healthy vein is straight.

Causes.—Long hours of standing; stricture of the flow of the blood.

Treatment.—Remove or lessen the cause. A perforated elastic bandage—allowing air to penetrate—is preferable to an elastic stocking, but one or the other should be worn.

In the event of a varicose vein bursting, the person should lie flat on the back, hold the leg up and put the thumb on and just below the bleeding point until assistance arrives. A pad of clean linen or lint and a bandage applied tightly will stop the hæmorrhage.

VARNISH, COMMON. Digest 1 part of shellac in 7 or 8 parts of alcohol.

VARNISH, FOR ENGRAVINGS, MAPS, ETC. Digest 20 parts gum sandarac, 8 parts gum mastic and 1 part camphor with 48 parts alcohol. Give the map or engraving one or two coats of gelatine before varnishing.

VARNISH, FOR FURNITURE. Take 1½ lb. shellac and 1 gallon naphtha and dissolve.

VARNISH, FOR OIL PAINTING. Mix 2 parts dextrine, 1 part alcohol and 6 parts water.

VARNISH, OAK. Two quarts boiled oil, 1½ lb. litharge, ¾ lb. gum shellac. Boil together and stir till dissolved. Then remove from fire and add 2 quarts turps. Strain into a bottle when settled and cork for use. Or:
Dissolve 3½ lb. clear pale resin and 1 gallon oil of turpentine. It may be made darker by adding a little fine lamp-black.

VARNISHING, to prepare new wood for. Give the wood a coating of either isinglass or gum-tragacanth dissolved in water to fill up all the pores. A coating of very thin glue will also serve the purpose.

VARNISHING. Before revarnishing, wash off all the old varnish with a strong solution of soda and warm water.

VEAL, to choose. Veal should always be chosen from a small animal; if large it is coarse and tough. The flesh should be find in grain and dry; it is not fit for food if moist and clammy. The lean should be pale pink and firm in the fibre; the fat firm and white. When buying veal two useful tests as to the condition are the state of the liver and the fat round the kidneys. The former must be clear and free from spots, and the latter firm, sweet and dry.

VEAL, BLANQUETTE DE (for 4 or 5 people).

1 lb. veal	2 oz. butter
2 onions	2 oz. flour
2 cloves	2 yolks of eggs
6 peppercorns	¼ pint cream
herbs	white stock or water
juice of 1 lemon	salt and pepper
cooked ham for garnish	

Put the veal into a stewpan with the onions, cloves, peppercorns and herbs, cover with stock or water, bring to the boil, skim and simmer gently till tender. Strain the liquor, put the meat on a hot dish, cook the butter and flour together, add the liquor gradually, stir till it boils, mix the yolks and cream together and add to the sauce, but do not boil. Season and add the lemon juice, pour over the veal and garnish with chopped ham.

VEAL BROTH.

1 lb. veal (meat and bone)	1 shallot
1½ pints water	½ oz. rice
few peppercorns	little milk
small blade of mace	salt and pepper

Put the meat cut up and bones into a white-lined saucepan with the peppercorns, mace and shallot, and simmer very gently till all the strength is extracted from the meat and bones. Strain, return to the pan with the rice and a little milk, cook till the rice is tender, season and serve.

Note.—A calf's foot makes very good broth.   Less veal will be required if one is used.

VEAL CUTLETS (5 or 6).

1 lb. fillet of veal	salt and pepper
1 oz. butter	potatoes
1 yolk of egg	3 or 4 rashers of bacon
1 dessertspoonful chopped parsley	vegetables for a garnish
	good brown or tomato sauce
1 teaspoonful grated lemon	egg and bread-crumbs

Cut the meat into neat fillets, dip them into a mixture made with the butter (melted), yolk of egg, lemon peel and parsley, seasoned; drop them into the bread-crumbs, then coat again with egg and crumbs, fry them in a sauté pan a nice brown colour, turning them occasionally. Mash some potatoes, make a mound in the centre of the dish, leaving a space in the centre, and place the fillets round on the potatoes with a roll of bacon on each fillet.   A suitable vegetable, such as peas of beans, should be cooked and piled in the centre, and a good brown or tomato sauce strained round.

VEAL, FILLETS OF, roast.

fillet of veal	½ lb. rashers
veal stuffing	1 pint béchamel sauce

Remove the bone from the fillet and stuff with veal stuffing—the quantity depends on the size of the joint—sew or skewer a piece of fat or skin on each side to prevent the stuffing from coming out, tie round firmly, bake in the oven till thoroughly cooked, basting frequently; cut the rashers, roll them and place on a skewer and put them in the oven with the veal for the last 10 minutes; dish up the veal, remove string, strain off the fat; pour the pint of béchamel sauce in the dripping pan, place it over the fire and stir till hot and a nice pale fawn colour. Pour it round the meat and garnish the dish with rolls of bacon.

VEAL, OLIVES AND TOMATO SAUCE (for 6 or 7 people).

1½ lb. lean veal	1 turnip
2 oz. ham	1 onion
3 or 4 mushrooms	1 oz. butter
1 oz. bread-crumbs	1 glass sherry
1 egg	½ pint tomato sauce
1 carrot	salt and pepper

Cut the veal into thin slices, make a forcemeat with crumbs, chopped ham, mushrooms, seasoning; bind with egg, lay a little on each slice of veal, roll up and secure with thread; prepare the vegetables, melt the butter in a stewpan, brown them lightly.   Also allow the olives to brown, add the tomato sauce and sherry, and cook very gently till the olives are tender; dish on a hot dish, removing the thread, season and strain the sauce over.

VEAL, STUFFED SHOULDER OF (for 7 or 8 people).

small shoulder of veal	bunch of herbs
2 carrots	veal stuffing (*see* Forcemeat)
2 onions	salt and pepper
1 oz. flour	

Take out the bone from the veal and fill with veal stuffing, roll up and tie with tape, place in a stewpan with the carrots, onions, herbs and enough water to cover and stew gently for 3 hours, remove the meat, thicken the gravy with the flour, season well, strain over the veal, garnish with the vegetables chopped neatly; this joint can be stuffed and roasted, served with good brown gravy and rashers.

VEGETABLE GARDEN. *See* under names of the various vegetables, directions for growing, and other headings for general cultural rules, fertilizing, pests, rotation and so on.

VEGETABLE MARROW. Sow seeds 3 inches apart on a gentle hot-bed early in May; when strong enough to handle, pot off singly, carefully harden off and finally plant out in June or end of May if forward enough and the weather mild. The seed may also be sown in the "open" late in May, and protected with hand-lights (*see* CLOCHES) until frost is past. The plants succeed best in very rich, heavily-manured soil and should be plentifully supplied with water during hot weather. An occasional application of liquid manure will also be beneficial. Allow lots of room for the long, trailing stems, see the young marrows do not rest in damp grass; a hurdle and some pea sticks for the shoots to rest upon is excellent.

VEGETABLE MARROW, BOILED.

1 marrow	½ pint whote sauce
salt	toast

Peel the marrow, cut in half and remove the seeds, then cut in neat pieces and place in a saucepan of boiling water with a little salt. Cook gently till tender—from 15 to 35 minutes—drain very well, place on a slice of toast in a hot vegetable dish and pour over the white sauce.

VEGETABLE MARROW, STUFFED.

1 marrow	herbs
minced meat	1 small onion
bread-crumbs	little brown sauce
chopped parsley	salt and pepper

Peel the marrow, cut in half lengthways, scoop out the seeds. Boil it in salted water till half cooked, drain it; make a stuffing with the minced meat, bread-crumbs, finely-chopped onion, parsley and herbs; moisten with a little brown sauce, season well, place it in the marrow, bind it together, place it on a greased baking tin, cover with greased paper and bake for half an hour. Sprinkle with brown bread-crumbs and serve with brown or tomato sauce.

VEGETABLE PIE (for 5 or 6 people).

short or flaky crust	2 carrots
2 oz. butter	2 turnips
2 onions	parsley
1 head celery	salt and pepper
boiled haricot beans	

Melt the butter in a stewpan, add the vegetables, cut in small pieces and cook till tender, season and add the chopped parsley. When cool put in a pie-dish, cover with a nice light pastry and bake in a quick oven, serve hot with a rich brown sauce.

313

VEGETABLE SAUSAGES.

2 medium-sized carrots	pinch salt and pepper
1 fairly large parsnip	2 eggs
3 medium-sized onions	8 oz. bread-crumbs
little chopped parsley	½ pint lentils or yellow peas

Soak and cook lentils or peas, then pound well in mortar. Chop the carrots, parsnip and onions very finely and mix with peas, add sprinkling of chopped parsley, salt, pepper, eggs and bread-crumbs. Make into sausage shapes, coat with egg and bread-crumbs and fry in boiling oil.

VEGETABLES, to boil. *See* GREENS.

VEGETABLES, BOILING. All vegetables grown above ground should be boiled with the lid off the saucepan, while those grown under should have the lid kept on. When cooking vegetables do not put too much water in the pot. A cupful of water, if the saucepan is covered, is all that is necessary for a saucepan full of vegetables.

VEGETABLES, SOWING AND MATURING. The quantity of seed required for two rows of 25 feet each, and the number of weeks after sowing when the results may be cropped are as follows:

Beans, Broad	1 pint	18
„ Dwarf	¼ pint	—
„ Runner	1 pint	16
Beet, Globe	1 oz.	—
Broccoli	1 packet	26 to 30
Brussels Sprouts	1 „	32
Cabbage, autumn	1 „	20 to 24
„ spring	1 „	34
Carrots	½ oz.	12
„ Main crop	½ oz.	24
Cauliflower	1 packet	24
Celery	1 „	36
Leeks	½ oz.	32
Lettuce. Sow a pinch.	¾ oz.	12
Onions, autumn and spring	½ oz.	24
Parsnips	½ oz.	30
Parsley	½ oz.	18
Peas	1 pint	16
Potatoes, Main crop	40 tubers	24
Radish	1 oz.	8
Savoys	$\frac{1}{16}$ th oz.	—
Spinach	1 oz.	9
„ Beet	½ oz.	8
Tomato (under glass)	1 packet	22
Turnips	¼ oz.	—
Vegetable Marrow	1 packet	14

VEGETABLES, STORAGE OF. Cabbages and so on are usually eaten as soon as cut, but the root crops can be stored for use during the winter in one or other of the following ways:

SHALLOTS AND ONIONS should be lifted before the frosts begin and stored in an airy damp-proof building; tie the tops together and let them hang in bunches.

CARROTS, TURNIPS AND BEETS should be lifted in October. The tops should be trimmed and the roots packed in boxes between layers of sand or soil. If stored out-of-doors stack in heaps with sand between and cover with straw or other material. When taking for use start at one end of the pile and continue thus, not taking out haphazard.

POTATOES after digging should be left 6 hours in the air to dry and then stored immediately in boxes in a frost-proof dark shed.

MARROWS should be harvested when really ripe and dry and hung in nets.

PARSNIPS, LEEKS AND SWEDES are best used from the ground as required. In early March parsnips should be lifted and stored, and leeks lifted and heeled in. This prevents spoilage.

VEGETARIAN COOKERY. See recipes for the following: Cheese balls, cheese cakes, cheese pudding, cheese pyramids, cheese soufflé, cheese straws; egg balls, eggs baked with tomatoes, eggs curried, eggs poached, eggs scalloped, eggs scrambled, eggs (Swiss); fritters (ground rice), fritters (potato), fritters (savoury); lentil cutlets; macaroni cheese, macaroni cutlets, macaroni savoury; nut cutlets, nut salad; omelettes (cauliflower), omelettes (cheese), omelettes (savoury); protose cutlets; rice (cheese); savoury pie; soup (chestnut), soup (lentil), soup (pearl barley), soup (potato), soup (vegetable), various vegetables; vegetable sausages.

Note.—All butter used in the above-mentioned recipes must be nut butter, and all oil vegetable oil.

VEGETARIAN CUTLETS.

1½ cupfuls finely chopped walnuts	1 cupful cooked marrow (chopped)
	1 egg
½ cupful fine bread-crumbs	2 tablespoonfuls butter
1 tablespoonful hot milk	1 cupful mashed potatoes
	1 teaspoonful salt

Mix all ingredients in a basin; stand half an hour. Shape into cutlets. Crumb then dip in slightly beaten egg diluted with ¼ cupful of milk. Crumb again and fry in hot fat till crisp and golden; serve with white sauce flavoured with onion.

VELLUM, to clean. Apply a little benzine on a sponge, or soft rag, to remove stains from vellum.

VELVET, to clean. Dip a cloth in powdered magnesia and rub the velvet. This will revive it to a freshness equal to new.

VENISON, ROASTED.

haunch of venison	gravy
flour (about 3 lb.)	red currant jelly
water	

Cover the haunch with flour and water paste and bake in the oven, basting constantly. Half an hour before it is served remove the paste and brown the venison well, taking care it does not burn. Serve with a good gravy and red-currant jelly. The gravy is improved by the addition of a glass of port or claret.

VERBASCUM. The pink variety yields a plant of tall and elegant habit with a stout stem, 4 feet high, from which spring many lateral branches covered in June with flatly opened flowers. The colour is a delightful pink shade with maroon eye. Easily cultivated in any normal garden soil with sunny situation, and a true perennial. Grow from seed; existing clumps can be divided in spring. The older yellow-flowered variety is popularly known as Aaron's Rod (which see).

VERBENA. A half-hardy perennial, brilliant in colour, excellent in habit and of long continuance in bloom. It may be raised from seed sown in the open in March on a well-prepared bed, though probably the more certain method is to sow in boxes (in March) put into a frame, the seedlings potted as soon as large enough, and planted out towards the end of May. A well-manured, well-dug, sweet soil is essential for their welfare. There is no difficulty in obtaining seed which will come true to colour, such as white, purple, violet, rose, pink and scarlet.

VERONICA (SPEEDWELL). A very large family embracing three distinct groups—shrubby plants, annuals and vigorous perennials. Plant the shrubby variety in April or September; lift and divide every fourth year, replanting only the younger outer crowns. Trim each year to keep in shape. Propagation is by cuttings of matured wood struck in a frame in August. The annual species should be sown in the open in September and thinned out to distances of 5 inches. The perennials are propagated by division in March or October. Blues and whites are more general, but there is a yellow (aurea) variety.

VINEGAR, AROMATIC. Here is a delightful cooling lotion for an invalid. Put a large handful each of rosemary, mint, and wormwood or lavender into a stone jar and cover with 1 gallon vinegar. Place near a fire for four days, then strain, add 1 oz. powdered camphor and bottle.

VINEGAR, CHILI. Infuse in 1 quart vinegar, 1 oz. cayenne pepper and 6 cloves.

VINEGAR, SPICED.

2 tablespoonfuls black peppercorns	1 dessertspoonful salt
1 tablespoonful allspice	3 bay leaves

Boil ingredients in vinegar for 10 to 15 minutes.

VINEGAR, TREACLE. Mix 6 tablespoonfuls of the best treacle with half that quantity of white wine vinegar. Keep well corked if not for immediate use. Take 1 tablespoonful in a tumbler of cold water night and morning as a cure for sickness, etc..

VINES. Grapes flourish best under glass, though they will grow in a warm situation. Spur-pruning should be employed late in September. Take a leading shoot at one, two or three years' growth and carry it the entire length of the wall. Leave spurs or lateral shoots to grow at regular distances along the leading shoot. Afterwards the pruning merely consists of cutting each spur back to the last eye at the base of the shoot.

VIOLA. *See* PANSY.

VIOLETS. Plant in frames in soil made up of calcareous (chalky) earth, leaf-mould and loam to obtain a steady succession of crops. The plants may be increased by runners or root-division. They do not take well to border planting.

VIRGO (THE VIRGIN). Sixth sign of the Zodiac, influencing persons born between 22nd August and 21st September. Such persons are suited for country life; they are quiet and reserved, with strong mentalities, persevering and industrious: science attracts and they set high value on money and possessions. Intolerance is a trait to be guarded against.

VITAMINS. A considerable percentage of the food-value of items of daily consumption lies in the vitamins, by which a balanced diet can be adopted, thus giving the maximum of sustenance in meals. The vitamins have alphabetic labels: A, B, C, D. Vitamin A promotes growth, as also does Vitamin D, to get both of which the diet must include butter, eggs, meat fat and, to remedy deficiency, cod-liver oil and malt. Vitamin B nourishes the nerves and is in liver, wholemeal of wheat, barley, oats, vegetables, eggs and milk. Vitamin C is good for general health, particularly in conditioning the blood, skin and pores, and can be taken in fruits, including lemons and oranges, fruit juices, watercress and green vegetables.

VOILE DRESSES. When washing these add to the rinsing water a teaspoonful of gum arabic previously dissolved in hot water. The dresses will look like new.

VOMITING. An effective means of stopping vomiting is to drink water as hot as can be taken, or cold water if the cause is billious nausea.

WAFERS, WALNUT.

3 oz. flour	2 oz. walnuts
2 oz. butter	2 eggs
2 oz. sugar	vanilla essence

Cream the butter and sugar well together, add the eggs and sifted flour alternately, beating well; chop the walnuts finely, and add with a little vanilla essence; drop in small spoonfuls on a greased baking sheet, not too near together and bake in a quick oven from 7 to 10 minutes.

WALL, DAMP, a paint for. Mix together 5 parts turpentine, $7\frac{1}{2}$ parts chalk, 5 parts boiled linseed oil and 5 parts resin, and use as a paint.

When walls are damp give them a coat of waterglass, which is very cheap, in order to prevent the damp coming through when new paper is put on. Apply before repapering.

To prevent pictures and mirrors hung on damp walls from being damaged, glue two discs of cork to the bottom inside corners of the frame.

WALLPAPER. The regulation "piece" or roll of wallpaper is 21 inches wide and 36 feet in length. In wallpapering, one piece in ten is allowed for waste in matching patterns, etc. The following table gives number of pieces required for rooms of varying measurements:

Feet round Room	Height of Room								
	7 to 7½ feet	7½ to 8 feet	8 to 8½ feet	8½ to 9 feet	9 to 9½ feet	9½ to 10 feet	10 to 10½ feet	10½ to 11 feet	11 to 11½ feet
28	4	4	4	4	5	5	5	5	5
29	4	4	4	5	5	5	5	6	6
30	4	4	5	5	5	5	5	6	6
31	4	4	5	5	5	5	6	6	6
32	4	4	5	5	5	6	6	6	6
33	4	5	5	5	5	6	6	6	6
34	4	5	5	5	6	6	6	6	7
35	5	5	5	5	6	6	6	7	7
36	5	5	5	5	6	6	6	7	7
37	5	5	5	6	6	6	7	7	7
38	5	5	6	6	6	7	7	7	7
39	5	5	6	6	6	7	7	7	7
40	5	5	6	6	6	7	7	7	8
41	5	6	6	6	7	7	7	8	8
42	5	6	6	6	7	7	7	8	8
43	6	6	6	7	7	7	8	8	8
44	6	6	6	7	7	7	8	8	8
45	6	6	7	7	7	8	8	8	9
46	6	6	7	7	7	8	8	8	9
47	6	6	7	7	7	8	8	9	9
48	6	6	7	7	8	8	8	9	9
49	6	7	7	7	8	8	9	9	9
50	6	7	7	8	8	8	9	9	9
51	7	7	7	8	8	8	9	9	10
52	7	7	7	8	8	9	9	9	10
53	7	7	8	8	8	9	9	10	10
54	7	7	8	8	9	9	9	10	10
55	7	7	8	8	9	9	10	10	10
56	7	8	8	8	9	9	10	10	10
57	7	8	8	9	9	9	10	10	11
58	7	8	8	9	9	10	10	11	11
59	8	8	8	9	9	10	10	11	11
60	8	8	8	9	9	10	10	11	11

WALLFLOWER. The seed is often sown too late. May, or even April, if the weather be favourable, is none too early, and enables the plants to attain a sturdy growth before being transplanted to their places (in limed soil) in autumn in readiness for blooming in the early spring. Keep the transplanted plants well watered till established. It seeds prolifically, hence select pods not only from the best bloom, but also from the plant of the best form and habit. The wallflower is not merely a border plant but flowers to perfection in the crevices of old walls—dwarfed, it may be, yet compact and full of blossom.

WALLPAPER, to clean. Clean with a large piece of dough slightly damped with ammonia. Stale bread may also be used for the same purpose.

WALLPAPER, to remove. Wet the paper thoroughly with a long-handled brush dipped in a bucket of warm water. Let it remain till the water has penetrated and the paper blisters and loosens, so that you can peel it off with your hands. Do not wet too much at a time. If any small bits are found still adhering, wet them afresh, and scrape off with a strong knife.

WALLPAPER, to remove stains. Cover the stain with a paste made of pipe-clay and water; allow this to remain about 24 hours. Then remove with a stiff brush.

WALLPAPER, VARNISHED, to clean. Add some cold strained tea to warm water and wash well. Dry thoroughly and polish with equal parts of sweet oil and turpentine.

WALNUT CAKE. *See* CAKE, WALNUT.

WALNUT FURNITURE, CHIPPED. If a chip is knocked off the leg of a walnut table, rub some iodine on the injured part and go over it with furniture polish and the place will hardly show.

WALNUTS, PICKLED. *See* PICKLES, WALNUTS.

WARDROBE. A portable wardrobe which can be folded into a very small space and carried in a suitcase can now be bought very cheaply. It is also useful in bedrooms which are too small to take an ordinary wardrobe. Made of cretonne it can be hung on any door or wall and is large enough to hang eight dresses.

WARTS. *See* CORNS.

WARTS. Mix together ½ oz. acetic acid and ½ oz. tincture steel and apply by rubbing well on the warts by means of an orange stick twice per day. The wart will shrink and fall off within a few days.

WASHERS ON TAPS. A new washer is required on a tap when it continues to drip no matter how tightly the tap is turned. Leather, rubber or composition washers may be used for cold-water taps, but for hot water the washer must be of red rubber or of composition. It is very desirable that the water should be turned off at the main or at the stop-cock in the house before the job is started. Unscrew the top by means of a wrench put round the neck of the tap. This enables the spindle to be taken out, also the washer with its attachment. The job is greatly simplified if the new washer and attachment is bought ready for use—it can be purchased at any ironmonger's. If this is not done, then the washer must be cut using the old one as a pattern. The washer is next put in and care must be taken to see that the brighter side is placed downwards. The head of the tap is replaced and screwed into position, using the wrench as before, and the water turned on again.

WASHING. After washing a knitted jumper put it on a coat-hanger and hang it on a line in the air to dry. It will keep its shape much better than if placed on the line.

The easiest way to sprinkle clothes is to use a clean whisk brush that should be kept for the purpose.

Starch made with soapy water prevents the irons from sticking and gives a better gloss to linen.

WASHING COLOURED FROCKS. Before washing a coloured frock soak it for a little while in a bowl of salt water. This will prevent loss of colour and "running" of the dye. When colours have faded, add a little vinegar to the last rinsing water. This is a wonderful reviver.

WASHING COLOURS. To prevent the colours in patterned materials from "running" and to freshen them up, add a few drops of ordinary blue-black ink or vinegar to both washing and rinsing waters.

WASHING, HINTS ON. Streaked clothes occur when they are blued in hard water and this can be avoided by the use of milk. Put a cupful of unskimmed milk in the water.

Another method is to use a lump of salt or washing-soda dissolved in water and added to the blueing water.

Add a handful of salt to the last water on wash-day and the clothes will not stick to the line in frosty weather. If clothes pins are boiled in a salt-water solution before using they will last longer, and will not freeze on the clothes when it is cold.

When washing coloured fabrics a little salt in the water will prevent the colours from running.

Do not allow silk or wool to get too dirty before laundering. They will last much longer if you do not.

Soap should not be rubbed into woollen garments. They should be dipped up and down in a lukewarm solution of soapsuds.

To wash chiffon, hang it in your bathroom and fill the room with steam. After a few minutes of this the chiffon can be taken into the open air and will return at once to a bright and fresh condition.

To wash embroidered fabrics put them in some cold water with a little blue and a little lemon juice. Let it boil for half an hour, rinse in cold water and dry in the air. The embroidery will come out white as snow.

For the clothes pegs, make a bag on a clothes hanger; this you can slip along the line with the pegs in as you hang out the clothes.

In the case of a rusty flat iron, when the iron is warm, not hot, rub it on a cloth dipped in paraffin and then on some sand or salt.

Old felt hats should be cut in squares and used for iron-holders.

WASPS, protecting fruit from. Place a small quantity of syrup of some kind, or a mixture of sugar and beer, into a high shouldered glass jar. Tie string around the neck of the jar, leaving two ends of about 6 inches long on each side. Suspend the jar, either from nails in the wall, or from the fruit trees, by these pieces of string. It will be found that this will form a tempting bait for wasps, and once in the jar, if it has the usual slanted shoulders, it is very difficult for a wasp to get out. The number of these traps required will, of course, depend upon the number of trees to be protected. Replenish syrup from time to time and kill any wasps which have been caught, but are not dead, by pouring in hot water.

WASP STING. *See* STINGS AND BITES, INSECT.

WATCHES, to clean. When a watch stops, the cause is generally dust. Cut a piece of blotting-paper slightly smaller than the inside of the watch, damp the blotting-paper in petrol, insert inside the watch next the works and close the case. Leave overnight and it will generally be found that the cause of the stoppage has been removed.

WATER, to purify. Add 1 oz. powdered alum to a hogshead of putrid water. This will purify it in the course of a few hours and make it fit for use.

WATER, to soften. If a teaspoonful of borax is added to a large jugful of water the latter will become quite soft. This will not hurt the most sensitive skin, and the solution is also useful in removing scurf grom the scalp. Or:
Glycerine should be used for softening water in which flannel articles are to be washed. Use 2 teaspoonfuls in a small tumbler of water.

WATER, to test for hardness. Dissolve ½ oz. good white soap in 1 pint rain water. Allow this to cool and settle and mix 1 oz. of this with 1 pint of water to be tested. Soft water will remain clear; hard water will become milky.

WATERING. When doing so, do it thoroughly and when the sun is not strong. Little and often causes the roots to come too near the surface and get baked by the sun, or bruised; a good soaking gets right down among the roots and they remain firmly in position. Plants differ in their needs, experience will tell; as a rule two good soakings a week will suffice in hot weather; once a week during mild spells. Always water seed-beds some hours before sowing. Give plenty of water to seedlings or transplanted plants at the time of putting in.

WATER PIPES, FROZEN. *See* FROZEN PIPES.

WATER SUPPLY. If anything goes wrong with the water supply, turn off the outside cock of main supply before making investigations. Then have a look at the cistern. Sometimes the ball sticks and in consequence the cistern runs dry. Put a little vaseline in the sliding hinge, work the arm up and down two or three times; then turn water on at the main, depress the cistern ball-cock and if water starts running it is all right. This failure of supply to cistern is also a cause of hot-water taps running dry; if so, as soon as the flow has filled the cistern beyond the hot-water supply pipe the water will start running again from hot-water taps. But in any case of failure of hot water the fire should be raked out to prevent danger from hot air exploding tank. If the cistern trouble is overflow of water, tie up the ball-cock as high as the lever will allow, if, after putting vaseline on sliding hinge and pushing the ball below the surface, the inflow does not stop. In overflow, turn off at main, turn on bath tap at full, so as to cause cistern to empty, but first tie up ball as indicated. Where these precautions do not succeed, send for plumber.

WATER TAPS. *See* WASHERS, *also* FROZEN PIPES.

WATERPROOF, to preserve. If your pram cover begins to wear and ceases to be properly waterproof you can prolong its life by lining it with a piece of rubber sheeting. Stick or sew this to the underside.

WAX PAINT. There is a cheap, easy way of covering ugly wallpaper. You can buy a wax paint which will give a flat, eggshell or semi-glossy surface, in several shades. If the exact shade you require is not on the list, colours can be blended to give the right shade. This paint is easy to apply to the walls and lasts a long time. Finger-marks can be washed off with hot water.

WEANING. A baby under ordinary circumstances, the mother being healthy and with plenty of milk, should be weaned at the eighth or ninth month. If the milk is deficient, or the mother is not strong, the baby should be weaned before this time. The milk after eight or nine months, though there may be plenty of it, becomes poor and watery. An over-nursed baby is, as a rule, flabby, fat, and may show a tendency toward rickets. A child should be weaned gradually, the bottle given once or twice a day at first; as the baby gets used to it, it may be given it more frequently, until at last breast-feeding is entirely done away with. A baby should not be weaned if it shows any signs of diarrhœa, but the mother must wait till the attack is better. Hot sultry weather is a bad time to change the mode of feeding and, if attempted, indigestion and purging may be the result.

WEDDING-DAY PREPARATIONS, ceremony and reception. It is not the custom for the bride to see her bridegroom until they meet in the church.

If her father is living and able to do so, be should give her away, otherwise her brother, uncle, or other male relation or an intimate family friend will take his place.

With him alone she drives to the church, being the last of the wedding party to leave the house.

All those invited to the church should endeavour to be quietly seated when the bride arrives, that is, with the exception of her own retinue, who await her in the porch.

In the Church.—Sufficient front seats on the right of the centre aisle are reserved for the relations and special friends of the bridegroom; on the left of the aisle for those of the bride. Other guests are shown into seats by the gentlemen ushers, who are usually young relations of both families.

When a large number of guests has been invited, it is well for the seating accommodation to be arranged beforehand, with due regard for respective claims.

The Ceremony.—On the arrival of the bride in the porch, her brides-maids—with pages or train-bearers if there are any—fall into their appointed order behind her and, taking her father's right arm, the bride passes up the aisle. (When the service is choral, she is preceded by the choir.)

Arrival at the chancel steps, she takes her place on the left of her waiting bridegroom, and her father then steps to the rear, on her left, but when the priest asks who gives her away, he steps forward again to make reply. The service proceeds as recited in the Prayer Book. At the conclusion, the bridegroom offers his left arm to the bride and they follow the clergy to the vestry, where they are joined by the parents of both parties, the best man and the chief bridesmaid—and sometimes by the other bridesmaids and any close relations and friends who have been asked to do so.

The register is signed, the bride writing her old name for the last time, and congratulations are given, but the groom is the first to kiss his bride.

The bride takes her husband's left arm and they return into the church, where the procession of attendants re-forms, and they pass down the aisle through the congregation, out to the porch, where they are followed by parents, best man, principal guests and, at length, by the remainder of the congregation.

The bridal couple drive off quickly so that they may be ready to receive the congratulations of the first of the guests arriving for the reception.

The Reception.—Bride and groom are quickly followed by the bride's parents, who remain near the doorway in the reception-room to greet their guests, who then pass on to the centre of the room to find the young couple and at once offer congratulations and good wishes; then the presents may be inspected and other friends greeted and chatted with until the time comes for the luncheon or whatever refreshments is provided.

If there is a luncheon, the bride and bridegroom go in first, next the bride's father with the bridegroom's mother, followed by the bridegroom's father with the mother of the bride, and the best man escorts the chief bridesmaid.

Except at really formal affairs where rank and precedence must be considered, one usually finds the remainder of the guests pair off as they will, it being left to good taste for precedence to be accorded where due, and the same rule will be observed in sitting down to table.

In the place of honour, or at the principal table, the bride sits on the left of the bridegroom, her father on her left, her mother on the right of the bridegroom. Where there are several tables, the bridal party, close relations and friends, will sit at the principal table.

Always the cake is placed before the bride.

Where refreshments take the place of a sit-down meal, it is usual to have them set out on a buffet from which guests are either served by attendants or help themselves, the gentlemen, especially the host and the best man ushers, looking after the ladies.

A number of toasts and speeches are not usual now, but all present will drink the health of the newly-married couple, this toast being proposed by some intimate family friend. The bridegroom replies for himself and his bride and may conclude by proposing the health of the bridesmaids, together with that of his best man.

It is then time to cut the cake. A large first slice should be cut by the bride, doubtless assisted by her groom, as it is not an easy task. This slice and others are cut up into convenient-sized pieces and handed round.

After she has cut the cake, the bride usually retires to prepare for her journey, acoompanied to her room by the chief bridesmaid, her mother, or whoever she may wish to be with her. The bridegroom also has to prepare for travelling.

When the bride reappears, the car should be waiting, then guests crowd round to shower good-byes, good wishes—and confetti!

It is not usual for guests to stay long after the departure of the happy pair. They take their leave with some kind little congratulatory word to the bride's parents.

WEDDINGS. *See* MARRIAGE, *also* WEDDING-DAY PREPARATIONS, etc.

WEDDINGS, GOLDEN. *See* GOLDEN WEDDINGS.

WEDDINGS, SILVER. *See* SILVER WEDDINGS.

WEIGHTS AND MEASURES.

MEASURES, HANDY, in cooking, etc.
A piece of fat the size of a small egg = 1 oz.
2 tablespoonfuls of flour = 1 oz.
1 breakfastcupful of "grains" = 4 oz.
1 tablespoonful of jam = 2 oz.
2 tablespoonfuls of cornflour = 1 oz.
1 tablespoonful of sugar = 1 oz.
3 penny pieces = 1 oz.
1 penny and 1 halfpenny = $\frac{1}{2}$ oz.
1 threepenny piece and 1 halfpenny = $\frac{1}{4}$ oz.
4 saltspoons = 1 teaspoon.
3 teaspoons = 1 tablespoon.
2 teaspoons = 1 dessertspoon.
2 dessertspoons = 1 tablespoon or $\frac{1}{2}$ oz.
6 tablespoons = 1 small teacup.
4 tablespoons = $\frac{1}{2}$ cup.
2 gills = 1 cup.
2 cups = 1 pint
4 cupfuls of flour = 1 lb.
2 cupfuls of sugar = 1 lb.
3 cupfuls of oatmeal = 1 lb.
1 cupful solid butter = 1 lb.
1 heaped tablespoonful of butter = 2 oz.
1 heaped tablespoonful of sugar = 1 oz.
1 tablespoonful of liquid = $\frac{1}{2}$ oz.

1 small teacup=1 gill or 4 oz.
1 breakfastcup=½ pint.
1 pint=4 gills or nearly 2 breakfastcups.
An ordinary tumbler measures ½ pint.
1 oz. dry substance=1 tablespoon.
1 oz. of butter=1 dessertspoon.
¼ lb. of flour=1 small teacup.
½ lb. flour=1 breakfastcup.

MEASURES, HANDY, for lengths.

A sixpenny piece measures ¾ inch.
A halfpenny measures 1 inch.
A half-crown measures 1¾ inches.

APOTHECARIES'.

20 grains   =1 scruple=20 grains.
3 scruples =1 drachm=60 grains.
8 drachms=1 ounce=480 grains.
12 ounces =1 pound=5760 grains.

APOTHECARIES' FLUID MEASURE.

60 minims =1 fluid drachm.
8 drachms=1 ounce.
20 ounces =1 pint.
8 pints   =1 gallon.

AVOIRDUPOIS WEIGHT.

27½ grains   =1 drachm (dr.).
16 drachms   =1 ounce (oz.).
16 ounces   =1 pound (lb.).
14 pounds   =1 stone.
28 pounds   =1 quarter (qr.).
4 quarters   =1 hundredweight (cwt.).
20 hundredweights=1 ton.

DRY MEASURE.

2 pints   =1 quart.
8 quarts =1 peck.
4 pecks   =1 bushel (bush.).
3 bushels =1 sack.
12 sacks   =1 chaldron.
8 bushels =1 quarter (qt.).
5 quarters=1 load (ld.).

LIQUID MEASURE.

4 gills   =1 pint (pt.).
2 pints   =1 quart (qt.).
4 quarts =1 gallon (gall.).
31½ gallons=1 barrel.
2 barrels =1 hogshead.

TABLE OF APPROXIMATE EQUIVALENTS.

60 drops *or* 1 teaspoonful   =1 dram ($\frac{1}{8}$ fluid oz.).

1 dessertspoonful	=2 drams ($\frac{1}{4}$ fluid oz.).
1 tablespoonful	=4 drams ($\frac{1}{2}$ fluid oz.).
1 wineglassful	=2 fluid oz.
1 teacupful	=4 fluid oz.
1 tumblerful	=8 fluid oz.

WELSH RAREBIT.

3 oz. cheese	2 tablespoonfuls milk
1 oz. butter	salt and pepper
$\frac{1}{2}$ teaspoonful mustard	buttered toast

Put the butter, milk, grated cheese, mustard, salt and pepper into a saucepan; stir over the fire until quite smooth. Pour over rounds of buttered toast and serve hot.

An egg added to the butter and melted cheese will take away all stringiness and improve the flavour. One egg is enough for 3 persons.

WET SHOES.
Boots and shoes which have dried hard after heavy rain should be well rubbed with oil and left to stand for several hours. This will soften them and also help to keep them waterproof. To avoid loss of shape stuff the boots while wet with plenty of newspaper and renew this from time to time as it absorbs the water from the shoes.

WHIPPED CREAM.
One teaspoonful of granulated gelatine, soaked in cold water for 5 minutes and then dissolved over hot water, can be added to 1 cupful of whipping cream before it is beaten. The cream is then sweetened and beaten as usual, then heaped on the sweet and put in the refrigerator to chill. This whipped cream will not separate and can be allowed to stand for hours.

Add the white of an egg to the cream before whipping. It will whip in half the time, be stiffer and go twice as far.

WHITEBAIT, FRIED (for 4 people).

1 pint whitebait	pepper and salt
flour	brown breat and butter
lemon	

Drain the fish, shake them lightly in flour so as to separate them, turn on to a sieve and gently shake away all loose flour. Plunge at once into very hot fat, shaking the basket gently all the time. Remove the fish, reheat the fat and plunge them in again to crisp them, drain them well and dish on a hot dish with a fancy paper. Season well and serve with quarters of lemon and thin brown bread and butter.

WHITE CRÊPE DE CHINE.
When washing this or any white silk, a little methylated spirit added to rinsing water will keep it a good colour.

WHITE PAINT, to clean.
Use a wet sponge and a little whitening.

WHITES, treatment of. Hot douches as many times a day as possible; a syringe may be used, or better still, a douche. A teaspoonful of boracic acid should be added to the water, especially if there is soreness of the parts. Or use Condy's fluid, only enough to make the water a rather dark pink in colour. The general health must be maintained.

WHITEWASH BRUSHES. *See* BRUSHES.

WHITEWASHING. When whitewashing or washing down walls with a whitewash brush, tie a piece of sponge round the handle and so prevent liquid running down on to the hands.

WHITE WOOLLEN SHAWL, to clean. Spread a sheet over a table; on this place shawl. Powder it all over with finely ground starch. Fold it up, powdering at each fold, press well together and leave for several hours wrapped in the sheet. Then squeeze and rub it together with both hands, finally shake out starch.

WHITING, BAKED. Cook fish in oven sufficient milk to cover, for about 20 to 25 minutes. Take out of milk. Melt a little butter, stir in a small quantity of flour and thicken the milk in which the fish has been cooked. Pour over fish and serve.

WHITLOW.
Causes.—Infection of the tips of the fingers around the nail. A splinter penetrating the part is generally the primary cause.

Symptoms.—The fingers become swollen and painful and the pain is worse if the arm is allowed to hang down, and at night-time. Matter forms which should be let out by the surgeon's knife, or allowed to burst on its own account.

Treatment.—Constant poulticing and the arm put in a short sling. The whitlow should be opened early and much pain and deformity will then be saved. Once it has been operated on, poultices should be discarded and hot fomentations applied. The arm should still be kept in a sling till the wound heals.

WHOOPING COUGH, symptoms and treatment of. Its onset is like a cold on the chest, but the cough increases and tends to come in paroxysms. Slight fever, running nose, inflamed eyes are symptoms. The "whoop" is heard after a week or 10 days.

Isolation and plenty of fresh air are necessary. The greatest care must be taken when the child is convalescent. Rub the chest with warm camphorated oil, and hang round the neck with some menthol crystals sewn in a muslin bag to ease the breathing. Do not apply poultices.

WICKER, to remove grease stains on. Grease stains may be removed from wicker chairs by rubbing with methylated spirit.

WICKER CHAIRS, to clean. If a wicker chair or table is scrubbed well with salt and water, as well as soap, it will look like new, as the salt not only cleans but stiffens the cane.

WILL, to make a. The simpler a will is phrased the better. There is no need to follow any particular form, but there is need to express clearly what is wished to be carried out. A will can be written *on* anything (an envelope, paper of any kind, linen, wood, etc.), and *with* anything (ink, pencil, typewriter, paint, blood, etc.). Any one can make a will on his (or her) own account, though where the items are varied and the value considerable, it is safer to have legal help. A will must be signed also by two witnesses at the same time: so long as these witness the signature a will is valid, even if by weakness or illiteracy the signature takes the form of a cross (in which case a clause explaining the reason and confirming that the witnesses know the circumstances is advisable to be inserted). It should be remembered that witnesses cannot receive any legacy under the will. A friend should be named as Executor (*See* EXECUTOR). It is necessary to be clear as to the meaning of special words: "worldly goods" does not include "real property"; the better wording would be "all my property whatsoever." "Real estate" means houses and lands. "Personal estate" signifies personal belongings such as furniture, clothing, shares, money at bank or in house. "Money" means actual money in house or bank, debts owing, including notes of hand. "My family" means children only, not wife. "Balance at Bank" means at death. "Balance now at Bank" means at time will is made. "Brother" includes half-brother, but not brother-in-law or step-brother.

The following is a simple and safe form of will, in which it is to be noted that no punctuation marks are used.

This is the last will and testament of me James Jones of 7 York Road Cardiff miner. I give and devise all my estate and effects real and personal of which I may die possessed or be entitled to unto .... absolutely and I appoint .... executors of this my will and I hereby revoke all former wills and codicils. Dated this tenth day of March One thousand nine hundred and fifty-seven.

James Jones.

Signed by the said James Jones in the presence of us who thereupon signed our names hereto in his and each other's presence {

Hugh Owen of 11 High Street Cardiff miner Jane Griffith of 2 High Street Builth teacher

WINDFLOWER. *See* ANEMONE.

WIND IN THE STOMACH. In the case of very young children a piece of ginger or a few carraway seeds should be boiled with the food. Older children should be given a few drops of strong peppermint water on a piece of sugar. For adults ¼ teaspoonful of ordinary bicarbonate of soda in hot water alone or with peppermint water gives relief.

WINDOW-BOXES. To whitewash these inside prevents rot and the presence of insects.

WINDOWS, to clean. Rub a damp paraffin rag quickly over the panes. Finish off the polishing with an old newspaper.

Fill a small cloth bag with crushed whitening. Sew it up and use it on your window which should be polished with a soft duster. Or: Add a few drops of paraffin and a touch of borax to hot water.

Another method is to wash them with a cloth soaked in vinegar and then polish them with a newspaper.

The best way to remove paint spots from windows is with an old razor blade.

Kitchen windows will not steam when cooking is in progress if wiped first with a velvet cloth moistened with glycerine.

WINDOWS, to frost. Lay a sheet of ordinary glass on a piece of thick, soft cloth, which should be spread over a flat surface. Some fine emery powder should be sprinkled over the glass and a little water added. Rub a piece of pumice stone over the glass until the desired effect is gained. Then wash the glass well.

WINDOWS, to make opaque. Dissolve 2 tablespoonfuls of Epsom salts in 1 pint of cold water or in warm beer and apply evenly.

WINDOWS, to prevent frosting. A thin coating of glycerine should be applied on each side of the glass to prevent the formation of moisture.

WINDOWS, to remove paint splashes from. Rub with strong hot vinegar to remove paint or putty.

WINDOW CURTAINS, to protect. Take one ½-inch board, 14 inches wide and as long as required to fit between side casings and window. Put a screw-eye at each end of upper corner of board. On each side of window casing put another screw eye in which tie cords 2 feet long and on ends of cords small hooks. The hooks on the cord fit into screw eyes on the sides of the board and the board is tilted back from the window; the window can then be opened as wide as the board is high; air enters but rain is kept out.

WINDOW LEATHERS. These can be prevented from becoming hard and stiff by placing them in an ordinary glass jam jar after use. They will retain their soft and damp condition and will not need to be soaked before being used again.

WINDOW SASHES. If the cords of window sashes are occasionally rubbed up and down with soap they will last as long again, and you will have no trouble in raising and lowering your windows.

WINE, to cool. The bottle should be covered with a wet cloth and stood in a draught or cold place until required for use.

WINE, BLACKBERRY. Take ripe fruit, measure and bruise. Add 1 quart boiling water to each gallon. Allow to stand for 24 hours, stirring occasionally. Strain off the liquid into a cask, adding 2 lb. sugar to each gallon. Cork tightly and keep till October before using.

WINE, BLACK CHERRY. Take 12 lb. small black cherries and 2 lb. sugar to each gallon of juice. Bruise the cherries, leaving stones whole. Stir well and allow to stand for 24 hours. Strain through a sieve and add the sugar. Mix again and stand for another day. Pour off clear liquid into a cask, and bung tightly when fermentation has finished. Bottle after six months.

WINE, COWSLIP. Boil 3 lb. white sugar in 1 gallon of water for half an hour, removing the scum as it rises. Pour into a pan to cool, adding the rind of 1 lemon. When cold add 2 quarts of cowslip flower with the juice of the lemon. Stir every 2 hours for 2 days. Strain and pour into a barrel and leave standing for 1 month. Bottle off, placing a piece of loaf sugar in each bottle.

WINE, CURRANT. Add 5 lb. sugar to 10 quarts juice and strain through a cloth into a stone jar. A further 3 lb. sugar should be added after 4 or 5 days and the liquid skimmed daily. When fermentation has ceased pour off into a clean barrel and allow to remain for about 8 months. After bottling, the wine should be kept in a dark, cool place and laid down to prevent bursting.

WINE, DAMSON. Use 2 quarts boiling water to every 4 lb. bruised fruit and 1½ lb. sugar to every gallon of juice. After bruising the fruit pour on the boiling water and allow to stand for 2 days. Strain into a cask, add the sugar and, when fermentation has stopped, fill up the cask and seal tightly. Bottle after 10 months. Though the wine may be used after a year it improves with age.

WINE, ELDERBERRY. Put the ripe elderberries into a pan adding ½ gallon of water to every gallon of fruit. Boil for 15 minutes; then strain through a hair sieve.

To every gallon of liquor add 3½ lb. moist sugar and the peel of 6 lemons. Place in a boiler and bring to boiling heat; then add the whites of 6 well-beaten eggs. Stir thoroughly, adding ½ lb. bruised ginger tied in a muslin bag; add spices to flavour. Allow the wine to stand for a week before bottling.

WINE, GINGER.

¾ lb. bruised ginger	12 oranges
18 lb. Demerara sugar	1 lb. raisins
12 lemons	2 oz. isinglass
6 gallons water	2 tablespoonfuls yeast

Boil the sugar in the water until no scum rises, peel oranges and lemons and add, with the ginger tied in a muslin bag; boil all together for 1 hour, remove into a tub and when lukewarm add 2 tablespoonfuls yeast on pieces of toast. Let it stand till next day, then put in cask with the juice of the oranges and lemons. Stir every day for 10 days, add isinglass to clear it and the raisins, then bung it down. It will be ready to use in 2 months.

WINE, MEAD. Heat 3 gallons of water and dissolve in it 3 quarts of honey and 1 lb. of loaf sugar. Boil for half an hour, removing all scum. Pour into a tub and add the juice of 4 lemons and the rinds of 2. Add 20 cloves, 2 roots of ginger, a top of sweet briar and a top of rosemary. When almost cool add 2 or 3 dessertspoonfuls of yeast spread on a piece of toast. Allow to stand 4 or 5 days before bottling.

WINE, MOCK PORT. Take 4 lb. beetroot, wash and cut up to pieces as quickly as possible. Put the pieces into cold water—1 quart to every 1 lb. (1 gallon)—boil until white, then strain off. To every quart of liquid add ½ lb. sugar and the juice of 1 lemon. Add cloves and ginger to taste. Stir well until sugar has dissolved, bottle when cold and cover for 10 to 14 days until fermentation ceases, then cork lightly.

WINE, MULLED. ½ pint wine and ½ pint water. Beat 4 eggs and add to the above while boiling, stirring rapidly. As soon as it begins to boil it is ready.

WINE, PARSNIP.

10 lb. parsnips
2 gallons water

little yeast
6 lb. preserving sugar
slice of toast

The parsnips should, for preference, be young. Wash, peel, thinly slice and weigh them. Put into pan with the water and cook thoroughly. Strain first of all through a colander, taking care to force out all the water, and then strain once more, this time through a fine sieve. Return the liquid to the pan with the sugar and boil for 45 minutes. Pour into a tub and allow to get cool. Then add the slice of toast thinly covered with yeast. Cover the tub with a cloth and leave for about 10 days, well stirring the liquid each day. At the end of this time strain the juice once more and pour into a cask. Leave, lightly corked, until fermentation has ceased, then close the cask securely and make it air-tight. Bottle at end of 6 or 9 months.

WINE, RAISIN. Choose large sound raisins, pick very clean and chop finely. Pour 1 gallon hot water on 10 lb. fruit and squeeze through a bag. Allow the liquor to stand for 12 hours, then add 1 lb. sugar and leave it to ferment. When fermentation has finished pour off into a cask, bung tightly and allow to stand for 2 months, after which it should be poured off into another cask which should be entirely filled. Seal this cask closely and bottle the wine after 10 months. It will be ready in a year.

WINE, RASPBERRY. Bruise ripe raspberries and strain them through a bag. Add 1½ lb. lump sugar to every gallon of juice, and boil. Then add the whites of eggs and boil again a quarter an hour, skimming constantly. Decant into a cask when the liquid is cold and settled and some yeast. When fermentation has finished add 1 pint white wine to each gallon and suspend a bag containing 1 oz. bruised mace in a cask. Keep in a cool place. The wine will be ready in 3 months.

WINE, STRAWBERRY. To 1 quart strawberry juice add 1 quart water and 1 lb. sugar. Stir well and allow to ferment in an open jar. When fermentation has entirely stopped, draw off in bottles and cork.

WINTER ACONITE. *See* ERANTHIS.

WIREWORM, to destroy. Dig in a thick sowing of quicklime and allow the ground to remain fallow for a winter. Traps may also be used in the shape of slice of potato, carrot or turnip buried about 1 inch in the earth. Stick a skewer with each piece to show its position and destroy the catch every morning.

WOOD, to prevent warping. Saturate wooden articles with copaiba balsam. If objects have already warped on one side they may be straightened by soaking the other side with the same liquid.

WOOD, EBONY STAIN. To give wood the appearance of ebony take 2 oz. borax and 4 oz. ebony; put this mixture on the fire and let them dissolve in 2 quarts of water until a perfect solution is obtained, then add 1 tablespoonful of glycerine. After mixing, add enough aniline black, soluble in water, and the preparation will be ready for use.

WOODEN POSTS, to preserve. Dry the posts thoroughly and place the ends in lime water. Remove and dry; then paint with diluted sulphuric acid. This will thoroughly harden them.

WOOD FERN. This will thrive under trees or in shady parts of the garden (even in a town garden) if given plenty of water. The more delicate sort should be grown in well-drained leafy loam.

WOOD LICE. This garden pest is very destructive where young and tender seedlings are concerned—especially in a frame. In cases where they have infested a frame, they can generally be destroyed by pouring boiling water along the sides of the frame. If this is not effective in ridding the frame of the pest, a sure way of getting rid of them is as follows. In common with earwigs, they love darkness and a dry, snug retreat, and a small-sized flower-pot, with a slice of fresh potato or apple as a bait and filled up with dry moss, will prove an alluring trap. Two or three of these pots should be placed in the frame or bed, and the next morning they will probably each contain a large number of the insects, which can then be destroyed by knocking the whole contents of the pot into a pail of hot water. The earlier in the morning the traps are cleared the better will be the catch, and, of course, the traps must be relaid from day to day until the pest has been completely removed.

WOODRUFF (ASPERULA). Is easily grown in ordinary garden soil from seeds sown thinly in March or April. A charming plant, but not so well known as it deserves to be; is useful as a diuretic and tonic.

WOODWORK, to wash. Bicarbonate of soda is useful for cleaning woodwork, but you must rinse the woodwork at once with clean water and not allow the bicarbonate to dry on it. Another method is to crush some eggshell to fine powder and shake it on the scrubbing brush.

WOOLLENS. *See* NEW WOOLLENS.

WOOLLY APHIS. *See* AMERICAN BLIGHT.

WORMS, to remove from furniture. The best way of getting rid of the little worm that works its way in wood is to dip a very small brush in paraffin and drop the oil freely into the holes.

WORMS, ROUND.
Symptoms.—Capricious appetite, itching at the nose: abdominal pains may be present. As a rule, however, the worms give rise to no symptoms. The first indication of their presence is that they are seen in the motions, or are vomited.

Treatment (1).—The person should take a dose of salts and abstain from food for a few hours. After the bowels have been moved, administer a worm cake, which any chemist can supply. When this has had time to work, a dose of licorice or Gregory powder will expel the parasite. This treatment should be repeated as the worms take a lot of killing.

Treatment (2) (*alternative treatment*).—To 1 teaspoonful of common salt add 1 pint of warm water. Inject night and morning and allow to remain in the bowels as long as possible. Give person plenty of fresh fruit.

Note.—For tapeworm and threadworm *see* TAPEWORM.

WRINKLES, to prevent. Gentle massage of glycerine and honey, apply a small quantity to the face on retiring. Wash in warm rain-water next morning, using unscented white curd soap.

WRITER'S CRAMP, to relieve. Rub the hand and arm with camphor and soap liniment during intervals between writing.

YEAST, to keep. Yeast will keep for several days if covered at once with cold water. When required the water can be poured off without disturbing the yeast. Mustard can be treated in the same way.

YOLK OF EGG. To keep this fresh until required, add a few spoonfuls of cold water.

YORKSHIRE PUDDING. *See* PUDDING, YORKSHIRE.

ZINC, to clean. Wash in warm soap suds; then dry and rub vigorously with a cloth soaked in either turpentine or paraffin.

ZINC PAIL, to mend. Apply a small piece of putty to the leak inside the pail and a larger piece outside; flatten out, and allow to dry.

ZINNIA. A half-hardy annual which ranks as one of the most effective of our bedding plants, especially the double varieties, which are shorter and more compact than the single. The plant is delicate and needs a sheltered, sunny situation and should not be bedded out before June, nor the seeds sown before the first week in April in heat, and hardened before bedding out. Transplant in good time, before seedlings have made much growth.

ZODIAC, SIGNS OF THE. The signs of the Zodiac are used in casting horoscopes from astrological calculations, accepted by many as a guide in domestic and social relationships, as well as in business affairs. They are twelve in number and represent the "houses" or divisions into which the heavens are charted by astrologer. The twelve signs are named: Aries, Taurus, Gemini, Cancer, Leo, Virgo, Libra, Scorpio, Sagittarius, Capricorn, Aquarius and Pisces. The significance of each sign is given under its own alphabetic order.

ADDITIONAL NOTES

ADDITIONAL NOTES

ADDITIONAL NOTES